The New and Cha Transatlanticism

In a world of more diffuse power and principles, Europeans and Americans are challenged to reposition their partnership for the twenty-first century. Yet they face a mismatch between the nature of the challenges and the institutional frameworks, strategic-action capacity, and practical tools at their disposal. This volume offers new insights into the governance of transatlantic relations and the evolving nature of the US–EU partnership.

Daniel S. Hamilton, *Center for Transatlantic Relations, Johns Hopkins University SAIS*

This is an interesting and informative collection of articles. I highly recommend the volume to a wide audience of those interested in transatlantic relations.

Joseph A. McKinney, *Baylor University*

The European Union and the US are currently negotiating the Transatlantic Trade and Investment Partnership (TTIP), with potentially enormous economic gains for both partners. Experts from the EU and the US explore not only the groundwork laid for TTIP under the "New Transatlanticism," but also the key variables – economic, cultural, institutional, and political – shaping transatlantic policy outcomes.

Divided into four parts, Part I, consisting of three chapters, contextualizes the transatlantic relationship with an historical survey, contemporary foreign relations and policy, and cultural dynamics. Together, these chapters provide the background for understanding the evolving nature of the EU–US relationship. Part II of this volume focuses on governance and comprises two chapters – one on transatlantic governance and the other on administrative culture. Part III consists of six policy chapters: competition, trade, transport, mobility regimes, financial services regulation, and GMOs. Part IV, consisting of three chapters, explores prospects and challenges associated with transatlanticism, including the TTIP. The last chapter concludes with lessons learned and future challenges with respect to policy convergence; the nature of the EU–US relationship; power, resources, and bargaining within the transatlantic partnership; and an assessment of the future of deeper cooperation and integration.

This insightful account into policy cooperation between the EU and the US is a welcome resource for policy specialists oriented toward comparative public policy wishing to enter the arena of Transatlantic Studies.

Laurie Buonanno is Professor of Political Science and Public Administration at SUNY Buffalo State and directs the postgraduate public administration division. She is a specialist in comparative public policy.

Natalia Cugleșan is Lecturer at the Faculty of History and Philosophy, Babeș-Bolyai University, Romania.

Keith Henderson was Professor of Political Science at SUNY Buffalo State. He helped establish the Master of Public Administration program at Buffalo State and developed internships for students in local, state, and federal government offices.

Routledge studies in governance and public policy

The New and Changing Transatlanticism

Politics and policy perspectives

**Edited by Laurie Buonanno,
Natalia Cugleşan, and Keith Henderson**

Routledge
Taylor & Francis Group

LONDON AND NEW YORK

First published 2015
by Routledge

2 Park Square, Milton Park, Abingdon, Oxon OX14 4RN

711 Third Avenue, New York, NY 10017, USA

Routledge is an imprint of the Taylor & Francis Group, an informa business

First issued in paperback 2017

Copyright © 2015 Taylor & Francis

The right of the editors to be identified as the authors of the editorial
matter, and of the authors for their individual chapters, has been asserted
in accordance with sections 77 and 78 of the Copyright, Designs and
Patents Act 1988.

All rights reserved. No part of this book may be reprinted or reproduced or
utilised in any form or by any electronic, mechanical, or other means, now
known or hereafter invented, including photocopying and recording, or in
any information storage or retrieval system, without permission in writing
from the publishers.

Notice:
Product or corporate names may be trademarks or registered trademarks,
and are used only for identification and explanation without intent to infringe.

Library of Congress Cataloging in Publication Data
The new and changing transatlanticism: politics and policy perspectives /
edited by Laurie Buonanno, Natalia, Cuglesan, and Keith Henderson.
  pages cm. – (Routledge studies in governance and public policy; 19)
  Includes bibliographical references and index.
  1. United States–Foreign economic relations–European Union
  countries. 2. European Union countries–Foreign economic relations–
  United States. 3. United States–Relations–European Union countries.
  4. European Union countries–Relations–United States. I. Buonanno,
  Laurie.
  HF1456.5.E85N48 2015
  337.7304–dc23   2014039189

ISBN: 978-0-415-53909-8 (hbk)
ISBN: 978-1-138-06665-6 (pbk)

Typeset in Times New Roman
by Wearset Ltd, Boldon, Tyne and Wear

Contents

Figures

Tables

Contributors

Federiga Bindi is Professor of Political Science and Jean Monnet Chair at the University of Rome Tor Vergata and Senior Fellow at the Center for Transatlantic Relations. Dr. Bindi holds a PhD in Political Science from the European University Institute and has been Visiting Professor and Researcher in a number of institutions in both the US and Europe (Brookings Institution, Norwegian Institute for International Affairs, Sciences Po in Lille, Université Libre de Bruxelles, Institut d'Etudes Européens). Dr. Bindi has won over 30 grants, fellowships, and prizes from national and international institutions among the European Commission, NATO, and the European University Institute in Florence. She has published widely in Italian, English, Portuguese, and Spanish; her most recent publications include: *The Foreign Policy of the European Union: Assessing Europe's Role in the World* (with Irina Angelescu, 2012); *Italy and the EU* (2011); *The Frontiers of Europe: A Transatlantic Problem?* (with Irina Angelescu, 2011).

Laurie Buonanno is Professor of Political Science and Public Administration at SUNY Buffalo State and director of the public administration division. She received a Ph.D. in Political Science from the Johns Hopkins University and an MBA from the University at Buffalo – SUNY. She has been the PI of several grants, including from the European Commission and a four-year Atlantis FIPSE/bilateral grant from the US Department of Education to fund transatlantic public administration curricular innovations, scholarship, and student and faculty mobility. She is co-author (with Neill Nugent) of *Policies and Policy Processes of the European Union* (2013). She has published articles and book chapters on European governance, policies, and identity. She served as Director of the Institute for European Union Studies at SUNY and co-chair of EUSA's public policy section. She is a recipient of the SUNY Chancellor's Award for Excellence in Teaching.

Alexander Caviedes is Associate Professor of Political Science at the State University of New York at Fredonia. He received a Ph.D. in Political Science at the University of Wisconsin–Madison in 2006, a J.D. at the University of Florida in 1993, and an LL.M. in European Community Law at the University of the Saarland, Germany in 1996. Before pursuing a career in academia, he practiced immigration law in Tampa, Florida. His research interests are in

comparative political economy, industrial relations, immigration, and, particularly, labor migration in Western Europe. He is the author of *Prying Open
Fortress Europe: The Turn to Sectoral Labor Migration* (2010) and co-editor
of *Labour Migration in Europe* (2010), together with Georg Menz. He has
published articles on European immigration policy, European identity, and
intellectual property in the *Journal of European Public Policy*, *Dialectic
Anthropology*, and the *Boston University International Law Review*. Recent
book chapters have been published in *Migrants and Minorities: The European Response* (2010), *Territoriality and Migration in the E.U. Neighbourhood* (2013), and *Migration in an Age of Restriction* (2014).

Natalia Cugleşan is Lecturer at the Faculty of History and Philosophy, Babeş-
Bolyai University, Romania. She received her Ph.D. in International Relations and European Studies from Babeş-Bolyai University. Her research
interest in European governance has resulted in the publication of several
articles and book chapters on multi-level governance (Romania and France),
decentralization and regional policy in Central and Eastern Europe, and
environmental policy. Dr. Cugleşan is the recipient of several grants from the
European Commission: Jean Monnet Module Multi-level Governance in the
EU (2010) and Jean Monnet Information and Research Learning EU at
Schools: 2.0 in Secondary Schools in Romania and Moldova (2013).

Carolyn Marie Dudek is Professor of Political Science and Director of Euro-
pean Studies at Hofstra University. She received her B.A. from Canisius
College and her M.A. and Ph.D. from the University of Pittsburgh. As a spe-
cialist in comparative politics, her regional interests include Europe and Latin
America. Dr. Dudek was a Jean Monnet Fellow at the European University
Institute in Florence, Italy, a post-doctoral fellow at Columbia University, a
Visiting Scholar at Harris Manchester College, Oxford University, and Visit-
ing Faculty at the University of Buenos Aires. She was also awarded Ful-
bright Scholarships to Argentina and Spain. Her field research in Europe and
Latin America has resulted in the publication of several articles and book
chapters on European regulation of GMOs, EU–Latin American relations,
Spanish politics, regional nationalism in Europe, and European Union
regional development policy. She is also the author of *EU Accession and
Spanish Regional Development: Winners and Losers*. Dr. Dudek has directed
and taught study-abroad programs in Australia, Central Europe, Spain, and
Italy, and was a lecturer in the Semester at Sea program.

Michelle Egan is Associate Professor and Jean Monnet Chair Ad Personam in
the School of International Service, American University. She received her
Ph.D. in Political Science from the University of Pittsburgh. She is the current
Chair of the European Union Studies Association (EUSA). Michelle is the
author of *Single Markets: Economic Integration in Europe and the United
States* (forthcoming). She is a member of the Transworld Project on Transat-
lantic Relations and Global Governance, which is funded by a European
Commission Framework grant (FP7 SSH). She has published on transatlantic

and regulatory issues, as well as European integration, including *Creating a Transatlantic Marketplace: Government Policies and Business Strategies* (Manchester University Press) and *Constructing a European Market: Standards, Regulation and Governance* (Oxford University Press). Michelle is the recipient of several fellowships, including the German Marshall Fund and Robert Bosch.

Keith Henderson was Professor of Political Science and Public Administration at SUNY Buffalo State and Coordinator of Public Administration in the MPA program. He received his Doctorate in Public Administration from the University of Southern California and did postdoctoral work at Columbia University. Prior to coming to Buffalo he was Associate Professor of Public Administration at the (then) Graduate School of Public Administration, New York University (now the Wagner School). He was Assistant Professor of Public Administration at the American University of Beirut on his first academic assignment, after completing five years in the government of the City of Los Angeles, including as Field Secretary to the Third District City Council Member. He edited (with O. P. Dwivedi) *Bureaucracy and the Alternatives in World Perspective* (Macmillan) and published widely in the field of American and Comparative Public Administration. He received two Senior Fulbright awards, the most recent (1998–1999) to teach and conduct research in the Law School, University of Rijeka, Rijeka, Croatia. Sadly, Dr. Henderson passed away in June 2014.

Holly Jarman is Assistant Professor within the Center for Law, Ethics, and Health and the Department of Health Management and Policy at the University of Michigan. She received a Ph.D. in Political Science from the London School of Economics & Political Science. As a political scientist, she researches the impact of trade agreements and economic regulations on domestic health and social policies, with a focus on the US and EU. Her work has been published in journals including the *Journal of Public Health Policy*, *Tobacco Control*, and *Public Policy and Administration*. Her book, *The Politics of Trade and Tobacco Control*, explores the consequences of trade law for tobacco control policies.

Neill Nugent is Emeritus Professor of Politics and Jean Monnet Professor of European Integration at Manchester Metropolitan University. He is also Honorary Professor at Salford University and Senior Fellow at the Centre for European Integration at the University of Bonn. He has published widely on the European Union and European politics. His books include: *Policies and Policy Processes of the European Union* (with Laurie Buonanno; Palgrave Macmillan, 2013); *The Government and Politics of the European Union* (7th edition; Palgrave Macmillan, 2010); *Research Agendas in EU Studies: Stalking the Elephant* (co-editor with Michelle Egan and William Paterson; Palgrave Macmillan, 2010); *European Union Enlargement* (editor; Palgrave Macmillan, 2004); *The European Commission* (Palgrave Macmillan, 2001); and *At the Heart of the Union: Studies of the European Commission* (editor;

2nd edition; Palgrave Macmillan, 2000). He is co-editor of two Palgrave Macmillan book series: *The European Union Series* and *Palgrave Studies in European Union Politics*. In 2013 he was awarded the Lifetime Achievement Award for his work in the area of European Studies by the University Association for Contemporary European Studies (UACES).

Michael O'Neill is Reader in Politics and Jean Monnet Chair in EU Politics at Nottingham Trent University, UK. He has published widely in the field of EU and comparative European politics. His books include: *The Politics of European Integration* (Routledge, 1996); *Green Parties and Political Change in Contemporary Europe* (Ashgate, 1997); *Democracy and Cultural Diversity* (Oxford University Press, 2000); *Devolution and British Politics* (Pearson, 2003); *The Struggle for the European Constitution: A Past and Future History* (Routledge, 2011).

Ellen B. Pirro is Professor of Political Science at Iowa State University and Adjunct Professor of Political Science at Drake University. Dr. Pirro has many years of teaching and research experience at a variety of educational institutions, including directing the Carrie Chapman Catt Center for Women and Politics. She was named teacher of the year at Iowa State University in 2012. She is co-author (with Eleanor E. Zeff) of *The European Union and the Member States*. Her recent work with co-author Richard Mansbach on the European Union's financial crisis has been delivered at conferences in Prague and Budapest. Her work on the EU and Central Asia was published in *Global Power Europe*, edited by Boening, Kremer, and van Loon. A series of pieces on EU transportation policy (with Eleanor E. Zeff) have been delivered at US conferences during the past five years. Dr. Pirro holds a B.A. from the University of New Hampshire and M.A. and Ph.D. from Yale University.

Reginald R. (Reg) Souleyrette holds the Commonwealth Chair Professor in Civil Engineering at the University of Kentucky. He is also Program Manager for Planning and Education for the Kentucky Transportation Center. Dr. Souleyrette has 25 years of experience in transportation research and education, and has completed over 100 projects ranging from simple task orders to complex, multi-year programs. He has led, organized, and conducted numerous tasks involving case studies, special studies, studies of institutional issues, and policy analysis. He is author or co-author of over 250 scientific papers and seminars and served as co-chair of the National Academies Transportation Research Board, Geographic Information and Science Committee (ABJ60), and as Chair of the Data and Information Technology Section. He currently serves on the Editorial Board for the *Journal of Transportation Safety and Security*, and is a registered professional engineer in Kentucky and Iowa. Dr. Souleyrette holds B.S. and M.S. degrees from the University of Texas and a Ph.D. from the University of California, Berkeley.

Nikolaos Zahariadis is Professor and Director of Political Science, Department of Government, University of Alabama at Birmingham, USA. He has been a Fulbright Scholar, an ESRC-SSRC Visiting Fellow, a Policy Studies

Organization Fellow, an adjunct Scholar at the Woodrow Wilson International Center for Scholars, and a National Bank of Greece Senior Research Fellow. He currently serves as co-Chair of the Public Policy Section of the European Union Studies Association and was President of the International Studies Association-South. Numerous agencies have invited him to speak on aspects of his work, including the US State Department, the governments of Romania and Greece, and many universities around the world, including Harvard University, New York University, the London School of Economics, University of Hamburg, the Wissenschaftszentrum-Berlin, University of East Anglia, and others. A native of Greece, he has published extensively on issues of comparative public policy and European political economy. His latest edited volume, *Frameworks of the European Union Policy Process: Competition and Complementarity across the Theoretical Divide*, was published by Routledge in 2013.

Eleanor E. Zeff is Associate Professor in the Department of Politics and International Relations and University Coordinator for Post-Graduate Scholarships at Drake University, Des Moines, Iowa. She received the Mentor of the Year Award in 2006. Dr. Zeff's publications include: *The European Union and the Member States* (with Ellen B. Pirro); a PEW case study on transatlantic passenger name records negotiations; a chapter on the EU's budget in Palgrave Macmillan's *European Union Enlargement*; articles about teaching the EU in *International Studies Perspectives*; and (with Ellen B. Pirro) on EU transport policies in *The Romanian Review of European Studies*. She has written conference papers and reviews on European policies and has worked on a recent mapping of EU studies. She participates on the Advisory Board of Annual Editions' *Comparative Politics*, and is a member of the European Union Studies and International Studies Associations. Dr. Zeff received a B.A. from Tufts University and M.A. and Ph.D. degrees from the Graduate Faculty of the New School.

Preface

This book is written to contribute to policy studies of the transatlantic partnership at a particularly auspicious epoch, namely during the negotiations for the Transatlantic Trade and Investment Partnership (TTIP) – an unprecedented trade and investment pact involving hundreds of government officials in the preparation of negotiation briefs. The potential of the TTIP for the Atlantic Community to produce economic gains, set international standards, and renew and strengthen transatlantic ties cannot be overemphasized and, perhaps, is best expressed in the informal term transatlantic observers have bestowed on TTIP – the "economic NATO." The potential growth benefits of a transatlantic free trade zone are staggering. If the TTIP produces a zero-tariff agreement, US and EU exports could each increase by 17%. Aligning regulatory standards in just half of all non-tariff barriers could add 0.7% to the size of the EU's economy and 0.3% to the US economy (Hamilton & Quinlan, 2014, pp. v–vi). Because most of the potential gains will be realized by harmonizing regulations or through mutual recognition, it is important to raise the question as to whether the EU and the US have the requisite foundation to enter into such a complex relationship requiring government officials and societal actors to work so closely together on a transatlantic basis to agree, implement, and monitor agreements across a wide range of industrial and service sectors.

Before 1990 such a book – where the North Atlantic Treaty Organization (NATO) is hardly mentioned – would have been inconceivable. This is so not because of any significant change in US attitudes toward Europe, but rather principally the result of European integration. When the then European Community (EC) and the US signed the Transatlantic Declaration on EC–US Relations in 1990, it was only five years since the EC had agreed to complete the internal market by 1992. This raised fears in the US of a "Fortress Europe" which, coupled with the fact that the EC was beginning to look to American policymakers like the single market that successive presidential administrations and American corporations had long desired, set the stage for the US to begin working with the EC as a partner, rather than through backchannels and directly through European states on an individual basis. Since the Declaration, interest among political scientists and policymakers in transatlantic relations has broadened considerably beyond security and foreign policy studies. And as the European Union (as the EC was re-named in 1993) has deepened (more integration) and widened (increased its membership from 12 members in 1986 to 28 members today), the transatlantic relationship, too, has adapted in order to respond to the EU's new policy competences and its greater economic power.

This book is being written during the critical first year of the TTIP negotiations (2013–2014). Rather than confining our analysis of the TTIP (which would be premature not only because the TTIP is ongoing), our main purpose is to give the reader a comprehensive study and analysis of the political and policy challenges, obstacles, and opportunities with which policymakers and stakeholders should be aware as they seek to establish an unprecedented partnership in which, if it produces an "economic NATO," will eliminate tariffs and align many regulatory standards between the EU and the US.

As is our editorial responsibility, we have endeavored to assist our authors to contribute to our goal of providing an integrated narrative, which is one of the principal challenges in edited books. Nevertheless, we recognize the different needs and objective of our readers. Therefore, we have both encouraged and tolerated some overlap in material and discussions across the chapters to ensure that each chapter could be read and comprehended on its own merit.

It is hoped that this book will assist current and future policymakers in understanding the complexities of past and present transatlantic policymaking in order to provide a more informed basis for their decision-making with respect to the changing nature of transatlantic relations. We hope, as well, to have contributed useful knowledge to the study of transatlantic policymaking, which may then serve as a base from which other scholars and practitioners can build in their continued examinations and recommendations for strengthening the transatlantic partnership.

Acknowledgments

The idea for this book began with an application for a four-year EU–US Atlantis bilateral grant – itself a result of the 1995 New Transatlantic Agenda which figures so importantly in transatlanticism. Laurie Buonanno and Neill Nugent co-wrote and served as principal investigators to their respective granting agencies (the US Department of Education, Office of Postsecondary Education) and the European Commission's Directorate General for Education and Culture).

Our first thanks and acknowledgment must go to the US Department of Education and DG Education and Culture for funding our project, and particularly to our program officers, Dr. Frank Frankfort, Senior Program Manager at the Fund for Improvement of Postsecondary Education (FIPSE), Michelle Guilfoil, Senior Program Officer at the International and Foreign Language Education Service (IFLE), and Klaus Haupt, Head of the Unit, Bilateral Cooperation with Industrialized Countries, at the Education, Audiovisual and Cultural Executive Agency (EACEA) of the European Commission.

We were assisted in our studies of transatlantic politics and policymaking by numerous colleagues and experts, who gave us both support and a large measure of patience, which we gratefully acknowledge. There were many members of the team involved in this project, including Adrian Ivan of Babeş Bolyai University, Frank Carr and Annabel Kiernan of Manchester Metropolitan University, and Henry Steck, at SUNY Cortland. Many government officials have facilitated student exchanges and fieldwork. Particularly, we would like to thank the City of Buffalo, Common Council – particularly Councilman Joseph Golombek – US Congressman Brian Higgins and his staff, and members and staff of the New York State Assembly for their willingness to provide internships for our American, British, and Romanian students.

We would be remiss if we neglected to acknowledge, thank, and express our pride in the many Atlantis scholars who have come through our program for their curiosity, ambition, intelligence, flexibility, and continued accomplishments after completing their undergraduate studies. We have been impressed with our Romanian, American, and British students. We have watched with pride the work so many of them have done since their time as Atlantis Scholars in terms of graduate study and the launching of international professional careers. We see them as part of a growing "Transatlantic Generation" that will be the successor to the generation that served both sides of the Atlantic well during the Cold War and in the quarter-century since 1989. Four schools, three nations, two continents and one commitment to working together; the Atlantis Mobility bilateral grant program has truly been one foundation stone for transatlantic understanding in the twenty-first century.

We would also like to thank Nikolaos Zahariadis, who as Chair of the Public Policy Interest Section of the European Union Studies Association assisted in publicizing the project and attracting contributors to it, and to the EUSA Public Policy Interest Section, in general, which sponsored two panels at the May 2013 conference in Baltimore where several contributors presented their book chapters. We would also like to thank Kathleen Dowley, Director of the Institute for European Union Studies at SUNY (IEUSS), who invited contributors to this volume to discuss transatlanticism at IEUSS-sponsored events.

We are grateful to the authors of the chapters who responded quickly and carefully to our editorial requests and were involved at all stages of the process in developing and refining our understanding of transatlanticism.

We would also like to thank the anonymous reviewers whose comments provided critical guidance in refocusing and fine-tuning our conceptual approach to transatlantic policymaking.

Finally, we would like to thank our editor, Natalja Mortensen at Routledge Press and her editorial assistants, Darcy Bullock and Lillian Rand. Natalja encouraged us to pursue this project, and without her encouragement, guidance, and patience we would not have been able to move this book from idea to finished product.

We hope this volume will be useful in university courses – such as comparative public policy and comparative public administration – and more broadly in studies of transatlanticism which focus on the numerous cooperative activities taking place between the EU and the US.

Laurie Buonanno
Natalia Cugleşan
Keith Henderson

Abbreviations

ACTA	Anti-Counterfeiting Trade Agreement
ALDE	Alliance of Liberals and Democrats for Europe – EP Political Group
APHIS	Animal and Plant Health Inspection Service (USDA)
ARM	adjustable rate mortgages
BAA	Buy American Act
BCA	Bilateral Competition Agreement
BIS	Bank for International Settlements
BIT	bilateral investment treaty
BRICs	Brazil, Russia, India, and China (sometimes BRICS, includes South Africa)
CAFTA	Central American Free Trade Agreement
CBP	Customs and Border Protection
CCP	Common Commercial Policy
CDOs	collateralized debt obligations
CDS	collateralized debt swap
CEECs	Central and Eastern European countries
CEPR	Centre for Economic and Policy Research
CETA	Comprehensive Economic and Trade Agreement
CFE	Conventional Armed Forces in Europe (Treaty)
CFSP	Common Foreign and Security Policy
CFTC	Commodity Futures Trading Commission
CGE	computable general equilibrium (models)
CIA	Central Intelligence Agency
CJEU	Court of Justice of the European Union
COREPER	Committee of Permanent Representatives
CRA	credit rating agency
CSDP	Common Security and Defence Policy
CSI	Container Security Initiative
CTP	Common Transport Policy
DG	Directorate General
DHS	Department of Homeland Security
DOD	Department of Defense
DOT	Department of Transportation

EABC	European–American Business Council
EAS	European Administrative School
EBA	European Banking Authority
EC	European Community
ECB	European Central Bank
ECI	European Citizens' Initiative
ECJ	European Court of Justice (pre-Lisbon Treaty name for the EU's court)
ECR	European Conservatives and Reformists – EP Political Group
ECSC	European Coal and Steel Community
EDA	European Defense Agency
EEAS	European External Action Service
EEC	European Economic Community
EFSA	European Food Safety Agency
EIOPA	European Insurance and Occupational Pensions Authority
EMIR	European Market Infrastructure Regulation
EP	European Parliament
EPA	Environmental Protection Agency
EPC	European Political Cooperation
EPP	European People's Party – EP Political Group
ERA	Office of European Union and Regional Affairs
ERS	Economic Research Service
ESA	European Supervisory Authority
ESDI	European security and defense identity
ESDP	European Security and Defense Policy
ESFS	European System of Financial Supervision
ESM	European Stability Mechanism
ESMA	European Securities and Market Authority
ESRB	European Systemic Risk Board
ESS	European Security Strategy
ETUC	European Trade Union Confederation
EU-12	European Union of 12 member states (Belgium, Denmark, France, Germany, Greece, Ireland, Italy, Luxembourg, the Netherlands, Portugal, Spain, United Kingdom)
EU-15	European Union of 15 member states (EU-12 plus Austria, Finland, Sweden)
EUPAN	European Public Administration Network
EUR	Bureau of European and Eurasian Affairs
FAC	Foreign Affairs Council
FASB	Financial Accounting Standards Board
FDA	Food and Drug Administration
FDI	foreign direct investment
FDIC	Federal Deposit Insurance Corporation
FED	Federal Reserve Bank
FHFA	Federal Housing Finance Agency
FINRA	Financial Industry Regulatory Authority

FMRD	Financial Markets Regulatory Dialogue
FSB	Financial Stability Board
FSOC	Financial Stability Oversight Council
FTA	free trade agreement
FTC	Federal Trade Commission
G-20	Group of Twenty
G-8	Group of Eight
GAAP	Generally Accepted Accounting Principles
GATS	General Agreement on Trade in Services
GATT	General Agreement on Tariffs and Trade
GDP	gross domestic product
GHG	greenhouse gas
GI	geographical indications
GIIPS	Greece, Ireland, Italy, Portugal, and Spain
GIS	Geographic Information Systems
GM	General Motors
GMO	genetically modified organism
GPA	Government Procurement Agreement
Greens/EFA	The Greens/European Free Alliance – EP Political Group
GUE/NGL	European United Left/Nordic Greens – EP Political Group
HHS	Department Health and Human Services
HLRCF	High Level Regulatory Cooperation Forum
HLWG	High Level Working Group on Jobs and Growth
HOG	head of government
HS	Homeland Security
IASB	International Accounting Standards Board
ICAO	International Civil Aviation Organization
ICC	International Criminal Court
IETEIG	Initiative to Enhance Transatlantic Economic Integration and Growth
IFRS	International Financial Reporting Standards
IGO	international governmental organization
IMF	International Monetary Fund
INGO	international non-governmental organization
IPR	intellectual property rights
ISA	International Services Agreement
ISAF	International Security Assistance Force
ISDS	Investor–State Dispute Settlement
ISIS	Islamic State in Iraq and Syria
ITS	Intelligent Transportation Systems
JHA	Justice and Home Affairs
LNG	liquefied natural gas
MEP	Member of European Parliament
MiFID	Markets in Financial Instruments Directive
MLAT	Mutual Assistance Legal Treaties
MLG	multi-level governance

MNC	multinational corporation
MRA	mutual recognition agreement
MSRB	Municipal Securities Rulemaking Board
NACC	North Atlantic Cooperation Council
NAFTA	North American Free Trade Agreement
NATO	North Atlantic Treaty Organization
NCUA	National Credit Union Administration
NGO	non-governmental organization
NHS	National Health Service
NHTSA	National Highway Traffic Safety Administration
NI	Non-attached Members – EP Political Group
NIH	National Institutes of Health
NIHRAC	National Institutes of Health Recombinant DNA Advisory Committee
NPG	New Public Governance
NPM	New Public Management
NSA	National Security Agency
NTA	New Transatlantic Agenda
NTB	non-tariff barrier
NTM	New Transatlantic Marketplace
OECD	Organization for Economic Cooperation and Development
OEEC	Organization for Economic European Cooperation
OLP	ordinary legislative procedure
OPM	Office of Personnel Management
OSCE	Organization for Security and Cooperation in Europe
OSTP	Office of Science and Technology Policy
OTC	over-the-counter
PNR	Passenger Name Record (agreement)
PR	proportional representation
PTA	preferential trade agreement
QM	qualified majority
QMV	qualified majority voting
RAP	Road Assessment Program
RCC	Regulatory Cooperation Council
Reg NMS	Regulation National Market System
S&D	Progressive Alliance of Socialists & Democrats – EP Party Group
SCFCH	Standing Committee on the Food Chain and Animal Health
SEA	Single European Act
SEC	Securities and Exchange Commission
SEM	Single European Market
SGP	Stability and Growth Pact
SLG	Senior Level Group
SMEs	small and medium enterprises
SPS	Sanitary and Phytosanitary (Agreement)
SRO	self-regulating organization
SSM	Single Supervisory Mechanism

SWIFT	Society for Worldwide Interbank Financial Telecommunication
TABD	Transatlantic Business Dialogue
TACD	Transatlantic Consumers Dialogue
TAD	Transatlantic Declaration
TALD	Transatlantic Labor Dialogue
TBC	Transatlantic Business Council
TBD	Tobacco Products Directive
TBT	technical barrier to trade
TEC	Transatlantic Economic Council
TEP	Transatlantic Economic Partnership
TEU	Treaty on European Union
TFEU	Treaty on the Functioning of the EU
TLD	Transatlantic Legislators' Dialogue
TPA	Trade Promotion Authority
TPP	TransPacific Partnership
TSCG	Treaty on Stability, Coordination and Governance
TTIP	Transatlantic Trade and Investment Partnership
UN	United Nations
UNCITL	United Nations Commission on International Trade Law
UNSC	UN Security Council
USDA	US Department of Agriculture
USPTO	US Patent and Trademark Office
USTR	United States Trade Representative
VEA	Veterinary Equivalency Agreement
WEU	Western European Union
WHO	World Health Organization
WMD	weapons of mass destruction
WTO	World Trade Organization

1 Studying Transatlanticism

Laurie Buonanno, Natalia Cugleşan, and Keith Henderson

Introduction

The purpose of this book is to examine transatlantic policy formulation and policy outcomes from politics and policy perspectives. While there is a considerable and growing literature on transatlantic relations, this literature contains empirical gaps with respect to understanding the nature and extent of policy cooperation and policy convergence in areas of mutual interest to the principal transatlantic partners – increasingly defined as the US and the EU (rather than between the US and the EU's individual 28 member states). The EU–US relationship is crucial for global peace, security, trade, and investment, and based on these attributes, merits book-length studies.

The contemporary transatlantic exchange is characterized by intensive involvement of government officials at both the cabinet and subcabinet levels meeting in summits, high-level working groups, and sector-level fora, resulting in a wide range of agreements in virtually every policy area in which Washington and Brussels have shared or sole competency. This more intensive exchange and the "policy communities" emerging in transatlantic policymaking represents a departure from relations carried out mainly through the traditional locus of power – foreign ministries and the US State Department. Ann-Marie Slaughter (1997, p. 194) was an early observer of this phenomenon and pointed particularly to EU–US relations in the early 1990s as an example of the centrifugal shift in international "relations" from the foreign ministry to other governmental agencies.

Because transatlantic relations operate at so many levels in a multiplicity of policy areas, this book adopts a multidisciplinary approach to transatlantic studies. Given the book's focus, it would have been inappropriate to ask all contributors to adopt a common theoretical approach or framework. However, the nature of the subject matter has led all contributors to draw primarily from variants of either international political economy or comparative public policy. The chapters are of two broad types: those that focus on the context of transatlanticism and examples of policy areas that have/are capable of developing strong transatlantic dimensions.

The first section of this chapter discusses the importance of the transatlantic relationship. The second section undertakes a review of policy competences in the EU and the US. The third section raises key questions to be addressed in this book. In the final section we explain the organization of the book.

Importance of the Transatlantic Relationship

The transatlantic relationship is crucially important to the EU and the US for three reasons. An obvious reason is security, an issue so well documented in the transatlantic literature as to be one that we need not belabor in this volume. The other two reasons, economic interdependence and the setting of global standards, are elaborated below.

Economic Interdependence

Hamilton and Quinlan (2014) provide a comprehensive assessment of the transatlantic economic relationship from which five general observations can be made. First, the transatlantic economic relationship is the largest in the world, generating $5 trillion in commercial sales, employing 15 million workers, and accounting for 50% of global GDP (40% measured as purchasing price parity) (Hamilton & Quinlan, 2014, p. v). Second, the trade relationship is quite compelling. Not only do the EU and the US account for 30% of world trade (US–EU High Level Working Group on Jobs and Growth, 2013, p. 1), when viewed at the US state and EU member state levels 45 of the 50 US states export more to Europe than to China (Hamilton & Quinlan, 2014, p. x). Third, the EU and the US are mutually invested: the EU and the US continue to be each other's primary source and destination of foreign direct investment (FDI), with the US accounting for 56% of total FDI in the EU and the EU accounting for 71% of total FDI in the US (Hamilton & Quinlan, 2014, pp. vi, ix). Fourth, the EU and the US are the world's two leading service economies and are each other's most important commercial partner in trade and investment of services (Hamilton & Quinlan, 2014, p. x). Within the financial services industry, no other regional relationship comes close to the transatlantic area's dominance: together, the EU and the US account for two-thirds of all financial services by transaction volumes, 74% of global insurance markets in terms of insurance premiums collected, and 72% in private and public debt securities outstanding (Transatlantic Business Dialogue, 2010, pp. 7, 9). Fifth, European majority-owned foreign affiliates directly employed 3.8 million US workers in 2012, while US affiliates directly employed about 4.2 million workers in Europe (Hamilton & Quinlan, 2014, p. xi).

It follows that with such a mutually dependent economic relationship, American and European policymakers would need to gain a working knowledge of the key policy areas shaping transatlantic economic relations. Accordingly, this volume contains chapters analyzing transatlantic policymaking in competition (a major influence on FDI); trade; genetically modified organisms (GMOs); financial services regulation (where the EU and the US hope to retain their collective global dominance); transportation policy (essential for the smooth exchange of goods in the transatlantic area); and mobility regimes (policies affecting the essential people-to-people links among interdependent regions).

Global Standards Setting

With generally low tariff rates between the EU and the US, negative integration is reaching limits on its return on investment (that is, governmental resources devoted to negotiating, implementing, and monitoring tariff reductions), prompting the transatlantic policy community to eye positive integration – particularly mutual recognition and harmonization of product and service standards and regulatory processes – as "new territory" for transatlantic negotiations. While it is certainly the case that both the EU and the US had aspired to utilize the World Trade Organization's (WTO) fora to promulgate global standards in nonagricultural products and services, the WTO's Doha Round, which began in 2001, failed to reach any agreement at all for over a decade. After suffering many near deaths, in December 2013 the Doha Round finally produced the "Bali Package" in which "trade facilitation" (simplifying and modernizing customs procedures) was to be its hallmark achievement. The developed world agreed to provide assistance to the developing and least developing countries to modernize their infrastructures, train customs officials, and costs associated with the agreement (World Trade Organization, 2013a). While *The Economist* (2013) concluded that the "completion of a WTO agreement reflects a broad appetite for trade integration and reduces the risk that regional deals degenerate into a world of Balkanised trade," it seems to us that the Bali Agreement suggests a rather different lesson: a variety of impediments such as varying levels of economic development and growth rates as well as domestic politics and government continue to undermine the ability of the advanced industrialized countries to reduce technical barriers to trade and investment within the WTO framework.

The renewed interest in negotiating and expanding regional trading blocs – for example, the Transatlantic Trade and Investment Partnership (TTIP), the Russian-led Eurasian customs union (more on its role in the Ukrainian separatist movement, below), the free trade agreements negotiated between South Korea and the EU (KOREU) and the US (KORUS), the EU–Canada Comprehensive Economic and Trade Agreement (CETA), the TransPacific Partnership (TTP – involving the US, Canada, Australia, Japan, New Zealand, Mexico, Chile, Brunei, Malaysia, Peru, Singapore, and Vietnam), and the EU's renewed efforts to expand its Eastern Partnership agreements with former Soviet republics (see the European External Action Service, 2014a for information on the Eastern Partnership agreements) – are at least partly, although not wholly, attributable to the slow pace of Doha (Hufbauer, Schott, Adler, Brunel, & Foong, 2010). Indeed, the TTIP and the EU's renewed assertiveness in negotiating Eastern Partnership agreements can be interpreted as a dual strategy of the Atlantic Community to expand markets for their goods and services. But as we noted above, the "easy" gains through negative integration have been realized. EU and US officials have been working in a variety of fields and for many years (see Chapter 5) to develop mutual understanding through non-binding agreements.

A report published by the Transatlantic Policy Network (2013) – an INGO devoted to promoting transatlantic ties – best summarizes a widely held point of view that the EU and the US had best cooperate if they wish to control and shape regulatory standards before Brazil, Russia, India, China, and South Africa (BRICS) are in a position to do so:

> The Transatlantic Trade and Investment Partnership is an opportunity to ensure that common transatlantic technical standards, based on the appeal of the world's largest market, become the prevailing global standard, especially for emerging information, bio, nano and similar cutting-edge technologies. And TTIP is the mechanism to enable European and American firms, workers and economies to reap the benefits of being those trend setters.

Members of European Parliament (MEPs) and US congresspersons echoed this view in their 74th Inter-Parliamentary meeting in 2013 in highlighting the benefits of equivalence, mutual recognition, and extraterritoriality, and agreed that a TTIP "based on these principles can also serve as a reference for further trade agreements and help revitalize the multilateral trade system, such as the WTO" (Transatlantic Legislators' Dialogue, 2013, p. 2) Echoing these concerns, David Martin, trade spokesman for the EP's Socialists and Democrats Group, suggested that TTIP could be the EU's "last chance to set global standards" (B. Fox, 2014b).

The continued strength of the transatlantic relationship was demonstrated as the pendulum in EU–US relations swung rather quickly from anger over the spy scandal to transatlantic solidarity in economic assistance for Ukraine (and shared humiliation over the inability of either the EU or the US to adopt short-term measures to thwart Russia's actions in Ukraine). The events in Ukraine reminded the EU and the US that their partnership is a mutually advantageous relationship grounded in trade and investment, but also of shared values and security needs.

So while the EU–US relationship is also one marked by fierce competition in which seemingly intractable differences can sometimes emerge in all sorts of areas from foreign policy to competition between American and European commercial airline manufacturers, on balance the transatlantic relationship is vital for economic and security reasons. Therefore, European and American policymakers need to understand their partners' values, goals, policy priorities, and domestic constraints as they attempt to fashion solutions to some of the more "wicked" policy problems facing the global community. This is an overarching goal of this book.

While the EU is not a fully fledged state, neither does it operate as an international organization. Described as *sui generis* or more colorfully as an "unidentified political object," the EU certainly shares features of federal systems and is perhaps best classified as a quasi-federal system. The next section of this chapter examines the extent to which Brussels and Washington enjoy policy competence in areas of key concern to both entities. This knowledge will help us to make meaningful policy comparisons throughout this book.

Policy Competences in the US Federal Government and EU Institutions

There are several ways in which policy competence is determined in federal and quasi-federal systems, the most important being legal (constitutions/treaties, statutes, judicial/case law) and political practice (majority party in federal and state governments). Irrespective of the mechanisms through which policy competence has been conferred, over time, policymaking power has shifted upwards to the national (US) and supranational (EU) levels.

In the EU, competence is laid out in the TFEU, divided according to shared competences (Article 4) and exclusive EU competence (Article 3) (see Box 1.1). TFEU, Title I "Categories and Areas of Union Competence," Article 2 (2) states:

> When the Treaties confer on the Union exclusive competence in a specific area, only the Union may legislate and adopt legally binding acts, the Member States being able to do so themselves only if so empowered by the Union or for the implementation of Union acts.

Box 1.1 European Union Policy Competences (TFEU)

TEFU Article 3
1. The Union shall have exclusive competence in the following areas:
    (a) customs union;
    (b) the establishing of the competition rules necessary for the functioning of the internal market;
    (c) monetary policy for the Member States whose currency is the euro;
    (d) the conservation of marine biological resources under the common fisheries policy;
    (e) common commercial policy.

TEFU Article 4
2. Shared competence between the Union and the Member States applies in the following principal areas:
    (a) internal market;
    (b) social policy, for the aspects defined in this Treaty;
    (c) economic, social and territorial cohesion;
    (d) agriculture and fisheries, excluding the conservation of marine biological resources;
    (e) environment;
    (f) consumer protection;
    (g) transport;
    (h) trans-European networks;
    (i) energy;
    (j) area of freedom, security and justice;
    (k) common safety concerns in public health matters, for the aspects defined in this Treaty.

The TFEU Title I, Article 2 (4) addresses the Common Foreign and Security Policy (CFSP) and the Common Defence Policy (CSDP) – policies in which EU competence is limited as laid out in the Treaty on European Union (TEU).

In the US, the "legal" foundation for federal policy competence is to be found in Articles I (legislative) and II (executive) of the US Constitution. Much of contemporary federal policy control has accumulated over time, however, especially during economic or security (war) crises such as mass emigration from Europe in the late 1800s (the federal government gained control over immigration policy), economic panics, recession, and depression (late 1800s–1930s, when the federal government gradually assumed responsibility for macroeconomic policy and the social safety net), and during times of war (especially the US civil war, during which time the federal government established a currency union).

Naturally, an important difference between the US and the EU is in the exclusive competence of the US federal government for foreign and defense policies (Article I, Section 8, Clauses 11–16 and Article II, Section 2, Clauses 1 and 2 of the US Constitution). Over the course of 200-plus years, the US Supreme Court has been an important arbiter in the tug and pull between federal and state power over policy competences, with the Court generally favoring the US internal market, basing its rulings on the "commerce clause" (Section 8, Clause 3) and the "necessary and proper" clause (Article I, Section 8, Clause 18) – "to make all laws which shall be necessary and proper for carrying into execution the foregoing powers, and all other powers vested by the Constitution in the government of the United States, or in any department or officer thereof."

Table 1.1 compares contemporary policy competences in the US and the EU. With the important exceptions of foreign and defense policies, the entries in Table 1.1 indicate that the loci of policy competences are remarkably similar in the US and the EU.

The information in Table 1.1 can be used in two ways to guide us in our exploration of transatlantic policymaking.

First, in those areas in which both Brussels and Washington have limited policy competence, it stands to reason that policy cooperation will be quite informal, taking the form of dialogue and information exchange among public officials. Accordingly, one expects that in the realm of housing, domestic crime, primary and secondary education, higher education, health, social welfare, transport, and defense, there will be little formal EU and US cooperation. While the EU has very little policy competence in external security, NATO's success would seem to weaken the assumption that there will be a lack of strong policy cooperation in those areas where the EU does not enjoy extensive policy competence. But it should be noted that NATO, while an example of highly successful transatlantic relations, is not an EU–US endeavor at all. NATO is a regional international governmental organization (IGO) to which individual countries are signatories and two of its most reliable European members – Norway and Turkey – are not EU member states. Furthermore, some EU member states have declined to join NATO.

The second point to be made is that where the EU and the US enjoy extensive, considerable, or shared policy responsibilities with their constituent governments

Table 1.1 The Varying Depths of EU and US (National Government) Policy Involvement

	Extensive EU/US Federal Involvement	Considerable EU/US Federal Involvement	Policy Responsibilities Shared Between the EU and the Member States/US and States	Limited EU/US Federal Involvement	Virtually no EU/US Federal Policy Involvement
EU	External trade Agriculture Fishing (exclusive economic zone) Monetary (for eurozone members)	Market regulation Competition/Antitrust Asylum	Regional/Cohesion Industry Foreign Development Environment Equal opportunity Working conditions Consumer protection Movement across external borders Macroeconomic (especially for euro members) Energy Cross-border crime Civil liberties (especially via the Charter of Fundamental Rights) Transport	Health Higher education Defense Social welfare Immigration	Housing Domestic crime Primary and secondary education
US	Defense Foreign Monetary Agriculture Fishing (exclusive economic zone) Movement across external borders Macroeconomic Crime (federal statutes and federal penitentiaries) Immigration and asylum Cross-border crime	Market regulation (include Financial Services Regulation) Competition/Antitrust	Environment Equal opportunity Working conditions Consumer protection Energy Interstate crime Civil liberties (through the US Bill of Rights) Health Social Welfare Transport Housing Industry Regional (through transfers of federal monies)	Higher education (financial aid) Crime (local/state) Primary and secondary education (mainly involved through financial incentives offered to the states to implement federal education initiatives such as No Child Left Behind and the Common Core)	

Source: Table adapted from Buonanno & Nugent, 2013, p. 11.

(the first three columns of Table 1.1) – such as in agriculture, market regulation, antitrust regulation, and trade – a great deal of transatlantic dialogue, whether cooperative or conflictual, would be expected.

In light of these two points, the level of policy control was deemed an important factor in selecting policies to consider for this book. Therefore, at least one policy was selected from the four columns in which there is both US and EU policy responsibility: external trade and GMOs (agriculture) were selected as representative policies in which there is both "extensive" EU and US federal involvement. Financial service regulation (market regulation) and competition/ antitrust policies were selected because they involve "considerable EU/US federal involvement." Transport policy was selected as representative of "shared" policy responsibilities. Two additional policies are considered in which the EU and the US do not have similar policy competences: high-skilled immigration and internal security (case studies of the Passenger Name Records Agreement and Container Security Agreement) to help us understand whether transatlantic policy cooperation can and does advance even in those areas where the EU enjoys very limited policy competence.

Policy Convergence?

Are policies converging or diverging? Adolino and Blake (2011, see, especially, chapters 2–3) helpfully suggest a grouping of explanatory variables to compare policies of advanced industrialized democracies as follows: economics (short-term economic conditions and longer-term economic trends); culture (family of nations, role of public opinion); institutional (intergovernmental relations; executive-legislative structures; bureaucrats); and politics (role and behavior of political parties; patterns of interest intermediation). This section briefly reviews how each of these variables may or may not contribute to transatlantic policy convergence, and the way in which contributors address these variables in their chapters.

Economics

To what extent do short-term economic conditions – such as the "Great Recession" which took hold in 2007/2008 – impact transatlantic policymaking? How might longer-term economic trends such as demographics, global competition, and the greater interconnectedness of trade and investment in the Atlantic Community shape transatlantic policymaking? The importance of economics varies in the policy studies in this book, but surely both short-term and long-term economic trends are impacting transatlantic relations and are almost certainly a factor in the TTIP. Several contributors identify economic factors in driving transatlantic cooperation: Neill Nugent and Michelle Egan in Chapter 2, where they examine the evolution of transatlantic relations; Nikolaos Zahariadis in Chapter 8, where he analyzes competition policy; and in Laurie Buonanno's examination of financial services regulation in Chapter 11.

Culture

Comparative studies of cultural influences on policymaking in the US and European countries have sought to address the perennial question of American exceptionalism, with, as of yet, no definitive answers. Seymour Martin Lipset (1996) advanced a persuasive argument on the side of American exceptionalism. More recently, Peter Baldwin (2009) marshals an impressive array of statistics in calling for a more nuanced approach, likening transatlantic differences to Freud's famous psychological observation "narcissism of minor differences." Baldwin implicitly draws on the federal nature of the EU and the US, presenting data at the EU member state and US state level to elucidate the sometimes striking disparity both among the EU's member states and American states on a wide host of issues – from religious values to attitudes about assimilation of immigrants. Therefore, to categorize values as "American" or "European" is to overlook the similarities between Californians and Germans and intra-European and intra-American differences. Michael O'Neill takes on this question in Chapter 4 as it informs transatlantic cooperation and provides contextual background to the relationship.

Different facets of culture appear in several of the policy chapters. While it is often presumed that postindustrial/postmaterial societies present similar risk aversion (see Inglehart, 1990, 1997), scholars and practitioners alike have identified disparities in risk acceptance within the Atlantic Community. This issue is particularly relevant with respect to trade in goods and services, and especially so given that one of the TTIP's key objectives is the reduction of non-tariff barriers (NTBs; such as regulatory rules and processes). So while US risk regulation is often a more "*ex post facto* litigation risk" (Transatlantic Business Council, 2013c), since the late 1990s the EU has adopted a decidedly more precautionary approach to risk assessment. (See D. Vogel, 2012 for a comparative study of "precaution" in EU and US health, safety, and environmental regulations.) Thus, on one hand we have the common-sense idea advanced by one advocate of mutual recognition of product testing and technical regulations: "it would be surprising, given broadly comparable stages of development, if consumers on one side of the Atlantic were more tolerant of unsafe products than the other" (Transatlantic Business Council, 2013c, p. 2). On the other hand, there is some evidence suggesting disparate risk tolerance informing regulatory practices between the EU and the US. Carolyn Dudek's analysis of GMO policy demonstrates the importance of public opinion and national culture in the shaping of what has become a long-standing dispute between the EU and the US over authorization of GMO cultivation, a dispute which has implications for the TTIP. (See, for example, US Ambassador to the EU's comments about GMOs and the TTIP in Vieuws, 2014.) So, too, it is sometimes assumed that American and European publics have different tolerances for financial risk, although the post-recession regulatory reforms on both sides of the Atlantic, which Buonanno details in Chapter 11, do not support this notion. She does, however, note that the Anglo-Saxon financing model is much more risk dependent than that of the continent. (See F. G. Castles, 1993 for his "family of nations" classification, which is widely referenced in comparative public policy studies.)

Institutional

Executive-Legislative Relations

As noted above, the EU is a hybrid system. It exhibits parliamentary features (the executive in the guise of the European Commission writes legislation) without fusion of power (the Commission is not part of the "government" in the same sense as the "government" of the British cabinet: commissioners are not simultaneously MEPs). Where does power lie in the EU and who speaks for Europe? The answer to this question, which has been somewhat of a moving target for many years, is crucially important in transatlantic policymaking because agreements are negotiated by the executive branch of the US government. The unified US structure with clear lines of command should be a more effective negotiating entity than a government (that is, the EU) with unclear and competing lines of authority. Egan and Nugent (Chapter 2) explore this question in the context of the EU's "maturation" into an entity which, since its founding in 1957, has gradually increased its power to have more authority to speak on behalf of its member states. Yet as Alexander Caviedes illustrates in his analysis of high-skilled immigration (Chapter 10) and Federiga Bindi argues in Chapter 3 (contemporary foreign policy), the EU has failed in these important areas to agree to common policies.

Another potential impact of institutional structure on transatlantic policymaking is the American separation-of-powers system, which was intended to produce fairly constant friction between the executive and legislative branches. While somewhat mitigated by the party system (when the same party holds both Houses of Congress and the presidency), "divided government" has become the norm in Washington. Therefore, while the executive branch may reach agreement with the EU, if the policy is subject to congressional approval the US president and his agents may fail to convince Congress to support the administration's position, especially when the oppositional party controls at least one house. This is of particular concern in trade negotiations, and currently the TTIP, as Holly Jarman argues in her analysis of transatlantic trade policy in Chapter 7 and Buonanno in her discussion of the controversy swirling around some of the TTIP chapters (Chapters 13–14).

The Bureaucracy

Bureaucrats – typically cabinet- and subcabinet-level officials – negotiate transatlantic agreements. Do bureaucrats at the European Commission and at the US federal executive bureaucracy view the "business" of government similarly (for example, through the lens of New Public Management)? Keith Henderson takes up this question in Chapter 6, finding some support for a shared administrative culture, but also identifying some significant differences between Eurocrats and US federal bureaucrats.

Another aspect of bureaucratic politics is the regulatory function's locus in the bureaucratic structure. So, for example, are the same "types" of agencies involved in formulating the policy under negotiation, or do these bureaucrats hail from agencies that are answerable to very different constituencies? The answer to this question is quite mixed. Zahariadis' analysis of competition policy finds a very different bureaucratic structure, while Buonanno identifies striking commonalities in the institutional structure for regulating financial services. Dudek finds a very significant difference in the regulatory locus for GMOs, where US regulation is housed in the US Department of Agriculture (USDA), while in the EU, GMO regulation is the responsibility of DG SANCO (Health and Consumer Safety). As Henderson explains in Chapter 6, bureaucrats will have very different orientations depending upon their agency location. This strongly suggests that USDA and DG SANCO officials will not share similar administrative cultures, and, it could be one factor impeding transatlantic policy understanding, agreement, and convergence around GMO regulation.

Intergovernmental Relations

Relations between the central government and constituent units (EU member states and US states) impact policymaking, and, therefore, should also affect transatlantic policymaking. While examining (domestic) intergovernmental or constituent relations is beyond the scope of our policy studies – our principal focus must be on EU and US policymaking – we recognize that federalism invariably complicates agreements made between Brussels and Washington.

A further complication is one of disparate regulatory regimes, where some EU member states and American states are regulatory "leaders" and others are "followers" (see P. Baldwin, 2009; Börzel, 2005; Liefferink, Arts, Kamstra, & Ooijevaar, 2009; and, D. Vogel & Swinnen, 2011). Implementation issues also feature in intergovernmental relations because in federal systems, and even more so in the EU's quasi-federal system, equal implementation of agreed polices cannot be assumed across time and space. While federal monitoring of US state implementation is hardly without obstacles – such as the costs of maintaining an "army" of federal inspectors and Americans' objections as intrusive such a large federal presence – the nature of cooperative federalism makes it easier to catch cheats. This is because federal and state agencies work in close cooperation to implement and enforce federal mandates. While states may gripe about "unfunded mandates," a great deal of money follows federal mandates to assist states with implementation. Second, businesses have long played a critically important role in reporting regulatory cheaters. And, third, civil society watchdogs operate in intersecting networks at the local, state, and federal levels. The EU, on the other hand, must rely on the EU member states to implement most policies and pan-European civil society organizations are less developed than national watchdog organizations in the US. Nevertheless, there are important exceptions where the European Commission is responsible for direct policy implementation, particularly in the areas of trade and competition policy which are so important in transatlantic policymaking. And as the internal market has matured, the European Commission has become increasingly adept at working with stakeholders to report implementation irregularities (European Commission, 2012c).

Politics

Political Party Ideology

While studies of transatlantic relations typically fall outside the traditional realm of party politics – namely, foreign and external security policy – much of transatlanticism, beginning with the 1992 New Transatlantic Agenda (discussed in Chapter 2), has been very much focused on economic issues. Furthermore, since 9/11 internal security issues such as individual privacy in any number of areas where data are collected (such as airline passenger data, social network websites, and financial transactions) have become increasingly controversial not just within the US and Europe, but in transatlantic negotiations. Because both individual liberties (which includes the expectation of the right to privacy) and the "proper" role of governmental intervention in the economy are the fodder of modern political party competition, transatlantic policymaking runs smack into political ideology and domestic politics when dealing with such hot-button issues as the EU agreeing to transfer airline passenger name records to the US and debates over whether government subsidies and tax breaks for domestic industries constitute unfair trade practices (see Hix, Noury, & Roland, 2007 on ideology and the European Parliament's (EP) political groups). Political ideology has affected transatlantic relations too, as can be seen in trade policy (Chapter 7), competition policy (Chapter 8), and personal privacy (Chapter10).

Elections and Electoral Systems

The EU and the US have disparate legislative electoral systems. The European Parliament (EP) is seated through proportional representation (PR) utilizing multimember districts, while the US utilizes a winner-take-all, single representative electoral system. The electoral systems are partially responsible for producing a two-party system Congress and a multi-party EP. And while it is true that the two main political groups in the EP – the center-left (Socialists & Democrats) and the center-right (European People's Party) – enjoy a majority (together controlling approximately 55% of the seats following the 2014 election), no single political group has a majority of the 751 seats. Reaching agreement in the EP, therefore, requires compromise and coalition of a nature that simply does not exist in the starkly left/right bifurcation in the US Congress. Furthermore, PR makes room for minor parties: in the EP, the Greens-European Free Alliance, which emphasizes postmaterial "quality of life" issues (see Inglehart, 1977, 1990) – holds 6.7% of the seats. The Alliance of Liberals and Democrats for Europe (ALDE) has 8.9% of the seats. The ALDE staunchly oppose governmental invasion of personal privacy. And the pro-business European Conservatives and Reformists (ECR) hold 9.3% of the seats. This complex calculus of control makes predicting the fate of the TTIP quite difficult.

How might such fierce competition in the American two-party system spill over into transatlantic policymaking? For example, does the nature of party competition in the US lead to greater politicization of transatlantic agreements such as the TTIP? The analyses in this volume do not offer a definitive answer, but there are "trends." So, for example, the anti-GMO stand has been able to gain traction in the EP because of the alliance of the S&D and Greens. So, too, the ALDE and S&D find common alliance in championing data privacy of European citizens by taking to task both the US government (NSA) and the data-mining practices of US IT companies such as Google and Facebook.

Representation

A common criticism leveled at the EU is that of a "democratic deficit," with the following three arguments typically advanced. First, European citizens have a weaker relationship with their MEPs than with their national legislative representatives, manifested in lower voter turnout for EP elections – 42.5% in 2014 (which held steady from the previous election) of that seen in national parliamentary elections. (See European Parliament, 2014b for EP election statistics.) Second, the Council of Ministers is an appointed body (government ministers of the member states) rather than an elected body (following a common historical pattern in a bicameral legislature's upper chamber). Third, the European Council's president is appointed by the heads of government rather than elected by European citizens.

Countering the democratic deficit argument is that the EP is an elected body. Moreover, in the 2014 EP elections, the EP managed to persuade the European Council to tacitly approve the concept of *spitzenkandidaten* (leading candidates), in which the EP's political groups nominated a candidate for commission president. As a result, the European Council selected Jean-Claude Juncker, the EPP's candidate (the political group which won a plurality of EP seats), for European Commission president.

The EU's democratic deficit could have important implications for transatlantic policymaking because the "distance" of EU institutions from the European polity seemingly affords it more leeway in negotiating agreements with foreign entities. The US Congress and President, however, must answer directly to their electorate and are forever, therefore, looking over their shoulders to public opinion. This vulnerability is most keenly felt in the US House of Representatives, whose members face re-election every two years, and must necessarily operate, therefore, under much shorter time frames than their counterparts in the EP who enjoy the "luxury" of five-year terms. Our studies suggest that the democratic deficit (or lack thereof) – could have an impact on the TTIP negotiations (see Chapter 13), and may be a factor in the Obama Administration's refusal to include financial services regulation on the TTIP agenda (see Chapter 11) or discuss changes to maritime shipping (the *Jones Act* requires shipping between American ports to be carried out by ships constructed in US shipyards, staffed by US merchant marines, and flagged in the US). Similarly, "Buy American" stipulations in congressional legislation will be very difficult for the Administration to horse trade in the TTIP's government procurement chapter. So, too, when it comes to homeland security, Congress is quite sensitive to public opinion. Zeff, Pirro, and Souleyrette (Chapter 9) discuss Congress' refusal to allow European companies to have a controlling interest in American-owned airlines. Similarly, Congress insisted on 100% screening of containers on ships leaving foreign ports bound for the US, despite the European Commission's protestations of the additional costs this program would place on European exports.

Interest Intermediation

Interest intermediation takes several forms in advanced industrialized democracies. On a continuum, with one pole "least amount of institutionalized links with government" and the opposite pole signifying "governments acting as partners with interest groups," there are three principal configurations: atomistic competition (Madisonian pluralism); issue networks (or the many variations such as "policy communities"); and corporatist arrangements. In Madisonian pluralism, competitive pressure groups have access to and exert greater influence on a relatively weak state. Corporatism involves a limited number of interest groups organized into hierarchical trade and peak associations enjoying monopolistic access and influence within particular policy areas and relative fixed relations with a "strong state." Issue networks (and its "tighter" variations such as the "policy community") occupy a midpoint on this continuum. According to Hugh Heclo (1978), the scholar who formulated the concept of issue networks, this type of interest intermediation is a communications network comprising a wide range of interested parties – from civil servants to lobbyists to journalists. Are different patterns of interest intermediation observable in the Atlantic Community? The answer seems to be "yes." So, for example, we know that interest intermediation is more "pluralist" in the US than the EU. Certainly interest intermediation in the EU seems to lean toward a more "elite" or privileged representation of business interests in Brussels (Coultrap, 1999) compared to that of Washington politics, the latter of which invariably includes weighty countervailing groups to business groups and trade associations. At the same time, scholars have documented the extent to which Brussels increasingly resembles Washington, with its plethora of lobbyists representing business enterprises, trade associations, regional and local governments, and civil society organizations. (The US literature on interest intermediation is prodigious. This subject is of increasing interest to EU scholars as well. See, for example, Chalmers, 2011; Damro, 2012; Eising, 2004; Greenwood, 2003; Klüver, 2013; Kohler-Koch, 2010; Rozbicka, 2013.) Adding to the complexity of interest intermediation is that "interests" may not always be pan-European, especially when a particular member state dominates in the manufacture of goods or delivery of services. Thus, when one of the more economically powerful member states opposes policy cooperation, it will be much more difficult for the EU to agree a common negotiating position. Audiovisual products represent a classic example of the point for the EU, where France has consistently opposed its inclusion in any trade talks whatsoever. (Conversely, it should be recognized that the EU can sometimes use international negotiations to force a recalcitrant member state to reach a compromise.)

Studies in this volume show that the EU and the US have sought to harness interests in unexpected ways. The high-level fora and consultations (inventoried and discussed in Chapter 5, and in Chapter 13 in terms of the TTIP) show the extent to which a "transatlantic" interest community is being fostered at the highest levels of government, and that this interest agglomeration has been dominated by business interests (at the expense of labor, consumers, and environmentalists). But business interests do not always reign supreme, as can be seen in Chapter 10's comparison of GMO policy in the EU and the US and the heated conflicts over inclusion of the Investor-State Dispute Settlement (ISDS) in the Council's negotiating mandate to the Commission for the TTIP. Interestingly, European interests opposing GMO approval have (likely) exported some of their anti-GMO sentiment to the US.

Chapter 13's analysis of the TTIP negotiations illustrates the different nature of interest group behavior in the EU and the US. In the EU, anti-TTIP EU groups are attempting to mobilize the public against the TTIP in a Stop TTIP campaign. This tactic was no more apparent than in the campaign by environmentalists and consumer protection advocates against the ISDS chapter in the European Council's negotiating mandate to the Commission. So, for example, the EP Greens leaked this negotiating mandate to the media in a rather naked effort to build public support against ISDS, in particular (and the TTIP in general). So, too, anti-TTIP forces sought to use the European Citizens' Initiative (ECI) to derail the ISDS chapter.

In the US, on the other hand, public mobilization is lacking, if not altogether absent. This is because American public interest groups have access to mainstream progressive politicians in Congress and the Administration's unit responsible for negotiating the TTIP (the Office of the US Trade Representative through institutionalized advisory groups as well as back channels) and, therefore, can focus their efforts on both negotiators and legislators in order to influence the TTIP during the negotiation phase. Thus, the institutionalized nature of American pluralism has enabled US interest groups to take a more "constructive" approach to the TTIP as compared to the European "protest" and "social movement" (outsider) "unconventional" participation tactics.

Nature of the Transatlantic Relationship: Conflictual, Cooperative, or Neither?

McGuire and Smith (2008, p. 3) characterize the transatlantic relationship as being based on an "adversarial partnership" in which there is an "interplay between competition and convergence." As they say, "in every aspect of their relationship the EU and the US are increasingly part of an integrated policy space, but ... within this space they are in often intense competition (sometimes formulated as 'competitive interdependence' or 'competitive cooperation')." Moreover, many of the issues that are the focus of much of this competition are partly underpinned by differing principles and values.

To state the obvious, the transatlantic partners are two sovereign states (taking the EU as a quasi-federal state) and, therefore, are not compelled to cooperate. In the absence of a hierarchical authority with police powers, to what extent does hard and soft power affect the EU–US relationship? In one sense, this is a key question running through this volume, but taken up directly in Chapters 2 (the evolution of the transatlantic relations) and Chapter 3 (contemporary foreign policy). Contributors to this volume report on long-running conflicts still unresolved in key policy areas: competition, trade, GMO cultivation, and data privacy.

Yet despite these incidents of highly publicized disagreement, a great deal of cooperation is taking place. Chapter 9 examines the progress made in the Open Skies Agreement. Chapter 3 reviews the foreign policy successes and the incidents when the EU and US have been "on the same page." Chapter 5 documents the large number of agreements that have taken place "below the radar" of the daily press – progress in biotechnology, security, energy, and so forth – while the financial services regulation case study in Chapter 11 documents the intensive communication and cooperation between American and European regulators.

Finally, there are mutual areas of concern where there has been neither conflict nor cooperation. Chapter 10 explores the lack of transatlantic dialogue on high-skilled immigration, despite the importance American and European policy-makers attach to attracting and admitting highly skilled immigrants. Caviedes finds that the reason for this lack of dialogue can be laid at the feet of the EU and its lack of "clear demarcation" of EU competence for immigration policy.

Power, Resources and Bargaining: Mutual or Imposed Agreement?

Are transatlantic agreements arrived at by mutual agreement or "imposed" by either the EU or the US? Famously, Robert Kagan (2003, p. 3) advanced the Realist perspective in which he concludes Europeans and Americans diverge fundamentally with respect to foreign and security policy:

> It is time to stop pretending that Europeans and Americans share a common view of the world, or even that they occupy the same world. On the all-important question of power – the efficacy of power, the morality of power, the desirability of power – American and European perspectives are diverging.... That is why on major strategic and international questions today, Americans are from Mars and Europeans are from Venus: They agree on little and understand one another less and less.

Power in international relations can be hard or soft. There are two truisms in EU studies: first, the US, with the largest military capacity in the world, can credibly wield hard power and the EU cannot; and second, the EU has enormous economic power (or expressed in EU shorthand: "economic giant, but political pygmy"). It has been argued that the EU's soft power can compensate for the lack of hard power because in most cases – as Keohane and Nye (1977) taught a generation of scholars – the exercise of hard power is rarely the appropriate or necessary response in international disputes. And certainly, the EU can point to some success in exercising collective soft power, such as the use of sanctions in forcing Iran to the negotiating table over uranium enrichment for weapons building.

Ten years after the Kagan thesis entered the transatlantic debate, allegations emerged of the US National Security Agency (NSA) spying on European External Action Service's (the EU's "foreign ministry") offices in New York and Washington (Castle, 2013). As the Edward Snowden documents – the former NSA contractor who had downloaded thousands of NSA documents – continued to be leaked, the NSA was discovered to have accessed thousands of French phone records, collected data on over 60 million phone calls in Spain, and spied on foreign leaders, which apparently went so far as to monitor German Chancellor Angela Merkel's mobile phone conversations (EurActiv, 2013; Minder, 2013). Months later a suspected double agent was arrested in Germany's Federal Office for the Protection of the Constitution (Germany's counterintelligence agency), ostensibly recruited by the US Central Intelligence Agency (CIA) (Baumgärtner et al., 2014). As the fallout from the NSA spy scandal continued, European business and government leaders reacted with renewed purpose and vigor to curb the power and practices of US internet companies with respect to data transfer, after having dropped the more controversial aspects of the initiative just two years earlier under pressure from Washington (Traynor, 2013).

In areas where economic power is not commingled with security issues, the EU and the US do seem to negotiate and achieve mutually advantageous outcomes. But as is illustrated in Chapters 2 (evolution of the relationship), 3 (foreign policy), and 10 (passenger name records), and in those cases where security is at issue, the US generally "gets its way." Furthermore, Henderson's comparative study of the EU and US bureaucracies (Chapter 6) brings to the fore their significantly disparate size, which invariably impedes the EU's influence in the various stages of the policy cycle.

Future Cooperation?

To what extent are the EU and the US currently seeking to build deeper cooperation or integration? Specifically, have the partners been more concerned with eliminating existing barriers to trade and investment (negative integration such as reducing tariff barriers) or with establishing a new basis of agreement (such as mutual recognition of standards or even harmonized standards, that is, reducing non-tariff and technical barriers to trade)? Chapters 2 and 5 document a very active pattern of deeper cooperation, which accelerated in the 1990s with the signing of the Transatlantic Declaration and the New Transatlantic Agenda (Chapter 2) and the increasingly "networked" nature of transatlantic cooperation (Chapter 5). The TTIP Agreement, the current "phase" of transatlantic (economic) cooperation, is the focus of Chapters 13 and 14.

Outline of Chapters

This book is divided into four parts. Part I, consisting of three chapters, contextualizes the transatlantic relationship with an historical survey, contemporary foreign relations and policy, and cultural dynamics. Together, these chapters provide the background for understanding the evolving nature of the EU–US relationship.

In Chapter 2, Michelle Egan and Neill Nugent examine the changing context and nature of the transatlantic relationship from the postwar era until the present. The authors discuss the principal transatlantic agreements and offer a broader perspective on a relationship that can be understood as both conflictual and cooperative. This chapter further shows the great extent to which the transatlantic relationship has been shaped by European integration and suggests that the ability of the EU's member states to agree common positions in relation to the US will continue to be a major factor in what they describe as the "New Transatlanticism."

In Chapter 3, Federiga Bindi discusses transatlantic foreign policy cooperation. This is a crucial area of study because the ability of the EU to speak as one voice on the world stage will continue to influence and even determine the ability of Brussels to "do business" on behalf of Europe. Naturally, if the EU and the US can cooperate in matters of foreign policy, they will be better equipped to shape the world according to Western values, goals, and objectives. Ideally, cooperation would also contribute to American and European security. Naturally, it is quite impossible to separate fully economics and politics. Indeed, East/West conflict in Ukraine reminds us of the interconnection between regional trade agreements and global politics and security. President Viktor Yanukovych's decision not to sign a trade association agreement proffered by the EU – edging Ukraine closer to Russia's Eurasian Customs Union – brought hundreds of thousands of Ukrainians into Kiev's Independence Square in November 2013 in protest (Herszenhorn, 2013). These protests triggered a chain of events culminating in Crimea's secession from Ukraine in 2014 and Russian annexation. Just hours after the Doha Round concluded in Bali, protestors in Kiev toppled and smashed a statue of Lenin while crowds cheered them on, chanting, "Ukraine is Europe!" (Walker, 2013), reminding the world that trade integration is as much about "politics" and "identity" as about "economics."

Michael O'Neill provides the much needed cultural context in Chapter 4. He asks to what extent might American and European cultures differ, and the political consequences thereof? He argues that "American exceptionalism" is an overstated and rather blunt concept, not allowing of the nuances inherent to the study of political culture. For O'Neill, the cultural legacy of the West "still fosters a familiarity conducive to shared endeavor and moral empathy."

Part II of this volume focuses on governance and comprises two chapters. Chapter 5, co-authored by Laurie Buonanno, Neill Nugent, and Natalia Cugleşan, has two purposes. First, it examines the governance architecture of transatlanticism. Second, it documents the many agreements to have been reached in a wide range of policy areas between the EU and the US. This chapter demonstrates that a great deal of transatlantic activity had been carried out by public officials and stakeholders (especially representatives of corporations engaged in transatlantic trade and investment) in the two decades prior to the opening of the TTIP negotiations, and has in many ways laid the basis for the TTIP.

Chapter 6, authored by Keith Henderson, compares the administrative cultures of the European Commission and US federal civil servants working in the executive branch. Unlike the traditional transatlantic relationship in which diplomats from foreign ministries interact on a regular basis (and are understood to be quite similar in their training, family background, acculturation, etc.), government officials are no longer drawn exclusively from the diplomatic corps, but from the government agencies responsible for economic and regulatory matters – agriculture, consumer protection, the central bank, homeland security, and the like. Thus, Henderson seeks to explain how the administrative cultures of the European Commission and the US executive bureaucracy might promote or hinder transatlantic policy cooperation, and concludes that there is some evidence to suggest similarities in administrative cultures.

Part III consists of six policy chapters. Holly Jarman writes on transatlantic trade policy in Chapter 7. Apart from the security relationship, trade is often thought of as the most important policy arena in which the US and the EU meet – both at the global level in the WTO and in EU–US bilateral relations (such as the ongoing TTIP negotiations). Jarman finds areas of agreement, but cautions readers against excessive optimism, at least in the near future, regarding some of the long-standing and seemingly intractable trade disagreements, many of which can be traced directly to domestic factors.

In Chapter 8, Nikolais Zahariadis analyzes cooperation in competition policy between the EU and the US. Competition policy, as with trade policy, is a policy that is unequivocally formulated and enacted in Brussels and Washington. Yet, despite the "federal" nature of competition policy in the policymaking systems of both partners, these policies are highly contingent upon domestic factors – making cooperation in establishing a shared and cooperative policy regime exceedingly difficult.

Chapter 9, co-authored by Eleanor Zeff, Ellen Pirro, and Reginald Souleyrette, focuses on the understudied area of transatlantic transportation policy. Naturally, with such a high volume of goods and large numbers of people crossing the Atlantic, transatlantic cooperation in transport is fundamental to facilitating people-to-people links, cross-investment, and trade. This chapter demonstrates that transatlantic transportation policy has been significant in continuing the liberalization processes associated with the transatlanticism of the 1990s. However, after 9/11 transportation security rose to the top of the transatlantic policymaking agenda, complicating negotiation and cooperation in transportation policy.

In Chapter 10, Alexander Caviedes offers a comparative examination of two mobility regimes – the Passenger Name Record Agreement and highly skilled migration. The purpose of this comparison is to further our understanding of areas where cooperation in transatlantic policymaking is deemed necessary. Significantly, this chapter offers empirical evidence for the Egan–Nugent contribution – where the EU's member states have not been able to agree to a common policy, little progress can be made in a policy area on the transatlantic level, regardless of whether it is an issue where transgovernmental actors recognize the advantages of cooperation.

In Chapter 11, Laurie Buonanno examines financial services regulation. She suggests that financial services regulation offers a classic example of the prisoner's dilemma, where regulatory arbitrage in the area of financial services regulation would benefit one or the other region, but cooperation would maximize the benefits of economic security to the transatlantic community. She also suggests that this policy has a federal dimension as well; specifically, there is a large disparity in expertise and market share in the provision of financial services among EU member states, an industry where the UK dominates and has been instrumental in shaping (or blocking) Brusselization of some aspects of financial services regulation. Financial services regulation policy also provides an opportunity to investigate the nature of transatlantic policy cooperation after a sudden and unexpected crisis (the global financial crisis that took hold in the US in the autumn of 2007, which precipitated the "Great Recession"), where Buonanno finds a great deal of policy convergence in regulatory reforms adopted since the Great Recession.

In Chapter 12, Carolyn Marie Dudek investigates US and EU policy in the regulation of GMOs. Unlike the sudden financial meltdown brought about largely by lax financial services regulation, the GMO case is an example of a long-standing and, to date, intractable policy disagreement between the EU and the US. Here a number of factors intersect and impede agreement, including the dominance of US companies in the development of GMO crops, the revolving door between industry and government prevalent in the US, and (historically) disparate cultural attitudes toward food both among EU member states and between Europeans and Americans.

Part IV, consisting of three chapters, explores prospects and challenges associated with transatlanticism. Chapter 13 is devoted to the politics, processes, costs, and benefits of the TTIP. Chapter 14 offers an in-depth examination of the three broad categories being negotiated in the TTIP – market access, regulations, and rules. Some of these issues are far too complex to reach within the confines of a "static" agreement, virtually ensuring institutionalization of a consultation mechanism for American and European public servants.

The book ends with Chapter 15, which revisits the themes introduced earlier in this chapter. Rather than a summary of the findings, this chapter seeks patterns which can help us to generalize about the nature of the relationship and predict the future direction of the transatlantic partnership.

Part I

Contextualizing Transatlanticism

2 The Changing Context and Nature of the Transatlantic Relationship

Michelle Egan and Neill Nugent

Introduction

In response to the changing geopolitical and economic contexts in which they are located, transatlantic relations have been adapted and adjusted in various ways over the years – especially since the early 1990s. While in the security realm the North Atlantic Security Organization (NATO) has shifted from being a defense-based territorial alliance into one based on crisis management, in the economic realm the relationship has become more institutionalized and has broadened beyond the traditional focus on trade to encompass a wide-ranging agenda spanning economic, monetary, and financial issues.

For more than 30 years after World War II the US and Europe did much to set the international agenda. Indeed, they were the main driving forces behind many of the global institutions and multilateral architectures of the postwar period – including the United Nations (UN), NATO, the General Agreement on Tariffs and Trade (GATT) and subsequently World Trade Organization (WTO), and the International Monetary Fund (IMF). The deeply intertwined close relationship that assisted the US and Europe in being able to exercise such influence on the world stage remains strong and is still characterized by a level of ties across the diplomatic, economic, and civil society realms that is unparalleled. Indeed, the number and scope of these ties have increased greatly in recent years. However, in response to structural changes at the global level as well as internal developments on both sides of the Atlantic, the past two decades have seen considerable debate about the future evolution of transatlantic relations, with analysts offering forecasts ranging from a fully functional and enduring global partnership to an increasingly episodic marriage of convenience (see, for example, Hamilton & Rhinard, 2011; Smith, 2009; Tocci & Alcaro, 2012).

So as to provide the context for the changes that have emerged in the post-Cold War era, this chapter begins with a brief overview of the key features of the transatlantic relationship in the period from the end of World War II until the end of the Cold War. The second section outlines the reasons why, from the late 1980s/early 1990s, an additional approach to transatlantic relations came to be seen as being desirable in response to the rapid changes occurring in the global geopolitical and economic environments. The establishment and nature of this additional approach in the 1990s – which was quickly dubbed "the new transatlanticism" – is outlined in the third section. The fourth section focuses on recent transatlantic relations by examining key features of the relationship during the Bush and Obama Administrations. In this section we identify a number of causal variables impacting on the relationship – including both structural and contingent variables and ideational and material variables – which should help contextualize subsequent chapters of this book that focus on specific policy domains. The chapter ends with some general conclusions and thoughts about the future of transatlantic relations.

Transatlantic Relations in Historical Context

In the years immediately after World War II, the US and the states of Western Europe established new and intensified relations of cooperation. The factors promoting these new relations were mostly a direct consequence of World War II, with the most important being the US abandonment of its prewar isolationism, its active engagement in assisting the economic recovery of Europe, and the need to respond to the onset of the Cold War through US–West European resolve to work together to resist the perceived communist threat. The impact of these factors was no more clearly witnessed than via the financial assistance that was provided by the US to Western Europe via the Marshall Fund and by the creation of two key transatlantic organizations: the Organization for Economic European Cooperation (OEEC) in 1948 and NATO in 1949.

Although the notion of a more integrated Europe was not at the center of American policy debates in the early post-World War II period, US policymakers did utilize American influence to promote European integration. So, for instance, the Marshall Plan was never simply an economic rescue for Europe, nor even a none too disguised effort to promote the ideology of market capitalism, but was crafted to require cooperation among the participating states of Western Europe (Hanhimäki, Schoenborn, & Zanchetta, 2012, p. 19). Such cooperation would, it was hoped, be in the interests of American business by, for example, resulting in some streamlining of the many regulatory and tax regimes in Europe with which American corporations had to work. For similar self-interested reasons, in the 1950s major US corporations supported the building of a West European common market, much more than they did the rival, UK-backed proposal for a free trade area (Committee for Economic Development – Research and Policy Committee, 1959).

The impact of these various factors emerging directly from World War II was soon being reinforced by exogenous factors promoting transatlantic cooperation. The most notable of these factors was the increasingly interconnected nature of the world and an increasingly perceived need in the US and Western Europe for the two to be working closely together to shape global economic and political governance. Certainly, the US was looking for strong allies. As Miriam Camps (1956, p. 18), a former US Department of State official, explained in her analysis of the potential for the viability of a European common market, "Our need for allies is not only a military requirement. In the struggle for the underdeveloped countries of the world, a Europe that has something to offer, both economically and ideologically, is an asset we badly need."

For many years after World War II, transatlantic cooperation did, of course, mean the US on the one side and the individual states of Western Europe on the other. However, with the establishment in 1952 of the European Coal and Steel Community (ECSC), US–European relations began to be based on an additional footing. The US was more than a cheerleader in this effort; for example, on Jean Monnet's first day of work as President of the High Authority at the newly established ECSC, US Secretary of State Dean Acheson sent him a dispatch in the name of President Truman granting the ECSC full diplomatic recognition (European Commission, 2004b, p. 11). In 1954 the ECSC opened a delegation in Washington and in 1956 the US reciprocated by creating a US Mission to the ECSC in Luxembourg. These initial steps were then followed, as the ECSC was broadened out into the European Community (EC) in 1957 and as trade and other forms of economic interactions between the US and Europe intensified, by increasingly wide and structured US–European relations.

President Kennedy signaled his Administration's desire for a deeper transatlantic relationship when, on American Independence Day in 1962, he delivered a speech on emerging global interdependence. At the heart of his speech was a call for a strengthened Atlantic partnership between the US and an increasingly united (Western) Europe:

> We do not regard a strong and united Europe as a rival but as a partner.... We see in such a Europe a partner with whom we can deal on a basis of full equality in all of the great and burdensome tasks of building and defending a community of free nations.
>
> ...The first order of business is for our European friends to go forward in forming the more perfect union which will someday make this partnership possible.
>
> ...the United States will be ready for a Declaration of Interdependence that we will be prepared to discuss with a united Europe the ways and means of forming a concrete Atlantic partnership.
>
> (Kennedy, 1962b)

But, as Kennedy foresaw, a prerequisite task for the building of a strong Atlantic partnership was the building of a strong Europe, which was still in its infancy. Accordingly, with the exception of external trade – which grew rapidly in volume in the postwar years and where the EC quickly assumed exclusive responsibilities to negotiate with trading partners on behalf of its member states – transatlantic relations remained, until well into the 1990s, mainly based on relations between the US and individual West European states. This was largely for three reasons. First, features of the fledgling EC made for difficulties: because of the Cold War it did not include Central and Eastern European states among its membership and – until the 1995 enlargement round – it was even missing significant Western European states; reflecting the laggardly pace of most of its policy development, the EC was very slow to acquire external policy responsibilities beyond trade (see Chapter 7 for a discussion of transatlantic trade); and when it did acquire such responsibilities – as with the (very tentative and slow) development from the early 1970s of a fledgling foreign policy (under the significantly vague name of European Political Cooperation) – it was frequently unable to present a united policy front, especially on matters where there were significant differences of interest and/or preferences between the member states.

Second, American presidential administrations vacillated with respect to the advantages of a united Europe for the American economy. Facing a growing European economy, a strong deutschmark, a falling dollar, and competition from European exports, President Nixon and his security advisor Henry Kissinger questioned what they increasingly saw as a one-sided relationship. Nixon complained, "They cannot have the United States' participation and cooperation on the security front and then proceed to have confrontation and even hostility on the economic and political front" (quoted in Lundestad, 2003, p. 180). At much the same time, Europeans – most notably the French President, Charles de Gaulle – complained about the inequality of the Bretton Woods System and US fiscal irresponsibility, prompting many European member states to push for changing the rules of the international financial institution. As Ludlow (2010, p. 46) has stated, "mutual incomprehension across the Atlantic was present in the financial sphere, as much as it was in the security sphere."

Third, until the Cold War ended, the US tended to see its relationship with Europe through the lens of anti-communism and containment. So, for example, in the 1960s and 1970s, when Europe did not support the US in Vietnam (the reason that President Johnson never made an official state visit to any European country) and later over policy toward Israel, the US was primarily concerned that Europe support America's unilateral perception of the prerequisites for global security (see Ludlow, 2010).

Naturally, these factors resulted in the US being somewhat uncertain, frustrated, and indeed wary of trying to work with the EC. For the most part, therefore, for many years after the EC was founded, transatlantic relations continued to be conducted directly between the US and individual European states, either on a bilateral basis or within the context of Western or Western-dominated international organizations.

Reasons for an Emerging New Transatlanticism

With the Cold War over, the 1990s witnessed a period of reflection about the future of the transatlantic relationship. Responding to predictions about the loss of Europe's strategic importance to the US, during a visit to Washington in April 1989 the President of the European Commission, Jacques Delors, argued that it was time to "reassess the [transatlantic] relationship.... Both partners now have to think about a wider political dialogue, leading possibly to joint action over issues of mutual interest" (quoted in Peterson, 1996, p. 46).

A few months later, in December, the US Secretary of State, James Baker, in a (now much-quoted) speech, stated:

As Europe moves toward its goal of a common internal market, and as its institutions for political and security cooperation evolve, the link between the United States and the European Community will become even more important.

We want our trans-Atlantic cooperation to keep pace with European integration and institutional reform. To this end, we propose that the United States and the European Community work together to achieve, whether in treaty or some other form, a significantly strengthened set of institutional and consultative links.

(J. Baker, 1989)

Thus was publicly set in motion a process that, as is shown later in this chapter, resulted in a number of initiatives being taken from 1990 with a view to both broadening transatlantic policy relations beyond the traditional concentration on Cold War security issues and supplementing existing transatlantic relations with more institutionalized relations between the US and the EC. As the process developed, it increasingly became clear that the intention was to lay bases for the creation of an EU–US partnership focused on policy cooperation and consultation in a wide range of, mainly economic-related, policy areas.

What explains this development? What transformed transatlantic relations into a multidimensional and complex network of formal and informal ties and links that have become increasingly institutionalized across a wide range of issue areas? A combination of several – in practice overlapping and interconnected – factors have driven developments.

The End of the Cold War

Prior to the end of the Cold War the East–West relationship was the most important defining feature of the international system. In that system, most Western European states were bound to the US within a defense and external security policy pact – NATO – which was based on their common resolve to resist communist expansionism. This binding between the US and the West European states was not a binding of equals: the latter were very much cast in junior, even subservient, positions. This uneven nature of the relationship was no more evident than in the way in which European leaders such as Margaret Thatcher and Francois Mitterrand were relegated to the position of interlocutors and advisors when in the 1980s US–Soviet relations thawed under Ronald Reagan and Mikhail Gorbachev.

The collapse of communism in Central and Eastern Europe and in the Soviet Union in 1989–1991 removed the shared transatlantic security challenge from the Soviet Union and in so doing greatly reduced the importance of NATO, which hitherto had been the pivotal base of the transatlantic relationship. However, external security policy remained important and indeed generated frictions as the EU's increasing foreign and defense policy ambitions, which were loudly proclaimed in the Maastricht Treaty and subsequently developed, resulted in the US becoming concerned about a possible decoupling of the security dimension of the Atlantic Alliance.

But although the end of the Cold War reduced the need for a transatlantic security alliance, it brought to the fore the need for other types of close transatlantic relations. In particular, there seemed now to be a more multi-polar and uncertain world in which economics and trade were key issues, and where there was a common effort to promote market economies and liberal democracy through emulation and diffusion of Western norms and ideas – with the Washington Consensus becoming the dominant paradigm.

The Increasing Policy Importance of the EU

Although it was initially created in the 1950s to establish a common market, until the mid-1980s progress in building the common market was rather slow and spasmodic. But, in 1985 the European integration process, and the common market project within it, was re-launched – partly via the Single European Market (SEM) program, which set December 1992 as the target for passing measures that would result in the market being "completed," and partly also via the Single European Act (SEA) which increased the EC's capacity for passing the necessary measures to achieve the 1992 target. In practice, this re-launch of the integration process in the mid-1980s stopped short of a true "completion" of the common market goal, but it did nonetheless result in a significant increase in market integration, trade liberalization and regulatory competition among European member states. As such, it was influential in persuading the US – especially when the American media and pundits suggested that the EC was creating a "fortress Europe" – that its relations with the European Union (the EC's new name after the 1992 Maastricht Treaty) needed to be upgraded.

While the EU often struggles to speak with a single voice, a key feature of its development has been its growing capacity to act as a single actor in respect of its external relations. Since the creation of the EU's Common Commercial Policy (CCP) in the 1960s, trade has long been the most important and developed policy where member states conduct their external relations as a single bloc – via the EC acting on the basis of instructions given to it by the Council of Ministers. However, in many other policy areas where there have been shared policy competences between the EU and its member states – such as the environment and internal security – the Commission's external policy roles have steadily increased over the years. Depending on whether there is an exclusive or a mixed policy competence, the Commission is sometimes authorized to act in external negotiations as the EU's sole representative and sometimes to act alongside the member states.

This international "actorness" on the part of the EU has been strengthened through successive treaty reforms, to extend well beyond trade and trade-related matters to cover – often on a shared basis with the member states – the external dimensions of most internal policies. Indeed, it even partly extends to foreign and security policy, with the Maastricht Treaty having laid the legal foundation for – what is still a very much under-developed – Common Foreign and Security Policy (CFSP) and the 2007 Lisbon Treaty giving the EU, for the first time, an international legal personality. The Lisbon Treaty also strengthened the institutional bases of the EU's external policies with the creation of a (revamped) post of High Representative of the Union for Foreign Affairs and Security Policy (in effect, an embryo EU Foreign Minister) and a European External Action Service (an embryonic diplomatic corps).

The EU has thus developed an increasing external policy capacity and importance and, correspondingly, has increasingly been seen by the US as an actor with which it can, and needs to, do business.

Globalization and Interdependence

For 30 or so years after World War II the US and Europe were able to exert effective leadership in global economic governance, but new international realities arising from globalization and international interdependence have increasingly resulted in this dominance being weakened. From about the late 1970s, and through to the present day, the hitherto dominant role of the US and Europe in world economic activity has come to be challenged by new economic powers. With Japan initially leading the way, joined more recently by the emergence of the BRIC (Brazil, Russia, India, and China) group, emerging powers have achieved much faster economic growth than Western countries and have increasingly asserted their presence in the global system. It is an assertion that has been hampered by problems between the BRICs in reconciling their different priorities, but on one matter they have been strongly in agreement: the current global system favors the transatlantic partners.

This increasing challenge to the West's shaping of the global order has heightened the sense that the US and the EU need to jointly respond to sociopolitical and economic transformation by creating a framework for cooperation that better enables them to shape global rule-making. Indeed, faced with an unclear world evolving to an unknown destination it is only natural and logical that they would do so. Unsurprisingly, therefore, as Steffenson (2005, p. 1) puts it, the transatlantic relationship has increasingly come to be viewed by many policy practitioners on both sides of the Atlantic "as a way to promote Western ideas of democracy and security in an era of change and uncertainty."

Mutual Interdependence

Many of the features of globalization and interdependence – and in particular the increased cross-border flows of economic activity – have long been, and still are, particularly intense in the transatlantic area. As is emphasized in the introductory chapter of this book, the US and EU are each the other's largest trading partner when all forms of trade are counted, and taken together their trade accounts for around one-third of world merchandise trade and for about 40% of world trade in services. There are even higher proportionate interactions in respect of foreign direct investment (FDI), with transatlantic FDI accounting for over 60% of global flows and with both the EU and US each accounting for over 50% of the other's FDI. (For a detailed analysis of the size and nature of the transatlantic economy, see Hamilton & Quinlan, 2014.)

The European integration process rests in large part on the belief that the removal of intra-EU barriers to cross-border economic activities will, all other things being equal, increase the volume of such activities. But, at the global level there are numerous such barriers, and attempts to remove them have been plagued with difficulties of many different kinds. So, taking trade, attempts since the early 1960s in the GATT and WTO frameworks to remove tariff, and even more so non-tariff, barriers have been slow and partial, and have become increasingly difficult given the growing heterogeneity of members. Inevitably, therefore, the world's two main trading partners have increasingly been motivated to look for bilateral arrangements involving the removal of trading barriers, in the belief that the volume of transatlantic trade will thereby be considerably expanded. The barriers they have sought to remove have been not so much focused on tariffs, which on most traded goods now average only 4%, although they are much higher on some sensitive products – especially foodstuffs. Rather, non-tariff barriers (NTBs) to transatlantic commerce have been, and are, the main problem. These NTBs take many different forms, including differing product standards, public procurement restrictions, and subsidies. As is shown in Chapter 7, tackling such problems has been a principal focus of the transatlantic agenda since the mid-1990s, and in 2013 was given a major advance with the opening of negotiations for the creation of a Transatlantic Trade and Investment Partnership (TTIP).

This mutual interdependence is resulting, as McGuire and Smith (2008, p. 53) have put it, in a degree of transatlantic governance which is no longer restricted to traditional military and trade issues, but is also becoming an important feature of regulatory policymaking in which diplomacy is increasingly networked through a range of public and private actors (see Slaughter, 2009; also Chapter 5 of this volume).

The New Transatlanticism of the 1990s

As was noted above, in December 1989 James Baker proposed that there should be "a significantly strengthened set of institutional and consultative links" between the US and the EC. This began to be given effect in the 1990s as the transatlantic relationship was given a broader and institutionalized base with the signing of agreements that resulted in the creation of new institutional structures and the issuing of joint declarations and statements of policy objectives. The nature of these agreements is described in this section of the chapter. (For fuller accounts than can be given here, see: Phillipart & Winand, 2001; M. Pollack & Schaffer, 2001b; Stefanova, 2001; Steffenson, 2005.)

The Transatlantic Declaration

The first important development in the new broadening and institutionalization of the transatlantic relationship was the 1990 Transatlantic Declaration (TAD), which was signed by the EC, its member states, and the US. Key inclusions in the TAD were:

- the identification of a number of common goals – including supporting democracy and the rule of law, safeguarding peace and promoting international security, and advancing market principles;
- a commitment by the EU and US to tackle a number of transnational challenges, in particular terrorism, illegal drugs activities, international crime, the protection of the environment, and the prevention of the proliferation of nuclear armaments, chemical and biological weapons, and missile technology;
- the laying of a framework for new forms of transatlantic policy cooperation and consultation, most notably with the initiation of high-level political meetings between the two partners, including on a bi-annual basis at the level of the US President on the one side and the Presidents of the European Council and of the European Commission on the other (European External Action Service, 1990).

Much of the contents of the TAD were rather bland. But it was nonetheless a very significant document in that it sought to move institutionalized transatlantic relations beyond their traditional main policy concern, namely defense, and also outside of their traditional main forum, namely NATO.

The New Transatlantic Agenda

The TAD was followed-up in December 1995 with the signing by US President Bill Clinton, EU Commission President Jacques Santer, and EU Council President Felipe Gonzales of a document entitled the New Transatlantic Agenda (NTA). Four priority areas were identified in the document (EU & US, 1995):

Promoting Peace and Stability, Democracy and Development around the World
Together, we will work for an increasingly stable and prosperous Europe; foster democracy and economic reform in Central and Eastern Europe as well as in Russia, Ukraine and other new independent states; secure peace in the Middle East; advance human rights; promote non-proliferation and cooperate on development and humanitarian assistance.

Responding to Global Challenges
Together, we will fight international crime, drug-trafficking and terrorism; address the needs of refugees and displaced persons; protect the environment and combat disease.

Contributing to the Expansion of World Trade and Closer Economic Relations
Together, we will strengthen the multilateral trading system and take concrete, practical steps to promote closer economic relations between us.

Building Bridges Across the Atlantic
Together, we will work with our business people, scientists, educators and others to improve communication and to ensure that future generations remain as committed as we are to developing a full and equal partnership.

Stuart Eizenstat, the US Ambassador to the EU for 1993–1996 and an important driver of the creation of the NTA, summed up the hopes of many of those who designed and negotiated the NTA when he wrote shortly after its signing (Foreword in A. L. Gardner, 1997, p. ix):

There is no question in my mind that the NTA is the most significant step in US–EU relations since the beginning of the European integration in the 1950s. It recognizes the prime importance of the transatlantic relationship and moves it from a largely consultative and trade-oriented one to a more broadly-based action agenda intended to further our common political as well as economic goals around the globe.... The NTA will enable the United States and the EU to harness our joint energies together across a wide range of political, economic, trade, diplomatic, science, health and private sector initiatives.

The NTA, which was accompanied by a *Joint US–EU Action Plan* (1995), was necessarily couched in rather general terms, but as compared with the TAD it was more specific about both the nature of shared transatlantic policy goals and how cooperation and consultation would be operationalized. The policy goals, as noted above, were grouped under and focused on four priority areas. The main instruments for giving effect to the goals were to be increased liaison and cooperation between EU and US policymakers and implementers and the deepening of people-to-people ties of various kinds through support for transatlantic dialogues between policy players and policy receivers. As Peterson (2003, p. 86) has observed, the NTA "locked both sides into a thick, multilayered set of exchanges between officials, representatives of civil society, and political leaders."

An important matter that was left open, and one that has in consequence subsequently given rise to uncertainty as to just what should and should not be regarded as being part of the new transatlantic agenda, was how defense and security matters fitted into the picture. For while the first policy goal (listed above) makes clear that foreign and security policy matters were certainly identified as being part of the NTA, there was also a strong statement about the continued importance of NATO (EU & US, 1995):

We reaffirm the indivisibility of transatlantic security. NATO remains, for its members, the centrepiece of transatlantic security, providing the indispensable link between North America and Europe.

The Transatlantic Economic Partnership

The NTA included provision for the creation of a New Transatlantic Market-place (NTM) "which will expand trade and investment opportunities and multiply jobs on both sides of the Atlantic." Quite what this would consist of was left vague, though it certainly was intended to include more market opening than was being sought within the WTO – a reason why some EU member states with protectionist leanings, led by France, were resistant to aspects of the NTA and the NTM.

In an attempt to inject momentum into the NTM, especially in respect of transatlantic trade liberalization, in March 1998 the EU Trade Commissioner, Leon Brittan, called for an acceleration of the removal of trade and investment barriers with a view to creating by 2010 a transatlantic marketplace based on free trade. This, however, met with resistance on both sides of the Atlantic, with the consequence that it was watered down and re-packaged into a Transatlantic Economic Partnership (TEP) that was agreed in May 1998. The TEP was designed to extend and intensify multilateral and bilateral cooperation and common actions on trade and investment by providing mechanisms for policy initiatives and agreements, including on regulatory cooperation and mutual recognition. The TEP agreement was followed in November 1998 with an action plan "based on intensive and detailed discussions between the US Administration and the European Commission" (United States Mission to the European Union, 1998).

Transatlantic Relations under George W. Bush

The Administrations of George W. Bush are commonly thought of as constituting a low point in post-World War II transatlantic relations. A key reason for this is the unilateralist tendencies displayed by the Bush presidency, especially in his first term (2001–2005), which resulted in much of Bush's years in office being accompanied by recurring transatlantic tensions. These tensions were at their greatest in the period leading to the 2003 American-led invasion of Iraq, which was launched on the supposition of the presence of weapons of mass destruction (WMD). The decision to invade Iraq over the objections of members of the UN Security Council split the EU on the issue, with the UK joining the US in overthrowing the Saddam regime and France and Germany strongly opposing the invasion.

Yet just two years before the Iraqi invasion, when Al Qaeda attacked the US on September 11, 2001, *Le Monde* ran the famous headline, "*Nouse sommes tous Américains*" (We are all Americans); such a spirit of solidarity could not be wholly expunged by the disagreement over Iraq, just as earlier such divergent positions on, for example, Vietnam and Middle East oil could not completely derail transatlantic cooperation. The rhetoric of neo-conservatives – Donald Rumsfeld's delineation of an "Old Europe" and a "New Europe" and Robert Kagan's categorization of Europeans as being from Venus and Americans from Mars – proved to be fleeting comments in the heat of argument. (See Cowles &

Eagan, 2012 for a discussion of the "neo-conservative moment" in the context of transatlantic relations.) When the dust settled, the conditions that since World War II had been strengthening the rationale for transatlantic relations still held: the US and the EU needed each other, arguably more than ever.

In consequence, the varying dimensions of growing transatlanticism continued under Bush, especially during the second Bush Administration (2005–2009) which sought and substantially achieved rapprochement in the transatlantic partnership. As part of this, Secretary of State Condoleezza Rice orchestrated an early 2005 Bush visit to Brussels that conveyed the message that the US needs Europe as a global partner. Bush's less strident rhetoric in his second term, coupled with such policy activities as anti-AIDS and development initiatives, were appreciated by Europeans and helped to smooth ongoing disagreements over Iraq, climate change, and other issues.

In the two most traditional areas of transatlantic cooperation – mutual defense and the pursuit of economic growth – the US and EU continued under Bush to evolve deeper levels of cooperation. As the then US Ambassador to NATO, Victoria Nuland (2008), noted in an address delivered in Paris in 2008 in which she set out the dependence of the two sides on each other:

> If we have learned anything since September 11, 2001 – or for that matter over the past 60 or 100 years – it is that we need each other. We, in the United States, need a Europe that is as strong and united as possible, ready and willing to bear its full measure of responsibility for defending our common security and advancing our shared values. And you, I would argue, need an America that is engaged, consulting and cooperating with Europe – finding common solutions to common challenges. Just as our unity in the 20th century ensured the defeat of fascism and Soviet Communism, in the 21st century we must also share the risk and share the responsibility for protecting and advancing the freedom we enjoy.

Varying sorts of NTA-inspired activities continued under Bush and were, indeed, advanced at the April 2007 EU–US summit when it was decided to refocus and give political impetus to the TEP by launching a "Framework for Advancing Transatlantic Economic Integration." This included the creation of a Transatlantic Economic Council (TEC), co-chaired by the EU Trade Commissioner and the US Deputy National Security Adviser for International Economic Affairs, which is a high-level forum that brings together governments with representatives from business, consumer, and other relevant interests to further transatlantic economic relations and coordination. It includes the advancement of regulatory convergence among its core tasks. A wide range of policy areas is covered – including trade security, financial services, investment, intellectual property, and numerous specialized issues. Many groupings, working parties, and dialogues are located within the framework of the TEC, some of which are standing and some of which are temporary and are created to fulfill a particular task (see Chapter 5 for an examination of this transatlantic architecture).

By the end of the Bush Administration, most displays of US unilateral behavior had disappeared, due in no small part to the global recession which took hold from the fall of 2007 in the US and spread to Europe by mid-2008. Transatlantic cooperation in the financial policy area, which heretofore had focused primarily on anti-competitive behavior in the financial services sector, broadened, at a near-frenzied pace, as the US and the EU struggled to reshape financial services regulation and establish much greater policy convergence (documented in Chapter 11 of this volume). Significantly, the pre-existing New Transatlantic networks facilitated the ability to move quickly to forge transatlantic policy consensus on key issues.

To the lengthening list of shared policy concerns, a new area of perceived need for transatlantic cooperation was added as a result of 9/11 and terrorist atrocities in Europe: internal security and counter-terrorism. However, this has been an area where many of the problems associated with much of the new transatlantic policy activity have been very much to the fore and where, as a result, policy agreements have been very difficult to find. One of these problems has been different perceptions of the nature of the policy challenge with, as Rees (2011, p. 169) puts it, the US tending toward a "war" approach and the EU toward a "crime" approach. This has led to the US taking a more hawkish and semi-unilateralist protectionist stance and has led also to significant differences between the EU and US on a number of specific issues – including on data privacy and on the collection and exchange of personal information (examined in Chapter 10 of this volume). A second problem has been that, partly as a consequence of differences in interests and value structures, but partly also as a consequence of the sensitivity of the internal security policy area, the EU and US have not been able to place particular policy problems within a wider context of an agreed overall policy strategy. As Hamilton and Rhinard (2011, pp. 71–72) have observed:

> For the most part ... the transatlantic homeland security agenda has fallen victim to ad hoc, reactive responses that are not commensurate with the challenges at hand or the depth of our interdependencies ... there is no overarching vision to guide and benchmark ongoing work between agencies and bureaucracies.

A third problem has been the location of policy responsibilities on the EU side. While the EU has assumed much greater responsibilities for Justice and Home Affairs policies since the mid-1990s, as Rees (2011, p. 160) notes, "Most of the operational counter-terrorism capabilities remain with national governments and they have been reluctant to cede sovereign powers to the EU." In consequence, the EU has generally been slow to negotiate and adopt transatlantic counter-terrorism measures, and when they have been adopted there have been variations between member states in respect of implementation.

Given these problems, a hierarchical approach to tackling counter-terrorism, and more broadly internal security, problems on a transatlantic basis was not possible. However, a networked approach brought added value from an early stage – "mainly in the capacity of networks to stimulate changes in environment and culture of their participants, to build relationships, and eventually to enhance international cooperation" (Pawlak, 2007, p. 19). As a result, a veritable web of networked interactions between EU and US agencies and officials was created during the first George W. Bush presidency.

Despite fits and starts, and difficulties with member state agencies cooperating in the exchange of information (a problem, by the way, which US state law enforcement agencies have long grappled with as well), the depth, breadth, and pace of transatlantic cooperation in Justice and Home Affairs (JHA – EU) and Homeland Security (HS – US), which has continued at full tilt during both Obama Administrations, is simply unprecedented since the establishment of the New Transatlanticism. This discussion will be continued below. (Also, see Chapter 5, where the architecture of the "New Transatlanticism" is inventoried and examined.)

Transatlantic Relations under Barack Obama

Europeans welcomed Barack Obama's 2008 election victory as an opportunity to move beyond the divisions that characterized much of the Bush period. Even more than within the US, Obama received much credit in Europe for simply being "not Bush" and for espousing a more multilateral and consultative approach to international policy. However, while Obama ostensibly promoted a more internationalist approach, he also affirmed that he would "reserve the right to act unilaterally if necessary to defend my nation" (quote by Sandy Berger, former National Security Adviser to President Clinton, in Combs, 2012, p. 469). In this regard, Obama was reviving the Clinton mantra: "Together when possible, alone when necessary" (Combs, 2012, p. 469).

Despite his warm reception from Europe, Obama initially pursued transatlantic relations in a manner quite similar to Bush in his second term of office. Both Bush and Obama shared a distinct lack of "love at first sight" for European leaders, especially in collective – European Council – settings, with Bush enduring a series of harangues on climate change and international cooperation at Gothenburg in 2001 (Sackur, 2001), while at Prague in 2009 Obama was subjected to a friendlier, but even longer, series of European criticisms following an address on non-proliferation (Wolf, 2009).

While Obama enjoyed a more extended "honeymoon" period than had Bush, the two were similar in both experiencing and causing disappointment in the transatlantic relationship. (For a review of the first year of the transatlantic relationship under Obama, see Council on Foreign Relations, 2009 discussion with Assistant Secretary of State Phil Gordon.) Regarding the "experiencing," Europe's perceived weak contribution to collective defense was a source of great irritation to both presidents. Regarding the "causing," Europe was rapidly disappointed by Obama's climate change policy, with the US staking out a middle position between Brazil, South Africa, India, and China (the BASIC group) on the one hand and the much "greener" EU on the other – resulting in frustrated EU aspirations at the 2009 Copenhagen Climate Summit (COP-15), which produced the "Copenhagen Accord." Explanations that the Obama Administration was limited by what could be passed through Congress did little to dispel the impression in Europe that Obama gave up on climate change at an early stage.

Looking at the overall picture, Europe was generally disappointed with Obama's first term of office and it frequently complained that the affections it bestowed on Obama were not returned (Harding, 2010). This sentiment reached its peak during the 2010 Spanish EU Presidency, when plans for a US–EU Summit in Madrid were scrapped by Obama on the grounds that there were no pressing issues that needed to be discussed at head of government (HOG) level.

Obama began his second term by providing reassurance to Europe by naming John Kerry and Chuck Hagel as his Secretaries of State and Defense, respectively, both of whom were widely viewed as having transatlantic instincts and a familiarity with the broad range of transatlantic issues. In his Senate confirmation hearing and in his initial meetings in 2013 with the EU High Representative (in effect his EU counterpart), Catherine Ashton in Washington, and with European Commission President, José Manuel Barroso in Brussels, Kerry stressed the importance of transatlantic ties and that he sees Europe as a "global partner." For his part, in his Senate confirmation hearing Hagel underlined the importance of Europe and NATO for US defense strategy. However, in the context of an environment of sequestration and reduced defense spending (in reality a reduction in the rate of growth in spending rather than the actual cuts seen in some European states), Hagel followed his predecessors in expecting Europe to share more of the burden.

A less noted development in US politics with potential impact on the transatlantic relationship is the widespread change among Members of Congress with responsibility for and interest in Europe. The defeat during the Indiana Republican primary of former Senate Foreign Relations Chair and Ranking Member, Senator Richard Lugar, and shifts in leadership among several key subcommittees, has led to what Barker describes as "depleted institutional memory of Europe" (Barker, 2012).

Defense and External Security

From the outset, the Obama Administration echoed a theme common to all US Administrations, namely dissatisfaction with European contributions to NATO's capabilities, with a particular focus of dissatisfaction being Europe's efforts in Afghanistan. In his parting address to NATO colleagues, George W. Bush's Defense Secretary, Robert Gates (2011), warned that

> if current trends in the decline of European defense capabilities are not halted and reversed, future U.S. political leaders – those for whom the Cold War was *not* the formative experience that it was for me – may not consider the return on America's investment in NATO worth the cost.

Nonetheless, the alliance did agree on a "New Strategic Concept" at the November 2010 NATO Summit in Lisbon. The allies underscored the centrality of NATO in the multi-polar era and continued their support of Article 5 and collective defense. They also called for a more comprehensive approach involving political, military, and civilian interaction – thus underscoring the Europeans' growing contributions of soft power. The alliance members also agreed that NATO would build an Antiballistic Missile Defense system. Coming out of the Lisbon agreement, it was clear that two constants would remain in the military alliance: the US would continue to play the leading role as "stabilizer of global security" and the European financial contribution to the alliance would be indeterminate (Smolar, 2011).

An indication of some possible "recalibration" of transatlantic relations regarding defense and external security policy was, however, displayed in 2011 when Libyan opposition forces confronted the Muammar Gaddafi regime. It was France and Britain – not the US – that called for Western involvement in proposed military action. When Obama agreed to participate in what became a NATO action, the American Administration made it clear that the US would play a limited role and, therefore, the Europeans would have to take the responsibility "in their backyard" (Hewitt, 2011). After the US military eliminated Libya's air defenses, France and the UK flew most of the bombing sorties. Behind the scenes, however, the US still played the critical role in air surveillance, intelligence, and refueling capabilities. Despite the Franco-British leadership, the shortcomings of European military capabilities were thus still very much evident (Combs, 2012, p. 481).

Internal Security and Counter-Terrorism

The developments in transatlantic cooperation in the areas of internal security and counter-terrorism that occurred under Bush have continued under Obama, and the mood of the relations – helped by Obama having toned down Bush's "war on terrorism" rhetoric – initially improved. An important step forward was the issuing in June 2010 of an important US–EU Declaration on Counter-Terrorism, which presented lists of principles and action items under the rubrics of: (1) respect for fundamental values and the rule of law; (2) bringing to bear all policy tools including law enforcement, judicial cooperation, intelligence, diplomacy, finance, and security policy; and (3) measures to address the long-term threat of violent extremism – including "home grown" terrorists (Council of the European Union, 2010). Targeting terrorist financing and implementation of the US–EU treaties on extradition and mutual legal assistance have furthered this cooperation (Mix, 2013).

However, while transatlantic cooperation on internal security and counter-terrorism has had some successes, problems arising from the Americans and Europeans having different approaches and capabilities in this area (which were referred to above) have continued under Obama. So, for example, Europeans have had considerable concerns on several issues, including data privacy (see Chapter 10 on this), the US's increasing reliance on targeted killings of suspected terrorists via drone strikes, and Obama's failure to close Guantánamo. The emerging issue of cybersecurity illustrates the difficulties such differences can create for effective transatlantic cooperation:

- A US–EU Working Group on Cybersecurity and Cybercrime was formed in 2010.
- In November 2011 the US Department of Homeland Security and the European Network and Information Security Agency conducted the first US–EU joint cyberattack simulation exercise.
- In early 2013 the EU was able to release a comprehensive cybersecurity strategy.
- Congress has been unable to agree on a similar comprehensive strategy, leaving the Obama Administration to do what it can via executive action to work with partners.

The "Asia Pivot"

During the first Obama Administration there was a perceived "pivot" in US policy towards Asia – both in the security realm, where US defense strategy increasingly focused on the South China Sea, and in trade and investment via the Trans-Pacific Partnership (TPP). Obama's shift was reminiscent of other US Administrations' turn to the outside: Nixon's overture to China in the 1970s, Clinton's involvement in NAFTA and APEC, and G. W. Bush's first-term willingness to seemingly look almost anywhere but Europe. However, in all these instances the transatlantic partnership was not fundamentally adrift: the Americans were simply looking to protect their interests elsewhere. Then Secretary of State Hillary Clinton repeatedly stressed that this continued to be the case under Obama, with the pivot not being intended as a slight to Europe. This theme was similarly adopted by Clinton's successor, John Kerry, during his confirmation hearings and first meetings with European counterparts, when he emphasized that he saw the US as pivoting "with" rather than "from" Europe to Asia.

According to Clinton, Europe remains the US "partner of first resort," as is witnessed in the remarkable "breadth and depth" of transatlantic cooperation – on challenges as important and complex as Afghanistan, Iran, and the Arab Spring (Clinton, 2012a). She expanded on these themes during her final address in Washington on EU–US relations, saying:

> Let me be clear: our pivot to Asia is not a pivot away from Europe. On the contrary, we want Europe to engage more in Asia, along with us to see the region not only as a market, but as a focus of common strategic engagement.
>
> (Clinton, 2012b)

For their part, European leaders have also publicly downplayed perceptions of the significance of a changing US pivot. As European Council President Herman Von Rompuy has noted, "Americans realize that the pivot is not an alternative to Europe and NATO. On the contrary, a strong transatlantic relationship is a precondition for America's focus on Asia" (Van Rompuy, 2012).

However, despite US reassurances, Europeans fear, and with some justification, that the US regards Asia as the region of the future. The trade numbers are compelling, with EU–Asia and US–Asia trade volumes exceeding EU–US trade and with cross-Pacific foreign direct investment (FDI) also rapidly increasing. At the same time, the EU itself is becoming increasingly enmeshed in trade and investment terms with Asia.

While fear from the outside can sow the seeds for transatlantic strife, the history of transatlantic relations demonstrates that it can also lead to closer cooperation: witness, for example, the fear of the Soviet Union in the post-World War II years which engendered the creation of the Atlantic Alliance and witness also the fear of a "Fortress Europe," which led to the first Bush Administration calling for a Transatlantic Declaration. To date, the record of transatlantic cooperation stemming from a "rebalancing" or "pivoting" to Asia is not fully formed, but both sides are professing a strong desire to work together, particularly in relation to China. In this context it was perhaps significant that during her April 2013 visit to Beijing for meetings with the new Chinese leadership, High Representative Ashton followed many of the same themes as US officials.

Trade and the Proposed Transatlantic Trade and Investment Partnership

The most important concrete US "pivot" to the EU under Obama was signaled at the very beginning of his second term of office when, in his 2013 State of the Union speech, he announced that he would seek negotiations for a comprehensive TTIP with the EU. The European Council President, Van Rompuy, and European Commission President, Barroso, issued similar statements the next day.

The proposed TTIP comes out of talks between the US and EU that began in November 2011 after leaders on both sides asked a High-Level Working Group on Jobs and Growth, co-chaired by EU Trade Commissioner Karel de Gucht and US Trade Representative Ron Kirk, to produce an assessment of the potential for a transatlantic free trade agreement (FTA). An interim report in June 2012 called for a comprehensive agreement to support growth, competitiveness, and general improvement in the performance of the US and European economies through the removal of tariffs, increased regulatory cooperation, and the reduction of non-tariff barriers in goods, services, and investment. A final report was issued the day after Obama's State of the Union address (US–EU High Level Working Group on Jobs and Growth, 2013).

The TTIP envisages a major advance in transatlantic relations, with the building of a US–EU FTA and the furthering of other trade and investment ties between the world's two major economic partners. As such it also involves an upgrading within the US of perceptions of the importance of the EU, following a 2012 US election campaign that featured more than a few disparaging remarks on the euro crisis and the EU's "socialist" regulatory model. However, despite the completion of four rounds of negotiation at the time of this writing, there is no assurance that the TTIP will ultimately be realized. Nor does the TTIP constitute a departure from the long-standing trade agendas of the US and the EU, which seek to open international trade wherever they can and to respond to recent steps by other countries to move forward with their own regional and bilateral trade agreements. So, for the US, the announcement of the TTIP came on the heels of the North and Central American Free Trade Agreements (NAFTA and CAFTA, respectively), as well as continuing negotiations over a TPP. Similarly for the EU, preferential trade agreements of various kinds have been/are in the process of being negotiated with an assortment of countries, included among which are Japan, Canada, and South Korea. (See Chapter 7 of this book for a detailed analysis of US and EU trade policy, and Chapters 13 and 14 for a comprehensive analysis of the TTIP.)

Conclusions

In the post-World War II era major changes have occurred in the nature of the transatlantic alliance, most particularly in the form of the changing geographical boundaries of Europe, Europe's increased ability to speak and act as a single entity rather than via its numerous states, and shifts in policy priorities – which have seen, especially since the end of the Cold War, military issues declining in importance relative to economic issues.

Reflecting these changes, the partnership has constantly transformed its institutions and operating practices in an effort both to manage the changes and conflicts that have been both internal and external to the alliance and also to adapt to an evolving external world. An important dimension of the transformation since the 1990s has been the greater institutionalization of transatlantic relations associated with the New Transatlanticism. Although policy practitioners now tend not to use the term "New Transatlantic Agenda" – because it has become the normal agenda – it is very much within the framework of NTA-based and -inspired thinking that much of the intensification of transatlantic relations since the 1990s has been developed.

Regarding this development, much has been made of the significance for the transatlantic relationship of the US "pivot" to Asia. Undoubtedly Asia is assuming an increasingly important position in US external policy thinking, but US leaders – including Presidents Bush and Obama and Secretaries of State Clinton and Kerry – have all stressed the importance of Europe as a global partner. Even though the BRICs, and particularly China, occupy a growing portion of Washington's attention, multiple impasses in the UN Security Council and varying responses to regional conflicts have served to remind the US that Europe provides by far the most reliable source of support for American goals. Moreover, the EU has become an increasingly important and viable international policy actor, and hence one with which the US can, and indeed must, deal. For not only has the EU increased its external policy responsibilities and acquired an ability to speak and act on behalf of its member states in relation to these expanding responsibilities, but it has also had some success on the world stage in acting as a norm setter which has used its market power to promote its market-related policies and regulatory practices beyond its territorial boundaries (Damro, 2012).

As for the foreseeable future, much will doubtless depend on, as Shapiro and Whitney (2009) have argued, Europe's ability to get its own policy act together, with individual EU member states abandoning hopes of retaining separate and "special" bilateral relationships with the US and instead agreeing on common positions in relation to the US. In some policy areas, especially trade, the EU is usually able to achieve this, albeit often only after considerable internal bargaining and compromising. But, in other areas, including foreign and defense issues, the EU's ability to act as one is limited, despite hopes that the Lisbon Treaty would lead to a more coherent EU internationally. The deep divisions in Europe on military action in Libya and Syria are evidence of the difficulties that often exist in Europe on achieving external policy coherence. Five years of economic crisis, which have displayed the constraints and weaknesses of the eurozone area, have also weakened Europe's role in global governance.

Nonetheless, the transatlantic relationship firmly endures. A successful negotiation of the current major item on the transatlantic agenda – the TTIP – would bode well for the future of the transatlantic relationship if it realizes projections for new and sustained growth on both sides of the Atlantic.

3 Transatlantic Foreign Policy Cooperation in the Obama Era

Federiga Bindi

Introduction

This chapter analyses transatlantic relations in foreign policy, primarily during President Barack Obama's first term in office. (As this chapter is being written in 2014, it is able to draw on some foreign policy events during Obama's first 18 months of his second term.) Over the past 25 years, transatlantic relations have changed substantially: Europe is no longer menaced from its Eastern border – its major challenges to security essentially come from the southern shore of the Mediterranean Sea – and traditional military hardware is not enough to successfully overcome such threats. In this new scenario, Europe is no longer a territory to be protected but perhaps, rather, has become the best partner to tackle these challenges. The central claim of this chapter is that while the first Obama administration was ready for a substantial upgrade in transatlantic relations, Europe was not.

As we will see in this chapter, Barack Obama is the first truly post-Cold War President and a person whose early foreign policy was the result of a combination of an idealist vision and a pragmatist approach. Europe, as a unified partner, well suited his approach to foreign policy; the almost simultaneous arrival of Obama to the US Presidency and the entry into force of the Lisbon Treaty thus potentially offered a unique chance for change. However, the EU's enduring disunity undermined this possibility. In other words, under Obama the US expected a more unified European actor in foreign policy than the EU could be.

This chapter proceeds as follows: the first section analyzes how transatlantic relations evolved before Obama. In the second section, we explore Barack Obama's aspirations and vision of foreign policy and discuss how these were eventually realized. In the third section, we examine transatlantic foreign policy cooperation in the years 2009–2013. In the conclusion we evaluate and discuss change and continuity in transatlantic relations with respect to foreign policy.

EU Foreign and Defense Policies and Transatlantic Relations: Historical Perspective

Foreign Policy

The foreign policy aspects of European cooperation evolved slowly (as compared, for example, to internal market policy). The early European Communities did not have a foreign policy *stricto senso*. In 1954, with the failed attempt to create a European Defense Community, the EU was left with the Western European Union (WEU) (a talk shop without military capability), essentially leaving European security exclusively in NATO's hands.

In 1957, the European Economic Community (EEC) included some provisions dealing with external relations, including a common external trade tariff (as a key feature of the customs union) and external trade (the Common Commercial Policy). Beginning with the 1963 Yaoundé Convention, the EEC took its first steps to form a development policy. In 1964–1967, the EEC represented its members in the General Agreement on Tariffs and Trade (GATT) Kennedy Round negotiations. In the late 1970s, the European Political Cooperation (EPC) was created, establishing the practice of regular meetings of EEC foreign ministers, of the heads of state and government, and of the political directors of the six EEC member states, as well as systematic consultation on all major questions of foreign policy. The subsequent Copenhagen Report of July 23, 1973 further specified the EPC's role and mechanisms. It established that the ministers of foreign affairs would meet four times per year and whenever they felt it was necessary.

The *Single European Act of 1986* (SEA) gave the EPC a treaty basis without changing its existing intergovernmental nature and methods of operation. In doing so, the SEA defined the role of the European Council (given the lead role), the European Commission (to assist the European Council), and the Parliament (minimal right to be informed) within the EPC. The EPC gave a treaty basis to what had already, in fact, been happening – where member states attempted to define common positions within international institutions or conferences, and to mutually assist and inform each other of foreign policy decisions and actions.

The year 1989 brought dramatic and unexpected changes in Eastern Europe. On December 8–9, the European Council in Strasbourg approved German reunification. German unification, however, was to be counterbalanced by a more integrated Community, which was realized with the 1992 Maastricht Treaty, or Treaty on European Union (TEU) establishing the "European Union." The Maastricht Treaty set the path for a European single currency and created the Common Foreign and Security Policy (CFSP).

The CSFP envisaged systematic cooperation between member states by, for example, adopting "common positions" in foreign policy matters; coordinating their activity within international organizations and conferences; engaging in joint actions; and refraining from any action which is contrary to the EU. The WEU was to be closely associated with the CFSP, acting as a bridge to NATO, and the CFSP was finally permitted to address the previously taboo question of "defense," with the possibility held out in the Maastricht Treaty of gradually moving toward a common defense system. The Council Presidency was to represent the EU in CFSP matters. Abroad, member state diplomatic missions and European Commission delegations were to cooperate, and the European Parliament (EP) was to be consulted.

However, Maastricht did not create a budget for the CFSP. Rather, it created a system for charging operational costs to the European Community (EC) budget and letting the Council decide whether to charge the EC budget of member governments for operational expenditures associated with joint actions (thus opening the door to endless procedural battles). Unfortunately for proponents of a strong EU foreign and security policy, the Iraqi invasion of Kuwait in August 1990 and the subsequent First Gulf War in 1991 coincided with the Maastricht Treaty negotiations and became a source of friction among EC partners, ultimately undermining the CFSP as a "European foreign policy."

In November 1990, the EU and the US agreed to the Transatlantic Declaration (TAD; see discussion of the TAD and high-level summits in Chapters 2 and 5 of this volume), which included the following foreign and security policy goal (Transatlantic Declaration 1990, p. 1):

> safeguard peace and promote international security, by cooperating with other nations against aggression and coercion, by contributing to the settlement of conflicts in the world and by reinforcing the role of the United Nations and other international organizations.

While the 1995 New Transatlantic Agenda (NTA), agreed during the Clinton Administration, primarily signaled an uptick in economic cooperation, this agreement also reaffirmed the Atlantic Community's commitment to foreign and security policy cooperation. In addition, the excellent personal relations that linked some of the European leaders to Bill Clinton, and the wide popularity he enjoyed in Western Europe, contributed to the decade and aura of harmony. The emblem of these excellent personal relationship are possibly the "Third Way" meetings which several heads of government and top government officials attended in 1998 at New York University and in 1999 in Florence, including British Prime Minister Tony Blair, US President Bill Clinton, German Chancellor Gerhard Schroeder, Dutch Prime Minister Wim Kok, French Prime Minister Lionel Jospin, and the Italian Prime Minister Massimo D'Alema (Castle, 1999).

Meanwhile, however, tensions had started to arise between two parallel processes: the integration of the new Central and Eastern European countries (CEECs) into the EU and into NATO. The end of the Cold War had opened the question of incorporating these recently democratized countries into the EU. Trade agreements had been signed by the EEC already in 1988 (Hungary and Czechoslovakia), 1989 (Poland), and 1990 (Bulgaria and Romania) and then replaced with Association Agreements (the so-called Europa Agreements) in 1992 (Hungary and Poland), 1993 (Czech Republic, Slovak Republic, Bulgaria, and Romania), and 1996 (Slovenia). However, the EU member states – fearing the costs of incorporating the CEECs into the EU – tried to delay the enlargement process by embarking on a number of more narrow negotiations over EU institutional reforms, considered as a precondition to enlargement. This strategy left Central and Eastern Europeans, who had previously looked at the EU as a source of inspiration against the Soviet system, frustrated.

Defense Policy

The US was quick in exploiting the political void left by the EU by speeding up the process of integration of the new European democracies into NATO. In November 1991, the North Atlantic Cooperation Council (NACC) was created to enable security discussions with the CEECs. In 1992 a "consultation forum" was created within NATO, which included the CEECs, but excluded Russia. In 1994 the WEU offered the CEECs the status of "associate partners," which would permit the CEECs to participate in Petersberg-like (peacekeeping) operations; but they were not offered the prize they most coveted – the West's security guarantee.

Meanwhile, the Europeans had begun talking of a European security and defense identity (ESDI). This idea, however, was not so well received in the US. The US Administration was in fact eager for the Europeans to bear more of the defense burden, but not if in the process an EU-led defense pact would rival NATO. As a result, in a June 1996 NATO Ministerial meeting in Berlin, EU defense ministers agreed to build ESDI within NATO, while simultaneously stressing the supremacy of the principle of transatlantic cooperation within the alliance (NATO, 1996). Subsequently, the US Administration pushed for speedy NATO enlargement. On July 8, 1997, the North Atlantic Council in Madrid invited the Czech Republic, Hungary, and Poland to begin accession talks with a view to joining NATO by its 50th anniversary in 1999. The EU had no option but to follow suit and in December of the same year invited the 10 CEECs as well as Cyprus to join EU membership talks.

The immediate post-Cold War period was not without tensions and developments, especially in the field of defense. France and the UK sent an important signal to the EU when, at a meeting in St Malo in December 1998, Prime Minister Tony Blair and French President Jacques Chirac, the leaders of the EU's two nuclear powers, agreed to establish European military cooperation within NATO. However, US approval came with conditions articulated by then US Secretary of State Madeline Albright – that the EU avoid the "three Ds": no decoupling (of European Security and Defense Policy [ESDP] from NATO); no duplication (of capabilities); and no discrimination (against non-NATO members). NATO members formally endorsed European defense cooperation at its 50th anniversary summit (April 25, 1999). (In December 2002, NATO and the EU negotiated a set of agreements, called "Berlin Plus," which governs the sharing of assets between the EU and NATO for crisis management and peacekeeping operations.)

Following the historic NATO summit, in the June 1999 Cologne Summit the EU heads of government (HOGs) announced their decision to absorb the WEU into a new European Security and Defense Policy (ESDP – renamed "Common

Security and Defense Policy" in the Lisbon Treaty). Former NATO General Secretary Javier Solana was appointed to WEU Secretary-General and High Representative for the CFSP.

The EU's first action under CDSP was in response to events in Kosovo, whereby at the Helsinki European Council in December 1999 it was agreed that by 2003 the EU would be able to deploy up to 60,000 troops within 60 days for at least one year to deal with Petersberg task operations. It was also agreed that new permanent political and military bodies would be established.

All in all, transatlantic relations in the 1980s and 1990s followed an ambiguous path. On the one hand, both sides claimed to attach great importance to closer cooperation and to stronger relations; on the other hand, they were involved in petty disputes, threats, retaliation measures, and counter-retaliations in economic matters (see the policy studies in Part III of this volume).

Tensions Build Between the EU and the US

After a bitter electoral dispute, George W. Bush took office in January 2001. Eight months later, the attacks of September 11 were to have lasting effects on US foreign policy and, consequently, on transatlantic relations. According to Petersen and Pollack (2003a), the new administration was at odds with its European allies on issues such as missile defense, climate change, and relations with Russia and the Balkans. September 11 and the subsequent War on Terror further contributed to tensions, which culminated in "one of the most serious transatlantic ruptures" with the Anglo-American attack on Iraq in 2003, which some EU member states supported and others strongly opposed. With the invasion of Iraq, US–EU relations thus reached a historic low: Secretary of Defense Donald Rumsfeld – asked by a Dutch reporter why America's European allies were not more supportive of US calls to hold Saddam Hussein to account – replied: "You're thinking of Europe as Germany and France. I don't. I think that's old Europe" (Bush, 2010, p. 88). Realizing the negative impact of such tense relations with Western Europe, the Bush II administration sought to correct its policy toward Europe, a process also eased by a number of changes in the new Administration's national security and foreign policy teams, most notably the replacement of Donald Rumsfeld with Robert Gates (see Bush, 2010, pp. 87–94; Reis, 2013). The damage, however, was done, and Bush's anti-European image lived on, thus contributing to high expectations in Europe about Barack Obama.

Meanwhile, in the attempt to repair divisions within Europe over Iraq – in particular those that had emerged between French President Jacques Chirac and British Prime Minister Tony Blair – the European Council agreed at the Thessaloniki Summit in December 2003 to a "European Security Strategy" (ESS) entitled "A Secure Europe in a Better World" (Council of the European Union, 2003). The text, drafted under Javier Solana's direction, was considered a counterpart to the US security strategy. It identified a list of key threats Europe needed to deal with: terrorism; proliferation of weapons of mass destruction; regional conflict; failed states; and, organized crime. Central to the ESS was the promotion of regional stability in Europe and its "neighborhood" (Council of the

European Union, 2003, p. 6), identifying the EU's strategic priorities to be in Europe (Balkans, Eurasia, Russia), the Mediterranean, and the Middle East. The European Defense Agency (EDA), established in 2004, was one of the new institutions to develop from this new strategy. Finally, on May 1, 2004, the Czech Republic, Estonia, Hungary, Poland, Slovenia, Cyprus, Latvia, Lithuania, Malta, and Slovakia joined the EU, followed on January 1, 2007, by Bulgaria and Romania.

Barack Obama's Foreign Policy Vision and Practice: An Overview

In his pre-election tour in the summer 2008, Obama was greeted rock-star style in Europe. However, unrealistic expectations often lead to disappointment and that was partially the case, too, with transatlantic relations during the Obama I years. In order to better understand transatlantic relations under the Obama I Administration, we will first need to look at Obama's vision of US foreign policy as a whole.

An excellent account of Obama's foreign policy is offered by Indyk, Lieberthal, and O'Hanlon (2012), three Brookings Institution scholars who advised the President and Secretary Clinton in various capacities. Obama's vision of foreign policy, they argued, was an integral part of the general narrative during the 2008 electoral campaign: A message of change, hope and audacity unified his domestic and overseas agenda under a common banner; Obama sought nothing less than bending "history's arc in the direction of justice, and a more peaceful, stable global order" (Indyk et al., 2012, p. 1). Obama argued for the need to pay more attention to the "global commons," which was threatened by terrorism, nuclear proliferation, climate change and pandemic diseases (Indyk et al., 2012, p. 5). In his July 24, 2008 Berlin speech, Obama spoke of a planet that needed to be saved from famine, rising oceans, and carbon emissions, a world without nuclear weapons and the redemption of those left behind by globalization by providing them with dignity, opportunity, and "simple justice" (Obama, 2008).

At the same time, Obama was promising toughness in Afghanistan and in handling terrorists and insurgents in Pakistan, as well as an exit strategy from Iraq. All in all, Obama was promising a major break with the past and an historic change for the future. Accordingly, Indyk et al. (2012) identify three pillars in Obama's foreign policy. The first pillar was a *changed relationship with the rising powers*, manifested in Obama's preference for the G-20 over the G-8, support for a permanent seat for India in the UN Security Council, and the Asia pivot (see Chapter 2). Except for the then British Prime Minister Gordon Brown and French President Nicolas Sarkozy – who both used the G-20 for the purpose of their domestic politics – the other G-8 Europeans and the EU showed uneasiness about a larger table for fear of being marginalized. Such fears were confirmed in December 2009 at the Climate Change Summit in Copenhagen, when a deal was made by the US with the Indian, Chinese, Brazilian, and South African leaders, leaving the Europeans and the EU literally out of the room.

The second pillar was *nuclear disarmament and proliferation*. In his Prague April 2009 speech, Obama (2009) declared he was seeking "the peace and security of a world without nuclear weapons." In September 2009, at the UN General Assembly, President Obama chaired a special meeting of the UN Security Council (UNSC) and then hosted in Washington the Summit on Nuclear Proliferation (April 2010) while at the same time launching the US *Nuclear Posture Review*, which spelled out the new US doctrine in the field: a "no first use" nuclear commitment towards those states that would foreswear nuclear weapons. Any achievement in this area was obviously linked to success in the "reset" of the relations with Russia. The main result of the reset was the signing of the new START Treaty and the positive vote of both Russia and China on the UNSC Resolution of June 2010 mandating tougher sanctions against Iran for its violation of the Non-Proliferation Treaty.

The third pillar was turning Bush's combative *relations with the Muslim world* into a positive partnership as Obama told the world in his Cairo speech (*New York Times*, 2009). Originally, Obama did not include the idea of "exporting democracy" – a principle arguably abused by Bush – and used a more abstract notion of "universal human rights": freedom of speech and assembly, equal rights for women, rule of law, accountable government. Only later, with the Arab Spring, the promotion of democracy became a foreign policy priority.

In his first four years in office, Obama experienced some notable successes in foreign policy: rebuilding America's standing in much of the world, resetting the relationship with Russia, effectively managing relations with China, achieving a UNSC agreement imposing harsh sanctions on Iran, announcing overdue but welcome free trade accords, negotiating a new START Treaty, eliminating Osama bin Laden and the weakening of Al Qaeda, withdrawing troops from Iraq, the beginning of downsizing US troops in Afghanistan, and intervening in Libya, culminating in the overthrow of the Muammar Gaddafi regime (Indyk et al., 2012, p. 21). However, Obama also suffered a number of setbacks, including a lack of progress in the Israeli–Palestinian conflict, continued tensions with Iran over its purported nuclear weapons programs, North Korea's continued development of its nuclear arsenal, deepening tensions in US–Pakistani relations, Mexico awash in drugs and violence, America's continued low standing in the Muslim world, and a major setback in combating climate change (Indyk et al., 2012, p. 22).

In addition, the contrast between Obama's visionary rhetoric and his "competent pragmatism" in governing (Indyk et al., 2012, p. 23; Lewis, 2012) became "a familiar landmark of Obama's Presidency" (Indyk et al., 2012, p. 139). Indeed, Obama's willingness to compromise often led to disappointment. For example, Vali Nasr's very critical account of Obama's Afghanistan policy reveals continuous difficulties and tensions between the State Department and the White House where – according to Nasr – major foreign policy decisions were funneled "through a small cabal of relatively inexperienced advisers whose turf as strictly politics was truly disturbing" (Nasr, 2013, p. 2).

Transatlantic Relations under Barack Obama's First Administration

One Phone Number?

As mentioned, the George W. Bush II Administration sought to improve cooperation and partnership with the EU, but eventually failed, thus leaving the task to his successor. Indeed, the new administration managed to reduce US–EU frictions. However, expectations about Obama in Europe were too high to be realistic.

Barack Obama was sworn into office in January 2009. At the end of the same year, in December 2009, the new Lisbon Treaty also entered into force. The new Treaty was seen in Europe and abroad as a substantial upgrade in the field of European foreign policy. The Lisbon Treaty finally entrusted the EU with legal personality and introduced a series of important innovations both in the fields of EU foreign policy and defense, now an integral part of CFSP. Most notably, it created the "High Representative for European Union Foreign Affairs and Security Policy," a "double-hatted" position combining the existing portfolios of the CFSP high representative and of the EU commissioner for external relations. However, this was not the EU "minister for foreign affairs" that was initially foreseen by the Constitutional Treaty; the negotiations leading to the Lisbon Treaty had modified it in order to ease the member states' fears of losing national sovereignty.

The person who was chosen to serve as the first High Representative in November 2009, Lady Catherine Ashton, was a relatively unknown figure. In her hearing for confirmation before the EP, Ashton candidly admitted her ignorance about foreign policy (European Parliament, 2010).

Ashton is assisted in her work by the "European External Action Service" (EEAS), a *sui generis* service comprising personnel recruited among the member states (one-third) and EU institutions (two-thirds). Frictions between the personnel coming from different departments still characterize the EEAS today, and to be fair to Ashton, she had a daunting task in front of her because of resistance from both the member states and the other EU institutions (Bindi, 2011).

The Lisbon Treaty also introduced a new position, the European Council President, to which the EU leaders appointed then Belgian Prime Minister Herman Van Rompuy. His activism in external relations initially led to confusion and difficulties with EU Commission President Josè Manuel Barroso and with the President in Office of the rotating EU.

Notwithstanding these shortcomings, the Lisbon Treaty raised expectations in the US about future EU foreign policy. In particular, people finally expected to have "one phone number" (see discussion in Chapter 2 of this volume). With such a prospect in mind, a number of adjustments were made in the US State Department to streamline its way of dealing with EU affairs.

In the US Department of State, EU affairs fall under the Bureau of European and Eurasian Affairs (EUR). The Bureau is structured to address multiple multilateral and bilateral issues: it consists of a cluster of functional offices, along with traditional, bilateral regional offices. Hence, in addition to the EU, EUR deals with NATO, the Organization for Security and Cooperation in Europe (OSCE), the Russian Federation, and non-EU member states in Europe. However, because it coordinates American action in international organizations that are so different in scope and in mission, EUR ends up coordinating operations also in countries geographically very distant from Europe, such as Afghanistan (because of the war) or the Horn of Africa (because of the maritime counter-piracy operations).

Yet, most of the work with the EU was still based on traditional bilateral channels, despite the fact that the different EU country "desks" are scattered around different "offices" (Office of Western Europe, Office of Southern European Affairs, Office of Nordic and Baltic Affairs, Office of Central European Affairs), each of which deal with different EU and non-EU member states. Not surprisingly, the Office of European Union and Regional Affairs (ERA), responsible for addressing US relations with the EU and its institutions, suffered a number of difficulties (US Office of Inspector General, 2011). In 2010, ERA's mission was finally charged to deal exclusively with EU affairs and a skilled diplomat, Elizabeth Dibble, was named as its head.

In addition, Assistant Secretary for European Affairs of State Phil Gordon – the same person who had crafted candidate Obama's very successful tour in Europe – embarked early in his tenure on a tour of European capitals to inquire about the Lisbon Treaty and its implications for the US. In most cases, the (national) diplomats informed him that, notwithstanding the Lisbon Treaty, bilateral relations with the member state capitals should stay as the core business in transatlantic relations. This was a short-sighted tactic, which had the effect of delaying the upgrading of transatlantic relations in the State Department. Thus, when the newly appointed Secretary of State Hillary Clinton traveled to Asia in her first trip overseas (US Department of State – Office of the Historian, 2009b) (in contrast to the two previous Secretaries of State, Madeline Albright and Condoleezza Rice, both of whom selected Europe for their first trips abroad), European officials began to worry, but did nothing, too soon comforted by the fact that President Obama's first "real" trip abroad, after a symbolic visit to neighboring Canada, was to Europe (US Department of State – Office of the Historian, 2009a).

In early 2010 President Obama announced that he was not planning to attend the US–EU Summit in May 2010 in Madrid (see further discussion in Chapter 5). Little did the Europeans reflect on the fact that the State Department indicated at the time that the confusion caused by changes to the EU's leadership and governance arrangements resulting from the Lisbon Treaty were one of the reasons that lead to the decision (Mix, 2010, p. 1; Rettman, 2010). The summit eventually took place at the margin of the Lisbon NATO summit in November 2010; according to unofficial comments of those present, Obama, however, dismissed it as too technical to be of interest for him. The announcement, in January 2012, of the removal of two of the four US Army brigades stationed in Europe seemed to confirm the Asian pivot hypothesis (Jaffe, 2012); so did the findings of German Marshall Fund's Transatlantic Trends 2011 survey (German Marshall

Fund, 2011), in which 51% of Americans surveyed responded that Asian countries were more important to US national interests than the EU.

Despite these shortcomings, examples of substantive transatlantic foreign policy cooperation are not lacking during the Obama years. Relations did progress well on a number of relevant issues, including the ongoing conflict in Afghanistan, nuclear talks with Iran, relations with Russia, the 2011 NATO operation in Libya, and the common problem of counterterrorism. Cooperation on these and other issues was seen, especially in the US, as proof of the continuing and deep vitality of the transatlantic partnership.

Examples of Successful Cooperation

Afghanistan

Over the past several years, many analysts have considered Afghanistan the most urgent and important international security issue for the transatlantic alliance. Afghanistan has been a focal point for transatlantic and international cooperation: as of February 2013, the NATO-led International Security Assistance Force (ISAF) consisted of over 100,330 troops from 50 countries, including all 28 members of NATO (NATO, 2013). After considerable force increases in 2009–2010, these numbers represent a substantial commitment of alliance and partner country resources. At the same time, Afghanistan has been a test of cohesion for the alliance. Amid concerns about flat or shrinking European defense budgets and persistent shortfalls in military resources, questions about the equality of commitments and burden-sharing in Afghanistan have at times caused tensions in the transatlantic alliance.

As agreed at the November 2010 NATO Summit, the Afghanistan mission entered a period of transition in which ISAF sought to gradually transfer responsibility for security to Afghan leadership, with Afghan forces leading in all functions and operations by the end of 2014. In early 2012 some indications about the details of the timetable began to emerge, suggesting the possibility of an accelerated transition. In January, France decided to move forward the date for ending its combat mission to the end of 2013, and French officials, in conjunction with Afghan President Karzai, suggested NATO should move the entire timetable up to that date. In late January 2012, France, Italy, and the UK each signed long-term bilateral partnership agreements with Afghanistan that outline military training and economic development commitments beyond 2014. Nevertheless, given Europe's economic difficulties and the sense of "Afghanistan fatigue" felt by many Europeans, the depth of the overall European commitment beyond 2014 remained uncertain at the time of this writing in early 2014. On the US side, the US signed a Bilateral Security Agreement with Afghanistan in November 2013, committing to withdrawal of all US troops by the end of 2014.

Iran

Transatlantic cooperation regarding Iran's nuclear program has been close and extensive. Since the discovery of Iran's covert enrichment activities in 2002, the "EU-3" (France, Germany, and the UK) have played a leading role in international efforts to curtail them. In 2006 the US joined the EU-3, along with Russia and China, to form the "Permanent Five Plus One" group that has attempted to conduct negotiations with Iran (Mix, 2013, p. 1). Between 2006 and 2010, the EU-3 and the US successfully pushed for UNSC approval of four rounds of sanctions on Iran (Resolutions 1737, 1747, 1803, and 1929).

With sanctions appearing to put considerable pressure on the Iranian economy, tensions between Iran and the West increased during late 2011 and early 2012. Following a November 2011 IAEA report about Iran's activities in pursuit of nuclear weapons, EU member states began discussing the dimensions of enhanced sanctions. On January 23, 2012, the EU adopted a major new round of sanctions on Iran. Among other measures targeting the Iranian Central Bank and Iran's petrochemical industry, the latest EU sanctions banned the import of oil from Iran. The EU had imported approximately 600,000 barrels of oil from Iran per day, accounting for about 20% of Iran's total oil exports. Three EU member countries – Italy, Spain, and Greece – accounted for the majority of the EU's Iranian oil imports; Greece, in particular, had come to rely heavily on Iranian oil procured on favorable terms. In order to allow time for the signing of new contracts with alternate oil producers, the EU sanctions allowed for previously concluded contracts with Iran to be carried out until July 1, 2012. Iran responded by threatening to preempt the EU embargo by immediately banning oil sales to European countries from its own end (Mix, 2013, p. 6).

Combined with the already extensive sanctions previously adopted by the EU, many American observers have been surprised by how far the EU measures have gone. In July 2010, the EU went beyond the measures authorized in UNSC Resolution 1929 in adopting a new round of tough sanctions, including measures targeting Iran's oil and gas industry and financial institutions. In the past, some Americans had pointed to European economic ties with Iran as a sign of European reluctance to press Tehran too hard, urging Europeans to adopt tighter sanctions. The EU's willingness to go beyond the UNSC authorizations sent a strong signal and brought US and European sanctions policy on Iran into broad alignment. The EU has stressed that its sanctions are designed to target sources of finance for Iran's nuclear program, and not the Iranian people or legitimate trade activities (Mix, 2013, p. 6). Negotiations resumed in November 2013, with High Representative Ashton as the chief mediator for the P5 +1. A breakthrough occurred when Iran agreed to a six-month temporary accord to freeze much of its nuclear enrichment program in exchange for easing some of the economic pressure on Iran (under the interim accord, Iran gains access to $4.2 billion of its money frozen in foreign banks as well as some easing of restrictions on trade in petrochemicals, automotive parts, and precious metals), which went into effect on January 20, 2014, in exchange for the time to negotiate a permanent accord that would require Iran to accept extensive verification, abandon plans to build a heavy-water reactor that can produce plutonium, and resolve long-standing concerns by the IAEA over past Iranian compliance (Dehghan, 2014; Gladstone, 2014; M. R. Gordon, 2014). Significantly, the European embargo of Iranian oil and the exclusion form a global communications network "that is critical to international finance" (Gladstone, 2014).

Libya

Both the EU and the US failed to foresee the coming of the Arab Spring and – most importantly – to resolutely act to support it. The response was slow and fuzzy, thus missing a chance to contribute to the democratic development of the area. In Libya, after years of confrontation, the Gaddafi government policy reversals on WMD and terrorism led to the lifting of most international sanctions in 2003 and 2004, followed by economic liberalization, oil sales, and international investments. Despite this apparent stabilization, the 2011 Libyan uprising occurred in the context of popular protest movements and political change in other countries in North Africa and the Middle East. In mid-February 2011, confrontations between opposition activists and government security forces in the eastern cities of Benghazi and Bayda resulted in the death of some unarmed protestors. Security forces used military force to subdue subsequent funeral gatherings and protests in incidents that reportedly killed or wounded dozens, if not hundreds, of civilians. Opposition groups seized several police and military facilities and took control of some eastern cities. In the weeks that followed, Gaddafi supporters' counter-attacks on opposition-controlled areas and opposition advances toward Gaddafi strongholds pushed Libya to the brink of civil war.

The French airstrike on March 20, 2011 marked the beginning of the allied operations in Libya (Kirkpatrick, Erlanger, & Bumiller, 2011). In the first week of Libya operations, the US dropped bombs from B-2 stealth planes flown from Missouri and roughly 200 missiles launched from submarines in the Mediterranean, causing alarm that any extended campaign would quickly cost billions more. But after the US military ramped up the operation, other NATO countries shouldered most of the air burden. Americans took a supporting role: aerial refueling tankers, electronic jamming, and surveillance. Hence, for the first time since the Cold War, the US decided to neither exercise leadership nor fully share risks in a war in which it was otherwise participating. However, although Washington took a back seat in the war, which the Obama Administration looked at skeptically from the start, the US still ran the initial stages, in particular the destruction of Libya's air defenses, making it safe for its NATO colleagues to fly. The US then provided intelligence, refueling, and more precision bombing assistance than Paris or London want to acknowledge (Erlanger, 2011).

A majority of NATO and EU members, including Germany, Poland, and Turkey, however, refused to support the war, notwithstanding an explicit UNSC resolution. In the case of Germany, 20 years of progress toward supporting participation in UN-backed and NATO-run wars was reversed. Even jointly owned assets such as NATO's fleet of AWACS radar aircraft were deprived of German personnel, although these were not strike aircraft. In addition, the EU played no identifiable part in the war. In the arena of defense, the war therefore exposed the EU structural insufficiencies and flaws (Heisbourg, 2011). Ironically, however, the Libya campaign is generally considered in Washington as an example of successful transatlantic cooperation, most especially because of the reduced costs and of (relatively) reduced direct US intervention. If "leading from behind" becomes the rule rather than the exception in US foreign policy – a plausible assumption given the current inward-looking mood in the US, the Asia pivot, and cuts in defense spending – European force planners will have to invest in some of these areas.

Counter-Terrorism

Homeland security and counter-terrorism also continue to rank at the forefront of transatlantic concerns. Europe remains both a primary target of radical Islamist terrorists and a potential base for cells seeking to carry out attacks against the US. In the years since the 9/11 attacks, transatlantic cooperation on counterterrorism has been strong. Spurred on by 9/11, the March 2004 bombings in Madrid, and the July 2005 bombings in London, the EU sought to strengthen and coordinate its internal counterterrorism capabilities. While the EU has thus been increasing its relevance in this area, bilateral intelligence sharing and cooperation between the US and individual European countries also remains key for efforts to disrupt terrorist plots and apprehend those involved. (See discussions in Chapters 5 and 10 as well as Tables 5.1 and 5.2 on pp. 87–90 for a list of agreements and transgovernmental groups related to cross-border crime, terrorism, and homeland security.)

There are also a number of issues in counter-terrorism that potentially divide the EU and the US. For instance, although some EU member states include Hezbollah on their national lists of terrorist organizations, the EU has for years resisted adding Hezbollah to its common list, despite repeated entreaties from members of Congress and US Administrations (Mix, 2013, pp. 10–11).

With the emergence of the Islamic State in Iraq and Syria (ISIS), Europe is now subject to a new and more deadly phase of counter-terrorism, with the immediate threat of "homegrown" terrorists (ISIS sympathizers with citizenship in EU member states). As Chapters 5 and 10 of this book document, homeland security cooperation has been mainly at the impetus of the Americans. This is now likely to change, and very quickly, as there are reports of a large number of European citizens fighting for ISIS in the Middle East (Sengupta, 2014). The problem is most acute for France, Germany, and the UK, but to a smaller degree in other EU member states as well. At the time of this writing, EU member states were considering various proposals, such as prosecuting citizens returning from Syria (UK), revoking the dual citizenship of an individual found guilty of joining a terrorist group (UK), preventing a citizen from leaving the country to go abroad (France), and revoking the national identity cards which allow Germans to travel to many countries (Sengupta, 2014). Thus, the EU and the US are now more likely to find a greater base for cooperation with respect to balancing civil liberties and security of citizens and property.

Russia

In the aftermath of its August 2008 conflict with Georgia, relations between Russia and the West reached a low level. In fact, relations had already grown increasingly tense in previous years, with numerous issues – including past and prospective NATO enlargement, and Western support for the independence of Kosovo – serving as points of irritation and contention. Against this backdrop, officials and observers in Europe and the US had routinely expressed concern about what they perceived as the increasingly authoritarian character of the Russian government, as well as its assertiveness and quest for influence in the Russian "near abroad" and beyond.

The Obama Administration's "reset" initiative helped alleviate some of the tension. At the April 2009 NATO Summit, it was decided to resume the meetings of the NATO–Russia Council, which had been suspended due to the Georgia conflict. President Obama traveled to Moscow for a summit in July 2009, and the two sides reached an agreement allowing the transit of US military material through Russia to Afghanistan, among other areas of cooperation. The Administration's September 2009 decision to alter US plans for missile defense installations in Poland and the Czech Republic temporarily diminished a primary source of past friction. In March 2010 the US and Russia concluded negotiations over the new START treaty; in June 2010 Russia backed UNSC 1929 authorizing tougher international sanctions against Iran, and in September 2010 Russia canceled the sale of air defense missile systems to Iran. President Medvedev also accepted an invitation to attend the NATO Summit that was held in Lisbon in November 2010. At the same time, however, there were standing and consistent US and European objections regarding Russian policy on many issues, including Georgia and Russia's recognition of the breakaway provinces Abkhazia and South Ossetia, Russia's unilateral suspension of its obligations under the Conventional Armed Forces in Europe (CFE) Treaty, and matters of internal governance and human rights (Mix, 2013, p. 8).

After a period of what appeared to be better relations in 2009–2011, tensions between Russia and the West increased following Russia's December 2011 parliamentary election. Following the vote, the US and the EU expressed serious concerns about allegations of widespread electoral fraud, procedural violations, lack of independent media coverage, and harassment of election monitors. Prime Minister Putin subsequently blamed the US for opposition protests which took place after the election, asserting that criticism leveled by Secretary of State Clinton sent a "signal" to Russian political activists (Mix, 2010, p. 8). Russia's March 2012 presidential election, which returned Putin to the president's office, and analysts' criticism of Russia's "managed democracy" further negatively affected US and European relations with Russia.

Russia also stepped up its criticism of US and European foreign policies. Russian leaders criticized the 2011 NATO operation in Libya, arguing that it exceeded its UN mandate. Russian officials have accused the US and European countries of seeking a Libya-style war with Syria to remove President Bashar al-Assad, and Russia has thwarted US and European efforts to address the violence in Syria through the UNSC. Russia has criticized the EU's oil embargo on Iran and accused the West of trying to foment unrest and revolution in Iran. Russia has also been critical of US moves in implementing revised plans for a missile defense system in Europe. Russian officials are unhappy about their exclusion from participating in the planned system and assert they have not received sufficient guarantees that the system is not directed against Russia (Mix, 2010, p. 9).

But the most important serious challenge for the EU since the Lisbon Treaty began in the fall of 2013, when Ukraine's President Viktor Yanukoych refused to sign the EU's proffered association agreement (see Introduction to this volume). As Edward Lucas (2013) of the Central European Policy Institute warned months before Ukraine was asked to sign the EU's Eastern Partnership Association Agreement in November 2013, there are a number of reasons why many Ukrainians would prefer to join Russia's common market:

> It would be a mistake to ignore other aspects of what Russia offers which are genuinely and widely popular. These include: visa-free travel to Russia (important for those with family ties); relatively open access to the labour market; cheap education (free of charge for Belarusians); and access to the huge Russian market for goods and services.... For countries, enterprises and individuals without the language skills and cultural familiarity needed for doing business in the EU, and facing the considerable bureaucratic and financial hurdles that it places in their path, the "eastern option" is highly attractive.

The EU's original reaction to "Russia's dismemberment" of Ukraine (the Russian annexation of Crimea; at the time of this writing, it is unclear if Western Ukraine will be able to keep its east from seceding and end Russian support for the east), was considered too slow by US standards – in a common American complaint about European foreign policy. Many EU member states have complex and interdependent relationships with Russia in terms of energy and economics, and therefore the EU has had a difficult time formulating a common approach to their eastern neighbor. Europe has for some time been divided between those who believe in a firm, vigilant stance toward Russia, and others inclined more toward pragmatism and engagement. Countries such as Poland and the Baltic states have tended to see Russia as a potential threat, looking to a US approach that robustly guards against Russian assertiveness. Advocates of engagement, on the other hand, notably countries such as Germany, France, and Italy, assert that the maintenance of extensive ties and constructive dialogue is the most effective way to influence Russia. They argue that Russia should be viewed as a strategic partner and observe that Russian cooperation is important on issues such as Iran, climate change, arms control, and energy. So, for example, between March and early July 2014, the US had imposed visa bans and asset freezes on members of Russian President Vladmir Putin's "inner circle," but the EU failed to follow suit, concerned with "antagonizing Russia" (Archick & Mix, 2014, p. 1).

Regarding energy, the EU as a whole is dependent on Russia for more than one-quarter of its gas and oil supplies. Additionally, in recent years Russia has been actively engaging in bilateral energy deals with a number of European countries and acquiring large-scale ownership of European energy infrastructure, while not applying Western standards of transparency and market reciprocity regarding business practices and investment policy.

European dependence on Russia's energy has been a major source of concern for the US and an issue that routinely appeared in all bilateral talks with the major importers of Russia gas and oil. There is in fact concern in the US over the influence that Russian energy dominance could have on European – and, by consequence, transatlantic – unity vis-à-vis Russia. For this reason, some officials have expressed the desirability of decreasing European reliance on Russian energy through diversification of supply, and supported European steps to develop alternative sources and increase energy efficiency. However, despite the enormous quantity of US gas reserves derived from hydrologic fracturing of shale available to export along with the building of ports to handle liquefied natural gas, the US is reluctant to lift its restrictions on the exportation of natural gas. (See Chapter 13's discussion of EU–US energy relations in the context of the TTIP negotiations.)

Nevertheless, by the fall of 2014 a common "transatlantic" response seemed to have taken hold in response to the crisis in Ukraine. Archick and Mix (2014, p. 2) point to several coordinated and common responses that entered into force in September 2014, including: restricting Russia's access to capital markets in the EU and the US; bans of future EU exports and imports of arms and related materiel; prohibition of sales of EU dual-use goods and technology for Russian military end-users of nine mixed defense companies; ban on EU sales of certain oil exploration equipment and technology. While there are qualifications to protections in the EU sanctions to protect particular industries, by and large these EU bans close up some of the "gaps" in the EU's sanctions regime against Russia: enough, apparently, to promote President Obama to observe that the "combined U.S.–EU measures would 'have an even bigger bite'" (Archick & Mix, 2014). At the time of this writing, there was a ceasefire in Ukraine, with some experts suggesting that "U.S.–EU tensions could resurface if some EU members begin pressing to roll back certain sanctions" (Archick & Mix, 2014, p. 2).

Conclusions

This chapter shows that there was substantial continuity in foreign policy between the Bush and Obama Administrations with respect to transatlantic relations for several reasons. The first reason is that the last Bush years were in reality less adversarial to Europe than they are usually thought to be because a few core ideas continue to underpin transatlantic relations: democracy, freedom, human rights, and the free market.

The second reason for this continuity is the transgovernmental nature of foreign policymaking, where the mid-level of the chain of command, diplomacies, and secret services on both sides of the Atlantic have become inextricably intertwined, with de facto institutionalized relations made of thick and constant flow of information, meetings, etc. Thus, civil servants are heavily involved in the day-to-day practice of transatlantic foreign policy.

The third reason lies in a commonality of interests between the US and the EU: in addition to the obvious economic ties, there is the need to combat diffuse threats such as terrorism or international criminality and to stabilize an increasingly unstable world.

This explains why Barack Obama was ready for an "upgrade" that would have meant also increasing dealings with the EU as such instead of the more time-consuming and stretching of an overstretched and overburdened federal civil service by dealing bilaterally with member states. When Obama was inaugurated to his first term of office, EU member states has signed the Lisbon Treaty the previous month and began the ratification process in the spring of 2008. But the EU member states may not have anticipated the extent to which the US was no longer interested in dealing with 27 (now 28) different member states when, to the US, the EU's goals and objectives, norms and values, looked near- identical to those of the Americans.

On their side, the Europeans did not help the situation. Though they liked Obama, they blamed his impatience on US disinterest with Europe, complaining Americans were too focused on the emerging powers and Asia at the expense of transatlantic relations. In reality, Europeans managed to be divided on almost anything that mattered to the US: from Afghanistan to Libya. And on Ukraine, the EU's Eastern Partnership strategy (which the US supported) utterly backfired, exposing the EU's inability to assist a humiliated and seemingly effete Obama Administration after Russia's annexation of Crimea. Indeed, EU–US drive to increase the Eastern Partnership – in completion with Russia's Eurasian Union – directly contributed to the dismemberment of Ukraine.

A "bite-and-go" transatlantic relation is of little long-run benefit to either partner. While in the past the EU has experienced difficulty speaking with one voice in foreign policy, three years since the Lisbon Treaty entered into force on December 1, 2009, High Representative Ashton has quietly gained the trust of her American counterparts and has represented the EU in extremely difficult situations such as in Cairo (ouster of President Morsi), Serbia and Kosovo, and with the Iranians over uranium enrichment.

But one person can only do so much. If Europe is to become a central global actor and a reliable US partner over the longer term, it needs to increasingly speak and act as one in foreign policy and security issues; to commit to deeper initiatives for pooling defense resources in order to gain capabilities and efficiency; and to emphasize the further development of soft power strategies that project influence through the attractiveness of European political, cultural, and economic values.

4 The Cultural Dynamics of Transatlanticism

Michael O'Neill

Introduction

Much is made nowadays of "Atlantic drift," once-close relations troubled by competing interests and conflicted values. This chapter examines this issue from the perspective of culture, the values and norms that give substance to identity and through which interests are defined. The critical question is whether Americans and Europeans still share "common" values and, if so, what sustains them in a mutable world. Cultural transmission cultivated over time a broadly shared idea of "the West," but how far common culture continues to bridge the Atlantic is debatable.

Some commentators answer this question by pointing to the Americanization of Europe, but cultural transmission is hardly one-way traffic. (For contrasting opinions into the direction of travel of transatlantic culture, see de Grazia, 2005; Pells, 1997. Both confirm the same direction of travel, but as Pells sees it Europeans have "Europeanized" American culture, whereas de Grazia remains mostly unconvinced by the "Old Continent's" efforts at cultural resistance.) Americans brought European values from the "old" world but recent cultural traffic has mostly been in the other direction, from Hollywood and popular music to supermarkets and "food to go" (Cross, 2015). The question here is not so much *difference* as *how much* difference, and its political consequences. Americans and Europeans share basic cultural values, albeit shaped by quite different experiences of state and nation-building, economic and social development. The West has modernized along similar trajectories, a transformative process characterized by democratic polities, free markets and the rule of law, though change here was variable, rooted in similar values maybe, but operationalized quite differently.

Some have even claimed an American exceptionalism, though Europeans, too, make their own claim to cultural singularity. Do these contending claims to difference confirm separate identities? (See for instance, Rose, 1985.) Americans, for example, do have greater faith in "the market" for efficiently allocating resources (Page & Shapiro, 1992, p. 128). Europeans, on the other hand, rely more on the state for macro-economic management (King, 1973, p. 300). Europeans, too, are mostly comfortable with publicly disbursed welfare (Keene & Ladd, 1990, p. 133). Americans on their side are generally averse to big government, less supportive of public welfare and hostile to redistributive taxation in order to pay for it, preferring welfare to be privately funded or voluntary (Kudrle & Marmor, 1984, p. 83).

Citing data from the *World Values Surveys* collected between 1980 and 1990, Lipset observed that "when asked to choose between the importance of 'equality of income or the freedom to live and develop without hindrance', Americans are more disposed to the latter" (Lipset, 1996). Yet before 1989 such marked cultural differences seemed not to matter, or at least were no threat to an abiding neighborliness. Indeed, over a half century and more the West succeeded in "building up more common understanding … than has ever been the case in history to date" (Weidenfeld, 1996, p. 99). What, if anything, has changed and why, and does anything survive of the once-familiar idea of the West?

America's postwar ascendancy prompted mixed reactions in Europe but transatlantic relations nevertheless remained settled, only experiencing real turbulence after 1989 and especially in the aftermath of 9/11. Since then, relations, have been more strained. The end of the Cold War, and with it the bi-polar world order, has undoubtedly weakened this sense of common purpose. But is this merely cultural dissonance or something more? Relations have certainly drifted, but whether transatlantic wrangling since the Iraq War is merely squabbling, necessary adjustment to changing times, or something worse, even an Atlantic identity crisis, is the critical question. Recent fall-outs have been in part about security, both sides reassessing strategic priorities as they confront new challenges, but there is more to it than that. The cultural fabric of Atlanticism as it has been understood over four centuries always gave rise to competing narratives about values and how these shape political identity, but recently cultural difference has acquired altogether new significance.

The Cultural Dynamics of Atlanticism: Theoretic Narratives

The dynamics of cultural similarity and difference impacted on Atlanticism from the start. But how do we explain the significance of this cultural variable? The influential realist narrative interprets international relations as *realpolitik*, the imperative for security to mitigate ubiquitous anarchy. Transatlantic relations on this reading are primarily about hard power; states make alliances to counter threat and by the same token unmake them when threat subsides. In this narrative Atlanticism is essentially instrumental, lacking affective meaning.

This much is true, but only so far. International relations are always about security, though not exclusively as other motives figure too, not least cultural affinity. Liberal theorists concentrate on these ideational factors, seeing international relations as mediated by values, cumulate cultural experience that both confirms "we-ness" and defines the "otherness" of "strangers" (Adler, 1997, p. 257). Cultural proximity may affirm common identity or not, but either way it contributes to framing the conduct and defining the purposes of international relations (Hellmann, 2008; Risse, 2008).

There are theoretical objections to this narrative too, the obverse of the realism critique. Values are indeed a useful prism for identifying the logics of international relations, but to the exclusion of hard power and functional interests. In fact, theoretic focus on any singular dependent variable, whether *realpolitik* or culture, distorts explanation. Atlanticism, or for that matter any other international relations, is not exclusively about values or interests, whether between neighbors or strangers. Accordingly, both of these classic narratives are unduly one-dimensional, failing to give an accurate picture of Atlanticism in as much as neither reflects the complex juxtaposition of the culture/values or interests/power dimensions of international politics (Joenniemi, 2009).

The social constructivist narrative, on the other hand, does meet this theoretic requirement, focusing as it does on the complex interplay between norms *and* interests, explaining how values define interests and shape values in turn, giving rise to a sense of common purpose and shared identity even across formal political boundaries (Hopf, 2005). Constructivist theory offers, then, a useful theoretic lens for explaining the cultural context of Atlanticism precisely because it acknowledges the very intermediation of normative and instrumental variables (Benhke, 2007).

Transatlanticism: Neighborly Difference or Culture Wars?

The idea of "the West" has cultural roots in the Enlightenment (Gress, 1998). But how embedded are those shared values and the interests they gave rise to? Is the cultural empathy that once bound close allies in common endeavor undergoing significant change, and if so, why and with what consequences for common identity and shared purpose in the new global order?

American Exceptionalism

American exceptionalism was a defining feature of Atlantic political culture from the very beginning, and for Lieven "one of the most important factors in alienating the United States from some of its closest allies in Europe and elsewhere" (Lieven, 2004, p. 19). Europeans saw America as an inferior outpost of their continent's values, but Americans responded in kind, extolling the moral ascendance of this first modern national state where old values acquired new meaning, not only a new country but a moral enterprise (Tyrell, 1991). As Hofstadter famously observed, "it has been our fate as a nation not to have ideologies, but to *be* one" (quoted in Lipset, 1996, p. 19).

Tocqueville found there a sense of historic mission grounded in uniquely civic virtue. The world's first democratic nation and one claiming to be the international exemplar (Restad, 2012). The Republic duly imported European norms into its law and governance but adapted them to state and nation-building, thereafter maintaining cultural distance from Europe, and even claiming manifest destiny (Polanyi, 1944). The claim to lead "the West" was more assiduously asserted after World War II, with the US as the sole Atlantic superpower. Lipset (1996, pp. 17–23) described this cultural reflex as the "American Creed." There is, of course, a paradox here, perhaps even hypocrisy for the claim to exceptionalism sits uneasily with America's own moral shortcomings, from slavery to bloody civil war, institutionalized racism to deep-seated social inequalities (Hodgson, 2009). Cynical use of military power for securing scarce resources or propping up morally bankrupt regimes on grounds of national security likewise raise questions about moral claims to leadership (Hofstadter, 1955). Gore Vidal (1998) even went so far as to describe the US as a "disguised Empire" that has "done the ... world incomparable harm."

One notable cultural difference between America and Europe relevant to the subject matter of this book concerns the relationship between citizen and state. The Republic's origins as resistance to hierarchic authority elevated individual over collective rights and embedded in political culture very different ideas about governance and society. This, in turn, shaped a distinctive capitalism that reified *laissez-faire* individualism over collectivism, a quite different interpretation of liberalism from that prevailing in Europe. And this despite the expansion of federal government in the New Deal's programs and agencies and the onset of the wartime command economy after 1941. (See Chapter 3, "The Late New Deal and the Idea of the State" pp. 37–62 in Brinkley, 1998.)

Another significant cultural marker is the role of religion in politics, and no less its impact on the public mind-set. In Lipset's (1999) view,

> Americans are utopian moralists who press hard to institutionalise virtue, to destroy evil people, and eliminate wicked institutions and practices.... They tend to view social and political dramas as morality plays, as battles between God and the devil, so that compromise is virtually unthinkable.

These particular cultural reflexes have influenced expectations about government and public policy on both sides and will certainly figure indirectly in the Transatlantic Trade and Investment Partnership (TTIP) negotiations. Whether or how far these different ideas have undermined common purpose, even an abiding sense of neighborliness, is critical for the success or otherwise of this latest endeavor at maintaining constructive relations.

Europe's Exceptionalism Turn

Europe's claim to exceptionalism is less strident than America's, but with its own moral purpose, albeit marked by ambivalence. No stranger to moral hubris as convenient cover for self-interest, its latest expression is less a claim to public virtue than apologia for historic failings, even an attempt to escape "tainted" history. The celebration of soft power is in part atonement for past failings, but also a positive assertion of difference from a more combative ally. In one account it is clear rebuttal of "what Europeans have come to think of (in their own Euro-centric way) as central patterns of post-1945 modernity, namely the overcoming of a culture of bellicose nationalism by modern civilisation and the replacement of nationalist unilateralism with international cooperation" (Lieven, 2004, p. 19).

Duchêne's (1973) assertion that

> Europe as a whole could well become the first example in history of a major centre of the balance of power becoming in the era of its decline not a colo-nised victim but an exemplar of a new stage of political civilisation

reflects ambition in Brussels to forge a new international identity, one grounded in soft power, *mission civilsatrice* as a novel claim to global "influence which can be wielded by a large political cooperative formed to exert essentially civilian forms of power." A Kantian excursion in the opinion of Monnet's official biographer perhaps, but not merely "utopian or second best but a quite deliberate choice" (Nicolaidis, 2005). Of course, an equally convincing neo-realist case can also be made for this EU project, less about creating a Kantian *Respublica* than making the most of limited political capital in the new world order in pursuit of national interests.

These competing exceptionalism narratives are fully in play in the current Atlantic debate, though this has not precluded a determined effort at continuing cooperation (Boon & Delanty, 2006, p. 169). Misunderstandings nowadays are certainly more frequent, though whether this is merely neighborly squabbling, the "narcissism of minor differences," or something more serious is the crucial question. Are these familiar transatlantic neighbors now so culturally disconnected from a broad understanding of shared values that they might even go their separate ways? (P. Baldwin, 2009). The constructivist narrative suggests a conditional rather than an absolute answer, seeing difference as an unavoidable outcome of changing times but by no means an impediment to continuing relations, common interests, and even to a shared if fragile sense of identity, albeit firmly rooted in shared values (Eichner, 2006; Fuchs & Klingemann, 2008).

Whither the West: Does Culture Bind or Separate?

By the end of the Cold War *the West* still had cultural meaning, an idea seemingly vindicated by that very event: military supremacy, economic power and prosperity, the legitimacy of governance, and the rule of law and entrenched human rights. On the purely functional level, transatlantic trade accounted for fully 50% of total global commerce and rising, with EU–US foreign direct investment (FDI) some 60% of the world's total. Technological innovation, predominantly though not exclusively American, was leading the world and driving globalization. Some saw the West's political triumph as heralding global leadership in perpetuity, for some foolishly it was even "the end of history" and for zealots justification for a mission to change regimes and remake the world in its own image (Ikenberry, 2000). The rise of multilateral organizations such as G-7 and G-8, though by no means confined to the Atlantic nations, confirmed Western hegemony. And though NATO is less important now, morphing into a broader alliance as much concerned with soft as with hard power, it continues to make an important contribution to international security.

The EU, though ambivalent about the West's role in this new international order, did contribute soft power, not least enlargement eastward, disbursing economic and other resources to its "near abroad." It seemed as if nothing could diminish the West's global dominance (Hogan, 1992). As one commentator saw it, "predictions that the loss of Europe's strategic centrality in US eyes would undermine the transatlantic bond failed to materialize. Occasional spats … were overshadowed by the degree of economic and strategic convergence …

the post-Cold War period witnessed a depth of transatlantic ties that would not compare unfavourably with Cold War standards" (Tocci & Alcaro, 2012). What, then, could possibly go awry?

When differences did arise over trade and security policy, the fault line was by no means exclusively transatlantic. European consternation about a "predatory" Wall Street following the sub-prime scandal of 2008 hit American just as much as European mortgagees, and muscular capitalism has found enthusiastic European disciples too. Growing social inequalities in education and health, and changes in labor markets, have fueled lively discourse on all sides about "irresponsible" capitalism. If there is a putative "crisis" of values it is a crisis facing the West as a whole rather than a cultural lacuna between Europe and America. The same can be said about changes in political as in economic culture. Declining election turnout confirms the growing disconnect between elites and citizens everywhere. The financial crisis and with it public concern that politicians are more responsive now to corporate lobbyists, more exercised by saving the banks than protecting jobs or maintaining ordinary people's living standards has reinforced widespread mistrust in governing institutions and especially of politicians on both sides. (See Stiglitz, 2013b, especially chapter 5, "Democracy in Peril" at pp. 118–145.)

The critical marker for transatlantic tensions is less cultural difference than events. September 11 is often cited as the signal event that sparked transatlantic crisis, Washington in its neo-con pomp unilaterally revising strategic options and adopting a confrontational approach to European allies, with some of them reciprocating in kind. But the main cause of contention here was strategic rather than cultural, though some (neo-cons on one side, arch Euro-federalists on the other) certainly saw this issue as evidence of cultural divergence (Pond, 2003). Critics and supporters of Atlanticism alike have claimed that America and Europe are indeed rapidly moving beyond each other's cultural orbits, with voices on each side blaming "the other." American neo-cons were strident in their condemnation of European "double standards" and "free-riding." Whereas some in Europe saw Washington as shamelessly cashing in on its hyper-power status, willfully disregarding its neighbors. (Kagan, 2003 is the classic statement of the former position; for a Europhile rejoinder see Rifkin, 2004.) The removal of the Soviet threat did weaken the idea of the West as a coherent cultural (defined by many as ideologically cogent) community of close neighbors with common values, but quite how far is open to question (Cox, 2004). Another interpretation of these same events suggests a more conditional conclusion.

To see even persistent difficulties as signaling the end of the West is certainly to exaggerate (Herd, 2010). The replacement of merely unequal partnership by an "American empire-lite [that] articulated, reinforced, but also exempted itself from global rules (the International Criminal Court, the Kyoto climate change protocol) according to the American interest" is only one interpretation of recent events, but there was less to these fall-outs than outright cultural angst (Tocci & Alcaro, 2012, p. 5). Of course we should not underestimate the fragility of even close relations; marriages sometimes end in divorce. And there is widespread doubt on both sides about future direction, not least whether and how far meaningful partnership based on shared purposes is possible in a much-changed global order (Stelzenmuller, 2010).

Differences there certainly are, from security policy to business culture and economic organization: how to manage markets and over the macro-economic role of the state, on welfare systems and regulatory rules. On one side a robust capitalism, on the other a claim to practice more humane economics and transnational politics, though this claim by some Europeans has certainly lost some of its moral salience after spectacular mismanagement of the sovereign debt and eurozone crises.

The critical question is not cultural disparity but how far cultural difference confirms growing separation or continuing neighborliness. The evidence indicates that, periodic fall-outs aside, there is still much to play for. Data on the extent of cultural transmission show more proximity than estrangement; for instance, in those indices that measure the frequency of tourism, academic and civic exchanges, and of electronic communications, patterns of trade and inward foreign investment, frequency of business take-overs, and interpenetration of labor markets. There is rivalry, too, on everything from trade tariffs to cyber-security, product and technical standards, to setting emissions targets for greenhouse gases and non-tariff barriers (NTBs) on services, and restrictions on free movement of people. But these are indices confirming regular interaction and no less of mutual interest than evidence of ineluctable difference, and as such resolvable.

And the evidence is by no means one way, for continuity coexists with conflict in those policy networks and epistemic communities that mediate transatlantic relations and negotiate exchanges of ideas, technical know-how, and policy practice on several fronts. What is clear from this range of activity is just how far cultural proximity facilitates cooperation by means of a dense matrix of interpersonal and institutional exchanges. As contributors to this volume show, the Atlantic community may be experiencing difficulties but this is hardly new turf. Meanwhile, strongly centripetal cultural flows confirm potential for constructive engagement, whether in government or business, the academy or civil society, the scientific community to the military. To say this is by no means to downplay difficulties. A former president of the influential Rand Corporation, James Thomson, gave timely warning a decade since against complacency, insisting that transatlantic solidarity does not just "happen" but requires sustained effort to maintain "a more deeply grounded willingness to negotiate and an interest in the partner's society" (Weidenfeld, 1996, p. 101).

On this point there are some worrying signs of distance, even of disengagement, with declining cultural and other exchanges of personnel as funding for cultural diplomacy is cut. The times are less conducive to close cultural encounters in a post-Cold War and multilateral world where both consensus on basic values and even mutual security are no longer the strong centripetal incentive to common understanding they once were. There is a problem, too, of balance. The US remains the principal Atlantic "partner" and behaves accordingly, a source of growing resentment in Europe.

The dynamic of transatlantic relations remains much as it was since 1945, a response by both sides to American hegemony. Europe's attempt to establish its own credentials as an autonomous actor, to enhance its international status by means of a common security policy and monetary union intended to rival, and for some zealots even to replace the US dollar as the leading global currency, has hardly been impressive. The Common Foreign and Security Policy (CFSP) has been more miss than hit in its attempts to police the European neighborhood. Consequently, ambiguity remains for both sides the principal cultural reflex of relations. A positive Atlantic future will depend on managing these competing, even divergent, interests and no less on modulating growing cultural differences rather than denying they exist.

What chance, then, of rebalancing Atlanticism to meet new circumstances? (Howorth, 2009). There are different views about this. Crisis rather more than cooperation is the appropriate descriptor of relations since the end of the Cold War, though even crisis can be an incentive to change, to rethink familiar shibboleths. And there are positive signs that, the negative externalities of the eurozone crisis notwithstanding, Europe remains an important region for Washington; if not as a partner to be emulated then one whose importance for global financial stability and commerce has to be taken seriously. Washington is rightly dismayed by Europe's mismanagement of its own domestic affairs, from the Bosnian *débâcle* to the eurozone crisis, but it does recognize there can be no adequate response to urgent global problems without Atlantic cooperation.

Europeans for their part tend to see recent problems in a different light, their principal cause due to lax American regulation of financial markets, proof positive for some Europhiles of abiding cultural disparities in the management of capitalism. That said, common ground does still exist, not least in the EU's preferred "solution" to sovereign debt and fiscal weakness, by following the neo-liberal supply-side reforms and embracing slash-and-burn austerity, an economic "remedy" for current ills that reflects America's economic culture more than it does Europe's. (These policy choices are discussed in Sachs, 2011.)

Over the medium term and regardless of occasional and sometimes deep differences, business lobbies and politicians on both sides acknowledge that stable capitalism, and no less social peace, depends on "efficient" and open markets, on expanding free trade, promoting a business culture favorable to competitiveness and entrepreneurialism, and not least on sound money. All of these fundamental values, despite local variations, are shared by Atlantic societies on both sides. The latest evidence of common purpose is the TTIP initiative, intended to harness the potential of the Atlantic economies to both expand and shape the global economy. Whether this ambitious project can revive transatlantic economies, let alone equip them for global leadership, will be determined in no small measure by cultural compatibility; how far differences of norms, values, and cultural expectations can be accommodated within a continuing idea of "the West."

Surviving Exceptionalism: Cultural Difference and its Consequences

Exceptionalism narratives are historically constructed stereotypes, whereas the cultural map of Atlanticism is altogether more nuanced. Closer reading of cultural history shows there is no unequivocal idea in Europe of "we" defined against the American "other," but instead a broad spectrum of opinion ranging from cultural mimicry to ambivalence and even hostility. Less a matter of cultural exceptionalism on either side, ideational coherence around an overarching idea of the "West," than disparate cultural reflexes, abiding differences within Europe per se as much as between that continent and America.

Examples abound; for instance, more tolerant attitudes to welfare in Scandinavia than in the UK, and likewise differences within Europe as much as across the Atlantic over multiculturalism or lifestyle choices, a fair social framework for capitalism, and no less about the purposes of government. A notable outlier of policy comparators is wholly different approaches to publicly funded health care, though Obamacare has made a start in reducing this disparity. In addition, more Americans are killed by guns, reside in penitentiaries for crimes, or are executed; fewer relatively belong to trades unions, and economic inequality is greater than in Europe. But would we realistically expect anything else? Differences here are markers of cultural distance, but this hardly amounts to a transatlantic culture war.

Disparities of outlook do matter but are by no means as great as exceptionalism voices on either side assert, and difference on many of these social indices is narrowing. America may have a different response to inequalities of wealth, affordable health care, and social deprivation and its impact on life chances. But cultural difference here is by no means exclusively transatlantic. Wide variations in social and political preferences exist in Europe too. The fact is that in surveys of public attitudes the US occupies a median position on many of these issues rather than always being the cultural outlier. American opinion fits well within the broad range of Atlantic opinion, which for one close observer of comparative social trends "at the very least ... suggests that far-reaching claims to radical differences across the Atlantic have been overstated" (P. Baldwin, 2009, p. 216).

The cultural fault line that has perhaps greatest significance for transatlantic public policy is American resistance to the idea of the interventionist state. This is a cultural leitmotif rooted in the founding idea of Liberty that still informs American thinking about public policy preferences. Though, again, differences here have narrowed. Many of Europe's new democracies, for instance, have forsaken conventional European economic and welfare models, preferring to take their ideological cue from American neo-liberalism. Western Europe, too, has embraced neo-liberal political economy fashioned in Chicago, though Western Europeans have never been hostile to free markets – not least because they invented them. Europe was already flirting with monetarism before the neo-liberal ascendancy in America, a reaction to growing doubts about Keynesian demand-led economics following the shock of multiple recessions and the hike in oil prices in the 1970s. The evidence of cultural transmission here is patent, not least the heavy footprint of Reaganomics and monetarist doctrine on the ideological mantras that impact on official economic policy in Europe.

Again we should avoid distortive generalization. Americans are reticent about the state, a legacy of the Republic's origins in popular rebellion against mercantilist autocracy. Comparison of public expenditure levels likewise confirms

American aversion to "big government," and attitudes to taxation, especially redistributive taxation, attests residual hostility to top-down meddling with "freedom." Yet actual data put such generalizations into proper perspective. America actually spends big on education and health, if not on social insurance, even if much public expenditure actually benefits powerful private sector lobbyists such as private medical insurance schemes and health care providers rather than patients, especially poorer patients and other consumers of public services. A familiar cultural defense of difference from Europe is the celebration of social mobility, the emotive imagery of "huddled masses," of a society that gave opportunity to live free, work hard, and rise, and thereby to take care of self and family without need of, or interference from, a "nanny state."

The cultural mantra of "freedom" is elemental for the very idea of America, but again polling data tell a different story: that welfare per se is by no means an alien concept though cultural resistance remains, ironically even from those who would benefit most. Another transatlantic marker that seems to confirm cultural difference is the American preference for civic localism, informal grass-roots networks of self-help that from the outset replaced the hierarchism of European feudal *noblesse oblige* and its subsequent embodiment as welfare capitalism. Yet declining civic identity is patent everywhere in the West, as captured in Robert Putnam's (1995) evocative "bowling alone" metaphor, and it confirms just how much contemporary transatlantic culture is marked as much by similar as by enduring and conflictual cultural reflexes.

To acknowledge common transatlantic cultural predispositions is not to deny that variance in attitudes, and no less of political culture, exists. Social change following remorseless globalization is modifying cultural disparities, but it has by no means removed them. It is misreading, though, to conclude that the cultural clichés that figure in some narratives on Atlanticism reflects, let alone explains, what remains as a complex cultural map. For example, a widespread European view of America's capitalism as a kleptocracy of mostly private power and capricious wealth where almost anything goes is to oversimplify what is an altogether more ambiguous attitude to money and power. The state does indeed play a key role there, albeit on a much tighter constitutional leash. Baldwin (2009, p. 220), among other cultural historians, has observed that "even by European standards [America] is quite meddlesome.... Many state activities are highly interventionist even though they are largely cost-free, compared to redistributive measures.... The American state has long micro-managed its citizens' bad habits" from drink to smoking, even showing European governments the way on smoking bans and restricting access to alcohol.

America has likewise given a positive lead on social inclusion, notably on proscribing race discrimination but also on disability, public health, and gender rights. It has been in the forefront of consumer protection, setting products and services standards, and in publicly funded research and development and legislating on public liability of private business. Even in the contentious area of climate change and related ecological issues, differences with Europeans are by no means as clear-cut as the much publicized political spats over reducing emissions and eco-taxation might suggest. Americans may be reluctant to pay more for gas, or indeed to use their cars less and public transport more, but these differences can be explained by history, the freedom to "go west" translated today as the right to cover huge distances encased in the modern version of the covered wagon!

Even here the notion of a deep Atlantic divide is misleading, with hard facts dispelling myth; Americans actually make fewer journeys, leaving smaller carbon footprints per capita, than do many Europeans. The sheer size of the country ensures that Americans are indeed less concerned about overpopulation, though surveys show that by and large they are no more in denial about climate change, and value landscape and clean water just as much as Europeans do. Threat of environmental depredation is readily acknowledged in attitude surveys, though when it comes to policymaking Americans prefer voluntarism over interference by national government, but even more from democratically unaccountable international agencies.

This brief survey of the comparative cultural impact of Atlanticism began by acknowledging competing exceptionalism narratives, but closer scrutiny shows how easily fable can prevail over hard evidence. Atlantic societies are indeed different, but they still have much in common, whether values or social preferences, as they confront similar policy dilemmas. This has implications for the TTIP, where the challenge of negotiating and implementing agreements on many key policies is considerable, given the range of interests in play. Difficult certainly, but by no means impossible given how much cultural ballast transatlantic societies still share.

The TTIP: Cultural Convergence or a Positive-Sum Game?

The TTIP is a response to formidable challenges that confront the Atlantic economies, and it confirms both the interdependence of the Atlantic community and its centrality in the global economy. EU–US trade has doubled since the turn of the millennium and now accounts for almost half of global GDP. Transatlantic financial markets are the most significant players in this critical sector, accounting for some two-thirds of global banking assets and private and public debt securities, and approximately 75% of global financial services and new international debt securities (Hamilton & Quinlan, 2014). Transatlantic fall-outs during the later WTO rounds were based less on insurmountable difference than reflecting the need to respond to urgent challenges.

The financial crisis confirmed economic interdependence, failures in the US sub-prime mortgage market spilling over to Europe, and contrariwise with spillback from the sovereign debt and eurozone crisis. Institutional machinery for reinforcing "strategic partnership," notably the Transatlantic Economic Council (TEC), was no guarantee of concerted let alone effective response. As the crisis worsened cooperation abated, each side opting for quite different policy responses. One contemporary commentary concluded from these events that "viewing the US–EU relationship through the lens of multilateral activities in the last five years might hint at a relationship that is stalling," with neither side "willing to take the lead and push for necessary structural reforms or immediate growth enhancement, least of all the US" (Zandonini, 2012). This was hardly unexpected because the crisis had quite different consequences for each side, though gradually some sense of common interests and even shared objectives did emerge, not least the need to boost slackening growth by expanding Atlantic free trade. From the America side this was in order redress declining primacy in global markets, and the no less urgent need to trade its way out of massive global indebtedness, notably to China. Whereas for Europeans it was the need to counter the negative impact of the sovereign debt crisis, the main obstacle to their economic recovery.

The TTIP is seen by both sides as a solution not only to particular concerns, but also for redressing structural problems in capitalist economies. The interim report of the High Level Working Group on Jobs and Growth (HLWG) set up to review the prospects for expanding bilateral trade and investment, and maybe even to accelerate transatlantic market integration, predicted a positive pay-off by way of more jobs, increased growth, and improved competitiveness. Neither side has underplayed the difficulties of reaching substantive agreement in areas where both the EU and US remain as commercial rivals and industrial competitors. Past experience shows how little has been achieved so far in these key policy areas. Yet cultural proximity is essential to this project, mutual interests rooted in common values ensuring that both sides are still broadly on the same normative page, prepared to learn from past mistakes and to try again to resolve long-standing differences. Economic advantage may be the principal motivation here rather than any nebulous idea of cultural affinity, but congruence of values does facilitate those positive-sum policy bargains that will determine success or otherwise. The European Commission's espousal of the TTIP, for instance, confirms that commercial interests rather than values are the key driver, predicting, for example, that removal of even 50% of extant NTBs would contribute some 0.3% per year to growth, worth some €41 billion annually (Berden, Francois, Thelle, Wymenga, & Tamminen, 2009). Such pragmatism is clearly echoed on the American side.

Seen in global context, this latest transatlantic initiative is not just about improving market access, but concerned also with all-round performance in a highly competitive international economy. Negotiations to date have mostly concentrated on lowering tariff walls and other barriers to freer trade, but the TTIP is more ambitious – or purports to be. Future discussions will show just how much (or how little) scope exists for settling differences in order to confront threats from elsewhere to commercial primacy and competitiveness. Some optimists see the process as following similar multilateral logics to those that have radically reshaped the EU's commercial diplomacy, notably finding common bargaining positions in wider global forums such as the GATT/WTO. Cultural proximity was by no means incidental to this outcome. But if EU multilateralism is seen as a model for the TTIP, the prognosis is rather less than encouraging; for even at this advanced stage of "ever closer union" national interests do still have priority over common objectives, and the European Single Market is far from complete (Kupchan, 2010). What are the likely prospects, then, for even moderate success in the more culturally diffuse and politically divided Atlantic community?

Skepticism is as patent here as optimism. Narrow atavistic instincts, a mix of competing interests and cultural resistance, may yet derail the TTIP program, though at the very least shared history and cultural proximity does improve prospects for successfully addressing mutual objectives such as fairer and freer world trade, and no less for ensuring commerce is underpinned by ethical concerns, whether observance of intellectual property rights, outlawing the employment of children or slave labor, labor market regulation and better environmental standard-setting, and so on. At the same time, structural imbalance in Atlantic relations will also play a part in determining outcomes, for these are hardly partners with commensurate political capital.

The eventual outcome may well have rather more to do with the usual logics of international relations even between close neighbors. Washington, for instance, might resort to its usual hegemonic default mode, the familiar tactic of divide and rule, using bilateral relations with "strategic" European partners to advantage if an effective "strategic partnership" with the EU per se proves elusive. Outcomes are far from certain, but if the TTIP can make even modest headway on problematic policy issues, its leverage in the multilateral regimes that manage global trade will be much enhanced. And this is precisely where cultural proximity and shared cultural values go hand-in-hand with and reinforce economic self-interest.

Some observers are more sanguine about the prospects. Myriam Zandonini (2012, p. 56), for instance, predicts a positive future for an Atlantic community that "is not just an artifact of the past, but is of paramount importance in handling the global economic and financial crisis. The relationship rests on solid trade and financial linkages, which are supported by shared values and ideas." More even than that, "the two partners (will) also use their link to lead international discussions and push forward the multilateral agenda."

Whether such optimism will be borne out is unclear at the time of writing, but regardless of outcome, the very juxtaposition of cultural proximity and abiding self-interest that has long defined Atlanticism is essential for cooperation going forward, in relations that "are still at the top of the world economy and at the forefront in setting the global agenda" (Zandonini, 2012, p. 57).

Does "the West" Have a Future?

The future of Atlanticism defies easy prediction. The consensus among close observers is that a range of outcomes is possible, from continuing cooperation to ineluctable drift, with all manner of hybrid relations in between that reflect variable cultural engagement alongside rising political tension and commercial rivalry. (See, for instance, the discussion in Tocci & Alcaro, 2012.) The options discussed below cover the broad range of potential outcomes.

Rivals

The outlier paradigm foresees greater transatlantic turbulence, rising perception of difference leading to further drift or worse; it fits a realist-inspired narrative.

The centripetal effect of shared values for resolving shared problems is mostly discounted, relations instead seen primarily in instrumental terms. In this account of events international relations are at most alliances of convenience for making positive-sum bargains between quite distinct and competing national interests, policy tradeoffs made for a specific purpose rather than durable alliances between culturally close neighbors working together to counter perceived threats (Daalder, 2003).

This paradigm figures most frequently in (and is more relevant to) the security discourse. If we apply the condition of common purpose to the security dimension of Atlanticism it is apparent that the implosion of communism, the resulting strategic vacuum, and the rise of new threats to peaceful order have eroded, perhaps fatally, the sense of abiding common interests, though without rescinding mutual security concerns as reason enough for continuing alliance. Cultural ballast, though implicit in security relations, was never NATO's most effective cement, yet there is acknowledgment here that alliances are more durable where parties share values. Clearly, functionality on its own is insufficient for maintaining close relations in circumstances quite different from the alliance constructed after World War II.

Other factors seem to have devalued functional interests as a reliable basis for Atlantic relations. Economic trends are also cited in this narrative as confirming ineluctable "drift." EU–Asia and US–Asia trade outstrips EU–US trade by volume, and likewise a trebling of EU–Asia inward investment compared with that between the EU and the US, with the emergence of China critical for both sides (Nye, 2011). Nevertheless, those who see economic and strategic trends confirming the remorseless decline of an historically grounded alliance simply miss the point. For though security and commercial exchange are indeed important for transatlantic relations, so too is cultural proximity, the transmission of shared values, norms, and ideas embodied in such multiple exchanges.

Friends

In the second paradigm prospects for continuing relations are rooted not merely in specific functional interests but in a sense of abiding common purpose, cultural affinity that partly defines interests rather than merely contingent cooperation. Common values and no less cultural affinity, the products of shared history are represented by dense interpersonal networks of policymakers and opinion leaders and conducive to good working partnership (Serfaty, 2008). Interests and values in this paradigm are complementary and mutually reinforcing. As such the policy community on both sides subscribe to "long-term visions and policy platforms ... based on shared interests, values and identities," with interests and policy goals tending "to converge and be complementary." The density of interpersonal ties and institutional connections might give rise to disagreement but not to cultural dissonance, and the very familiarity and frequency of these exchanges, "the institutionalized web of relations embedding the transatlantic partners [provides] effective conflict management mechanisms" (Tocci & Alcaro, 2012, p. 11).

Cultural proximity here has centripetal impact, the cause and direct consequence of close and historically grounded relations. Normative complementarity is both familiar and has binding effect: in particular, commitment to liberal democracy, primacy of individual rights, and free markets, all of them distinctively Western values that no other global partnership can remotely match, and for that very reason a strong disincentive to fractured relations and no less positive encouragement to resolve disagreements (Tocci & Alcaro, 2012). Fall-outs may be unavoidable in a friable and multi-polar world, but cultural proximity lessens their potency (Ikenberry, 1996; Serfaty, 2005). Partnership may be conflictive in strategic affairs but are no less so in commercial relations. Yet the sheer prolixity of these contacts reinforces determination to confront and where possible resolve differences, and no less to avoid serious fall-outs.

The facts offered in support of this narrative are persuasive enough: a world economy dominated by transatlantic trade and investment flows accounting for something like one-third of global exchanges of goods (especially in high-tech and value-added goods), but also in the vital services sector, with some 40% of the global total. The EU and US likewise accounts for 63% of global inward foreign investment and for 75% of outward FDI, 75% of global financial markets, and 80% of international development aid. Moreover, this advanced and integrated economy generates $5 trillion of annual sales and 15 million jobs (Hamilton & Quinlan, 2014).

The abiding interdependence of the Atlantic economy was patent during the recent financial crisis. Dysfunctional asymmetries and just plain competitive angst are normal outcomes even in closely integrated economies, but for all that the Atlantic economy remains inextricably connected and structurally interdependent. Of course, common interests are as important as cultural sentiment for facilitating cooperation. But structural interdependence depends, too, on the density of abiding patterns of cultural transmission and exchange, the sheer volume of interpersonal linkages in this vast and profitable market that have persuaded Washington and Brussels to embark on an ambitious project to find solutions to public and private indebtedness, and to reduce the structural barriers to efficient and open markets. The TTIP on this assessment is the logical extension, a clear outcome of a dense web of macroeconomic exchange and joint efforts at crisis management in the aftershock of 2008. And rather easier to deliver because building on existing networks, drawing on mutual experience of free markets, open competition, shared technical expertise, entrepreneurial disposition, and no less on abiding cultural empathy.

This undertaking is hardly risk-free, nor without difficulties given the history of Atlantic fall-outs over trade and tariff barriers, differing product and environment standards, and with abiding differences in business culture, and no less rising mistrust after years of what both sides regard as unduly protected national markets. The TTIP project is ambitious precisely because it aims to go beyond merely mutual reduction of tariffs (already at quite modest levels, with some 90% of Atlantic trade already exempt from duties and tariffs) and to initiate measures to reduce thinly disguised protection of "local" markets, but also to enhance structural interdependence: for instance, removing barriers to job creation, expanding transatlantic investment flows, reforming financial markets, liberalizing trade in the services sector, eliminating discriminatory technical standards and product and services regulation, removing state subsidies and improving labor market rules, and so on.

Cultural proximity figures prominently in this paradigm though it is no guarantees of success. What it does ensure is that parties to these negotiations are on a similar normative wavelength when addressing their differences. But this paradigm makes rather too much of cultural and ideational proximity, as does the Liberal international relations narrative from which it takes its theoretic cue, failing to see how much successful outcomes actually depend in even the closest relations on accommodating mutual values with competing interests.

Partners

A more realistic (rather than merely realist) paradigm of Atlantic futures takes a middle course between these preceding paradigms. It foresees neither fracture nor ineluctable friendship, but instead an altogether looser arrangement that some commentators describe as structural or "elective" partnership (Risse, 2012; Steinberg, 2003). Cultural proximity, though still in play, is conditional, as some argue it always was in transatlantic relations, more dependent on contingent circumstance than cultural affinity, let alone on ontological identity. Values do figure, but they are not sufficient per se for ensuring close engagement, certainly not compared with the Cold War years when persistent threat to the West's security was a powerful incentive to work together. To survive and prosper in changed times requires an altogether new type of partnership, flexible but designed for mutual advantage, loosely underpinned by cultural proximity but by no means defined by it a priori.

The multilateral and multi-polar world order that emerged after 1989 has altered perceptions all-round of both national and common interests, in this region as elsewhere. Atlantic relations are more fluid now, shaped only in part by residual institutional memory and shared norms sustained by habits of cooperation and empathy fashioned from shared ideological affinity and embedded cultural reflexes generated by a common history. These partners now confront entirely novel challenges for which shared memory is no sure guide to action. The Atlantic states can no longer take for granted the ideological or cultural solidarity that once underpinned Cold War bipolarity. Relations going forward will operate according to quite different logics, a compound of mutual empathy and competing interests, of convergence and conflict, cultural similarity and difference (Steinmo & Kopstein, 2008). As this paradigm sees it, transatlantic relations will continue, but on more conditional terms as cultural familiarity shrinks, residual empathy fades with growing circumspection, and with that rising political uncertainty.

This much is already clear from recent events: mutual recriminations over the Iraq War, urgent rethinking on all sides of NATO's primary purpose, even exigent rethinking of the very idea of the West. Yet this revisionism is modulated by the very habit of "doing business" with familiar and mostly friendly partners wherever circumstances allow. This reflex is evident in the efforts on all sides to find a way through post-2008 economic turbulence, notwithstanding mutual complaints about the principal causes of this rolling crisis, and no less competing views about how to rebalance the Western economy to prevent a repeat of the crisis (Ruggie, 1994).

In the quarter-century since the end of the Cold War, Atlantic relations have experienced unprecedented flux and deep uncertainty over future direction. Before 1989 "the West" did experience a sense of shared political identity, not merely vested in a mutual strategic interests but drawing on common values that defined imminent threat in terms of "us" and "them." This cultural fundament was shaken to its core by the sudden demise of that threat, and since then relations have experienced cumulative aftershocks.

Of course, political bargains built on shared concerns hardly imply convergent interests, let alone common identity. Nevertheless, Atlanticism as depicted by this paradigm is more than merely cumulative and contingent bargains fashioned from ad hoc interests as it is in the realist narrative, though it is much less the cultural and ideational community of the liberal narrative. The current state of EU–US relations are an altogether better fit with the constructivist narrative, interests, and values inextricably connected, each mediating and shaping the other. Economic diplomacy as played out in recent inconclusive WTO rounds does suggest something less than close relations, at most disjointed incrementalism, willingness to engage in cutting deals in trade diplomacy, though by no means always with successful outcomes. Economic diplomacy seen from here (or for that matter in the TTIP) hardly conforms to that commonality of purpose, those mutual agendas occurring even in the intergovernmental European Single Market and eurozone regimes. Again this is to be expected. Disputation has long marked Atlantic trade relations, from fall-outs over bananas, tariffs, state aid for the aircraft industry and many other industrial and commercial sectors, to EU import restrictions on GM foodstuffs and chlorine-washed poultry products and much more.

The list of contested issues is a long one and shows vested interests actively lobbying for specific national and sectoral interests. There have been fall-outs also on how to respond to ecological depredations and climate change. Both sides broadly acknowledge the "problem" yet differ over solutions. Europeans promote an emission standards regime with caps and taxation as preferred instruments, whereas Americans advocate non-regulation and new technologies to deliver greater energy efficiency. Again political culture plays a part here. Europeans tend to see government as the fount of creative solutions, a view that clashes with American aversion to "the state," resistance to regulatory intervention, and unflagging trust in the rationality of markets.

Further evidence of how far cultural difference remains as a source of discord is the issue of human rights, a commitment at the broad level to universal values that accords with Western ideas about freedom and democracy, though with quite different ideas regarding application and enforcement. Americans and Europeans alike subscribe to the principle of human rights, yet differ as to agency in a world where trust in "others" is, to say the least, tenuous. Many

Europeans are averse to what they see as muscular interventionism, the use of military force to enforce regime change in the name of democratic values. Europeans are generally better disposed to impartial international justice, not least to judicial arbitration by the ICC, whereas deep hostility to that institution has placed the US uncomfortably in the same camp of some of the world's most despicable regimes.

There are cultural and no less ideological leitmotifs in play in the growing debate about the international enforcement of "rights." Europeans tend to be rather more measured in their response to international crises, a consequence of their violent and no less imperialist history. Americans, on the other hand, are inclined to see the world through the pristine lens of realism, but a lens ground in part too by liberal idealism that defines the world as an unduly simplistic stand-off between good guys and bad – familiar in the plot-line of any western movie, only with "Uncle Sam" rather than capricious foreign justices as the self-appointed sure-shot sheriff, the preferred arbiter of "justice." This is a view of the world constructed as one famous variant of this narrative sees it as a straight zero-sum "clash of civilizations," good and evil juxtaposed, an outlook that at times has bordered uncomfortably on the messianic idea of America's destiny, mentioned above (Huntington, 1993).

Insofar as this paradigm accommodates values and interests in line with the social constructivist narrative, it offers the closest fit with the situation currently facing the West. It mostly avoids crude stereotyping, notably an "outward-looking" supposedly post-national Europe and an assertively nationalistic US that figures in some contemporary international relations discourse. Cultural differences do, of course, impact on policy, those disparities of norms and practices embedded in quite different histories and heterogeneous political cultures. Yet something remains in this paradigm of Atlanticism that is familiar to all sides, even of an abiding idea of the West, and especially so among those political and business elites who populate the policy networks that frame public policy. Shared values and mutual expectations, just plain "knowing" familiar associates in established and elaborate networks who confer not quite as "other" or "strangers" but as collaborators with a shared history, common instincts, and interests does facilitate cooperation, even if relations nowadays are by no means always harmonious (Peterson & Pollack, 2003b).

There is evidence of such culturally conditioned cooperation in response to current global challenges. Europeans are more attuned nowadays to market forces, committed to removing inefficient state monopolies in the services sector and public utilities, telecommunications, and media, with both sides developing joint intellectual capital to move beyond merely national solutions and seeking instead transnational outcomes to common problems. In effect, a transatlantic learning and research community with synergies and exchanges running in both directions. Differences remain, but periodic squabbles are too often exaggerated by both media and politicians for their own narrow purposes, choosing to downplay or even ignore the exponential growth of transatlantic cooperation at every level, ensuring that much of it happens below the public's radar.

This median paradigm reflects the unique mix of conditionality and reciprocity of recent endeavors in the Atlantic region, the disposition to make common cause on many current policy issues. The stakes could not be higher. Globalization's insidious challenge, the rapid development of technology and communications, problematic demographic trends, unprecedented shifts in trade and investment flows, unpredictable economic cycles, competing perceptions of comparative advantage and disadvantage that are impacting on the once familiar and reassuring Western presumption of global dominance, have all massively raised the stakes. The consequences of such mutability for a stable international order are clear to see and they reinforce the perception on both sides that there is still advantage from cooperating with long-standing allies and familiar neighbors. Of course, much has changed along the way, as it was bound to do with the sudden collapse of the familiar bi-polar order. Cultural flux and competing interests in a world no longer defined by ideological dogma has freed both sides to rethink preferences and redefine strategic options, and they have done so with alacrity.

Things can never be quite what they once were for these neighbors. Over time, certainly within two generations, the cumulate impact of these global shifts will undoubtedly alter public mind-sets and further change expectations on all sides. Whether for the improvement or not of Atlantic relations will depend less on residual cultural norms and rather more on the short-term and contingent nature of diplomacy, how both sides respond not just to policy challenges but also to the prospect of working together to find mutually acceptable policy outcomes. The prognosis here, however, is not as bleak as some have suggested. Familiarity persists and old habits die hard, and accordingly accommodations in public policy will always be easier to negotiate with close neighbors than with complete strangers.

Constructing an Atlantic Future: Prospects and Problems

It is impossible to predict the future state of Atlantic relations, but for the foreseeable future at least there is a reasonable expectation of accommodation on matters of mutual concern. TTIP is some indication that those policy stakeholders on both sides who determine public policy are committed to a broadly shared agenda, even predisposed to cooperate with close neighbors in a capricious world. A notional idea of "the West" does survive in the official mind, though perhaps less so with the wider public. Somewhat diminished maybe, certainly not the close cultural encounter that characterized relations after World War II, but with sufficient cultural proximity to sustain common purpose. Relations now are more ambivalent, "Western" identity more nebulous, though nevertheless reflecting broadly shared values as much as merely narrow and competing self-interest. This much was apparent during the economic crisis.

The causes and consequences of seismic turbulence in global financial markets raised widespread concern and no less mutual recriminations, its impact felt well beyond the narrow circles who manage Atlantic affairs. Loss of public trust, the end of permissive consensus that allowed policymakers license to manage affairs without effective public scrutiny, let alone meaningful accountability, has been damaged – possibly beyond repair. Declining trust in the political class everywhere has changed the way government is regarded by publics who ended up footing the bill for what they see at the very least as political dereliction. This has consequences, in turn, for the political culture of liberal democracies and no less so for market economies going forward, with public accountability now very much on the line. A narrative of political culture that was once commonplace in Atlantic societies is now widely challenged, doubts voiced on both sides about everything from the competence and no less the trustworthiness of politicians to the reliability of markets for ensuring prosperity and creating jobs. But this erosion of public trust is common to all Western polities and as such confirms a common liberal democratic political culture on all sides of the Atlantic, even if one in crisis.

This has consequences, too, in as much as Atlanticism remains a cultural construction rather than merely a contingent alliance of mutual convenience, one based on broadly shared values, policy preferences, and aspirations about how to do politics, manage economies and ensure security against the "other," what the great English bard called "the envy of less happier lands." Garten Ash (2004) makes the connection between Shakespeare and the idea of English Liberty when he cites lines attributed to William Wordsworth in his *Poems Dedicated to National Independence and Liberty*: "We must be free or die, who spake the tongue that Shakespeare spake." In a very real sense this cultural ballast still exists even in adversity, the West's political and public preferences conditioned by a shared and broadly progressive narrative about freedom, democracy, free markets, social justice, and individual rights. But there are limits to such common cultural ballast. Shared values and mutual interests do not necessarily ensure commonality of purpose, let alone cultural convergence. What this cultural legacy does still foster, however, is familiarity conducive to shared endeavor and moral empathy, a reflexive response that looks for compromise on policy differences as a first instinct of diplomacy. The TTIP will certainly put this familiar reflex to the test.

A suitably tentative conclusion might be "so far so good," though complacency about cultural affinity as a sure solvent of difference should be avoided. Residual values there may well be and they retain the capacity to bind, but rivalries over interest and normative disjunctions are still very much in play. There are other shared cultural problems confronting Atlantic political culture. Public anxiety fueled by loss of trust has ratcheted up nationalism everywhere and diluted the very idea of interdependence, the propensity among even close neighbors to settle for positive-sum rather than zero-sum bargains.

This is a problem for the EU as much as it is between the Atlantic partners. Politicians seeking re-election are only too aware of these constraints on negotiations, rather more prone nowadays to indulge in glib populism as a convenient political shortcut for recovering electoral support among restive domestic constituencies. In these circumstances, narrow political calculation too readily panders to atavism and hinders constructive negotiations, though again this is hardly new in Atlantic relations. Europeans, on their side, have a more skeptical outlook after the sub-prime mortgage crunch about "socially irresponsible" American capitalism, whereas on the other side there is widespread scorn of self-indulgent, over-regulated, and welfare-dependent Europeans.

Again stereotypes have always figured in the Atlanticism discourse, confirming both in the public and political mind cultural disjunction alongside familiarity. Accommodations may well be made in the TTIP negotiations because they have to be, and in the end hard interests usually trump even rooted prejudice in diplomacy, not least between neighbors. After all, it is not the public at large that negotiates, but those elites who populate the critical policy networks of trade, business, finance, and investment, influenced by the epistemic communities who advise them, all of them aware of the remorseless logics of globalization and for that reason rather better disposed to positive-sum bargaining. Pragmatists more than ideologues, these policy wonks are more inclined to see beyond distortive stereotypes and be more amenable to compromise. Both sides of the Atlantic community have a clear interest in accommodating their own abiding interests, and no less defending their common values in the face of insidious challenges. The Atlantic polities have enough in common to give this ambitious project fair wind. There will be disputation, even clashes over both interests and values, but this is normal politics in any partnership and by no means signals the end of a community grounded in shared values as much as "merely" contingent interests.

None of the three paradigms discussed here remotely captures the complexities of Atlantic relations past or present. Elements of all three are to be found in actual relations, though the closest approximation, the most appropriate descriptor of Atlantic relations since the end of the Cold War is the conditional friendship, the elective partnership identified in the concluding paradigm. Atlantic relations are underpinned as they always have been by something more than security concerns, exclusive definitions of strategic or commercial self-interest. These interests define deeper values and in turn are expressed by them, the critical feedback loop suggested by Max Weber in his classic work on social action; the causal linkage between value-oriented action and rational ends (*sinnzusammenhänge*) that figures as a crucial dynamic of the constructivist paradigm utilized here. Common values, the cultural cement that enables international relations to survive periodic discord, is an essential medium for effective transatlantic diplomacy: namely, shared ideas about governance, the moral purpose of human society, rule of law, and free markets. Competing policy preferences and even serious fall-outs there will be as in any common endeavor, but this too confirms what remain as close encounters between neighbors rather than skirmishes with strangers. As the constructivist narrative acknowledges, it is the very smallness of differences over fundamental values that can make for strife in any family. Though as one contemporary writer has put it, "basic American and European values have not diverged – and the European democracies are certainly closer allies of the United States than the inhabitants of any other region" (P. Gordon, 2003, p. 74).

As the Atlantic Community assimilates the fact that the world is no longer remotely molded in its own "Western" image, nor aspires for the most part to embrace its elemental values, at least not in the way these values have been fashioned from distinctive historic experience, these close neighbors are well enough disposed to affirm what they still hold in common as they respond to formidable challenges in a turbulent world. The cultural dynamics of Atlanticism endures, then, drawing on a shared past, though whether this will be quite enough to meet contemporary challenges, and in the process to provide effective leadership in a new international order, remains to be seen.

Part II
Governance

5 Transatlantic Governance

Laurie Buonanno, Neill Nugent, and Natalia Cugleşan

Introduction

In Chapter 2 Michelle Egan and Neill Nugent explained that the advent of "New Transatlanticism" was tied to a number of changes including the increased policy importance of the EU, globalization and interdependence, and the mutual interdependence of the Atlantic Community. This chapter takes up the story where Chapter 2 ends, by exploring, cataloging, and analyzing the governing infrastructure of New Transatlanticism and the many fora which have been established and agreements made since the signing of the Transatlantic Declaration (TAD). Egan and Nugent observed that as European integration deepened, a path was opened (from the early 1990s) to replace numerous bilateral sector-level agreements between the US and EU member states with an umbrella framework between the EU and the US. While there are long-standing institutional global and regional fora in which EU member states, the EU, and the US interact (NATO being an obvious example), the New Transatlantic Agenda (NTA) (and its offshoots – particularly the Transatlantic Economic Council [TEC]) can be a seen as a combination of action plans and umbrella structures which not only lay out the need for cooperation around the major issues of concern to the EU and US, but also provide an arena for policymaker interaction to promote discussion, understanding, and, hopefully, cooperation.

This chapter utilizes the Pollack and Schaffer (2001b) three-level approach to transatlantic governance in order to chart the institutional development and increasingly complex architecture of transatlantic cooperation and governance. The first section of this chapter contains an overview and catalog of the transatlantic architecture and agreements prior to the Transatlantic Trade and Investment Partnership (TTIP). (The TTIP Agreement is covered in Chapters 13 and 14.) The second section reviews the Pollack and Schaffer three-level model. The third section focuses on the intergovernmental level, where heads of government (HOGs) and the most senior officials operate. The fourth section explores transgovernmental links among subcabinet officials. The fifth section covers transnational actors. The sixth section of the chapter analyzes variations in the operation and use of the structures identified and examined in the previous sections. The seventh section evaluates the "success" of transatlantic governance. The chapter closes with conclusions with respect to the "state of play" of transatlantic governance.

Fora and Agreements

What is sometimes referred to as "The New Transatlanticism" is legally based on post-Cold War agreements, in particular the TAD (1990), the NTA (1994), and subsequent overarching agreements focusing on the economic partnership, particularly the now defunct Transatlantic Economic Partnership (TEP; 1998), and the TEC (2007). The implementation of these agreements required both the establishment of new institutions and the inclusion of new actors, thus leading to the substitution of intergovernmentalism by governance (M. Pollack & Schaffer, 2001a; Smith, 2009; Steffenson, 2005). Table 5.1 contains a list with brief descriptions of the framework agreements forming the foundation of this New Transatlanticism.

Table 5.2 lists several of the many sectoral agreements (some which take the form of treaties while others operate as Memoranda of Understanding) between the EU and the US. The table includes the year the agreement came into effect, the purpose, and the key institutional actors.

The rapidly evolving nature of transatlantic relations in the early post-Cold War period is seen in major differences between the TAD, NTA, TEC (and proposed TTIP) framework agreements.

The TAD raised the level of consciousness for Americans and Europeans with respect to the role the EU was playing and would play as an intergovernmental actor in US–Europe relations. The TAD also confirmed that the Atlantic Community was founded on shared values. Finally, when the US negotiated and signed the TAD with the EU, it also reconfirmed its long-standing support and encouragement of European integration, which the US had consistently welcomed since the EEC's founding during the Eisenhower Administration.

The NTA, on the other hand, was drawn up as a strategic plan to identify areas of mutual interest with which the US and the EU would work together as equal partners. In effect, the NTA explicitly recognizes the importance of transgovernmental and transnational communication by encouraging the establishment of transgovernmental and transnational fora.

Subsequent overarching framework agreements – notably the TEC, the TEP, and the proposed TTIP – focus on the various actions necessary to strengthen the Atlantic Community's economic relationship. If the TTIP is agreed, it will "integrate" the EU and the US to a much greater extent than any of the subsequent agreements in achieving both negative integration (zero tariffs) and positive integration (single product testing, mutual recognition or harmonization of regulatory processes and standards).

Transatlantic Governance

A significant contribution to the study of transatlanticism is provided in a book edited by Mark Pollack and Gregory Schaffer (2001b), which proposes a three-level model – intergovernmental, transgovernmental, and transnational actors – as a framework in which to study transatlantic governance. The "transnational" level is straightforward – these are civil society actors and other non-executive

Table 5.1 Overarching (Framework) Agreements

Framework Agreements	Year Signed	Purpose	Institutional Actors
Transatlantic Declaration	1990	Identification of common goals, including democracy, crime, and agreement to high-level political meetings on a bi-annual basis between the US president and the presidents of the European Commission and the European Council	US and EU member state heads of government, European Commission president
New Transatlantic Agenda	1995	Creation accompanied by *Joint US–EU Action Plan*, guiding transatlantic cooperation in several policy fields	Heads of government (US and EU country presidency), European Commission president
Transatlantic Economic Partnership	1998	To extend and intensify multilateral and bilateral cooperation and common actions on trade and investment by providing mechanisms for policy initiatives and agreements, including on regulatory cooperation and mutual recognition	Heads of government (US and EU country presidency), European Commission president
Transatlantic Economic Council (Transatlantic Economic Council, 2014)	2007	Superseded TEP; primary plenary forum for transatlantic economic dialog	Co-Chaired White House Deputy National Special Advisor for International Economic Affairs and European Commissioner for Trade
Transatlantic Trade and Investment Partnership	Launched February 2013	Trade agreement being negotiated by the EU and the US including tariffs, unnecessary regulations, and restrictions on investment	Heads of government (US and EU country presidency), European Commission president, European Council president

Table 5.2 Sectoral Agreements

Sectoral Agreements	Year in Force	Purpose	Negotiating Bodies
Justice and Home Affairs/Homeland Security			
Container Agreement	1997, updated 2004 to include US Container Security Initiative	Updated and upgraded the 1997 agreement to include security screening; established the EU–US Joint Customs Cooperation Committee as implementing body	The EU–US Joint Customs Cooperation Committee
Personal Data Exchange between US and Europol	2002	To enhance the cooperation of EU member states, acting through Europol, and the US in preventing, detecting, suppressing, and investigating serious forms of international crime (EU and US, 2001)	US Ambassador to the EU and Europol Director
Personal Data Exchange between US and Eurojust	2006	To enhance cooperation among judicial authorities with respect to cross-border crime and terrorism	US Justice Department and Eurojust Director
Declaration on Counterterrorism	2010	Renewed commitment for cooperation in combating terrorism, including recognition of the EP's role in counter-terrorism	Adopted at EU–US summit (June)
Extradition and Mutual Legal Assistance (treaties)	2010 (signed 2003)	Enhances and modernizes law enforcement and judicial cooperation, including authorizing the participation of US criminal investigators and prosecutors in joint investigative teams in the EU; contains a provision allowing extradition to be conditioned on non-application of the death penalty (US Department of Justice, 2010)	Signed by US DOJ and JHA Commissioner; ratified by US Senate, ratification bodies of all EU member states, Council (of Ministers) agreement, and EP consent

The US–EU Terrorist Finance Tracking Program – TFTP II (SWIFT Agreement)	2010	After the EP rejected TFTP, new safeguards negotiated, including a role for Europol in vetting data transfers to the US Department of Treasury – covers all personal and business financial transactions (Buonanno & Nugent, 2013, pp. 244–245)	Treasury Department, Commission DG Finance
Joint Statement on Supply Chain Security	2011	To secure the transatlantic supply chain	DHS Secretary and European Commission – VP for Transport, VP for Taxation and Customs Union, Audit and Anti-Fraud, DG Home Affairs
Passenger Name Record Agreement (PNR)	2012	Rules for processing and transferring PNR data by air carriers to the US	Signed in 2004, struck down by ECJ in 2006, revised and signed in 2007. DHS and the Council and Commission
US–EU Framework Agreement for Data Privacy and Protection	Negotiations launched 2010, expected in mid-2014; NSA spying scandal may delay agreement as the Commission undertakes a review of the alleged mass surveillance of US and EU citizens	Proposed as an umbrella agreement which would specify how personal information would be exchanged for law enforcement purposes. Sticking points: (1) EU wants the US to extend judicial redress for EU citizens; (2) EU wants the agreement to apply retroactively	DOJ, European Commission (JHA and Citizen Rights – two commissioners); DHS officials and interior ministers of EU member states holding the EU Council presidency

continued

Table 5.2 Continued

Sectoral Agreements	Year in Force	Purpose	Negotiating Bodies
Other Agreements – Various Purposes			
Mutual Recognition of Certificates of Conformity for Marine Equipment (EU/US, 2004) (another MRA negotiated between the US and EEA/EFTA countries)	2004	A company that receives approval of their product under the US–EC MRA is able to market that product in the US, EU member states, and the EEA–EFTA countries while complying with only one set of regulatory requirements	US Coast Guard and European Maritime Safety Agency (European Maritime Safety Agency, 2012)
Open Skies	2007, expanded in 2010	Reciprocal takeoff and landing rights for EU and US carriers; open up carriers to foreign ownership	US Department of Transportation, EU Council of Ministers (transport ministers from EU's member states), DG Transport and Mobility
eHealth/health IT MOU (US Department of Health and Human Services and European Commission, 2010)	2010	Cooperation surrounding health-related information and communication technologies	Secretary of US Department of Health and Human Services and Vice-President of Commission & Consumers
Joint Declaration Child Internet Safety Pact	2012	Cooperation on several joint projects to support safer internet	DHS, VP European Commission & Consumers
Shared Principles for International Investment	2012	Open, transparent, and non-discriminatory international investment policies	USTR, DG Trade & DG Industry and Enterpise

governmental actors (such as national and state legislators), and thus, populated by actors ranging from multinational corporations, NGOs, national and local legislators and government officials, and private foundations and philanthropists.

But what is the distinction between intergovernmental and transgovernmental actors? Keohane and Nye (1977) suggested that transgovernmental actors are those public officials working in subunits of government (below HOGs and their cabinets or the "intergovernmental" actors). For Keohane and Nye, power and control are the key distinguishing characteristics because, they reasoned, it is more difficult for governments to control bureaucrats and to coordinate their activities below the cabinet level. On the other hand, cabinet-level officials in the US and EU Commissioners (those officials reporting directly to HOGs or the European Commission President – admittedly, the latter being complicated by the fact that the "College of Commissioners" is the decision-making body in the European Commission), should be seen as "intergovernmental actors." While not the classic Weberian "bureaucrat" versus "politician" argument, intergovernmentalism and transgovernmentalism can be seen as proxies for the disparate orientations of the two policymaking actors. (See Aberbach, Putnam, & Rockman, 1981 for a classic study of the differences between bureaucrats and politicians in Western democracies.) Furthermore, in Ann-Marie Slaughter's (2005) "New Diplomats" thesis, central bankers, judges, and regulators replace career diplomats in foreign ministries as the central actors in international relations. Indeed, in an early exposition of her new diplomats thesis, Slaughter (1997, p. 194) identified the NTA as a "leading example of transgovernmentalism in action."

Thus, at the intergovernmental level, EU and US HOGs and cabinet-level senior officials frame and negotiate the key issues of the day. The actual policy coordination among governments, however, takes place at the second level of "transgovernmentalism," among subcabinet governmental officials – central bankers, heads of regulatory agencies, assistant and deputy ministers, and so forth. And while it is clear enough that EU–US Summits are meetings of inter-governmental actors, it must be recognized that this black-and-white distinction between intergovernmental and transgovernmental agreements shades to gray as we move from the overarching framework agreements to the many working groups and numerous informal interactions that together comprise contemporary transatlantic governance.

Intergovernmental Level

EU–US Summits

At the apex of intergovernmental consultation is the EU–US summit, which the 1990 TAD established and has been held since 1991. The key participants of the EU–US summit are the US President, the European Council President (after entry into force of the Lisbon Treaty), and the European Commission President. Other high-level EU and US officials participate, including the EU's High Representative and the US Secretary of State. Other US cabinet secretaries and their Commission counterparts attend, depending upon the agenda topics.

Originally established as a biannual summit, it was reduced to one per year early in the George W. Bush presidency, and is now held "only when necessary" (Pop, 2010). The 2010 summit, for example, was canceled when there was little on the agenda that top officials needed to discuss, and the November 2011 and March 2014 summits were the only ones held under the Obama presidency at the time of this writing.

But the lack of an annual summit should not imply that the EU and the US are not meeting regularly at the highest levels. So, for example, the G-8 summits (which include the "Big Four" EU member states of France, Germany, Italy, and the UK, and the EU as a "ninth" member) provide an opportunity for the US President, EU HOGs, and EU high-ranking officials (including the Commission President and President of the European Council) to meet on an annual basis. Indeed, President Obama and EU leaders selected the June 2013 G-8 meeting to announce the opening of negotiations of the new TTIP (Castle & Calmes, 2013).

Significantly, all of the major architecture discussed in this chapter was agreed within the EU–US summits, which cabinet and subcabinet levels were then directed to establish, depending upon how broad or specific was the mandate given by the political leaders. Foreign policy always features in these summits, but matters related to trade, investment, energy, climate change, cross-border security, and innovativeness also have been discussed, as well as issues that have generated intense public concern, such as the Great Recession.

The EU–US summits end with the release of a "joint statement," which consist of broad pronouncements on a wide range of policy areas; direction to intergovernmental and transgovernmental working groups to carry out the initiatives identified in the summit; and, where deemed necessary, authorization to establish new institutional structures which will carry forward cooperation in those areas identified by political leaders. (See European External Action Service, 2014b for joint statements of EU–US summits.) Box 5.1 contains a sample of policy areas covered in the 2014 summit (Council of the European Union, 2014).

Intergovernmental Groups at the Cabinet Level

Transatlantic Economic Council

The intergovernmental group responsible for overall economic cooperation is the TEC, which superseded the TEP because the latter was thought no longer up to the task of managing and advancing transatlantic relations. The TEC's purpose is to "strengthen transatlantic economic integration, with the goal of improving competitiveness and the lives of our people" (European Union and United States, 2007, p. 2).

The US–EU High Level Regulatory Cooperation Forum (HLRCF) originally was established under the TEP and incorporated aspects of all three levels of transatlantic governance. This arrangement seemed to offer a promising model to advance economic cooperation across sectors, and, thus based on its successes in the area of mutual recognition agreements (MRAs), TEC was then set up to be both a council body and a framework (Steffenson, 2005, p. 46).

Box 5.1 EU–US Summit, 2014

Sample of the topics addressed at EU–US summits (March 2014)

- TRADE   We seek a landmark Transatlantic Trade and Investment Partnership to build our common prosperity.... We call on other negotiating partners to contribute to the prompt conclusion of a balanced and commercially significant expansion of the Information Technology Agreement (ITA) by offering commitments reflecting the high level of ambition shown by the EU and the US.
- ECONOMIC GROWTH   We commit to continue our efforts through the G-20 to promote strong, sustainable and balanced growth across the global economy by developing comprehensive growth strategies for the Brisbane Summit. We aim at implementing the G-20 commitments to create a more stable financial system. Fiscal sustainability in advanced economies remains critical for a stronger and sustainable recovery. We also welcome the ambitious G-20 agenda to fight tax evasion.
- NEW TECHNOLOGIES   Our collaboration in the space domain also contributes to growth and global security, including on an International Code of Conduct for Outer Space Activities. We will combine wherever possible our efforts as we did in the Transatlantic Ocean Research Alliance and through the GPS/Galileo agreement. The Transatlantic Economic Council will continue its work to improve cooperation in emerging sectors, specifically e-mobility, e-health and new activities under the Innovation Action Partnership
- DATA PRIVACY AND PROTECTION   The transatlantic digital economy is integral to our economic growth, trade and innovation. Cross border data flows are critical to our economic vitality, and to our law enforcement and counterterrorism efforts. We affirm the need to promote data protection, privacy and free speech in the digital era while ensuring the security of our citizens. This is essential for trust in the online environment.
- ENERGY   The EU–US Energy Council fosters cooperation on energy security, regulatory frameworks that encourage the efficient and sustainable use of energy, and joint research priorities that promote safe and sustainable energy technologies. The situation in Ukraine proves the need to reinforce energy security in Europe and we are considering new collaborative efforts to achieve this goal. We welcome the prospect of US LNG exports in the future since additional global supplies will benefit Europe and other strategic partners.
- ENVIRONMENT   The EU and the United States demonstrate leadership and are intensifying their cooperation, including: phasing out fossil fuel subsidies, phasing down the production and consumption of hydrofluorocarbons (HFCs) under the Montreal Protocol, in promoting sustainable energy, energy efficiency and renewable energy, fighting deforestation, and mobilizing private and public finance.
- MOBILITY   We reaffirm our commitment to complete secure visa-free travel arrangements between the United States and all EU Member States as soon as possible and consistent with applicable domestic legislation.

- COUNTERTERRORISM   We welcome our increasingly close cooperation in building the capacity of partner countries to counter terrorism and violent extremism within a framework of rule of law, particularly in the Sahel, Maghreb, Horn of Africa region and Pakistan. We pledge to deepen and broaden this cooperation through the United Nations, the Global Counterterrorism Forum, and other relevant channels. We have also decided to expedite and enhance cooperation on threats directly affecting the security of EU and US diplomatic staff and facilities abroad.
- DEMOCRATIC REGIMES   In the EU's southern neighbourhood, we are coordinating closely to assist countries in transition in north Africa, including the worrying situation in Egypt. We welcome the adoption of a new constitution respectful of human rights and fundamental freedoms in Tunisia, following an inclusive national dialogue. As agreed earlier this month in Rome, we also aim to intensify coordinated assistance to Libya, a country facing significant challenges to its democratic transition and stability.
- DEVELOPMENT   Building on the progress made through the EU–US Development Dialogue, we will continue to utilize this forum to pursue cooperation and a division of labour to build resilience and address food insecurity. Attention should also be given to universal access to sustainable energy in Africa and other underserved regions, through public and private investment, and appropriate investment security.
- UKRAINE   The EU and the US support the Ukrainian people and their right to choose their own future and remain committed to uphold the sovereignty and territorial integrity of Ukraine. We strongly condemn the illegal annexation of Crimea to Russia and will not recognise it. Further steps by Russia to destabilise the situation in Ukraine would lead to additional and far reaching consequences for the EU's and US' relations with Russia in a broad range of economic areas. The EU and the US stand by the Ukrainian government in its efforts to stabilise Ukraine and undertake reforms, including through assistance.
- EUROPEAN INTEGRATION   We support the ongoing process of political association and economic integration of interested Eastern Partnership countries with the EU, an expression of the partner countries' free choice. The Association Agreements, including their Deep and Comprehensive Free Trade Areas, have the potential to support far-reaching political and socio-economic reforms leading to societies strongly rooted in European values and principles and to the creation of an economic area that can contribute to sustainable growth and jobs, thereby enhancing stability in the region.
- FOREIGN POLICY   We have undertaken joint intensive diplomatic efforts through the E3/EU+3 to seek a negotiated solution that resolves the international community's concerns regarding the Iranian nuclear programme. The strong and credible efforts of the E3/EU+3 that resulted in agreement last November on a Joint Plan of Action, are widely supported by the international community.

(European External Action Service, 2014b)

The TEC framework was established at the April 2007 EU–US summit in the form of the "Framework for Advancing Transatlantic Economic Integration" (European Union and the United States, 2007) with the "Council to oversee the efforts outlined in the Framework" (Transatlantic Economic Council, 2007). Thus the framework operates through transgovernmental working groups feeding into the intergovernmental level (the Council).

The composition and the work of the Council will be discussed in this section, with the transgovernmental framework of working groups postponed for the next section of this chapter.

Section II of the agreement establishing the TEC lays out the priority of the agreement (European Union and United States, 2007, p. 2):

> In light of our shared commitment to removing barriers to transatlantic commerce; to rationalizing, reforming, and, where appropriate, reducing regulations to empower the private sector; to achieving more effective, systematic and transparent regulatory cooperation to reduce costs associated with regulation to consumers and producers; to removing unnecessary differences between our regulations to foster economic integration; to reinforce the existing transatlantic dialogue structures in regulatory cooperation both by intensifying our sector-by sector EU–U.S. regulatory cooperation and our dialogue between the European Commission services and the U.S. Office of Management and Budget on the methodological issues: we resolve to achieve the goals set out in Annex 1 in a timely manner.

Areas of TEC cooperation topics have included finance, innovation and technology, intellectual property rights, pharmaceuticals, safety and regulations, and use of standards. The current TEC workplan consists of cloud computing, e-Vehicles, e-Health, energy efficiency, ICT trade principles, innovation and action partnership, investment, limiting regulatory divergence, nanotechnology, raw materials, secure trade, and small and medium enterprises (SMEs) best practices (US Department of State, 2011).

Section IV of the agreement establishes the Council, which is co-chaired by a US cabinet-level official in the Executive Office of the President and, on the EU side, by a member of the European Commission.

The TEC Agreement charged the Council with 11 duties (see Box 5.2), including the mandate to "Guide work between the EU–U.S. Summits with a focus on achieving results, including setting goals for achieving the purposes of the Framework, developing metrics, setting deadlines and targets, and monitoring progress" and to "Convene a group comprised of individuals experienced in transatlantic issues drawing in particular from the heads of existing transatlantic dialogues to provide input and guidance to the EU-U.S. Summit on priorities for pursuing transatlantic economic integration" (European Union and United States, 2007, pp. 2–3).

Box 5.2 Transatlantic Economic Council: Duties

Section IV – Transatlantic Economic Council

1. Oversee the efforts outlined in this Framework, with the goal of accelerating progress;
2. Guide work between EU–U.S. Summits with a focus on achieving results, including setting goals for achieving the purposes of this Framework, developing metrics, setting deadlines and targets, and monitoring progress;
3. Adopt a work program, drawn initially from the existing work program under the 2005 U.S.–EC Economic Initiative, with the goal of achieving the objectives of this Framework, and shall adapt this work program and otherwise organize its activities in the manner best suited to achieving those objectives;
4. Review at least semi-annually its progress in achieving the objectives of this Framework;
5. Facilitate joint action under this Framework to advance its purposes;
6. Review ongoing EU–U.S. economic engagement in order to maximize progress in existing transatlantic dialogues with a view to consider phasing out technical dialogues that have completed their work or are otherwise no longer necessary;
7. Meet at least once a year at such time as the co-chairs decide;
8. Oversee preparation of annual reports to the EU–U.S. Summit leaders on goals, metrics for meeting those goals, deadlines, achievements, and areas where more progress is needed;
9. Facilitate closer cooperation between the European Union and the United States and our legislators and stakeholders;
10. Convene a group comprised of individuals experienced in transatlantic issues drawing in particular from the heads of existing transatlantic dialogues to provide input and guidance to the EU–U.S. Summit on priorities for pursuing transatlantic economic integration; and
11. Include representatives of other governmental entities as the Council determines to be appropriate.

(European Union and United States, 2007, pp. 2–3)

EU–US High-Level Working Group on Jobs and Growth

Despite the history of institutional creations, policy declarations, and cooperative agreements, there was a feeling by the beginning of the second decade of the new century that the "New Transatlanticism" was responsible for only very modest policy achievements. The limited extent of trade and investment liberalization was viewed as being especially disappointing given that: the international trade liberalization talks in the World Trade Organization (WTO) Doha Round had virtually stalled; trade and investment had long been the single most important policy consideration in New Transatlanticism deliberations, but the business community complained little had been accomplished to free-up transatlantic trade and investment; and, unlike the security relationship within NATO, the trade and investment relationship was perceived (and this point is especially important for the EU) as one of equal partners (see, for example, Smith, 2009). This was the one area where the EU could and should exercise its market power in US relations, yet despite the completion of the EU's internal market, the US was proving an intractable force in all sorts of areas, including in regulatory rules for products and services as well as in the lucrative government procurement market.

In response to the lack of progress, and also the problems associated with the international economic and financial crises and the continuing problems of relatively low growth and high levels of unemployment, the November 2011 summit created a joint High Level Working Group on Jobs and Growth (HLWG) under the auspices of the TEC. The HLWG's brief was essentially to explore opportunities for expanding transatlantic trade and investment.

The HLWG issued its final report on February 11, 2013. It called for a new wide-ranging trade agreement (which was to become the TTIP) based on market-opening principles. (See Chapter 13 for details of the HLWG's recommendations.)

Other Cabinet-Level Intergovernmental Configurations

In addition to EU–US summits and the TEC are meetings between teams headed by very senior political representatives, who are usually the appropriate departmental secretaries on the US side and Commissioners on the EU side. The most frequent such meetings involve the Secretary of State and the Secretary for Commerce and/or the US Trade Representative and the High Representative of the Union for Foreign Affairs and Security Policy and the EU Commissioner for trade.

The EU–US Energy Council, which was created in 2009, is another high-level forum, with the EU side chaired by the EU High Representative, the Commissioner for Energy, and energy/environment minister of the EU country holding the rotating presidency, and the US side by the Secretary of State and the Secretary for Energy. Among items it considers in its annual meeting are cooperation on energy policies and strategic energy issues, climate change, and research collaboration on sustainable and clean energy. As the following excerpt from the EU–US Energy Council Joint Press Statement notes, the 2014 meeting focused on ways to jointly address energy security in light of the Russian annexation of Crimea and ways to assist Ukraine in diversifying its energy supplies (European Commission, 2014b):

> The Council affirmed its strong support for Ukraine's efforts to diversify its supplies of natural gas including through the rapid enhancement of reverse flow capacities, increased gas storage capacity, and decisive measures recently announced with the IMF to build a competitive energy economy.... The EU and the United States will work with Ukraine and international partners to extend best international practice as Ukraine takes these steps. The EU and the United States also welcome the determination of the Ukrainian government to pursue energy efficiency, market transparency, and the long

overdue restructuring and reform of Naftogaz. The Council emphasised that all near-term actions to improve Ukraine's energy security should be pursued in the context of a strategic vision of full integration into the European energy market. In this context, the Council reaffirmed its commitment to work with Ukraine on the legislative and regulatory reforms necessary to realise this vision and support it along its path.

The US also utilized this meeting to discuss the building of ports in Europe that could handle importation of US liquefied natural gas (LNG) and the EU to affirm its goal of creating a common European energy market (European Commission, 2014b).

The high-level political meetings are prepared and underpinned by a multitude of exchanges and meetings between groupings of US and EU officials in both formal (as in working groups) and informal (as in emails and telephone conversations) settings. At the apex of these groupings is the Senior Level Group (SLG), which prepares summits and meetings of Foreign Ministers. Since the Lisbon Treaty and the creation of the double-hatted High Representative of the Union for Foreign Affairs and Security Policy (Catherine Ashton was the first occupant of this post, followed by Frederica Mogherini), foreign policy meetings and joint statements have been common between the US Secretary of State and the High Representative.

Of course, such formal transatlantic meetings do not exhaust the number of high-level political contacts between the EU and US. Supplementing them are numerous less formal meetings that are arranged as and when they are required. So, for example, in April 2013, to the background of US concerns about a number of matters, including the continuing eurozone crisis and the proposed financial transactions tax by 11 eurozone states, the US Treasury Secretary spent time in Europe meeting with the Presidents of the European Council, the Commission, and the European Central Bank, plus the finance ministers of the two key eurozone states – France and Germany.

Table 5.3 contains a sample list of the wide range of fora – both high-level fora and groups (co-chaired by cabinet-level officials) and working groups managed by subcabinet-level officials.

Transgovernmental Level

This level involves subcabinet US and EU officials attempting to cooperate – often through working groups, expert groups, task forces, and dialogues of various kinds – in a wide range of policy areas on a networked basis. As such, this level of EU–US bilateral relations is based on a particularly intensified form of the networked governance.

TEC Framework

Many groupings, working parties, and dialogues are located within the TEC framework, some of which are standing and some of which are temporary and are created to fulfill a particular task. An example of a standing group is the Working Group on Investment, which is a dialogue of subcabinet officials normally led on the EU side by the Commission's Director of Services, Investment, Intellectual Property and Public Procurement, and on the US side by the Principal Deputy Assistant Secretary of State for Economic and Business Affairs. The Working Group helped to develop, and now operates on the basis of, a set of Shared Principles for International Investment that was agreed in April 2012. An example of a temporary grouping arose from the November 2011 meeting of the TEC, which agreed to a raw materials work plan that would include the preparation of a joint inventory of raw materials data and analysis on both sides. This resulted in increased sharing of information and an EU–US Expert Workshop on Mineral Raw Material Flows and Data, which issues to the TEC a set of recommendations for further action and joint work.

Thus, a core focus of much of the activity at this level has involved dealing with restrictions on free movement arising from varying domestic regulatory standards. Much of the work that is undertaken on regulatory issues is overseen by the EU–US High-Level Regulatory Forum ("the Forum"), which is co-chaired on the EU side by the Director General of the Directorate General for Enterprise and Industry and on the US side by the Administrator of the Office of Information and Regulatory Affairs in the Office of Management and Budget. Within the framework of the Forum, senior officials from both sides of the Atlantic meet in dialogues and workshops of various sorts to discuss specialized issues of both sectoral and cross-sectoral kinds. Examples include the EU–US Financial Markets Regulatory Forum and the EU–US Insurance Regulatory Dialogue.

The approach taken in these transgovernmental settings has not involved the removal of specific restrictions by regulatory harmonization or by formalized mutual recognition, both of which would involve the making of transatlantic law. Rather, there has been a reliance on the promotion of non-binding understandings and cooperation between regulators regarding the facilitation of free movement. In this context, there have been many significant cooperation agreements, including on such matters as the recognition of each other's certification procedures, the application of competition policy, and the operating practices of officials at borders.

Justice and Home Affairs/Homeland Security

Beyond dealing with regulatory issues, transgovernmental networking also involves many other sorts of activities. So, for example the EU–US Task Force on Biotechnology, which oversees many working groups of experts dealing with such specialized matters as molecular biology, bioinformatics, and applications of biotechnology to sustainable development, has as its main purpose the coordination and promotion of transatlantic biotechnological research. But without doubt, the major policy area shaping the New Transatlanticism is counter-terrorism, which since 9/11 and the subsequent attacks in London and Madrid, have brought a level of cooperation simply unprecedented in the

Table 5.3 Fora and Working Groups

Forum/working group	Year Signed/ Agreed	Purpose	Institutional Actors
High-level Fora			
High Level Political Dialogue on Border and Transportation Security	2004	Marked the beginning of homeland security officials' dialogue about border security – issues such as biometrics in passports, sky marshals, etc. (Pawlak, 2007)	DHS, State, DOJ JHA, External Relations, Transport and Energy, Customs Union
US–EU High Level Regulatory Cooperation Forum (HLRCF) (US Office of Management and Budget, n.d.)	2005	Provides a setting for officials from all areas of the government to come together to discuss regulatory policy matters of mutual interest. The Forum aims to improve the quality of regulation on both sides, through sharing regulatory best practices such as risk and impact assessments, and techniques related to reducing the costs to business and consumers that arise from unnecessary differences in regulatory requirements (US Office of Management and Budget, n.d.)	Director-General of the DG Enterprise and Industry and the Administrator of the Office of Information and Regulatory Affairs in the Office of Management and Budget
High-Level Contract Group on Data Protection	2006	To discuss privacy and personal data protection in the context of the exchange of information for law enforcement purposes to prevent and fight terrorism and serious transnational crime (Council of the European Union, 2008)	Senior-level officials from the Commission, US DOG, DHS, and State
EU–US Energy Council (US Department of State, 2009a)	2009	To deepen the dialogue on strategic energy issues of mutual interest, foster cooperation on energy policies, and further strengthen research collaboration on sustainable and clean energy technologies (Council of the European Union, 2009). Three working groups – energy security and markets, energy policies and regulation, energy technologies and research cooperation	US Secretary of State, EU High Representative, EU Commissioner for Energy, US Energy Secretary, representative from the Council of Ministers (member state holding the rotating presidency)
High Level Consultative Group on Development (HLCGD) (EU–US Development Dialogue)	2009	Information sharing, coordination and policy alignment in several areas including food security and agricultural development, climate change, the Millennium Development Goals, and security-development (Gaus & Hoxtell, 2013)	EEAS, State Department as well as Commissioner for Development, administrator for USAID (State Department) various other officials based on meeting discussions

Name	Year	Objective	Lead agencies / participants
High Level Working Group on Jobs and Growth (HLWG) (High Level Working Group in Growth and Jobs, 2013)	2011	Identify policies and measures to increase trade and investment to support mutually beneficial job creation, economic growth, and competitiveness, working closely with public and private sector stakeholder groups, and drawing on existing dialogues and mechanisms, as appropriate (Office of the United States Trade Representative, 2012)	US Trade Representative Ron Kirk and EU Trade Commissioner Karel De Gucht

(Sample) Sectoral Working Groups

Name	Year	Objective	Lead agencies / participants
EU US Task Force on Biotechnology Research (European Commission, 2011d)	1994	To promote information exchange and coordination between biotechnology research programs funded by the European Commission and the US government	Variety of US and EU agencies, co-chairs USDA, Agricultural Research Service and Agricultural and Food Directorate, DG Research and Innovation (European Commission, 2011d)
Transportation Security Cooperation Group	2004	Inform each side in advance as to planned changes/initiatives and to achieve cooperation in transportation security, such as at airports	Transportation Security Cooperation Group
Working Group on Cyber-Security and Cyber-Crime	2010	To identify common strategies and goals on fighting cybercrime	DG Home Affairs, DHS, US Attorney General (DOJ)
Joint Customs Cooperation Committee	1997	Expand scope and increase levels of customs cooperation; overseas the joint customs agreements (e.g. container agreement).	DHS, DG Taxation and Customs Union
EU–US Financial Markets Regulatory Dialogue	2002	To increase EU–US cooperation in both market liberalization and regulation of financial instruments	SEC and DG Industry & Enterprise
EU–US Insurance Dialogue	2012	Increase mutual understanding and enhance EU–US cooperation to promote business opportunity, consumer protection, and effective supervision (US Department of Treasury, 2012)	Treasury, Commission, EIOPA, US state regulators

Atlantic Community. Table 5.2 (pp. 88–90) contains a list of the many agreements and declarations since 2001, which together far exceed any other sectoral agreement.

These cover a wide range of cooperative activities, such as sharing financial data (the SWIFT agreement) and the November 2010 EU–US summit's establishment of an EU–US Working Group on Cyber-Security and Cyber-Crime to "tackle new threats to the global networks upon which the security and prosperity of our free societies increasingly depend" (Europa Press Release, 2010a). Within the framework of the Working Group – which is not purely transgovernmental in that it also involves representatives of and experts from outside bodies – expert sub-groups focus on such matters as cyber incident management, public–private partnerships, and cybercrime. As Archick (2013a, p. 4) explains in her Congressional Research Service report to US Congress on EU–US cooperation in counter-terrorism, this is a rich area of cooperation both at the intergovernmental and transgovernmental levels. The US State Department is the interagency coordinator for "enhancing US–EU police, judicial, and border control cooperation," while the Justice and Homeland Security Departments "provide the bulk of the legal and technical expertise." So, too, the US Treasury Department is involved by leading the effort to cut-off terrorist financing. Archick (2013a, p. 4) reports an impressive level of interaction. For example, cabinet-level officials meet at least once per year; a Working Group of senior officials meets once every six months to discuss police and judicial cooperation against terrorism; and engage in a high-level policy dialogue on border and transport security to discuss issues such as passenger data-sharing, cargo security, biometrics, visa policy, and sky marshals. Cooperation also takes place at the transgovernmental and transnational levels through "liaison relationships." Archick (2013a, p. 4) reports that:

> Europol has posted two liaison officers in Washington, DC, and the United States has stationed an FBI officer in The Hague, Netherlands, to work with Europol on counterterrorism. A U.S. Secret Service liaison posted in The Hague also works with Europol on counterfeiting issues. In 2006, a U.S. liaison position was established at Eurojust headquarters in The Hague as part of a wider U.S.–Eurojust agreement to facilitate cooperation between European and U.S. prosecutors on terrorism and other cross-border criminal cases.

In conclusion, in order to give effect to cooperation envisaged in the EU–US annual summits, the Atlantic Community has established a wide range of transgovernmental groups, which are managed at the subcabinet level (assistant and deputy secretaries in the US; directorate generals and below in the European Commission; heads of administrative agencies; and central bankers).

Transnational Level

No policy is implemented in democratic societies without wide consultation of stakeholders; this is especially true when governments are dealing with issues that directly affect business profits (see Lindblom, 1977; Olson, 1965). Furthermore, as the New Transatlanticism has expanded into areas requiring legislative approval, recent examples being data privacy protection and the TTIP, the need for the key committee chairs in the EP and the US Congress to form linkages has become nothing short of urgent if there is to be progress made in mutual recognition and harmonization (given that regulatory authority is subject to legislative oversight) and for agreements requiring legislative approval.

The NTA attempted to foster stakeholder and legislative input by establishing three "dialogues": the Transatlantic Business Dialogue (TABD), the Transatlantic Consumers Dialogue (TACD), and the Transatlantic Legislators' Dialogue (TLD). Furthermore, the TEC includes a wide range of formal stakeholders and advisors as follows: the Atlantic Council, the Bertelsmann Foundation, Business Europe, European American Business Council, TABD, TACD, TLD, Transatlantic Policy Network, and the US Chamber of Commerce

Business Actors

The Transatlantic Business Council

The Transatlantic Business Council (TBC) began as the TABD within the framework of the NTA in 1995 at a conference in Seville of European and US business leaders. In 2013 the TABD merged with a smaller transatlantic business association, the European–American Business Council (EABC), to form the TBC. Within the TBC structure, the TABD continues to function as a distinct program, "preserving its important and unique role as the official business advisor to the Transatlantic Economic Council" (Transatlantic Business Council, 2013b).

Today the TBC comprises approximately 70 EU and US manufacturing companies and service providers which have a significant involvement in transatlantic economic activity. In broad terms, the dialogue seeks to identify, and to make joint policy recommendations in respect of, ways in which European and American business interests may be advanced, especially regarding the further opening of transatlantic trade and advancing MRAs, and in this capacity has been involved in all of the transatlantic fora, including the extensive consultation that preceded the launch of the TTIP and throughout its negotiations. (See, for example, Transatlantic Business Council, 2013c.)

Trade Associations

Business interests cooperate outside of the TBC/TABD framework as well, notably through US and EU trade and business associations. Recent evidence of such cooperation can be seen in the EU and US call for joint statements in advance of the TTIP negotiations (Office of the United States Trade Representative, 2012). Box 5.3 contains a list of the EU and US trade associations that submitted joint statements. Most of the statements seek transatlantic regulatory compatibility, even convergence, and MRAs as the statement below, submitted

---

Box 5.3 Joint Stakeholder Comments to EU and US Call for Input on Regulatory Issues for Possible Future Trade Agreement

- Active Pharmaceutical Ingredients Committee/European Fine Chemicals Group/Society of Chemical Manufacturers and Affiliates
- Airports Council International – North America ("ACI-NA") and Airports Council International Europe ("ACI EUROPE")
- American Automotive Policy Council/European Automobile Manufacturers Association
- American Chemistry Council/European Chemical Industry Council
- Association of the European Self-Medication Industry/Consumer Healthcare Products Association
- EuropaBio/Biotechnology Industry Organization
- Business Europe/US Chamber of Commerce
- The Business Roundtable (BRT)/the TransAtlantic Business Dialogue (TABD)/European Round Table of Industrialists (ERT)
- Cosmetics Europe/Personal Care Products Council
- European Crop Protection Association/CropLife America
- European Federation of Pharmaceutical Industries/Association/Pharmaceutical Research and Manufacturers of America
- European Generics Medicine Association/Generic Pharmaceutical Association
- European Radiological, Electromedical and Healthcare IT/Medical Imaging & Technology Alliance
- European Services Forum/US Coalition of Services Industries
- European Starch Industry Association/Corn Refiners Association
- Motor and Equipment Manufacturers Association/European Association of Automotive Suppliers
- Toy Industries of Europe/US Toy Industry Association
- Transatlantic Coalition on Financial Regulation (EU–US Coalition on Financial Regulation)
- Transatlantic Industry Contribution (numerous US and EU-based trade associations)

(Office of the United States Trade Representative, 2012)

---

by the two major US and EU chemical trade associations, indicates (American Chemistry & European Chemical Industry Council, 2012, p. 14):

> It is difficult to quantify the savings that would result from the above proposals. However, addressing the opportunities for regulatory cooperation in these areas can help minimize the potential for duplication of effort by government and industry, create efficiencies by ensuring high-quality, reliable information is the basis for decision-making, enhance the value of transAtlantic chemicals trade and offer guidance to the rest of the world in setting justifiable and usable regulation. Developing and agreeing on principles in these areas would help guide future cooperative work and set the stage to leverage all the efficiencies and effectiveness possible.

Labor Unions

The Transatlantic Labor Dialogue (TALD) was established in 1996 following an agreement between the representatives of the EU and US peak labor organizations, the European Trade Union Confederation (ETUC) and the American Federation of Labor and Congress of Industrial Organizations (AFL-CIO) (Knauss & Trubek, 2001, p. 235). The TEP Joint Action Plan had called for the need for "increased dialogue on labor between workers, employers and NGOs," although labor unions were skeptical about their presence on the agenda of the EU–US summits (Meyer & Barber, 2011, p. 108; Steffenson, 2005, p. 86). Not surprisingly, the TALD has been characterized by a low level of activity and although not formally abolished has had "only a handful of meetings" (Compa & Meyer, 2010, p. 5).

Compa and Meyer (2010, p. 8) argue that the failure to address labor standards and enforcement in a transatlantic context "means that no signal is sent to the rest of the world on its importance to the global trade system." They offer the Boeing–Airbus dispute as an example, suggesting that Boeing engaged in a "new form of unfair trade practice: de-unionizing to gain competitive advantage. With the implicit promise of greater job security, workers voted to surrender bargaining rights." Compa and Meyer (2010, p. 13) also point out that high-level working groups have not included officials from the European Commission DG Employment, Social Affairs and Inclusion and the US Department of Labor.

Environmental and Consumer Protection Actors

Two dialogues addressing the "social dimension" were established in the NTA, one for consumers and the other for the environment, but only the consumer dialogue continues to operate and is included in the TEC framework. The Transatlantic Environmental Dialogue was disbanded in 2001, only two years after its initiation. The TACD, established in 1998, comprises representatives of EU and US consumer organizations. The TACD promotes consumer interests, including via the advancement of policy recommendations through the TEC and also directly to EU and US decision-makers. Among specific areas of consumers' interests that are covered by TACD policy committees and special taskforces are food policy – including GMOs and growth-promoting hormones in cattle, which have long been the subject of transatlantic disputes – intellectual property, and financial services.

While, as in the business dialogue, there is support in the consumer dialogue for close EU–US economic and regulatory cooperation, the TACD has often expressed concerns that consumer interests are too often bypassed. Indeed, in this context the TACD has voiced considerable reservations about the likely merits of the proposed TTIP, stating that "We are very sceptical that a trade partnership built around regulatory convergence will serve consumer interests" (Transatlantic Consumer Dialogue, 2013a).

Legislative Actors

Exchanges between the European Parliament (EP) and the US Congress date back to 1972, when a congressional delegation visited the EP in Brussels and Luxembourg. Since that time, exchanges have generally taken place twice per year (Archick, 2013b, p. 14) and were institutionalized in 1999 when the EP and Congress (the House of Representatives) launched the TLD as part of the NTA. The TLD was further strengthened when it was named as an advisor in the TEC framework (Archick & Morelli, 2010, p. 1). The TLD, however, has been characterized in the past as "the weakest link in the NTA framework" (European Commission, 2004a, p. 8). As will be discussed below and taken up again in Chapter 9 (financial services regulation) and the concluding chapter in this volume, Member of European Parliament (MEPs) and congresspersons are slowly beginning to "connect."

Archick (2013b, p. 15) reports a number of activities taken by the EP to enhance its links with Congress, including the EP's establishment of a liaison office with the US Congress in Washington, DC – leading observers to conclude that the EP is "far out in front of Congress in pursuit of a stronger relationship" (Archick & Morelli, 2010). While Archick (2013b, p. 15) explains previous controversial agreements (Passenger Name Records and the SWIFT agreements) needed the EP's consent, in the US they were "negotiated by the United States as executive agreements under existing U.S. law." Thus, Archick (2013a, p. 24) notes particularly in her review of EU–US cooperation in counter-terrorism that:

> given the European Parliament's growing influence in many of the areas related to counterterrorism and its new role in approving international agreements – such as the U.S.–EU SWIFT and PNR accords – Members of Congress may increasingly be able to help shape parliament's views and responses.... Some Members of Congress and European Parliamentarians have recently expressed interest in strengthening ties and cooperation further. Such exchanges could provide useful opportunities for enhancing transatlantic dialogue on the wide range of counterterrorism issues facing both sides of the Atlantic.

Furthermore, the TTIP negotiations – involving as they do such a wide range of interests – "may heighten Congress-EP engagement in the years ahead" (Archick, 2013b, p. 15). (See Chapters 13 and 14 for an in-depth analysis of the TTIP, and Chapter 15 for more on the role of Congress and the EP in future transatlantic relations.)

Variations in the Operation and Use of the Structures

The extent to which and the enthusiasm with which the three levels of New Transatlanticism relations have operated and been conducted has varied both between policy areas and over time. Regarding variations between policy areas, a key factor has been the ability of the EU to speak and act with authority, which in turn has depended essentially on the EU's policy competences. It has to be remembered that the EU is not a state but rather is a uniquely developed organization of states. As such, although it can frame some common external policies and conduct some external actions, it does not have such capacities in all external policy areas. (See the introductory chapter in this volume for an overview of EU and US policy competences.) Moreover, where such capacities do exist, they are not always strong because they necessarily have to be exercised on the basis of internally negotiated agreements that are reflective of the (often differing) views and preferences of most, if not all, of the member states.

Where the EU's and US's competences are strong – as with external trade, competition policy, and market-related regulatory standards – then EU–US bilateral relations at the three levels tend to be at their strongest. (See subsequent chapters in this volume for in-depth analyses.) Where one of the partners' competences are weak – as with most social policies and foreign and defense policies in the EU – then EU–US bilateral relations tend to be not much developed, with most transatlantic relations being channeled through the member states on the EU's side. And where the member states share competences with the EU – as in such policy areas as macroeconomic and cross-border transport (see Chapter 9) – the nature of transatlantic relations is often based on a mixed package. Moreover, it can be a package that is subject to fluctuation, with the Commission and member states sometimes disputing representational rights and with the US sometimes preferring to take advantage of internal policy preferences in the EU to deal either with the Commission or particular member states. But the sense of the US as a unified actor should not be pressed too far and would risk overlooking the long history in American public administration of fractured authorities among regulatory agencies (see Chapters 8, 11, and 12 on this point with respect to antitrust, financial services, and GMO regulation, respectively). Thus, as Ahearn (2009, p. 9) writes:

> U.S. regulatory agencies have the mandate and funding to focus on domestic regulatory issues and they enjoy a fair amount of independence on policy implementation matters. However, the United States lacks a clear-cut institutional mechanism to coordinate cooperative efforts. And neither the Commerce Department nor the Office of U.S. Trade Representative (USTR), the lead agencies for U.S. undertakings in the realm of transatlantic regulatory cooperation, have authority to overhaul domestic regulatory policymaking. While Commerce and USTR may bring the heads of U.S. regulatory agencies to the negotiating table, the regulatory agencies are not usually funded nor mandated to engage in TRC (transatlantic regulatory cooperation) activities.

Regarding variations over time, an important factor has been the tenor set by the White House. As Pollack (2005, p. 904) has pointed out, "the Clinton era did represent an effort by both sides to create a privileged, and largely collusive, bilateral relationship between Washington and Brussels." During this period institutional arrangements were put in place that offered considerable potential for significant advances in policy cooperation and collaboration. Progress continued during the Bush years, and in some respects was even intensified by 9/11 insofar as it highlighted issues that the EU and the US have in common – not least in combating a shared terrorist threat. But the Bush presidency also hampered New Transatlanticism development in that it fostered a less favorable political climate via its more hawkish and in some respects unilateralist foreign policy stance. This stance resulted in a number of high-profile EU–US disputes – including on the authority of the International Criminal Court (ICC), climate change, and the invasion of Iraq (which also resulted in internal EU disputes). Under Obama, advances have continued to be made, although they have been rather moderate – a consequence in no small part of his first term Administration seemingly prioritizing relations across the Pacific over those across the Atlantic. However, relations with the EU came back to the fore at the beginning of his second term, with the importance of transatlantic relations being specifically mentioned in Obama's 2013 State of the Union speech, with the announcement by the US and the EU in February 2013 of their intention of opening negotiations on the TTIP, and with the explicit connection with the EU's Eastern Partnership agreements to the civil and political turmoil in Ukraine and Russia's annexation of Crimea.

Conclusions

The architecture supporting the New Transatlanticism was established and built primarily for the purpose of opening more, and more direct, Washington–Brussels links, especially in policy areas affecting economic activity across the Atlantic and, thereby, also on each side of the Atlantic. In these, and increasingly also neighboring policy areas, it was hoped that the New Transatlanticism would contribute to policy cooperation and coordination. Although, perhaps misguidedly given its focused policy aims, the New Transatlanticism system is prone to being criticized for not having been much directly involved in resolving high-profile, politically sensitive, and disputed issues – see, for example, Chapters 7 (trade), 8 (competition), and 12 (GMO food) – it has had some success in what it is supposed to do. As Peterson and Steffenson (2009, p. 41) argue, NTA institutions have "helped keep both sides focused on a pragmatic, co-operative policy agenda regardless of 'political noise' over Iraq, human rights, climate change, and so on."

6   Comparing Administrative Cultures

Keith Henderson

Introduction

This chapter uses the paradigm of "administrative culture" as an explanatory construct to understand differences and similarities between two sets of partners, US federal officials and counterparts in the European Commission (the administrative arm of the EU). The first section explores the variables that affect the ability of EU and US officials to agree to policies of mutual concern. The second section explains the importance of "administrative culture" to bureaucratic culture in executive departments and agencies. The third section compares and contrasts EU and US administrative cultures. The fourth section examines the background and orientation of EU and US bureaucrats. The chapter assesses the extent to which EU and US administrative cultures may or may not be converging.

Governmental Officials and Transatlantic Cooperation

There are a number of variables that should affect the ability of the EU and the US to agree on policies of mutual concern. Such exogenous variables include sector-level EU and US competition and dominance, attitudes about the role of government in the economy, terrorist threats, shared environmental concerns (e.g., climate change), and political institutions (variable policy implementation in the EU – a quasi-federal state) as compared to the US (a full-fledged federal state).

In the literature on EU–US transatlantic policy development, differences between the Commission and US federal officials have not been well researched nor have the implications for other cooperative partnerships been analyzed. Thus, the significant literature on the business sector and public–business, public–voluntary pairings – along with intergovernmental linkages – should be supplemented by additional study of transatlantic strategic partnerships and the policy roles of bureaucrats. A recent study – the largest internal survey ever undertaken in the EU (Kassim et al., 2013) – coupled with ongoing analyses by the Office of Personnel Management, the Merit System Protection Board, and others in the US will facilitate our ability to undertake a comparative analysis.

As summarized in Table 6.1, officials working in the European Commission and the US executive branch bring their own backgrounds, experience, and

Table 6.1 Comparison of EU and US Bureaucracies

	European Commisison	*US Federal Bureaucracy (Executive Branch)*
Size	23,803, official and temporary	2,061,569
Language	Tend to be multilingual	Tend to be unilingual
History	Approximately 50 years	Long-standing administrative culture
Territory	Europe (tempered supranationalism)	US (national)
Legislative role	Right of initiation (writes legislation) in a wide-range of policy areas.	Acts as executive agent in a separation-of-powers system advising on legislation
Tradition	European civil law traditions (UK common law tradition, the exception)	US common law tradition
Training	System-wide programs	By agencies themselves
Recruitment and hiring	By EU with balancing by national origin	By agencies themselves
Diversity emphasis	National and gender	Ethnic and gender

Sources: European Commission, 2013c; LRP Publications, 2014.

career circumstances to the interactions in addition to simply reflecting organizational goals and policy considerations. The size of the European Commission and US federal (executive bureaucracy) is not at all comparable, with approximately 24,000 employees in the European Commission compared to two million in the US federal bureaucracy. This latter point is important, but taking it up here will lead us astray from the principal task of this chapter – to compare and contrast administrative cultures. Therefore, the capacity inquiry will be delayed until Chapter 15 (policy implications).

Administrative Culture

Administrative culture is the "culture of administrators … whose activities are restricted to the administrative environment" (Sharma, 2002, p. 65). Based on a six-year study involving numerous interviews, Carolyn Ban (2013, p. 44) characterizes the administrative (organizational) culture of the European Commission as follows: "It is clear from the preceding discussion that, within the Commission, there is a common culture that binds the organization together." Henderson (2004, p. 239) observes in the US context: "Administrative culture is related to the broader political culture, from which it derives, and can be further discussed in terms of sub-cultures." In the US federal government, a broad and inclusive culture with a history of merit-system values is acknowledged by officials.

Students of comparative public administration have long asked: "Do administrative cultures differ among nation-states?" As public administration has evolved from the Wilsonian politics–administrative dichotomy to New Public Management (NPM) and to New Public Governance (NPG), so administrative cultures "are in flux" to reflect these changes in public management (Jamil, Askvik, & Hossain, 2013, p. 901). And key for the accomplishment of the policy convergence sought through the TTIP vehicle is the extent to which administrative cultures may be converging in the US and the EU around these two new paradigms. This is an important question because earlier, in a landmark study of administrative culture, Aberbach, Rockman, and Putnam (1981) interviewed politicians and bureaucrats in several Western European countries and the US, finding that the administration–policy split was much stronger in Western Europe. But as the values and skills prized in NPM (which began to take hold in the 1980s) and NPG (a rejection of rigid hierarchy and recognition of the incompatibility of the market model with the administration of collective goods) became prominent, accountability, operational efficiency, and networking are increasingly shaping the administrative cultures of both the EU and the US.

Do behavioral variables exist that affect operation of agreements, agendas, dialogues, and summits beyond organizational and policy differences? Are career bureaucrats on either side of the Atlantic socialized (in the sense of acquiring a particular orientation leading to values and beliefs) and motivated in sufficiently different ways as to affect transatlantic relationships? These are important questions given the widely discussed policy variations between the EU and the US, and the high number of interactions taking place among career bureaucrats in the Atlantic community.

Another important question is the extent to which the interaction of EC and US public administrators empower one another. Kassim and Stevens (2010, p. 82), in a study of EU air transport policy, argue: "US policy opened up a debate about the regulation of the sector, empowering the supporters of a more liberal aviation policy and led to a growing chorus for Community action." Some policy areas reflect US dominance. This was the case with overall air transport policy, which emphasized the US approach to deregulation and Open Skies and required removal of restrictions on capacity and fares (Kassim & Stevens, 2010, p. 165).

Dual Administrative Cultures

Overall, in the US, a decentralized system in which most departments and agencies undertake their own recruiting and hiring may be characterized as merit-based. A general federal system is supplemented by agency-specific systems – also merit-based – in the Foreign Service, Forest Service, Public Health Service, FBI, and elsewhere. It has evolved over time with post-9/11 changes in Homeland Security (a newer Department) and the Defense Department, which have the effect of providing more flexibility to management and – from the standpoint of public employee unions which opposed the moves – loss of Civil Service protections. Vastly larger than its EU counterpart with proportionately few personnel directly involved in US–EU agreements, agendas, dialogues, and summits, it admits of numerous nuances and sub-sets in its application.

Certainly one important difference between the EU and the US administrative cultures is that Commission officials usually undergo *two* socialization processes, one in their home country and another in the Commission, the latter contributing to the Commission's supranational character. It is a neglected concern since the values, attitudes, and beliefs of officials are typically taken for granted as representing the agency. US federal officials, on the other hand, typically begin their career in the federal government after completing their undergraduate education or move from the private or non-profit sectors (rather than from civil service in the local and state governments).

At the same time, among the European Commission's Directorate Generals (DGs), which are roughly equivalent to national-level departments or ministries, different values can be found – just as is found in national ministries. As an illustration, in the European Commission's DG Competition (tasked with antitrust and competition policy), neo-liberal values have been identified as well as a legalistic style of working (Cini, 2000, 2009). Conversely, the DG Employment and Social Affairs DG is a highly corporatist culture, while DG Information Society is more pluralist and concerned with technical expertise (Hix, 2005, p. 47).

The existing literature includes some attention to national cultures and national identities as they impact performance within the European Commission (Cini, 2000; Kassim et al., 2013; Nugent, 2010). Cultural complexity, in the broader sense, arises from the multitude of national traditions which are only partly obscured in what Nugent calls the "cultural compromise" (Nugent, 2001, chapter 2, pp. 182–183). As Nugent points out, officials understandably take a particular interest in the impact of policies on their own country even though this does not require that they function as advocates of policies:

> So, for example, an Italian official in the Agriculture DG working on a sensitive land-usage proposal with environmental implications may well be prepared to informally explore options and possibilities with Italians in the Environment DG but be wary about doing so with non-Italians.
>
> (Nugent, 2001, p. 183)

Recognizing these factors, attempts have been made in the EU to override national differences through such devices as a "SEM 2000 program" and codes of conduct for officials. Contrasted with the US federal government, the representational and linguistic aspects of administrative behavior in the EU are substantially more prominent. And European Commission officials are virtually all at least bilingual in contrast to English-only US officials.

In the US federal government – a federal system – the 50 state governments do not contribute state perspectives in the EU sense, where national origins are in constant evidence. In their comprehensive survey Kassim et al. (2013) explore attitudes of employees toward the Commission and reform efforts, toward each other, and toward policy. E-12 employees (the original group) are distinguished from E-15 (the enlarged group) and breakdowns are given by organizational level. The massive amount of data do not admit easy generalizations, but provide a point of comparison to the US. EU data show a more legalistic, rule-bound approach in addition to matters of size, national loyalties, and morale. Most European countries and the EU itself, which has a body of administrative law (Craig, 2012), derive their legal systems from Napoleonic revival of Roman Law, emphasizing control agencies, transparency, citizen access and redress, and contributions made by Community courts. In contrast, the US Common Law legal system derives from English traditions of standards within the Community There is less reliance on strictly legal interpretations of rules and regulations but more involvement with lawsuits relating to regulation and control. Similarities of the two cultures lie in competency-type orientations and efforts to fend off political controls from outside. Expertise is typically the basis for the latter in both administrative cultures.

Absent in the available surveys are conscious attempts to make transatlantic comparisons. Similarly, the large volume of public administration information available through the European Public Administration Network (EUPAN), Euro-barometer, the European Administrative School (EAS), and elsewhere is over-whelmingly concerned with only the EU and member countries.

The European Commission is involved in all EU decision-making and is organized under individual commissioners in charge of particular policy areas who act collectively as a "College of Commissioners." Commissioners have their own cabinets and advisory committee networks consisting of expert com-mittees and consultative committees, the latter system known as "comitology" (Nugent, 2010, chapter 8). With its legalistic legislative and oversight role, the EU is substantially different from its US counterpart but, nevertheless, coopera-tion with US officials is the norm.

Other administrative officials – some interacting with US personnel – are found in the EU but about three-quarters of all EU staff are in the Commission, including those on permanent and temporary assignments to administrative tasks. Unlike their US federal government counterparts, officials in the European Commission do not share a common tradition of fundamental reform directed at a previous pattern of spoils. Although some nation-states (notably the UK in 1854 with the Northcote–Trevelyan Act) did have such a tradition, it is not a uniform pattern.

The designation "competency-based and supranational," therefore, is used to characterize a similar but more diffuse behavioral pattern than "merit." Techni-cally, the EU Commission – like the EU itself – is multinational but functions – or attempts to – as supranational. The term goes back to the original European Coal and Steel Community (ECSC) in 1951 and the dissatisfaction with the auto-nomy of the "High Authority" (the administrative arm) when the European Eco-nomic Community was formed in 1958. The EU is sometimes characterized as "federal" and students often first experience it in the context of "international" and "regional" organizations. As in other organizations, reforms have been undertaken with the objective of making it *more* supranational and less national (see Chapter 2 on this point). Part of broader trends toward globalization and internationalization along with networking and partnering, which have become increasingly important in the study of public administration, current textbooks and course content, recognize its significance and an overall shift from "national" to "international" seems to be occurring.

In postindustrial societies business and civil society actors take on more importance and cooperative linkages increase. Additional contextual factors relate to the NPM, NPG, the pervasive distrust of "bureaucrats" in pejorative usage, and the interdependencies of financial reregulation and technological developments providing a vast quantity of instantly available information. This is common to both administrative cultures.

In the European context, the EU is expected to expand beyond its current 28 members and to continue reforming and modernizing its bureaucracy. Unlike the US, it has its own school of administration (the EAS) and a large professional network of academics, practitioners, and others.

Background and Orientation of Officials

In response to the question "Is there a typical EU official?" (Kassim et al., 2013, pp. 264–266), the newest member states are found to be widely diverse in cultural background, administrative tradition, and social attitude from Western European member states. These findings make generalization difficult; nevertheless, a significant variable is whether the originating state is unitary or federal. Other variables include Northern or Southern Europe origins and position in the organization.

Kassim and associates profile top-level officials separately and characterize answers by organizational unit. Their findings correlate with those of Ellinas and Suleiman (2012, pp. 114–115), Buonanno and Nugent (2013, pp. 226–231), and others on bureaucratic attitudes and action programs.

As in the US administrative culture, in spite of considerable differences in beliefs, attitudes, and values among the various groupings, there is arguably an administrative culture made up of commonalities for all: Ellinas and Suleiman (2012, pp. 125–126) ask

> Does the European bureaucracy have a common culture that complicates political efforts to make it more responsive? There are good reasons to think so. The first one relates to the legal foundations of the European bureaucracy. Two other reasons are the functional uniqueness of the organization and the remoteness of the Commission from European citizens.

Work habits may be influenced by nationality, with officials from northern member states adhering to a more rule-driven style than those from southern member states. Nordic state officials may be particularly disposed toward more transparency (Nugent, 2010, pp. 182–183). Ellinas and Suleiman (2012, pp. 114–115) note that "One of the striking findings in the survey is … EU-12 officials are considerably more right wing in economic terms and less social liberal than their EU-15 colleagues."

The European Commission bureaucracy, in its behavioral dimension, is dynamic rather than static, with changes over time as new member states join the EU and enlist their nationals. The addition of 10 countries in 2004 made a difference in the concerns analyzed here. Between 2004 and the end of 2010, 4,004 officials and temporary agents were recruited, significantly above the target of 3,508 (European Commission, 2012a). EU enlargement has also had a positive effect on the gender balance in the Commission, with women now outnumbering men in the organization. Many women work in the largest DG, Translation, which totals 2,309 employees. A "representative bureaucracy" is a goal in the US, with important developments in minority and gender representation. Gender representation is also a goal in the EU but – more prominently – "representation" reflects national origins and attendant educational/social/linguistic characteristics. Ban (2013, chapters 6–7) indicates that gender "matters more than expected" in her findings but that nationality and region "matter less than expected."

EU officials are socialized into the EU but retain loyalties and connections to their originating countries and affinities among fellow nationals. Principal–agent theory provides insight and interpretation of bureaucratic behavior but recognition is also required of independent action by officials. Pollack (2003, p. 36) writes:

> As an empirical matter, it is unquestionably correct that the Commission is composed of hundreds of bureaucratic sub-units and thousands of individuals; that these sub-units and individuals often have distinct policy preferences and that internal Commission politics is frequently depicted as a haven of bureaucratic politics and intra-organizational struggle.

This is not different than the well-documented interdepartmental rivalries in the US and the "sides" are much the same in the Commission as in the US federal bureaucracy. So, for example, in Chapter 12 of this volume Carolyn Dudek demonstrates how the rivalry between agricultural technology interests (championed by the US Department of Agriculture and DG Agriculture) and environmentalists (US Environmental Protection Agency [EPA] and DG Environment) were identical as genetically modified organisms (GMOs) were leaving the lab for field tests in the mid-1980s. Her analysis strengthens the argument that the Commission must constantly seek to balance national and supranational interests. But it also demonstrates that transatlantic cooperation may be facilitated by the similar administrative cultures and orientation in respective policy areas such as biotechnology, agriculture, research and innovation, competition, and even in foreign policy. Thus, in many cases Commission and US bureaucrats in the same sector (e.g., US Department of Commerce and DG Enterprise and Industry) may have more in common with one another than with their counterparts in rival agencies such as DG Environment and the EPA. Likewise, one would expect bureaucrats in DG Home Affairs to be more attuned to their counterparts in the Department of Homeland Security (DHS) than they would be with officials working in DG Agriculture or the US Department of Agriculture.

Reforms over time – along with EU enlargement and, in the US, presidentially initiated reorganizations – have changed appointment procedures, rotation in office, and recruitment of more women in senior management positions. Additionally, staff have been moved from over-resourced to under-resourced offices and from low-priority to high-priority assignments. More emphasis upon professionalism and a more flexible grading arrangement have occurred, although it should be noted that selection and promotion based on skill and ability (competency-based) are affected by pressure, negotiation, and maneuvering by member states in a highly competitive and contested atmosphere (Nugent, 2010, pp. 116–122).

Within the broader category of US administrative culture are orientations of officials which we will label subcultures. American administrative culture can be understood as having three subcultures: traditional, self-protective, and entrepreneurial (Henderson, 2005). These concepts change over time with, for example, evidence that "self-protective" takes on more importance in an era of austerity when downsizing and bureaucrat bashing are prominent in the discourse. It is a category in which many officials are cautious in their actions, bond together in shared decision-making, and feel that legislators and the public do not appreciate their efforts. The "traditional" category is still the most common as of early 2014, encompassing routines of public service focused on formal duties and responsibilities competently performed with a sense of accomplishment. "Entrepreneurial" is a reflection of the business-like orientation of the marketplace and flexibility associated with NPM and "reinventing government" beginning in the 1980s. More recently – as a shift has occurred toward NPG – the entrepreneurial element draws heavily on performance measurement in a context of second (business) and third sector (non-profit) involvement and public participation.

Of importance to this study are the behavioral characteristics evidenced by civil servants themselves, as shown in case studies, empirical surveys, and theories/notions of bureaucratic behavior. All are problematic in developing understandings and making comparisons. The latter, for example, reflect a range of views from the more extreme bureaucratic pathologies and their wide discussion (e.g., Hummel, 2008) to positive views more compatible with career preparation and public appreciation (e.g., Goodsell, 2003). These kinds of interpretations typically are thought to extend beyond a particular administrative agency.

Numerous case studies, reaching back at least to Kaufman's (1960) forest service provide important insights. Empirical studies which are based on systematic methodologies also provide insights but in surveying attitudes, values, beliefs, and job satisfaction they suffer from overlap of the personal with the formal. Socialization factors and supervisory review of findings – even if responses are anonymous – may introduce a bias away from full and frank disclosure (see Amitin, 2010 for a good overview). Of course, this would also be true of the EU.

Along with the Merit System Protection Board and the Federal Office of Personnel Management (OPM), the Partnership for Public Service and Office of Management and Budget conduct systematic surveys of government employees. In a 2002 "Human Capital Survey," the OPM questioned over 100,000 randomly selected employees and found that 91% believe they do important work. Sixty-seven percent were satisfied with their work but there were doubts about rewards for good performance, with only 30% agreeing that awards programs provide incentives to do their best. Subsequent surveys revealed generally positive results and the Federal Employee Viewpoint Survey (the successor to the Human Capital Surveys) is now conducted annually to measure job satisfaction, commitment, and engagement; over 600,000 government employees responded to the survey in 2012. The OPM reports that confidence is shown in employees' leaders, pride is evident in work, and the vast majority believe their agency is accomplishing its missions and would recommend it as a good place to work (US Office of Personnel Management, 2010). A job satisfaction index has been developed showing agencies with the highest increases since 2008: the Department of State, Department of the Treasury, and Department of Transportation are the top three. A new section has also been added to the survey on work–life programs (e.g., worksite health and wellness, dependent care, telework) to better understand the impact of various programs designed to create "flexible, supportive environments" (US Office of Personnel Management n.d.). A current trend – reflecting downsizing and privatization – is toward lower morale among employees. This would be expected in the austerity mode of the moment. The OPM surveys illustrate that the goal of "merit" needs to extend beyond recruiting, hiring, promoting, disciplining, and similar matters. Ingraham (2006, p. 487) expresses it well:

> Merit is having not only the necessary skills and competencies to fill the job in question, but also a *public service character* – a desire to act, not for individual self-interest but for a broader good. Merit is related to values, ideals, and ethics, to the appropriate role of the civil service in a democracy and thus to governance in a democratic society.

Conclusions

Administrative culture is a useful conceptual framework for understanding the relationship between the behavioral aspects of the European Commission and the US federal government. Both reflect management challenges in confronting service delivery and coordination problems in a time of austerity, and both work together or in parallel on a variety of issues. Although trade, homeland security, and financial regulation have received the most attention in the considerable transatlantic literature and have focused more on policy than administrative issues, public officials deserve attention for their roles.

This chapter has found important differences between the Commission and the US federal bureaucracy. The Commission is designed to be a supranational organization, or as Buonanno and Nugent (2013, p. 45) observe, "tempered supranationalism"; the US federal civil service is national. Commission officials perform a variety of duties including proposing and developing policies and legislation in a structure not familiar in the US federal government. The EU's civil service is much smaller in size but includes officials from 28 countries. The EU has a relatively short history; the US has an administrative culture of long standing. EU officials are multilingual and typically first socialized in the administrative system of their home country; US officials may come to the federal government from other positions, but have only one country of origin. They are generally unilingual. A more integrated professional orientation is found in the EU than in the US.

In spite of differences in policy, procedure, and structure, the EU and US administrative cultures are alike in important ways. They respond similarly to external pressures and share among their members common professional backgrounds. Transatlantic communication among officials has been facilitated both by global communication networks and language. Increasingly, EU and US officials are working interactively across the Atlantic, utilizing new electronic technologies as well as traditional meetings. Language has become another area where transatlantic collaboration has become possible because, increasingly, meetings (especially at the committee level where civil servants, rather than politicians, would predominate) within the EU are conducted in English or "Euro-Globish" with only occasional additions in other languages so that, as *The Economist* (Charlemagne Column, 2014) puts it, "interpreters sometimes feel they are speaking to themselves." This trend has accelerated since the enlargements that brought in member states from Central and Eastern Europe.

Several examples should further illustrate similarities between the two current administrative approaches on opposite sides of the Atlantic. In the realm of trade and investment, negotiations are underway on the Transatlantic Trade and Investment Partnership (TTIP; a comprehensive trade and investment agreement between the EU and the US discussed elsewhere in this volume). The TTIP, which it should be emphasized is as much "process" as "outcome," will ultimately restructure relationships because civil servants will be crucial to its implementation and monitoring, and should bring EU and US officials closer together in their working relationships, and would be expected to influence administrative culture in both of the partners.

Looking at the sector level, similarities in administrative culture can be quite pronounced. Taking one policy area of considerable concern among advanced industrialized countries – the environment – staffing in both the EU (DG Environment) and the US (EPA) is in large measure by professionals oriented to environmental protection, alleviation of climate change, problems such as carbon emissions, and regulation/subsidy/coordination of intergovernmental programs. In a second example – education – both Brussels (DG Education and Culture) and Washington (US Department of Education) take a supporting role (policy coordination, subsidies, and overall standards) because in both systems education is controlled by constituent units (EU member states/US state and local government). Therefore, similar sensitivities to local culture and standards must be balanced with the educational needs of the federal/quasi-federal state, and government officials must be skilled at coordinating partnership agreements and monitoring recipients for compliance with the requirements of funding streams.

Given the basic similarities in the two administrative cultures on formal public service commitments, contrasts may be more subtle and elusive. In attempting to strengthen strategic partnerships and networks – even if basically functional – there is usually room for improved relationships; but broader attitudes among the public may intrude on the efforts of civil servants. As is brought out in some of the chapters in Parts II and III of this volume, differing views exist between Americans and Europeans on major security, trade, and economic regulation issues, as well as less dominant concerns such as the death penalty, organic farming, and business subsidies.

Part III
Policies

7 Transatlantic Trade Policy

Holly Jarman

Together we make up ... the greatest aggregation of economic power in the history of the world. We now have the means to make certain that we build our strength together and that we can maintain this preeminence.

President John F. Kennedy (1962a), upon signing the Trade Expansion Act in 1962

A clever American once said "neither we nor the members of the European Common Market are so affluent that we can long afford to shelter high cost farms or factories from the winds of foreign competition."

Karel de Gucht (2013), European Union Commissioner for Trade, quoting President Kennedy's 1963 State of the Union address

Introduction

The EU–US trade relationship remains one of the most important in the world. The EU and the US are the world's two largest traders in goods and services, and export a significant proportion of those goods and services to each other. Connected to this trade, and perhaps even more significant, a huge amount of money crosses the Atlantic in the form of investment, much of it transferred from companies to their affiliates.

Much of the close relationship between the US and EU described elsewhere in this volume can thus be attributed to trade and investment. The formal institutions that attempt to deepen the transatlantic economic relationship between the two regions are often described as the most developed of their kind in the world (Hänggi & Roloff, 2006; Meyer & Barber, 2011). The adoption of the New Transatlantic Agenda (NTA) in the mid-1990s was only the first in a series of institutions that have iteratively attempted to improve trade and investment between the two regions. Yet these mechanisms have also been disappointing to many on both sides who are impatient to see real increases in the volume and efficiency of trade and investment as a result of closer transatlantic cooperation.

This chapter argues that this is unsurprising given the substance of contemporary trade policy. Today, the most substantial transatlantic barriers to trade are frequently not tariffs, but "non-tariff barriers" (NTBs), regulations and technical standards identified by businesses as impediments to economic exchange

(Hamilton & Quinlan, 2014; Young, 2009). While ministers and governments may find it easier to turn the "high politics" of security and defense into tangible results, trade and investment policy as we currently understand them are arguably not as sensitive to high politics. Ministerial brinkmanship can motivate a trade deal, or push for its conclusion, but high-level summitry is a poor mechanism by which to harmonize webs of conflicting rules and regulations.

Trade harmonization is therefore as much a product of public administration and policy as it is of raw politics. Regulations perceived as trade barriers – such as health and safety standards, environmental regulations, standards governing use of personal data, or labor market regulations – are likely to have been designed for some other public purpose. They are the business of bureaucrats and agencies, not presidents and cabinets. Identifying which regulations truly serve a legitimate public purpose, and preserving that purpose while making them more efficient and harmonized across jurisdictions – something that EU officials claim they can and will do – requires taking a scalpel to domestic policies, something quite different from swinging the sword of tariff cuts. In its FAQ on the Transatlantic Trade and Investment Partnership (TTIP), the European Commission (2013l: 7) states: "The negotiations will not be about lowering standards: they are about getting rid of tariffs and useless red-tape while keeping high standards in place. There will be no compromise whatsoever on safety, consumer protection or the environment."

Characterizing regulations as barriers to trade is also problematic in that rules designed to protect health or the environment frequently attempt to protect the public at large rather than any specific group within the population or set of organizations. The public in the US and European states often disagree about important issues surrounding the food chain and the environment, giving these issues different levels of political salience in different countries or regions. Even when the EU and US agree in principle that a particular area of human activity, such as actions affecting public health, should be regulated, there are significant differences in the mechanisms that the two polities use to regulate those areas. There are therefore many constellations of actors which are potentially affected by contemporary trade negotiations, not just businesses and trade unions.

Despite these difficulties, the two trading powers have considerable economic and political incentives to coordinate their trade policies and form a more cohesive bloc – not least increased competition from expanding markets elsewhere in the world or poor economic conditions at home. Anticipating increased international competition, the EU and US have launched a new round of trade talks that will further harmonize their economies and cement their dominance in the global economy.

In the context of the recent economic downturn, this chapter reviews promises and progress to reduce both tariff and non-tariff barriers to trade between the US and EU. I explain why these two large polities, which have such complex economic links and so many common problems, are finding it hard to cooperate on trade policy – not because of friction between the two powers, which is relatively low, but because the remaining unresolved trade issues involve a combination of intricate regulations and political flash-points. The following section explains some of the history and symbolism that lies behind transatlantic trade relations, before detailing the various iterations of more formal transatlantic institutions designed to promote transatlantic trade, including the NTA, the Transatlantic Economic Partnership (TEP) agreement, and the forthcoming TTIP. The chapter then explores the changing institutional landscape at the domestic level, in order to further explain these international dynamics. I conclude by drawing these elements together to explain the resilience of transatlantic efforts to foster trade and investment.

The Symbolism of Transatlantic Trade

With 28 member states, the EU constitutes the world's largest market. By 2013, the volume of both the region's merchandise trade and its trade in commercial services was greater than that for all other WTO members, even after excluding intra-EU trade. The most important destination for the EU's merchandise exports is the US (17%), followed by China (9%) and Switzerland (8%). Seventeen percent of its merchandise imports are from China, 12% are from Russia, and 11% are from the US.

The volume of US trade flows is only slightly smaller. The state remains the wealthiest economy in the world. It exports merchandise most often to Canada (19%), the EU (18%), and Mexico (13%), and imports merchandise most often from China (18%), the EU (17%), and Canada (14%). The US and EU are the world's largest service economies, with trade in services forming a large part of their economic exchange with each other (Cooper, 2014; World Trade Organization, 2013c).

A large proportion of the economic activity in both the EU and US can be accounted for by exchange between the two countries. The amount of investment that moves back and forth between the two regions is particularly significant. Each is the greatest destination for, and source of, investment for the other. In 2011 the US and EU together accounted for 57% of inward foreign direct investment (FDI) and 71% of outward FDI. Much of the economic activity between the two trading powers is generated by affiliate sales (Hamilton & Quinlan, 2013, pp. 7–8), demonstrating the deep economic integration that exists between the two polities.

But statistics can only tell us so much. In order to understand the contemporary transatlantic trade relationship, it is also important to reflect on the political motivations for forging a trade partnership between the US and Europe.

Poor trade relations between the US and prominent European states in the early twentieth century exert a powerful symbolism that persists to this day and influences current transatlantic trade relations. Trade protectionism in the early decades of the twentieth century on both sides of the Atlantic is frequently credited with deepening and prolonging (and sometimes, erroneously, with causing) the Great Depression of the 1930s. Logrolling in the US Congress, where elected representatives supported protectionist tariff increases for interests in each other's districts, contributed to high tariff levels in the early decades of the twentieth century (Schattschneider, 1960). As a result of this political bargaining, high tariffs were imposed on new consumer goods from Europe, from radios to cars and Swiss watches. European states retaliated against these tariff increases by imposing higher tariffs of their own. And although the history surrounding the role of tariffs in economic growth during this era is far more complex than can be detailed here, the impact of this "high tide" for tariffs on subsequent trade negotiations, as well as diplomatic relations, should not be underestimated (Eckes, 1995; Irwin, 2011). Trade protectionism as practiced by the US and European countries during this period played an important role in shaping attitudes toward trade policy in subsequent decades – fostering a strong desire among policymakers to avoid the perils of protectionism.

The move toward the reciprocal lowering of tariffs from the mid-1930s onwards in the US is, conversely, associated with improved economic prosperity by both economists and politicians. In the subsequent decades, the US and key European states worked together to establish international institutions to manage trade relations. Under a banner of peace and economic stability, the General Agreement on Tariffs and Trade (GATT), signed in 1947, served to cement both the economic and the political relationship between the US and Europe. GATT signatories began the first in a series of negotiations that would eventually see tariffs drop to much lower levels worldwide.

In the 1960s, one such round – the "Kennedy Round" – of multilateral trade negotiations set about reducing tariffs between the US and European states. This was, in part, a response by the US to the fledgling European Economic Community (EEC) and an attempt to prevent US goods from being shut out of Europe's large marketplace. Again, the US and European governments ultimately attempted to cooperate rather than compete with one another, fearing the political, not just the economic, ramifications of a weak transatlantic relationship.

It is this symbolism, the image of a lasting partnership of political stability and economic prosperity, that EU Trade Commissioner Karel de Gucht (2013) invoked in a speech at the Harvard Kennedy School in 2013. De Gucht's visit was designed to promote the most recent in a series of attempts by the US and EU to cement their trade relations – the TTIP.

But the reality of the Kennedy Round was somewhat different from the rhetoric. The negotiations were far from harmonious, as might be expected from such a complex and ambitious task involving so many countries. Significantly, the Kennedy Round was the first to include negotiations on a wide range of NTBs to trade, facing problems that would only become more apparent in later rounds, and the first to tackle agriculture. The EEC's Common Agricultural Policy was still being formed when the round began, and EEC members found it difficult to present just one single position during the negotiations. Likewise, America's newly created Strategic Trade Representative's office struggled with challenges to their mandate. The final agreement was only reached just before US trade negotiating authority was due to expire (Eckes, 1995, pp. 60–68).

In hindsight, many commentators have criticized the Kennedy Round – both for failing to achieve the substantial economic gains promised by the political rhetoric of state leaders, and as the root of several key problems that contribute to making current multilateral trade negotiations unmanageable. Starting with the NTA, the next section examines the transatlantic institutions created between the US and EU to promote trade. As we will see, many of the hopes and fears of the Kennedy Round are no less salient for transatlantic economic cooperation today.

Transatlantic Institutions Designed to Promote Trade

Despite being perhaps the most developed interregional economic partnership in the world, and one of the biggest in terms of the volume of trade and investment, formal attempts to govern transatlantic economic relations are widely viewed as disappointing in terms of their economic impact. Announced in 1995, the NTA aimed to achieve both political and economic goals. Yet, in practice, trade frequently took a backseat to more high-profile political issues. Trade politics was the province of mid-level officials whose actions were largely unaffected by the high politics of the biannual intergovernmental summits (Meyer & Barber, 2011). The TEP agreement of 1998 established that a core objective of the TEP was the abolition of tariff and non-tariff barriers to trade and investment (Meyer, 2008), but it was equally disappointing in terms of its economic results.

The underlying cause of this inability to make progress was that much of the so-called "low-hanging fruit" had already been picked (Pollack & Schaffer, 2001b). With the exception of sectors such as agriculture and textiles, highly visible barriers to trade such as tariffs (taxes imposed on imports and exports) and quotas (limits on the quantity of a good that can be produced abroad and sold domestically) are minimal between the EU and US (World Trade Organization, 2013b). And while the implementation of tariffs can be complex, they are a relatively simple policy instrument. The authority of a government to set tariffs is highly centralized and rarely contested, the economic effects of tariffs are easy to observe, and their costs usually fall on specific firms or sectors of the economy.

The trade barriers that remain between the EU and US are either the result of differences in regulation between the US and EU, or long-standing unresolved trade disputes in sensitive, and politically salient, sectors. In the past decade, the EU and US have pursued a trade agenda that attempts to deal with these two issues. Transatlantic economic relations have been dominated by a "deep" trade agenda, with pressure from economic actors on both sides to negotiate agreements on domestic rules, not just measures at the border (Arujo, 2013; Young & Peterson, 2006). Issues where firms would like to see greater regulatory harmonization include product safety standards (for example, in food, pharmaceuticals, and the auto industry), data privacy issues, procurement rules, and specific measures in sectors such as aviation and telecoms. Duplicative product testing and requirements for different packaging and labeling in these areas, they argue, cause unnecessary costs which are then passed onto consumers (Hamilton & Quinlan, 2013, p. 27).

The focus on regulation and standards rather than tariffs has turned trade negotiations into something of a regulatory arms race. On the European side, the emphasis on improving competition within the single market has put pressure on trade negotiators to emphasize regulatory change in external negotiations (De Bièvre, 2006; McGuire & Smith, 2008). Particularly in the earliest stages of the Doha Round, the EU showed its willingness to push its own regulatory standards forward in an attempt to propagate them (McGuire & Lindeque, 2010, p. 1338).

The New Transatlantic Economic Partnership was established in 2007 to do the same for transatlantic trade relations, negotiated under the influence of the Merkel and Bush Administrations. This agreement created the Transatlantic Economic Council (TEC), a bilateral institution charged with the task of creating a more integrated transatlantic economy.

The TEC initially had a very narrow focus, attempting to deal with persistent trade disputes between the two polities. However, over time, its agenda has evolved to become an instrument of the "deep" transatlantic trade agenda, attempting to both reduce existing regulatory barriers to trade, and to ensure that new regulations (dealing with emerging technologies, for example) are designed to be compatible between the two trading partners. The TEC has made some progress, including on an agreement to promote cooperation on agriculture, and greater consensus surrounding sanitary/phytosanitary and food safety standards, financial regulation, and intellectual property rights (Ahearn, 2012, p. 5).

The key problem is that the high politics of agreeing to cooperate are distinct from the low politics of operationalizing regulatory harmonization, which are much more difficult. The EU and US genuinely have very different ideas about how to regulate things like food (including GMOs), cars, chemicals, and pharmaceuticals. Both have well-developed existing standards and industrialized economies, so there is no "natural" underdog, no trade-dependent state that can be induced to adopt the standards of the hegemonic power. In areas where there has been substantial progress between the EU and US, for example on the transatlantic recognition of products certified as organic, this progress relies heavily on mutual recognition of standards rather than harmonization. In this process, rather than making standards identical US product standards are recognized by the EU as equivalent to its own standards, and vice versa. Mutual recognition agreements can therefore produce real economic benefits, but their effectiveness in preserving existing levels of public protection in some areas is questionable.

The many civil society dialogues set up under the NTA (see Chapter 5) proved ultimately to be weak mechanisms with which to construct a robust transatlantic agenda for trade. The environmental dialogue ceased to exist in 2001 (when the Bush Administration dropped all efforts to include environmental issues in the US trade agenda), and the labor dialogue quickly petered out when trades unions expressed the opinion that the dialogue was worthless given the strong influence of businesses over the process. The result was a narrow transatlantic agenda that did not receive "buy-in" from many key actors outside of business interests (Compa & Meyer, 2010; Meyer & Barber, 2011).

The TTIP is the latest attempt by the US and EU to address regulatory barriers to trade. Announced in February 2013, negotiations for the TTIP began in July 2013, with the aim of reducing barriers to trade (both regulatory barriers as well as tariffs) and improving the harmonization of investment rules between the two trading powers.

Why do the EU and US want this new agreement? The most recent multi-lateral round of trade negotiations overseen by the WTO, the Doha Development Round, was suspended in 2006 after years of sporadic negotiations. The US and EU trade delegations returned home in ignominy after the negotiations degraded into name calling and vitriol. Trade conflicts between the US and the EU, most prominently over agricultural policy and trade in services, played a significant part in this collapse. The WTO process has since ground on behind the scenes, and although progress has been made, the measures agreed to date are substantially less ambitious than those envisioned in the original Doha Development Agenda.

Why start a new round of complex negotiations now, given that many fundamental disagreements between the US and EU remain? According to statements made by Karel de Gucht, the EU's Trade Commissioner, there are three main reasons for negotiating the TTIP.

The first argument posits that enabling more trade will increase economic growth. De Gucht points out that the EU and US together constitute 50% of global economic output. The negotiators estimate that the trade agreement will add half a percentage point of GDP growth to the US and EU economies. De Gucht (2013) has described the TTIP as "the cheapest stimulus package you can imagine," estimated to add a significant number of jobs to the US and EU economies. (See also Chapter 13's discussion).

The US enters this new round of negotiations in a slightly better economic position than the EU. At the time of writing, the US is slowly pulling itself out of recession, painstakingly adding jobs, and its housing market is recovering, although all this could still change. Major economies in the EU, however, face severe economic challenges and their ability to recover is uncertain. In contrast, the south of Europe is in dire straits – rapidly losing population and facing incredibly high unemployment, especially among young people. Europe's "success story," Germany, is barely growing, and faces manufacturing competition from emerging economies such as China.

Second, the rhetoric behind the TTIP is somewhat defensive. Negotiators point out that emerging economies are becoming more competitive markets for trade and investment, arguing that a new agreement is necessary in order to "keep up" with large, growing economies such as China and Brazil and to protect European and American businesses and investors from unfair practices in other states. Today's transatlantic trade agenda is notably distinct for its emphasis upon protecting the rights of investors and intellectual property holders. What business lobbies crave in this time of uncertainty is not "free" trade, per se, it is legal certainty and harmonization. Businesses and investors want to lock-in rules and get rid of regulatory impediments to transatlantic trade.

Finally, the EU and US see the new transatlantic agenda as a key catalyst for the slowly progressing Doha Round of trade negotiations. Because the transatlantic economic relationship weighs so heavily on the global economy, any EU–US consensus on key standards also significantly influences the baseline for multilateral negotiations. Given the Bali Package of measures agreed at the WTO ministerial meeting in December 2013, and the progression of the negotiations from this agreement to trickier trade issues, it is in the interests of these two trading powers to cooperate to secure a satisfactory conclusion to the round.

Domestic Institutions and Transatlantic Trade

Because modern trade policy deals with regulation, trade and investment agreements have become the source of even more intense political conflict. Companies that manufacture goods mainly for export are likely to support low tariffs and regulatory harmonization, while firms or farms that produce for the domestic market are more likely to demand protection from foreign imports. Consumer groups might desire the cheaper products that result from increased trade, but also have concerns about the quality or safety of imported products. Trades unions raise objections to trade agreements that they feel will undermine the position of their members at home and/or increase the ability of multinational corporations to exploit foreign workers (Elliott & Freeman 2003). Environmentalists likewise oppose the exploitation of environmental resources, as well as the expansion of trade in goods that might harm the environment, such as GMO crops (made from genetically modified organisms). Development and human rights NGOs question the ability of industrialized countries to impose the rules of trade upon less developed, less powerful, states. And public health advocates criticize trade and investment agreements that could potentially undermine public health goals such as expanding access to cheaper pharmaceuticals or decreasing the use of tobacco products (Shaffer, Waitzkin, Brenner, & Jasso-Aguilar, 2005). On many of these issues, substantial disagreements exist between groups in the EU and those in the US.

Understandably, in order for any trade policy to exist at all, this political conflict must be mediated. Most industrialized states do this by delegating the authority to negotiate trade agreements from the legislature to the executive branch. By making trade policy a more technocratic matter and less an issue of the ballot box, it is argued, governments can negotiate agreements with other states without being extensively tied by domestic interests.

This is, of course, an overly simplistic notion, and the successful negotiation of a trade agreement does not guarantee its successful ratification. In the US Constitution, the power to negotiate international agreements lies with the executive, while Congress has the sole power to regulate commerce with other states (Destler, 2005). US Administrations since the mid-1970s have sought to overcome this impasse by persuading Congress to delegate trade negotiating power to the executive. Under this "fast-track" negotiating authority (renamed Trade Promotion Authority in 2002 by the Bush Administration in order to avoid the negative connotations of the fast-track debates under Clinton) trade agreements are negotiated by the executive branch in consultation with Congressional committees, then put forward for an up or down vote in both the House and the Senate. Amendments to the implementing bill are not permitted, and the measure cannot be filibustered.

The trade policy process in the EU owes much of its intellectual origins to the procedures adopted by the US. For much of the EU's history, bureaucrats in the

European Commission have negotiated trade agreements, acting on an agenda proposed by the Commission and approved by the Council, with very little input from the European Parliament (EP). Trade policy has thus been somewhat removed from the purview of elected representatives.

But recently, this institutional separation has changed. The Lisbon Treaty (TFEU) gives the EP the authority to approve or reject trade agreements and places framework agreements under the co-decision procedure, now known as the "ordinary legislative procedure" or OLP. Under the OLP, regulations can only be adopted if they are approved by both the Council and the EP. The TFEU also expands the EU's Common Commercial Policy to bring important issues such as FDI, services, and trade-related intellectual property rights more firmly under the purview of the central EU institutions rather than leaving them to individual member states, at least in theory (Hillman & Kleimann, 2010, p. 3). The balance of power between the Community and member states in trade policy is complex and has varied by issue and over time as a result of the Court of Justice of the European Union (CJEU) jurisprudence and inter-institutional bargaining. (See, for example, Meunier & Nicolaidis, 2000.) This means a longer legislative process, particularly if the Council and EP do not agree (Hillman & Kleinmann, 2010, p. 3).

So far this theoretical greater influence has only been empirically tested on a few occasions. The TTIP could prove a major test of the OLP and the ability of member state governments and the Commission to overcome factions in the EP and the lobbies that will attempt to influence parliamentarians.

There is already some evidence that a more influential parliament has attracted greater attention from large corporations and their lobbies. In recent months, the tobacco and food industries have proven that their considerable resources make them effective lobbyists for corporate interests in the EP (Kurzer, 2013). There is every reason to hypothesize that rather than better representation of the views of Europeans in trade policy, the TFEU may well strengthen the representation of already powerful corporate interests in trade negotiations. The future of EU trade policy could prove to be more US-style lobbying, without the presence of the mandatory lobbying reporting found in the US. The EU's system is substantially more voluntary, and not nearly as transparent.

Nevertheless, the EP has demonstrated that it can reject international trade agreements that it does not like. In July 2012, the EP rejected the ACTA, the Anti-Counterfeiting Trade Agreement negotiated between the EU, US, and nine other industrialized states, by 478 votes to 39, with 165 MEPs abstaining. A press release issued by the EP after the vote claims that "Parliament experienced unprecedented direct lobbying by thousands of EU citizens who called on it to reject ACTA, in street demonstrations, e-mails to MEPs and calls to their offices" (European Parliament, 2012a).

Intellectual property provisions in trade and investment agreements are almost unique in that they are essentially protectionist in nature. Where most other elements of trade policy are concerned with liberalizing markets and removing barriers to trade, intellectual property provisions are designed as legal tools to protect the rights of property holders against unfair competition, for example from generic medicines or counterfeit merchandise. If it enters into force, ACTA would establish an international organization to oversee intellectual property rights – separate from existing bodies such as the WTO or World Intellectual Property Organization. MEPs expressed opposition to the agreement on the grounds that the agreement was vague and could therefore be construed in such a way as to be harmful to the civil liberties of EU citizens (European Parliament, 2012a).

It remains to be seen whether big lobbies or public opinion will hold more sway over the EP's trade policy decision-making. The TTIP is likely to include an investor–state dispute mechanism, intended to allow investors to sue national governments for compensation over changes to domestic regulations that damage the value of their investments, as well as many ACTA-like elements that many NGOs consider to be harmful to the public interest.

Last, but by no means least, member state governments themselves have a tendency to disrupt trade negotiations. Although the EU is supposed to speak with "one voice" in trade negotiations, this does not mean that member states are content to sit silently on the sidelines of the negotiations. France, for example, is a frequent offender in this regard, and it is not uncommon to see French ministers in the international media openly criticizing the current state of the negotiations for failing to protect groups such as farmers or the film industry. With regard to the TTIP, France has voiced opposition to the negotiations on the grounds that the EU should not be negotiating with a trading partner that has been caught spying on European institutions (France24, 2013).

These changes in the EU's legislative process have resulted in a degree of convergence between the trade policy process in the EU and in the US. In the US, the potential for the legislature to cause disruption to trade negotiations is already substantial. The Obama Administration does not currently have fast-track negotiating authority – and in order to obtain it, Congress must vote to constrain its own power. Michael Froman, confirmed as the United State Trade Representative (USTR) in June 2013, has communicated the Obama Administration's intention to pursue fresh fast-track authority, and at the time of writing draft legislation was under consideration. (See Chapter 13 of this volume for further discussion of fast-track authority.) This authority will be required in order to negotiate two major trade agreements – the TTIP and the TransPacific Partnership (TPP) with a group of other countries bordering the Pacific. Notably, the draft legislation attempts to clarify and strengthen Congressional input into the trade negotiation process in response to concerns raised by representatives about being unable to access the draft text of trade agreements.

Despite the frequently cited (and somewhat overblown) existence of Congressional "bipartisanship" on trade issues, the Obama Administration will find it difficult to get Congress to agree to delegate its power over trade in the current political environment. Trade is frequently a wedge issue for Democrats, and many Democratic candidates want to reassure businesses of their free trade credentials, while key trades union supporters in industrial swing states frequently oppose free trade agreements (FTAs). Even if the Obama Administration should hold fast-track authority as well as control of the Senate, conservative and anti-global representatives in the House are an unpredictable element of the equation.

Transatlantic trade and investment cooperation relies, in part, on the ability of domestic political institutions to provide a clear mandate for negotiations. But when the trade agenda focuses more heavily on regulatory harmonization, that mandate can be harder to achieve.

Conclusion: How Deep Is Your Trade Agenda?

Much of modern transatlantic trade policy emerges from "low politics." The transatlantic economic relationship as a whole is undoubtedly important to the survival of the US and to European states. But it is a very healthy relationship, resilient even during the recent economic downturn. And it is an economic relationship largely characterized by free exchange. Tariffs in most sectors are low. Inter-regional investment is very high, as are levels of protection for investors. Serious formal conflicts between the two trading partners do exist (for example, over hormone-treated beef, bananas, and airplanes) but most of the time diplomacy alone is enough to settle trade disputes.

Despite this, firms on both sides of the Atlantic see economic benefits in tackling the remaining barriers to trade. Many of these are regulatory rather than tariff barriers. There are undoubtedly many inefficient and costly regulatory barriers to trade between the EU and US that could be removed or updated. But to what extent is it possible to separate inconvenient red tape from important rules that protect public interests? There are legitimate differences of opinion between the US and EU on food safety and environmental regulations. And one important area of conflict between the US and EU, the regulation of personal data, has been the subject of disturbing revelations on both sides of the Atlantic, making public opinion on the issue highly salient to any negotiations. To what extent will there be effective public scrutiny of this process? We might well ask: Should regulatory harmonization be sought in this way, through relatively closed bilateral negotiations, with comparatively little transparency?

This is not an academic or marginal question. The economic crisis in the EU has seen a great deal of decision-making power ceded to bureaucrats – both technocrats in member states and officials in the European Central Bank, European Commission, and International Monetary Fund. European citizens themselves have arguably had few opportunities to influence the debates that have led to formal balanced budget requirements and austerity plans, despite widespread protest and the defeat of several member state governments in elections (Greer, 2013). Civil society groups and the wider public have already indicated their opposition to the TTIP process on many of the same grounds. We should not expect future transatlantic economic integration to be forthcoming without considerable political turmoil.

8   Transatlantic Competition Policy

Nikolaos Zahariadis

Introduction

Despite considerable promise since the inception of the New Transatlantic Agenda (NTA) in 1995, transatlantic cooperation in competition policy remains uneven and somewhat limited. Some cooperation has been achieved in the form of annual meetings, exchange of information, and enforcement processes, but significantly less in other competition areas than analysts had come to expect. Why? I use the concepts of positive and negative integration to argue the limits of cooperation are framed by escalating transaction costs in two areas: (1) the preferences of political leaders and government officials; and (2) business firms. Institutional divergence, disinterested leadership, and periodically adverse macroeconomic conditions expose weaknesses in the current international framework. I conclude that a framework resembling negative integration under certain conditions reduces transaction costs and propels business firms to demand enhanced cooperation.

Competition policy is very important. It is the essence of Adam Smith's invisible hand and a main staple of the NTA. Its goal is to stimulate competition in order to give transatlantic consumers the greatest choice of goods and services at the lowest possible prices. Markets operate most efficiently, and benefits to society are maximized, when markets are fully competitive. Sometimes they are not. Increased economic activity across borders, especially a flurry of global mergers and acquisitions since the 1990s, as well as technological progress and liberalization of domestic markets, pose major challenges for governments and consumers alike (Monti, 2001). For this reason, governments have developed regulatory mechanisms which enhance, or prevent abuses to, competition among business firms. The scope of mechanisms ranges from regulating mergers to preventing predatory behavior to punishing cartels.

The chapter follows a "most likely" case design. The case is an important area of economic activity where the European Commission enjoys almost exclusive competence, making negotiations and agreement more likely. Because many firms operate on both sides of the Atlantic, they are expected to demand similar sets of rules and procedures to reduce friction and increase profitability of their global operations. Yet less progress than expected has been achieved so far. Why? Competition policy is first placed within the context of globalization.

I identify the globalization paradox and specify the impact of transaction costs in cases of positive and negative integration. These costs escalate depending on the degree of institutional divergence, the strength of political leadership, and domestic business preferences which influence political willingness to cooperate. I then identify the obstacles inhibiting further cooperation in competition policy since the early 1990s and draw implications for the future of transatlantic economic relations.

The Globalization Paradox and the Cost of Positive Integration

The NTA was established in response to problems emanating from increasing global integration, a process that is encapsulated by the term globalization in the form of increased economic activity and interdependence across national economies. I am only interested in a single dimension, competition policy. In a thoughtful book, Slaughter (2005) identifies a peculiarity of increasing globalization. On the one hand, she informs, globalization creates a series of collective problems, e.g., financial crises, climate change, and others. What makes these problems important are size and destructive potential. Because they are enormous in scale and scope, only global responses can hope to address them. On the other hand, world government is both unrealistic and indefensible from a democratic point of view, limiting the scope of meaningful responses. The way to foster greater firm competition across national jurisdictions is to reduce transaction costs when firms move across national boundaries. Cooperation (or progress toward agreement) in the transatlantic area takes the form of policy harmonization through the diffusion of superior norms, which former US Federal Trade Commission (FTC) Chairman William Kovacic (2008, p. 10) defines as best practices that promote accurate diagnosis of competition problems and design timely, corrective government intervention. How can this be achieved?

The literature on European integration identifies two distinct modes of enhanced cooperation: positive and negative integration (Majone, 2005, chapter 7; Pinder, 1968). Decoupling the argument from its European context, positive integration, or enhanced cooperation, involves creating international agencies which apply commonly agreed rules to iron out national and regional differences. Negative integration achieves the same goal by lowering barriers to economic transactions across national boundaries in the form of sharing information or improving enforcement capabilities, but not changing legal or institutional frameworks. The transaction costs between the two modes are significantly different. In the case of positive integration, costs are much higher for two reasons. The first refers to additional resources that need to be found in order to create and staff the agencies which will monitor activities. The second refers to political and diplomatic resources that need to be expended to come up with commonly accepted rules. Negative integration achieves agreement by reducing costs via the elimination of barriers. Preference for one mode over the other depends on issue area and who bears the cost and benefit of adjustment.

Prospect theory claims actors are loss averse, that is, they value losses more than they do gains (Kahneman & Tversky, 1979). The implication is that because transatlantic agreement is very difficult, success is more likely when negotiations focus on losses rather than benefits from regulatory cooperation. Keeping the issue area constant, competition policy, the analysis focuses on lowering cost. International regulatory cooperation often raises significant conflicts over distributive consequences because the cost of alternative proposals falls on different actors. Once adopted, standards frequently face enforcement problems because "states are tempted to defect from the cooperative solution under pressure from domestic constituencies" (Verdier, 2009, p. 115).

Costs are borne by regulatory providers and/or consumers: either government officials and policymakers or business firms. Individual consumers are less important actors because, first, cost is small and widely distributed and benefits are not immediately obvious, and second, consumers are not well organized or politically powerful (Olson, 1965). Therefore, cost fluctuates according to the willingness of governments to supply regulatory coordination and the demand by firms to lower trans-jurisdictional costs. Of course both the US and the EU have well developed and distinct competition regimes, implying significant institutional divergence in both structure, i.e., the agencies that supply regulation, and norms, i.e., the rules and logic that define and regulate competition among firms in a particular jurisdiction. Differences between the two regimes are such that the cost and nature of change are considerable. New agencies must be staffed by individuals trained to operate under different rules. Agreement at the transatlantic level also implies zero-sum gains and losses. For the Europeans (Americans) to agree, their system must become a bit more like the US (EU) system in which US (EU) firms will have a first-mover's advantage.

Looking at each side separately, who bears the relatively higher cost of change: bureaucrats and policymakers or business firms? It is clear change affects the core activities of agencies so governments will have to change more. Firms will also bear some cost because of changes in the regulatory environment, but change will not necessarily affect their core activities or substantially change their profits. Demands for change of the status quo, i.e., more transatlantic regulatory agreement, will have to come from changes in the cost structure of business firms. Assuming things stay the same, governments have incentives to agree to disagree. Therefore, firms must demand change. They do so when their cost of additional business across national boundaries increases relative to their regulatory burden.

There are three ways to change this ratio. The first is through changes in institutional structure and/or legal norms. Businesses that operate in more than one jurisdiction have an incentive to ask for similar procedures in other jurisdictions or one-stop-shop to minimize the cost of seeking approval or complying with regulatory demands. *The greater the divergence in institutional structure and/or legal norms, the greater the cost of positive integration will be.*

The second way is through political leadership. No changes are possible without political support or pressure because changes involve negotiations among governments. Specifying a common regulatory framework involves considerable economic and political cost that is unevenly spread. Businesses and politicians have incentives to gain concessions on their own terms, in effect minimizing the cost of adjusting to new rules. For this reason, *political cost is lower and cooperation is more likely when forms of negative integration are sought*, such as soft law or strengthening enforcement, as opposed to positive integration, which may involve the creation of new agencies or changes in domestic legislation.

The third way to alter cost structure is through changes in the macroeconomic environment. The two factors already enumerated explain why policymakers or firms may demand cooperation. Macroeconomic conditions affect when these demands are most vocal. Periods of lower economic growth, higher government budget deficits, or financial crises, reduce the intensity of calls for more regulatory cooperation. The regulatory burden stays the same, while economic activity falls. When times are good, the loss of potential added business relative to regulation increases. Firms demand more cooperation because they stand to lose more if cooperation is not forthcoming. However, in light of reduced economic activity or in countries which are less exposed to world markets and are therefore stuck with fewer choices for expanded activities, there are fewer demands for cooperation. Stated more formally, *cooperation in competition policy is more likely under favorable macroeconomic conditions*.

There is one more factor to reducing cost: rapid advances in technology. Such changes lead to the multinational spread of enterprises (Vernon, 1998), which in turn demand common rules to maximize profits. The best way to test this argument empirically is to compare periods of rapid (and not) advances. Unfortunately, my time frame is too short; there is no reason to assume that any year since the NTA's inception is more or less conducive to technological advances. For this reason, a relatively constant rate of technological innovation is assumed during the period under examination.

The argument has a policy implication: Remove barriers to economic exchange across jurisdictions while leaving regulatory structures and norms in their current state. Enhanced economic opportunities for some increase losses of potential profits for others. Assuming the denominator stays the same, the ratio increases, implying added pressure by business on governments. Agreement will lower the cost of doing transatlantic business. In other words, agreement is more likely in the case of negative rather than positive integration.

Cooperation and Competition under the NTA

As explained in Chapter 2 of this volume, one of the reasons why transatlantic negotiations often break down is the inability of Europe to often speak with one voice. There is a difference between institutional and political authority. Even in areas where the European Commission is charged with negotiating external agreements (Article 218 of the Treaty on the Functioning of the European Union [TFEU]), there is considerable political pressure to support or oppose the Commission either on the part of European governments, eager to protect national interest, or on the part of the US government, eager to soften opposition to demands for concessions. The EU–US Bilateral Competition Agreement (BCA) (Damro, 2006) and EU–US Open Skies (Delreux, 2011) negotiations are good examples of the power and limitations of the Commission. Nevertheless, cooperation has progressed most in competition policy, an area where the Commission has been delegated exclusive competence and implementation (a model that Coeuré & Pisani-Ferry, 2007 label unconditional delegation). Theories stressing bargaining power as the determinant of leverage in negotiations hypothesize that market size and the number of negotiators determines the ability of one side to gain the upper hand in getting concessions from the other (Meunier, 2005, p. 43). Yet there is still considerable resistance to pursuing forms of positive integration on the part of both EU and US officials.

There are several reasons why transatlantic cooperation in competition policy has not moved further along. To be sure, much has happened since the BCA was signed in 1991 which led to the NTA and the broader Transatlantic Economic Partnership (TEP) launched in May 1998. On the basis of the TEP's Action Plan, a memorandum on guidelines for regulatory cooperation was drafted and approved in 2002. The purpose has been to remove barriers to merchandise trade and improve dialogue between the EU and the US. By 2005 the Initiative to Enhance Transatlantic Economic Integration and Growth (IETEIG) was launched. One of its priorities calls for building "effective mechanisms to promote better quality regulation, minimize unnecessary regulatory divergences to facilitate transatlantic trade and investment and increase consumer confidence in the transatlantic market" (United States and European Union, 2005, Annex 4). In 2007, the Transatlantic Economic Council (TEC) was established as a political body to promote integration and enhance regulatory compatibility. Despite progress, however, institutional divergence, weak political leadership, and adverse economic conditions have kept the two sides apart. These factors in turn increase the cost of positive integration.

Institutional Divergence

Despite some similarities in institutional structures, the two sides are still quite apart in terms of norms and legal philosophies.

Structures

The US has a complicated, litigation-oriented environment. It is centered on two main agencies: the Antitrust Division of the Department of Justice and the FTC. Both agencies have extensive jurisdiction although they differ significantly in terms of enforcement capabilities. The FTC makes decisions and renders opinions which can be subject to litigation in the court system, while the Antitrust Division operates in a more litigious fashion, prosecuting cases and enforcing antitrust laws. In contrast to the EU system, companies in the US run the risk of criminal sanctions and civil lawsuits (Damro, 2005; E. M. Fox, 1997, p. 66).

The EU system is more bureaucratic, broader, and regulatory in nature. The laws are enforced through a system of notifications, exemptions, and block exemptions. Approval is based on negative clearance, meaning that it is the default decision unless the European Commission's relevant Competition Directorate General (DG Comp) decides to open an investigation or requests additional information with a view to rendering a negative decision. The biggest problem with enforcement in price-fixing, predatory pricing, and the like is the level and quality of enforcement. The US system employs more legal experts, including a substantial number of specially trained economists. The EU system is thin on human resources, relying far more on national experts seconded to the Commission for specific tasks. While DG Comp used to be staffed mainly by lawyers (Cini & McGowan, 1998), it has since acquired more economic expertise with the addition of the Office of Chief Competition Economist in 2003 following a string of decisions overturned by the ECJ (Röller & Buigues, 2005). Moreover, DG Comp is charged with monitoring, approving or rejecting state aid, an issue that has no comparable agency in the US.

The essence of institutional divergence leads to different incentives for both governments and firms. On the one hand, even US-based firms operating on a global scale and engaging in international mergers prefer the EU system in some instances. Despite its bureaucratic nature, the process contains specific rules, stages, and deadlines which make it more predictable (Dewatripont & Legros, 2009, p. 91). On the other hand, global trade might magnify divergences because both jurisdictions must rule on the same case. It is possible they may seek cooperation and compromise in the process, but it is unlikely either jurisdiction will rule in defiance of domestic law or politics. The General Electric-Honeywell (2001) case is instructive in the different ways evidence is used to make a ruling. But politics is clearly evident in some cases, especially those that involve major domestic companies. For example, while the Boeing–McDonnell Douglas merger was approved by the FTC possibly for reasons of industrial policy, it was rejected by DG Comp for similar reasons, i.e., to protect Airbus (Dewatripont & Legros, 2009, p. 92). The point is not that there will only be divergence; rather institutional differences are highlighted to stress higher costs shaping the limits to convergence.

Norms

The statutes covering competition issues in both jurisdictions differ significantly. US statutes are concise and subject to judicial interpretation. Through more than a century-old litigation, a body of law has been established that leaves little room to the federal government for policymaking or adjustment. In contrast, EU law is governed by the Treaties of Paris and Rome, later incorporated into the TFEU (Articles 101–109) and interpreted by the European Commission subject to appeal before the General Court (formerly the Court of First Instance). First, the statutes operative in both economies are worded differently (Rosch, 2012). The Sherman Act in the US forbids unreasonable restraints on trade (Section 1) and outlaws monopolies or attempts at establishing monopolies (Section 2). In contrast, the relevant Articles (101 and 102) of the TFEU are broader in scope and more specifically worded. Article 101 forbids restrictive, preventive, or distortive practices to free trade but permits undertakings that meet specific criteria, such as those that promote economic development but also supply consumer benefits. In other words, although the US criterion of unreasonableness is left up to appellate courts to decide, EU law explicitly prohibits most undertakings but it permits some as determined by the European Commission and subject to adjudication.

Second, the different legal cultures provide for significantly different interpretations of the law and legal procedures. EU competition law is inspired by a different legal culture from the US. The fact that Europe did not have a rigorous competition regime in place until recently (at least relative to the US) suggests that different national legal traditions vied for controlling EU competition processes. Most countries in the EU did not have a solid competition regime in place, save for the UK and Germany, until the late 1980s. The deepening of integration through the single market provided the impetus for the development of such regimes inside most member states (Amato, 1997), in addition to giving EU institutions more de facto and *de jure* competence vis-à-vis national authorities (Woolcock, 2007, p. 224).

There is a tendency in the EU to acknowledge non-economic factors as major components of EU competition policy. Part of the rationale goes back to the Treaty of Paris, which sought to diminish discriminatory practices on national grounds, linking transnational competition policy to trade liberalization (Motta, 2004, p. 14). The Treaty of Rome later added the aim of forbidding practices that distort the Common Market (Scherer, 1994, p. 35). Writing in 1995 as Competition Commissioner, Karel Van Miert clarifies his stance: "Competition policy does not operate in a vacuum. It must take into account its effects on other areas of the Commission action, such as industrial, regional, social, and environmental policies" (cited in Kingston, 2012, pp. 32–33). Critical of this tendency, Amato (1997) argues that fundamentally political institutions, like the Commission, are bound to make economically inefficient decisions which can only lead to suboptimal outcomes. Central to this view is the broader theory of ordoliberalism (the so-called Freiburg School), which views private economic power as inherently antithetical to the competitive economic process (Gerber, 2001).

In contrast, US competition law has been influenced by the Chicago School of microeconomics (E. M. Fox, 1997; Rosch, 2012). It sees competition in much narrower terms, especially when considering the role of dominant position and monopolistic behavior. For US legal scholars and economists, potential harm and economic power are seen as short-term effects on price and output. As FTC chairman Thomas Rosch (2012, p. 7) confirms, there is no inherent, long-term abuse of private economic power unless it can be demonstrated in short-term consequences. Even in areas where the two legal traditions are in broad agreement, such as that competition policy should promote consumer welfare, there is disagreement between established traditions in the US, which defines welfare as that of all consumers in society as opposed to the narrower EU view of welfare only in relevant output markets. For this reason, the two jurisdictions differ in terms of how they view predatory pricing, bundled discounts, loyalty discounts, price squeezes, and the like (Hay & McMahon, 2012; Rosch, 2012, pp. 12, 15).

The end result implies norm convergence is costly. This is especially true when considering the cost of creating new agencies or seeking to draft new legislation with exacting monitoring requirements that addresses existing problems. The institutional structures are significantly different to not justify the cost of creating new institutions or legislation through positive integration. Besides, the cost of harmonizing laws and regulations to boost cooperation would simply be politically insurmountable as it would involve policymakers from both sides of the Atlantic seeking to shape the outcome to lower the cost of their home-based business expanding in the other jurisdiction's territory. As early as 2000, Evenett, Lehmann, and Steil (2000, p. 19) note the limited appetite by both sides "to harmonize competition policy standards or to adopt core minimum standards." Part of the continued state of divergence has to do with uncertainty over distributive consequences and differences in enforcement styles. Competition policy and its remedies rely heavily on market structure, e.g., ease of entry, horizontal and vertical obstacles, firm size and access to distribution networks, taxation regimes, and others. Because US and EU markets are structured differently, the same remedy to the same infraction would have dramatically different consequences in each market. Moreover, as Nicholas Forwood, Judge at the General Court in Luxembourg, noted at a roundtable, 90% of enforcement in the US still depends on private civil action lawsuits. In Europe, enforcement is very much the task of European or national regulators (Friends of Europe, 2010, p. 13).

Weak Political Leadership

Leadership in improving transatlantic cooperation may take two forms. On the one hand, bureaucrats may seek out cooperation under their discretionary authority in order to limit domestic political intervention. Such cooperation is limited, however, because it magnifies information asymmetries. On the other hand, policymakers might seek to undermine cooperation by not pursuing it vigorously as a result of extraneous issues and concerns. In both cases, more cooperation is better achieved through less costly "soft" regulation, which essentially means non-binding, information-seeking cooperation subject to domestic legal and political constraints.

Bureaucrats might seek to enhance cooperation in order to increase their discretionary authority. Using a principal–agent model, Damro (2006) explains the signing of the BCA in 1991 by reference to three points. First, economic globalization raises the likelihood of concurrent jurisdictions. To avoid making divergent decisions, regulatory agents seek enhanced cooperation. Second, the form cooperation will take depends on the ability of agents to minimize the cost to their discretionary behavior. Third, policymakers will intervene to prevent agent shirking, i.e., increasing discretionary authority, when the cost of non-intervention exceeds the cost of intervention. I add to this argument the increasing cost of positive integration. Enhanced cooperation is more likely when integration takes the form of negative integration, i.e., removing barriers to trade and exchanging information. Such market-making mechanisms are at the heart of negative integration. They are also more likely to be the provenance of non-majoritarian institutions, such as the European Commission. Because the latter lack democratic legitimacy, they are more likely to be effective in addressing issues in ways that lower the cost of governance (Majone, 2005; Scharpf, 1999).

By early 1990 it was clear that increasing economic exchange improved the chances of overlapping jurisdiction of competition cases, especially cases of mergers and acquisitions and abuses of dominant position. Sir Leon Brittan, Competition Commissioner at the time, opted not to increase EU legal extraterritoriality. By preventing or limiting transatlantic disputes, regulatory authorities hoped to increase access to non-confidential information and establish channels of consultation that limited economic and political cost. Seeking to avoid lengthy ratification battles by establishing a formal treaty, US authorities sought to create a non-binding agreement (Damro, 2006, p. 184). Sensing a possible political challenge, Commissioner Brittan quickly moved to do the same. However, a legal challenge by member states led by the French government nullified the BCA. The Court ruled the Commission had overstepped its institutional boundary. As a result, the Commission later presented a request for approval to the Council of the European Union. It succumbed to principal demands to respect confidentiality of information and engage in transparency of process, which essentially mandated the Commission would notify relevant member governments should it receive information by US competition authorities that might adversely affect their national interests (or businesses). Following clarifications and concessions, the Council and the Commission officially approved and implemented the agreement by making it one of the high priorities of the NTA. The NTA noted the need to address "technical and non-tariff barriers to trade" in what it called "a New Transatlantic Marketplace" (EU & US, 1995, p. 5).

Factors Exposing Political Weakness

Cooperation has since improved through the TEP. Nevertheless, two major factors mark the political climate and help shape and limit transatlantic cooperation. The 9/11 attacks on the US and the subsequent War on Terror have had a profound effect on US politics and its foreign relations. Similarly, the launch of the world trade talks in Doha and its subsequent demise since Cancun in 2003 have given pause to initial enthusiasm for cooperation by exposing fundamental political and economic differences (but see Chapter 7 for guarded optimism following trade talks in Bali in December 2013).

The War on Terror

Although driven by security concerns, the War on Terror has had a significant effect on competition cases in two ways. First, of particular interest are the Mutual Assistance Legal Treaties (MLAT) negotiated by the US and several EU member states, including one with the EU as a whole. The US–EU MLAT supplements existing treaties offering assistance in criminal investigations. For example, it "explicitly permits requests for bank and financial institution account information regarding persons or companies convicted of, or 'otherwise involved in', a criminal offence" (Sinan & Laciak, 2004, p. 32). Of particular significance is the ability of national competition authorities to seek assistance in connection with investigations with a view to prosecution. In a sense, authorities that do not have prosecutorial authority may now request information that aids in the prosecution of companies or individuals by the prosecuting authority in a different national jurisdiction.

The War on Terror has had both positive and negative effects. As noted above, it has provided a platform for enhanced cooperation in certain competition areas that were not possible before. However, it has also limited cooperation by exposing potential abuse of information gained within the framework and by turning public opinion in many European countries against more robust forms of cooperation (Hoese & Opermann, 2007). For example, in testimony before the US Senate in 2004, James Dobbins (2004) of the RAND corporation argued that following the terrorist attacks in Madrid, public opinion in Spain and other European countries turned resolutely against robust cooperation on fighting the war in Iraq and by extension giving more support to enhanced cooperation with the US government in this matter. The rationale is that support has increased the likelihood of attack on domestic populations in ways that were not likely before. Moreover, allegations of extraordinary rendition in Europe, such as the existence of "secret prisons," put pressure on policymakers to distance themselves from the US government. As Julianne Smith (2007, p. 9) said in her testimony before the US House of Representatives, political elites in Europe began to feel that "standing shoulder to shoulder with the United States" had become "a political liability." According to another observer, differences over the Iraq question "led many in Europe to look for alternatives to the existing structure of transatlantic relations," focusing on more European integration as a balance to perceived US hegemony (Sloan, 2011, p. 6). While these developments were unrelated to competition policy, they helped shape preferences for transatlantic cooperation, including competition policy, among many European policymakers. Unfortunately, the revelation of wiretapping telephone conversations of European private individuals and public officials by the National Security Agency (NSA) in 2013 was a major setback, eroding any gains in European trust and good will that had been built since President Bush left office.

World Trade Talks

The second factor of restraint was the launch of world trade talks in Doha. Their subsequent demise and the emergence of bitter rivalries in state aid and mergers epitomized by *Boeing v Airbus* dented appetite for additional cooperation. The TEP placed competition at the forefront of multilateral cooperation. Implicit was the commitment to begin world trade talks. This was achieved with fanfare in Doha, following unsuccessful attempts in Seattle and Genoa. However, inability to agree on the agenda and the subsequent collapse of talks in Cancun in 2003 became a major setback. There is room for guarded optimism following talks in Bali, where agreement was reached on simplifying customs procedures and improving access for goods from least developed countries (Elliott, 2013). Nevertheless, the main issues of discord remain intact. While competition is not at the heart of trade talks, inability to agree on subsidies to agriculture and the treatment of foreign direct investment (FDI) has exposed a serious rift in the transatlantic alliance in addition to more complicated issues among G-20 countries. More importantly, it has clarified interconnections between trade and competition. The drop in tariff barriers through several multilateral trade talks unfortunately have led to an increase in non-tariff barriers (NTBs) to economic entry (Blais, 1986; Scherer, 1994, p. 15). As governments began to limit their protection options at the border, they started contemplating protection inside domestic economies through the use of subsidies, national champion strategies, national security provisions, and employment-enhancing adjustment measures (Bhagwati, 1988; Zahariadis, 2008). Such behavior has led to more transatlantic acrimony by sharpening differences between the two regimes. Despite lobbying pressure to the contrary, there is a realization on both sides that international trade liberalization is an indispensable tool to strengthen competition in domestic markets (including public procurement) ranging from airlines to defense (Anderson & Kovacic, 2009). Nevertheless, trade disputes raise cost and limit cooperation in competition policy.

The dispute epitomizing the limits of cooperation is the bitter rivalry between Boeing and Airbus. To be sure, it is not representative of all differences between the two jurisdictions and it does not imply that relations are largely acrimonious. It simply illustrates the cost of competition in a highly visible case involving multi-level governance issues (because it involves national and sub-national governments and EU institutions). It also demonstrates linkages between trade and state aid (an area of direct purview by EU competition authorities) and limitations imposed by politics. Apart from skewing trade flows, state aid directly affects market structure in frequently opaque ways by discouraging new entrants and favoring domestic producers over their foreign counterparts (Zahariadis, 2008, pp. 5–6). The large civil aircraft industry is economically very important. Since the 1990s it has been mainly a duopoly with thousands of employees and high numbers of suppliers and customers spread around the globe. Moreover, it has considerable national security implications in light of heavy involvement of both companies in the defense sector.

Although disputes between the two companies go back to the early 1970s, the latest round began in 2004, with the US government withdrawing from bilateral negotiations and filing a complaint with the World Trade Organization (WTO) alleging German, French, British, and Spanish governments violated the WTO's agreement on subsidies and countervailing measures by providing illegal launch aid to the new Airbus A380 and A350 (WTO DS316). The EU immediately countered with its own complaint charging Boeing has benefited from decades of illegal NASA and defense contracts (WTO DS317 – no longer pursued – and DS353). The trigger appears to be Boeing's declining market share. By 1998 Airbus had gained 50% of global sales of large civil aircraft and in 2003 it sold more aircraft than Boeing for the first time ever (Kienstra, 2012, p. 577). Following nine years of litigation and appeals, the verdict gave both sides partial victory. In separate cases, the WTO Appellate Body found that Boeing had received at least $5 billion in illegal launch subsidies for the 787 and other aircraft while Airbus benefited from subsidized $15 billion loans and several billion in EU and national grants to develop its aircraft (Clark, 2012). Naturally, each side charged the other of not complying and sought WTO permission to retaliate.

There are two major challenges that keep the sides apart (Kienstra, 2012). The first revolves around the role of state aid. The fact that each company has benefited from different types of government support – more indirect aid in the form of contracts and tax breaks in the US and more direct aid in the form of grants and loans in the EU – poses difficulties in conducting direct comparisons of effects in the two jurisdictions. More importantly, "the differences will allow additional room for argument as to the comparative effects and permissibility of the respective programs and will require the parties to haggle over the limitations to be set on each form of subsidy rather than *setting a single standard applicable to both parties*" (emphasis added, Kienstra, 2012, p. 601). In other words, positive integration in the form of common standards is unlikely. The second obstacle refers to the entry of new competitors from Canada and Brazil in the near future. Bombardier and Embraer already compete successfully within the regional aircraft market, with Bombardier recently entering the low end of the narrow-body (737/A320) market. The Airbus–Boeing duopoly may be coming to an end (Ostrower & Van Hasselt, 2013). Under these conditions, neither the EU nor the US may want to set limits on their own activities without ensuring they also apply to emerging competitors. Confirming our expectation, transatlantic cooperation in this area is limited largely by political discord and to an extent issue linkages.

Adverse Domestic Economic Environment

The argument predicts more economic cooperation in good economic times and less when things go badly. To test it I examine robust calls for cooperation in the 1990s and contrast them with cooperation whispers since 2008. Figure 8.1 shows US and EU-27 economic growth rates since 1996. It sets the background against which preferences are articulated. Although both economies dipped in the early part of the 2000s, there is one main recessionary period: 2008–2010. Both economies came out of the recession in 2010, but US economic growth has hovered around 2%, whereas the EU has gone back into recession.

Serious divergence, in other words, has been experienced since 2010. Unemployment follows a somewhat similar trajectory (Figure 8.2). Although US unemployment has been consistently lower than that of the EU by an average of roughly 3% since 2000, both economies experienced massive layoffs since 2008. By 2010 the US rate spiked faster, reaching that of the EU-27 at 8.2%. However, as the US economy began to improve, unemployment declined to 6.8% in 2012. In contrast, the EU-27's rate continued to climb, reaching 10.9 in February 2013 (Eurostat, 2013). The EU average hides considerable variation. In Greece and Spain unemployment reached a gargantuan 26.4% and 26.3%, respectively, in

Figure 8.1 Economic Growth in the US and Europe, 1996–2012.

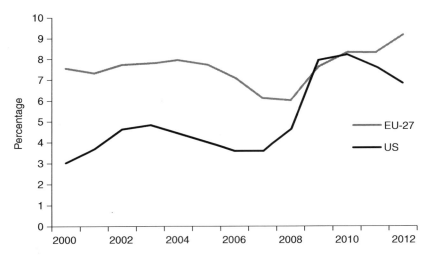

Figure 8.2 Unemployment in the US and Europe, 2000–2012.

February 2013 while it remained low at 4.8% and 5.4% in Austria and Germany during the same period (Eurostat, 2013).

These data indicate a period of covariance until 2010 but considerable divergence since then. We can draw two implications from these trajectories. First, despite similar conditions at roughly the same time, the two economies have responded very differently. Second, there are significant differences in impact across countries, leading to divergence in incentives and preferences for enhanced cooperation.

Despite some convergence in areas of information sharing and enforcement, analysts and practitioners alike question the need or utility for commonality of competition approaches. Adding a political dimension to macroeconomic conditions, Sophie in 't Veld, Vice Chairwoman of the European Parliament's Committee on Civil Liberties, Justice and Home Affairs and Rapporteur on Competition Policy, warned of growing reluctance and lower citizen confidence in the Commission's intervention. "If we have witnessed one thing coming out of the crisis," she added, "it is that the reluctance of people to accept EU competence is growing" (Friends of Europe, 2010, p. 11). Echoing this sentiment, Olli Rehn, then Commissioner for Economic and Monetary Affairs, admitted one year later the Commission faced strong challenges in the short-run in steering member states toward a common goal: "We have a support fatigue in some European countries, and there is a reform fatigue in others" (Friends of Europe, 2011, p. 17).

If nothing else, the crisis showed the difference between the US and the EU in tackling economic problems at home. US Ambassador to the EU William E. Kennard highlights the relative ease of the US to "act quickly, dramatically, and comprehensively" because it "does not depend on several sovereigns reaching consensus to implement reform" (Friends of Europe, 2011, p. 15).

Thus, this case study corroborates the discussion in Chapter 2 of this volume: it is precisely the absence of leadership in times of crisis that has undermined (or at least limited) EU response. Blyth and Matthijs (2012) boldly concur: "the structure – twenty-seven radically different member states and no leader – remains the main obstacle."

Not surprisingly, the number of initiatives and substantive cooperation has dropped in recent years following the surge of interest in the early 1990s. Between 1996 and 2005 only 10 EU competition agreements were signed with non-member states and international organizations relative to 17 in the previous 10 years (Coeuré & Pisani-Ferry, 2007, p. 59). Only one major initiative was signed since 2008; in 2011 the Best Practices agreement was revised. First signed in 2002, it provides advice for interagency cooperation and contains guidelines for prospective mergers between firms. Between 1991 and 1999, EU and US authorities notified each other in 689 merger and antitrust cases of mutual interest (Devuyst, 2001, p. 138). Although the number of merger notifications increased exponentially in each jurisdiction in subsequent years, the number of notifications of mergers of mutual interest remains subdued. For example, in 2002 the Commission received 277 merger notifications while US authorities dealt with 1,187 cases. Of them, 27 were notifications made by US authorities (9.7% of the Commission's workload) and 56 by the Commission (4.7% of the US workload) (European Commission, 2003; Gibson Dunn, 2012). After peaking in 2007 in both the EU and the US, merger cases continue to hover at 309 and 1,450 cases, respectively. These levels, reduced significantly since 2009, are still below those of 2005 and only 15% higher on average than 2002 levels (Gibson Dunn, 2012).

Conclusions

This chapter has considered the progress of convergence in transatlantic competition relations. Echoing Pollack's (2005) assessment that cooperation has been uneven with a highly variable pattern of effectiveness, the study proposes three major factors that explain why cooperation in competition policy has so far been limited. Structural divergence, weak political leadership, and adverse economic conditions inhibit further cooperation by increasing political and economic cost. This does not imply there will be no cooperation. The argument simply reflects the difficulties to be encountered should cooperation proceed in the form of positive integration.

There are three implications for theory and policy. First, trade and competition are linked policy areas: more trade leads to greater cooperation in competition policy. However obvious this linkage appears, it bears repeating. Unimpeded flows of goods, services, and capital raise competition concerns and fuel the need for more cooperation. To be sure, the two issue areas are different in the sense that trade issues tend to be settled politically through the use of countervailing measures despite quasi-intergovernmental arbitration instruments through the WTO (see Chapter 7). In contrast, competition authorities are far less reliant on politics and more reliant on the courts (Devuyst, 2001). The point is that cooperation will improve when economic growth and trade pick up in both economies. It will be an uphill battle for the EU because of its inability so far to deal decisively with its financial crisis.

In February 2013, EU and US leaders announced the launch of negotiations for a Transatlantic Trade and Investment Partnership (TTIP) (see Chapter 13 of this volume for a detailed discussion). It aims "to go beyond the classic approach of removing tariffs and opening markets on investment, services and public procurement and focus on aligning rules and technical product standards." Moreover, "both sides envisage a 'living agreement' that allows for progressively greater regulatory convergence over time against defined targets and deadlines" (European Commission, 2013d).

The findings of this study leave room for pessimism. While it is too early to draw any definitive conclusions, interest in pursuing some form of positive integration is premature. The cost of financing monitoring and adjudication regimes, as well as the need to change legislation to align it more closely with commonly agreed standards, especially in Europe, is for the moment too high for national policymakers to support.

Second, contrary to Pollack and Shaffer (2009), more intergovernmental contacts will not be very helpful. While these contacts help diffuse legal norms, they do not by themselves lead to greater cooperation because agents do not have the incentives to cooperate more fully. More contacts lead to greater understanding and narrow the distance of opinion between the two sides. However, each side has very different incentives to cooperate because they are affected differently by the global economy. The EU side is still greatly affected by the financial crisis. Focusing on austerity policies detracts leaders from creatively addressing competition issues because domestic EU actors struggle to minimize losses.

As, such they are less likely to agree on fewer regulations and greater market liberalization. Increased competition from abroad is likely to increase losses or at least increase adjustment costs in the short run. When already facing high unemployment and the loss of government protection, the prospect of more losses due to increased competition from abroad limits appetite for cooperation and increases labor discontent, which in turn raises political cost. There may be business interest for cooperation but less EU political interest for agreement.

Third, and despite increasing global integration, domestic politics continues to shape the preferences and limits of cooperation. System-level variables interact with domestic politics to shape preferences and incentives just as two-level theorists predict (e.g., Evans, Jacobson, & Putnam, 1993). Global economic conditions define the limits of the possible but they do not necessarily determine the outcome; they merely provide the context which contains both constraints and opportunities. While regulators sought to establish non-treaty cooperation in order to limit political intervention (Damro, 2006), political will, to an extent, undermines the process by establishing more formal avenues of cooperation and by exposing the magnitude and cost of information asymmetries. Although a cooperative arrangement was initially viewed as the most efficient way to foster non-political cooperation, political winds may eventually blow in the opposite direction. Supplementing Damro's (2006) argument, enhanced cooperation is more likely under the guise of negative integration not so much because doing so increases bureaucratic discretion, but because it implies less political and economic cost. Negotiations will achieve more by doing less: negative integration is the key.

9 Transatlantic Transportation Policy

Eleanor E. Zeff, Ellen B. Pirro, and Reginald R. Souleyrette

Introduction

As noted in several chapters of this volume, the EU–US trade and investment relationship is the largest in the world. While it has been increasingly recognized that economic liberalization between the EU and the US is necessary to grow their economies and create more jobs (see, for example, the discussion in Chapters 13 and 14 with respect to the ongoing TTIP negotiations and Chapter 8 on competition/antitrust policy), the mechanisms for increasing circulation of goods and people – transport – is often overlooked by policymakers. Yet mutual recognition of maritime equipment, facilitation of air transport, and agreements regarding motor vehicle standards – from safety to air pollution mitigation equipment – are crucial to increasing the free exchange of persons and goods in the Atlantic Community.

Transatlantic cooperation is essential in the transportation sector, both in terms of facilitating trade, but also because the various elements of transportation – from automobile manufacturing to maritime shipping – are hugely important to the EU and US economies.

While there are a number of polices tied to "transportation," including fishing, marine life, environmental conservation, and the privacy of passenger data, this chapter will focus on issues related to aviation, maritime shipping, and roadways. In the US, competence rests mainly with the Department of Transportation (DOT) (motor vehicles and open skies), the US Coast Guard (maritime equipment standards), and in the EU, DG Mobility and Transport and the European Maritime Safety Agency. However, when "security" is at issue, the US Department of Homeland Security and DG Home Affairs are the major negotiating actors, with DOT and DG Mobility and Transport taking a supporting role. The empirical case studies in this chapter will assist us in answering the questions raised in Chapters 1 and 2 – namely, despite the advances in the EU–US partnership attendant with the New Transatlanticism, whether the EU can be an "equal" partner with the US when the high politics of homeland security outweighs the low politics of trade and competition.

Another interesting aspect of transportation policy compared to other policies negotiated under the New Transatlanticism (e.g., competition policy, trade policy, and financial services regulation) is the locus of governmental control in the different stages of the policymaking process. Table 1.1 (p. 7) compares and contrasts the EU and the US in terms of supranational/national competence in the major policy areas for which advanced industrialized democracies are responsible. It can be seen that transport policy in both the EU and the US is a "shared" competence with its member states and states, respectively. Indeed, as Nugent (2010) points out, while the Treaty of Rome establishing the European Economic Community (EEC) envisaged the EEC would be heavily involved in transport policy, national governments resisted the Europeanization of transport policy, in many instances in order to shield national transportation entities from competition from foreign carriers. For a variety of reasons (including pressure from the European Parliament on the Council of Ministers – see Nugent, 2010), the EU's transport policy competence has increased from 1970 when "all, or virtually all, major policy decisions [were] taken at the national level" to the contemporary state of play where "major policy decision [are] shared between EU and national levels" (Buonanno & Nugent, 2013, p. 7). Thus, as the EU became more involved with European transport policy, it became "ripe" for transatlantic policy negotiation and cooperation. Accordingly, the first section of this chapter examines transportation policy through the lens of multi-level governance/federalism.

The second section of the chapter considers the institutional and political dynamics of transportation policy in the EU, the US, and within the transatlantic context. The purpose is to compare and contrast the formulation and implementation of transportation policy in the EU and the US in order to contextualize successes and failures in transatlantic cooperation.

Because transportation policy varies by mode of conveyance, this chapter then offers an analysis of transatlantic policy cooperation in three principal transportation sectors. This sectoral analysis begins with a discussion of transatlantic aviation accords, specifically the "Open Skies" agreement. Our analysis of Open Skies enables us to explore EU–US transport cooperation in the context of market competitiveness. Next, the chapter reviews the principal post-9/11 transatlantic maritime agreement dealing with container security. This agreement opens a window into the US negotiating behavior when the most salient issue is one of security. The final case study – transatlantic vehicle and roadway agreements – is selected for three reasons. First, trade in automobile and automobile parts is the largest export sector between the US and the EU. Second, EU member states and the US have significant cross-national foreign investment in the auto industry. Third, vehicle and roadway policy is an example of "cooperative federalism," in which the US executive bureaucracy and the European Commission must work closely with member states and US states, respectively, the latter holding a great deal of policy power in this area. And, fourth, there are a great number and variety of civil society actors involved in transportation policymaking. With respect to this fourth point, we are curious to know to what extent transatlantic cooperation will have infiltrated a "localized" transportation policy.

The last section of this chapter places transportation policy into the larger policy milieu on New Transatlanticism, paying particular attention to lessons learned which can be applied to the broader challenge of transatlantic policy cooperation.

Multi-level Governance and Transportation Policy

Multi-level governance (MLG) provides a useful theoretical guide to examine transatlantic transportation policies because transportation policy can be characterized as having multi-level administrative systems, with differentiated polities. MLG, as originally defined by Gary Marks (1993, p. 392) consists of "continuous negotiation among nested governments at several territorial tiers – supranational, national, regional, and local." Hooghe and Marks (2003) further clarified the concept of MLG governance by identifying a "Type 1" (related to vertical federalism – hierarchical allocation of power) and "Type 2" (related to horizontal federalism – multiple and task-specific jurisdictions – such as special districts in the US). Transportation policy in the US and many EU member states exhibits elements of both Type 1 and Type 2 MLG because the EU/US federal government, member states, regional governments, local governments, and special districts (such as port, bridge, waterway, and highway authorities) share in the governance of transportation policy. So while multiple levels of governance have long been the norm in US transport policy, increasingly, EU scholars have shown that MLG is a fruitful paradigm for understanding the evolution of EU transportation policy as well (see, for example, Szydarowski & Tallberg, 2013).

What this means in practical terms is that increasingly the EU and the US are demonstrating similar governance structures in the transportation policy area – a form of governance that is not neatly hierarchical, but one that can be characterized by overlapping jurisdictions, horizontal relationships, and networks composed of a variety of governmental and non-governmental stakeholders. But the extent to which a transport policy sector is closer to Type 1 MLG or Type 2 MLG may have implications for the ability of the EU and the US to achieve cooperation in transport policy. Based on the policy studies in other chapters of this book, one might hypothesize that for the EU and the US those transportation policies characterized as Type 1 are precisely those policies that will need transatlantic cooperation. This is because Type 1 policies are those that the polity has already determined need hierarchical, centralized coordination, such as safety standards in air, road, and maritime transportation. (Safety standards, being a particularly salient form of market failure, typically are in the central government's policymaking sphere in both unitary and federal systems.)

The Historical and Institutional Context

The US

The US is a federal union where the states have designated powers under the US Constitution, but where the federal government – whether Congress or the presidency and the executive branch – have primary competence in a number of areas enumerated in the US Constitution and as interpreted by the federal judiciary. Although states have considerable control over their own transportation systems, the westward expansion of the US, urbanization, and recently, globalization necessitates greater mobility and citizen protections, blurring the lines between regional, national, and international transport issues. Therefore, the federal government has been involved in both the regulation of transportation and the promotion of new transportation networks and modalities.

The federal government began regulating interstate transportation in the late nineteenth century with the establishment of the Interstate Commerce Commission, America's first regulatory agency, tasked with regulating the railways and later trucking. (The Interstate Commerce Commission was abolished in 1995.) Subsequent legislation strengthened the Interstate Commerce Commission's regulatory powers and since the early twentieth century the federal courts have tended to rule in favor of federal supremacy in the area of interstate transport. (In general, both the US Supreme Court and the Court of Justice of the European Union [CJEU] have interpreted the US Constitution and the EU treaties so as to strengthen their respective internal markets.)

The US DOT was not established until 1966, its functions being scattered throughout several federal agencies, including an Undersecretary of Transportation in the US Commerce Department. Box 9.1 lists the "Operating Administrations" for which the DOT is responsible, which cover the entire gamut of transportation from maritime, to pipelines, to mass transit. The DOT is a large department with an annual budget of approximately $77 billion and 57,000 employees.

Despite the controversy of establishing a federal DOT (it had been proposed in the Congress for nearly 100 years prior to its establishment [US Department of Transportation – Office of the Historian, 2009]), in postwar America transportation had become too complex, continuously spilling over into many other policy areas so that in the 1960s and 1970s the US was confronted with one transportation crisis after another: national security (this was the era of airplane hijackings), environmental concerns (overbuilding, environmental degradation, supersonic air transport), bankrupt railroads (New York Central, Penn Central), continuing financial crises in mass transit funding, labor concerns (striking air traffic controllers), the oil crises of 1973 and 1977, and unsafe roads and automobiles (an early example of the latter was brought to the public's attention by consumer advocate Ralph Nader's "Unsafe at Any Speed" 1965 campaign for mandatory safety features on American cars). Environmental mitigation, particularly the reduction of greenhouse gases (GHGs) and energy conservation continue to be federal priorities, both acting under federal authority and through partnerships with states (US Department of Transportation, n.d.).

The DOT has periodically developed strategic plans which involved partnerships with other governmental entities – the most recent being the High-Speed Rail Strategic Plan (US Department of Transportation – Federal Railroad Administration, 2009) – but the most far-reaching is the postwar building of the Dwight D. Eisenhower National System of Interstate and Defense (completed in the 1980s), consisting of 48,867 miles (US Department of Transportation

Box 9.1

US Department of Transportation

Operating Administrations:

- Federal Aviation Administration
- Federal Highway Administration
- Federal Motor Carrier Safety Administration
- Federal Railroad Administration
- National Highway Traffic Safety Administration
- Federal Transit Administration (urban transit)
- Maritime Administration
- Saint Lawrence Seaway Development Corporation
- Research and Innovative Technologies Administration
- Pipeline and Hazardous Materials Safety Administration
- Surface Transportation Board
- Office of Inspector General

DOT number of employees: 57,000
Fiscal year 2013: $77 billion.

EU DG Mobility and Transport

Oversees:

- European Aviation Safety Agency (EASA)
- European Maritime Safety Agency (EMSA)
- European Railway Agency (ERA)
- Trans-European Transport Network Executive Agency (TEN-TEA)
- European Agency for Competitiveness and Innovation (EACI)
- SESAR Single European Sky ATM Research Joint Undertaking.

DG Mobility and Transport number of employees: 400
Annual budget: 1.5 billion (mostly for co-financing European transport network infrastructure and transport research)

(European Commission DG Mobility and Transport, 2010;
US Department of Transportation, 2013, pp. 9, 21)

– Federal Highway Administration, n.d.). While about 90% of the cost of building the interstate highways system was borne by the federal government, the states own and operate the interstate highways, including setting the speeds and enforcement. The federal government influences state operations of interstate highways through financial incentives (see below).

Despite the important role of the federal government in interstate transportation, each state has its own DOT to regulate infrastructure design, construction and maintenance, licensing, safety regulations (such as traffic flow, speed, motorcycle helmets, and motorist cell phone use).

Each state receives federal funding (and fines) for complying (or not) with federal regulations on interstate highways. The federal government has involved itself in a number of controversial public safety and conservation issues involving transportation by not only informing the public about the hazards of underage drinking, distracted driving (e.g., mobile texting), helmet use in motorcycles, and blood alcohol content, but also at times, the US Congress or the President has tied federal highway funding to adoption of federal requirements such as reducing the speed limit to 55 during the 1970s oil crises (*Emergency Highway Energy Conservation Act of 1974*). One of the more controversial federal initiatives was passage of the *Uniform Drinking Age Act of 1984* (23 U.S.C §158), which reduced federal highway funding by 10% to states permitting drinking under the age of 21. So while states are empowered to set the legal drinking age, the federal government used the power of the purse to bring about uniformity across all 50 states regarding the minimum legal drinking age. Similarly, since 1967 federal funding has contained a provision for mandatory motorcycle helmets for states to qualify for certain federal safety programs and highway construction funds; thus, by the early 1960s nearly all of the states had passed universal motorcycle helmet laws (Insurance Institute for Highway Safety, 2014). The federal government has also used highway funding to persuade states to enact laws reducing the allowable blood alcohol content (Zimmerman, 2002, p. 13).

In addition to the shared responsibility of the federal government, states, and territories for transportation policy, there are also numerous special districts/ public authorities that deal exclusively with transportation, such as the Metropolitan Transit Authority serving New York City and the Los Angeles County Metropolitan Transportation Authority. Added to these authorities are the numerous interstate administrative transportation compacts such as the Port Authority of New York and New Jersey, the E-Z Pass-consortium of eastern states radio frequency tag interagency agreement, and the I-95 Corridor Coalition of states from Maine to VA formed to employ Intelligent Transportation Systems (ITS) (Zimmerman, 2002, p. 204).

This discussion illustrates that US transportation policy is a "messy" amalgamation of Type 1 and Type 2 MLG. One might question whether transatlantic cooperation could develop in a policy area where, unlike foreign and defense policy, so much of the power is vested in the states and territories, there are multiple societal stakeholders, and it is a highly salient policy issue with the public.

The EU

The EU has envisioned a Common Transport Policy (CTP) since the EEC's establishment (Zeff & Pirro, 2006, 2011). The CTP is governed by Title VI (Articles 90–100) of the Treaty on the Functioning of the European Union (TFEU). The TFEU clarifies the division of policy competence in the EU, which can be exclusive, shared, or supporting (Europa, 2010a), with transport and trans-European networks granted shared competence in the TEFU (Article 4 g and h). In the EU, however, policy competence is limited by the principles of proportionality ("the content and form of the EU action should not be more than what is necessary in order to achieve the objectives of the Treaties") and subsidiarity ("the EU has competence to legislate if the objective of the proposed action will be better achieved at the EU level, and cannot be sufficiently achieved by the member states individually" (Eftestøl-Wilhelmsson, 2010, pp. 36–37).

The EEC originally sought a CTP as a key component of the internal market; namely, reducing barriers to competition and ensuring a good transport system throughout the Community (Council of Ministers, n.d.). As with the US, concerns over traffic congestion, safety, and sustainable development are currently the principal focus. But unlike the US, the EU has faced a unique challenge in last 20 years supporting the modernization of transportation systems in the Central and Eastern European countries (CEECs) and integrating CEEC transport with Western Europe. The EU has carried out this goal mainly in the context of the internal market and contributed to the modernization and integration of CEEC transportation systems through cohesion funds. Another set of challenges for the EU has been in coordinating energy, environment, and transport policies to conserve energy (the EU is heavily dependent on external sources for its energy) and reduce GHGs (the EU is the policy leader in this area) – both of which are directly impacted by transport.

At the EU level, the Commission, the Parliament, and the Council of Ministers are involved in setting EU transportation policy, while the Court of Justice of the European Union (CJEU) has adjudicated many cases in the transportation sector. The Commission is responsible for writing transportation legislation. And since the Lisbon Treaty came into force, transportation policy has been legislated under the ordinary legislative procedure. Therefore, the Council and the Parliament "co-decide" transport legislation. Since 2002, the Council configuration responsible for transport policy has been the "Transport, Energy and Telecommunications Council," which consists of the respective cabinet ministers from the 28 member states. The European Parliament (EP), as with the US Congress, works through the committee system with a standing committee (Transport and Tourism) responsible for EU transport legislation.

The EU advances transportation policy through "Action Programmes" in transportation sectors (e.g., road safety action programs) and for general strategies such as intelligent transport systems and increasing multimodal transport. Most EU transportation policy has been advanced through regulations (technical and specific adjustments to EU law that are immediately binding on all individuals and effectively become part of domestic law) and directives (broad principles and frameworks of law applicable to the member state with some latitude for the member states when transposing the EU directives into national law). EU transport directives and regulations cover air, road, waterborne, and rail transportation, passenger rights, intermodality and trans-European networks, intelligent transport, and transport/environment/energy (Europa, 2014).

As can be seen from the list contained in Box 9.1, the EU's role in transportation policy is very much a regulatory relationship, a finding that dovetails with Majone's (1996) identification of the EU as a regulatory state in parallel with the evolution of US federal power. Network governance – an important element of the MLG approach – is a regular feature of EU transportation policy because member state governments and society stakeholders are represented on the EU's transportation agency boards. So, for example, the European Maritime Safety Agency's administrative board is composed of one representative from each member state, Iceland, Norway, four Commission members, and four non-voting representatives of the maritime industry (European Maritime Safety Agency, 2013).

The European Commission's most recent White Paper on transport policy lays out an ambitious road map consisting of 40 initiatives (European Commission, 2011e, pp. 18–30). One of the key factors driving these initiatives is the plan by 2030 that transport will reduce GHGs to around 20% below 2008 levels, and by 2050 a reduction of at least 60% of 1990 levels (European Commission, 2011e, p. 3). Achieving these overall cuts in GHGs will have an impact on transatlantic trade in terms of product standards, sales of US cars and commercial aircraft, and transportation equipment, rules and regulations regarding multimodalities, and shipping insurance. (Multimodalities are considered key to reducing road freight, and thus pollution; see Eftestøl-Wilhelmsson, 2010.) Specific EU goals include no more conventionally fueled cars in cities, 40% use of sustainable low-carbon fuels in aviation, and at least 40% cut in shipping emissions; 50% shift of medium-distance intercity passenger and freight journeys from road to rail and waterborne transport. But to accomplish such a reduction in GHGs, the EU will need to work with the US (and other major trading partners) with respect to emission standards on motor vehicles. This is no small matter because automobiles represent the largest manufacturing and exporting sectors in both the EU and the US (Blunt, 2012, p. 1). So, too, the US insurance industry will be affected by liability rules regarding multimodal shipping. The manufacture and sales of commercial aircraft (particularly the Airbus–Boeing commercial airline duopoly) are also affected by GHG targets; so, for example, subsidies by EU member states to Airbus to achieve the EU emission targets could become a point of contention in the long-running disputes between the EU and the US within the WTO. (See Chapter 8 for a discussion of the Airbus–Boeing subsidies dispute in the context of competition policy.)

The Transatlantic Dimension

Since 9/11, the US and the EU have included transport issues in their negotiations.

In contrast to the authority of the US DOT (or Homeland Security in transportation areas involving security issues) to negotiate transatlantic transport policies, the EU employs a more complex institutional process for reaching consensus on transport policy. Although the Commission negotiates foreign treaties and agreements, it does not act on its own. The double-hatted High Representative/Commission Vice-President (currently Frederica Mogherini) is involved with transatlantic policy, including transport and trade issues. Whereas Janet Napolitano, as US Secretary of Homeland Security, was the sole signatory on the EU–US Joint Statement on Supply-Chain Security covering maritime and aviation security and trade (European Commission, 2011b), three EU commissioners (Home Affairs, Taxation & Customs, and Transport) signed on behalf of the EU.

Transport experts from the EU Commission's DG for Mobility and Transport (DG MOVE) have been included in transport-related transatlantic policy discussions (DG Mobility and Transport, personal interviews with top-level officials, June 2012). In carrying out these activities, DG MOVE is assisted by the expert input from several European agencies and a Joint Undertaking, which it oversees (see Box 9.1).

While originally the NTA focused on transatlantic economic liberalization and trade and did not specifically discuss transport policy, the events of September 11, 2001 (9/11) prompted governmental officials to recognize the importance of including transport issues and transport officials in transatlantic discussions to improve both transatlantic mobility and security (DG Mobility and Transport, personal interviews with top-level officials, June 2012).

The US and EU began exploring more avenues for fruitful cooperation on transport issues, first in the annual summits and then also in lower-level conferences and exchanges. The annual US/EU summits (see Chapter 5) now routinely include transport issues related to aviation and maritime concerns (such as streamlining transfers, cabotage, ownership by foreign firms, transit lanes, environmental concerns, use of electronic devices, emergency situations), and increasingly important topics of transatlantic transport policy discussions (aviation and automobile technology exchanges, aviation and maritime security, and containers and similar transport issues related to facilitating trade).

There have been several transatlantic agreements in the transportation sector regarding aviation competition (Open Skies); maritime safety and standards; common standards on automobiles; and aviation technology, safety, and transport emissions. And despite the wide variety and number of stakeholders and governmental officials (see earlier discussion of MLG), the EU and the US have been able to achieve cooperation. The EU and the US also are actively working in international fora, particularly through the UN's International Civil Aviation Organization (ICAO). to establish voluntary emissions standards (US Department of Transportation, n.d.).

It can be concluded that the Atlantic Community is highly engaged in transport sector negotiations, both at the transatlantic and international levels, in a wide variety of issues. The next three sections review the principal transatlantic activities in three transport modalities – aviation, maritime, and roadways.

Aviation Policy: Open Skies

There have been two major agreements concerning aviation – one, the Passenger Name Record (PNR) agreement is detailed in Chapter 10, and the other, EU–US Open Skies (Stages 1 and 2), is examined here. PNR is as much about security as transportation, while Open Skies is mainly about deregulation, competition (even if, as is often the case in protectionism, opponents opposed Open Skies utilizing the rhetoric of national security).

The Atlantic Community had long wished to negotiate an EU–US Open Skies. Per the norm in transatlantic accords, there were bilateral "Open Skies" agreements between the US and 16 individual EU member states (the first having been signed between the US and the Netherlands in 1992, over the EU's objection), a fragmented system that stymied competition (Europa, 2007). Progress toward EU–US Open Skies, however, had to wait until the US felt it had made substantial progress on its air traffic and travel security system post-9/11. By the 2004 EU/US summit in Ireland, the US and the EU agreed to "work together to enhance trade and transport security while facilitating the movement of people and goods." The US Congress rejected the first attempt – the 2005 Air Transport Agreement – prompting the EU to make several (temporary) concessions between 2004 and 2007.

The first EU–US Open Skies was agreed by the EU and the US in Washington, DC in April 2007 and took effect in March 2008. There were five main objectives of EU–US Open Skies: first, permitting European- and American-owned airlines to fly any route between any city in Europe to any city in the US and vice versa; second, allowing foreign ownership of US and EU airlines; third, granting antitrust immunity to joint ventures among previous competitor airlines (Centre for Aviation, 2013); fourth, winning cabotage rights in each other's markets; and, fifth (connected to the first goal), lowering prices for transatlantic flights.

Open Skies achieved the first goal: European carriers can fly from any point in the US from Europe (not just from their home countries) and US carriers have the same reciprocal relationship. Almost immediately, carriers announced flights from airports where they had been previously denied landing rights. The second goal of permitting foreign ownership proved contentious for American negotiators – Congress, organized labor, and the Pentagon opposed foreign ownership – thus, the agreement fell short of full ownership rights. Europeans would now be able to own up to 50% of an American airline, but hold no more than 25% of its voting stock (Europa, 2007); Americans could control up to 49% of European airlines (BBC News, 2008). The fourth goal, cabotage rights, was granted to American, but not to European airlines. And, because of increased prices for jet fuel in the time period (March 2008 to the present), the fifth goal of cheaper transatlantic flights has not yet been realized, with only modest evidence for some increase in transatlantic traffic (Centre for Aviation, 2013).

Because the US emerged with the more advantageous deal – opening up ownership and cabatoge (the US has the largest intercontinental continental passenger volume (Centre for Aviation, 2013), which are both critically important to European airlines – the EU placed stipulations on the 2007 deal, or Stage 1 as it came to be called, that required a new agreement be negotiated by 2010 that would open up US airlines to foreign control. The third goal immunized the three big alliances – Sky Team, Star Alliance, and One World (which together control 83% of the capacity across the North Atlantic) from antitrust action (Centre for Aviation, 2013).

In May 2008 the EU and US began second stage negotiations on the unresolved issues of the first stage Open Skies agreement. Following seven rounds of talks, negotiations ended with the initialing of the Second Stage Agreement on March 25, 2010. This second stage of the "Open Skies" Agreement included: granting EU air carriers cabotage rights in the US (allowing them to pick up passengers in the US and then go to a further destination); a promise by the federal government to seek relaxation of US laws on airline ownership and control; and an agreement to begin discussions on a roadmap to reduce GHG emissions (Kanter & Clark, 2010).

Maritime Policy

Ninety percent of global trade is carried by sea (International Maritime Organization, 2012), and thus is a crucially important element in US–EU trade. Maritime shipping between the US and EU accounts for 17% of all US trade and a significant proportion of EU external trade (Bank, Craig, & Sheppard IV, 2005). Furthermore, the Port of Rotterdam is ranked as the tenth largest port by shipping volume. Finally, based on gross tonnage (2010 data), shipping by fleets owned by EU and US companies is substantial – Greece (second), Germany (third), US (fifth), UK (sixth), Denmark (ninth), Italy (thirteenth), France (nineteenth), and Belgium (twentieth) – accounting for 47% of total maritime shipping (International Maritime Organization, 2012, p. 12).

Maritime cooperation between the nations of Europe and the US dates back to the 1800s and helped to forge extensive commercial relations (US Department of Transportation – Maritime Administration, 2010). A variety of international agencies under the auspices of the UN deal with maritime issues, with the International Maritime Organization (responsible for maritime safety, shipping security, and prevention of marine pollution by ships) and International Standardization Organization (standardized container shipping), particularly important to the maritime shipping industry.

Maritime concerns, like aviation issues, are also multifaceted, spilling over into other areas of governance, particularly competition, security, and the environment. Security concerns have become important to the Atlantic Community, especially after 9/11. Since that time, fictional and "reality" scenarios have portrayed container ships with nuclear materials hidden among regular commerce. Commercial and liberalization concerns involve expanding routes, securing and opening ports and their accommodations, maritime regulations, and a host of other concerns involving the speedy transfer of goods. Furthermore, the Atlantic Community has worked together on agreements to deal with emergencies that arise from oil spills and other environmental or security disasters. This section examines EU–US negotiations regarding the principal transatlantic maritime shipping agreement enacted post 9/11 – the Container Agreement of 2004.

The Container Agreement of 2004

The *Customs Cooperation Agreement of 1997* followed soon after the New Transatlantic Agenda (NTA) came into effect. The *Container Agreement of 2004* significantly updated and upgraded the 1997 Agreement to include security screening, and established an EU/US Joint Customs Cooperation Committee to implement it. Although the Committee meets annually, a "working committee" named by the Joint Customs Cooperation Committee does the real work. This working committee is composed of representatives from the full committee, representatives from the US Customs and Border Protection, and representatives from interested EU member states. In this way, additional stakeholders are involved in the ongoing process of expanding, developing, and regulating maritime shipping. Among the "working committee" mandates are defining minimum standards and best practices in all areas; establishing levels of information and exchanges of information; establishing industry partner programs; and identifying needed legislative changes. In the security area, the working committee identifies high-risk cargos at their homeports, where measures can be taken to secure them. The working committee reports to the full committee and also to the US Commissioner of Customs and Border Patrol and to the DG of Taxation and Customs Union. It has been the practice of the full committee to adopt the measures put forth by the working committee.

Significantly for EU–US cooperation, the US established the *Container Security Initiative of 2002* (CSI), which permits US Customs and Border Protection (CBP), working with host government Customs Services, to examine high-risk maritime containerized cargo at foreign seaports before they are loaded on-board vessels destined for the US. All the major European seaports (23) participate in the program (US Department of Homeland Security, 2012), adopting it through a clause in the 1997 Customs Agreement which permitted adding new elements without re-negotiation. However, on August 3, 2007, US Congress enacted the "Implementing Recommendations of the 9/11 Commission Act of 2007," setting a deadline of July 2012 to implement 100% screening at foreign ports (European Commission, 2010b, p. 7; Schneidmiller, 2012). This proposal met with EU opposition for a number of reasons such as the lack of proof that 100% screening would increase security, the economic hardships it would cause to the EU, a potential trade protection measure, the diversion of resources from EU security, and the non-reciprocal nature of the proposal (European Commission, 2010b, pp. 7–12). The EU proposed an alternative security system based on "multilayered risk management." In the meantime, the US Department of Homeland Security (DHS) has had to account for the delay in implementing 100% screening in congressional hearings, with Congress continuing to insist that the program go forward (Schneidmiller, 2012). The DHS piloted 100% screening under the *Safe Port Act of 2006* at several ports around the world, finding that at busy ports only about 5% of the containers were scanned (Schneidmiller, 2012). Eventually, however, the scanning systems were put into place, so that according to DHS "these systems (now) scan 100% of all containerized cargo and personal vehicles arriving in the U.S. through land ports of entry, as well as over 99% of arriving sea containers" (US Department of Homeland Security, n.d.).

This outcome has important implications in understanding transatlantic cooperation. It demonstrates that in an area characterized by security issues (high politics), the "equal partnership" of the New Transatlanticism can be empty rhetoric. Despite the Commission's evidence (and the DHS's own skepticism with respect to both the feasibility and effectiveness of 100% screening of shipping containers), domestic politics triumphed (US Congress). In the end, the US was able to impose unilaterally its security requirements on the EU. This supports the findings with respect to PNR (see Chapter 10), which suggest that when the goal of US negotiators is to protect US citizens, the EU has been unable to prevent the US from implementing a unilateral policy, even when this policy increases the cost of trade for EU member state businesses and taxpayers.

Highway and Motor Vehicle Policy

The Road

As in the aviation and maritime transport issue areas, automobile and road issues are both multifaceted and have gained transatlantic importance. However, roadway issues differ considerably from the other transport issue areas. First, they are removed from transatlantic security problems. Second, transatlantic negotiations incorporate more stakeholders from different levels, including business, environmental, and safety interest groups and transport NGOs, and third, many negotiations occur at lower levels of policymaking, rather than at the national departmental level, and fulfill a different mandate of the NTA, which was to promote transatlantic exchanges of information, such as university and business technology exchanges and information on safety practices.

Road Assessment Programs

Road Assessment Programs (RAPs), developed in Europe and the US, are efforts to systematically summarize and synthesize crash data and statistics – spatially and temporally – as well as to conduct road safety reviews and establish road safety ratings based on design features of specific roadway segments (Midwest Research Institute, May 2006). Both the EU and the US collaborate with the International Road Assessment Program (International Road Assessment Program, n.d.), an international non-governmental organization (INGO) that conducts road safety assessments, provides training, and assists in determining benefits of safety investments by tracking road safety performance.

Traffic Safety Information Systems

The quality and completeness of traffic safety information systems are vital to evaluating roadway safety design and operations on both sides of the Atlantic, yet resources for data collection are shrinking. The US established a multi-level panel in October 2003 to conduct an international review on how agencies in the Netherlands, Germany, and Australia design, develop, and operate innovative traffic safety information systems. Key findings emerged from their collaboration, including the idea of supplementing police-reported crash data with public surveys, insurance agency data, and hospital emergency room data. In addition, they discovered that there were already inter-agency agreements for sharing roadway design characteristics and useful methodologies for identifying areas with high crash rates or "blackspots," which could be mutually beneficial. Three components emerged to improve roadway safety and driver behavior: cost–benefit analyses, public education programs, and driver sanctions. The multinational panel also suggested that free training and crash data collection software should be provided to law enforcement for more efficient and consistent crash data collection and that Geographic Information Systems (GIS) are useful for displaying and analyzing crash data by location.

The US review team also identified three themes – strategic issues, efficiency issues, and utility issues – which pertain to a unique coordinated approach for collecting, managing, and using safety data (US Department of Transportation – Federal Highway Administration, 2004, p. 39):

> Themes included as strategic issues focus on considering safety a core business function of government and placing emphasis on making resources available for using safety data for strategic decision making. Themes included as efficiency issues focus on ensuring that the right safety data are collected simply, accurately, and at a reasonable cost. Themes included in utility issues relate to the ability to use data for research and analysis, including the analytical tools available to do so.

Road Geometric Design Standards

The US and the EU share a common road design philosophy: design based on standards with exceptions to allow for a balance between mobility and safety and community needs and values (context-sensitive design). In the US, the principal design reference is the AASHTO Policy on Geometric Design of Highways (aka the Green Book). The US DOT's FHWA Office of International Policy together with AASHTO (state DOT CEO organization) sponsored scanning tours of European countries to share experiences with design policy and context-sensitive design in the early 2000s.

The Automobile

Motor Vehicles: International Harmonization

Automobile production represents the largest manufacturing and export sector in both the EU and the US (Blunt, 2012, p. 1). In May 2008, Vann Wilber of the Alliance of Automobile Manufacturers and Paul Eichbrecht of General Motors presented a paper which detailed the long-term transatlantic collaboration between the EU and the US on global motor vehicle regulatory harmonization (Wilber & Eichbrecht, 2008). Their paper chronicled several cooperative efforts, including the 1995 Transatlantic Business Dialogue (TABD), the 1996 Transatlantic Automotive Industry Conference on International Regulatory Harmonization, and the 1996 Enhanced Safety of Vehicles Conference. Commenting on the 1998 Agreement – World Forum for Harmonization of Vehicle Regulations

(WP29), which is a subsidiary body of the UN Economic Commission for Europe, Inland Transportation Committee (United Nations Economic Commission for Europe, 2012), the authors argue:

> The most significant, tangible success to come out of the TABD effort was the drafting and ratification of the "Agreement Concerning the Establishing of Global Technical Regulations for Wheeled Vehicles, Equipment and Parts Which Can Be Fitted and/or be Used on Wheeled Vehicles" ... it established a world forum to develop global technical regulations (GTRs) for motor vehicle safety, environmental protection, energy efficiency and anti-theft performance.

WP.29, which began as a UN regional (European) forum, later transformed into a world forum, meets three times per year to discuss various vehicle regulation issues. WP.29 produces informal documents, working documents, final documents, and adopted proposals (UNECE – World Forum for Harmonization of Vehicle Regulations, n.d.).

Yet, despite considerable progress and multiple transatlantic conferences and agreements involving participants at multiple levels of government and industry (such as the US–EU High Level Regulatory Forum), the EU and US systems for setting standards, testing and certifying motor vehicle safety and environmental performance are not yet harmonized. In addition, harmonization is still lacking in the technical requirements necessary to achieve common vehicle safety. While motor vehicle regulatory harmonization is desired, the 1998 Global Agreement recognized that there could be unique situations in individual countries that require some flexibility in setting standards and regulations. And, as noted in the Introduction to this volume, international fora are not always suitable for reaching agreements, especially when participants have different goals arising from disparate levels of economic development. Therefore, the EU and US automobile industry have been lobbying for the Atlantic Community to undertake to resolve their concerns. In response to a call seeking comments on regulatory burdens in advance of the TTIP negotiations (US Department of Commerce – International Trade Administration, 2011), Matt Blunt (2012, p. 2), representing the American Automotive Policy Council – European Automobile Manufacturers Association in a joint letter to the US Trade Representative (Ron Kirk), EU Commissioner for Trade (Karel de Gucht), and EU Commissioner for Industry and Entrepreneurship (Antonio Tajani), wrote:

> efforts were undertaken to bridge these regulatory differences and establish a global model. This culminated in the important but limited progress made under the auspices of the United Nations Working Party 29 (WP29). AAPC and ACEA call for ambitious, bilateral cooperation on automotive technical regulations and standards. Under the auspices of the U.S.–E.U. trade agreement negotiations, this cooperation could include different steps such as the mutual recognition or functional equivalence of existing regulations and standards, and a stronger and comprehensive process to internationally

harmonize upcoming regulations within the United Nations WP29 structure. The effort should draw on recent collaborative experience, led by industry, to establish common standards for e-mobility and electric vehicles under the auspices of the Transatlantic Economic Council.

Electric Cars

The US and the EU have been able to collaborate at different levels of negotiations and reach agreements of benefit to both entities in the new area of electric cars. There is now a better "roadmap" for cooperation on regulatory issues, standardization, and research programs, as well as a manufacturers' agreement to harmonize electric vehicle recharging ports. Negotiations included agency conferences such as the Conference on Electric Vehicles held during World Standards Week in October 2011, where US and EU automobile and regulatory agencies participated.

While there has already been significant progress between the EU and the US related to electric vehicles, two initiatives signal even closer collaboration for the future. The first initiative is a preliminary joint proposal for the development of test facilities for electric vehicles. Second, a November 2011 proposal would establish EU–US–Japan informal electric vehicle working groups with the objectives of exchanging information on current and future regulatory requirements for electric vehicles in different markets, minimizing the differences between these regulatory requirements, with a view toward facilitating the development of vehicles to comply with such requirements and, where possible, developing common requirements in the form of one or more UN Global Technical Regulations (UNECE – World Forum for Harmonization of Vehicle Regulations, 2011).

Conclusions

Studies of transatlantic relations tend to overlook the transportation sector, emphasizing instead competition, trade, and foreign relations. Trade and competitiveness, however, depend upon transatlantic cooperation in the transportation sector. Post-9/11 policymaking has added a security dimension to transportation policy, further complicating the Atlantic Community's long-running attempts to achieve cooperation in aviation, maritime, and roadways (especially with respect to mutual recognition in the production of motor vehicles).

The responsibility for transportation, unlike foreign, security, and trade policies, are a shared responsibility of the US federal government/EU and constituent units (mainly the states/member states, but also special districts/authorities/compacts). Where the US and EU enjoy the major policy responsibility – airline competition (through the US interstate commerce and the EU's internal market) – progress has been made in transatlantic cooperation (Open Skies). But even here, where national security is raised as a concern (foreign ownership of US airlines), the EU has been unable to obtain all of its negotiating goals (the ability of European airlines to own a controlling interest in US airlines), and most of the new events with Open Skies concern security issues and not the TTIP.

Despite the significant trade occurring between the EU and the US and the predominance of container traffic in this trade relationship, security concerns have, again, relegated the EU into a position of accepting US demands with respect to container screening. There are few new developments in the areas of maritime transport or roadways. Instead, it seems that everyone is awaiting the TTIP, and what work is being done is to create inputs for the negotiations for the customs facilitation chapter. In this regard, the US Maritime Administration has issued a document listing items it would like covered, including materials to be used in merchant vessels, inspection criteria, etc. Furthermore, the Obama Administration has refused to include the commercial airline and maritime sectors in the TTIP. This is not surprising given that the US practice has been to exclude these sectors from trade talks on national security grounds (MM&P Wheelhouse Weekly, 2014).

In a repeat of policy outcomes in other chapters in this volume, the EU was unable to speak with a unified (and thus powerful) voice to refuse the US demand for 100% screening, reducing the Commission to sending a well-researched, empirical report (ignored by the US Congress) questioning the wisdom and proposing alternatives to the 100% screening requirement in the CSI (European Commission, 2010b).

The case of roadways demonstrates that there is a great deal of "transnational" exchange in a policy area that is not controlled at the center, but rather resembling Type 2 MLG (horizontal interactions with intensive involvement by civil society actors). In the newer member states, "despite the remarkable growth performance (especially in the automotive sectors), the overall impact of the TTIP on the region is, however, not at all obvious" (Novak, 2014).

When it comes to the critically important motor vehicle sector, however, most of the achievement has taken place through the auspices of the UN (WP.29). WP.29, however, has been unable to address the mutual recognition needs of US and EU automobile manufacturers. Thus, the ability of the TTIP and the US–EU High-level Regulatory Cooperation Forum to achieve cooperation and agreement with respect to mutual recognition in the automobile industry will be an important test for the future of transatlantic cooperation with respect to the New Transatlanticism. Due to the many factors discussed in this chapter (trade, investment, safety, security, GHGs), transatlantic cooperation will become increasingly important in transatlantic policymaking. As this chapter has illustrated, however, achieving agreement in this complex and wide-ranging policy area, characterized by a variety of decision-makers, will continue to be a challenge to the Atlantic Community.

10 A Comparison of Transatlantic Mobility Regimes

The Passenger Name Record and Highly Skilled Migration

Alexander Caviedes

Introduction

The New Transatlantic Agenda (NTA) was established to generate an infrastructure to implement general points of transatlantic interest and concern. As many of the other chapters attest, various formal transatlantic agreements have their genesis in the process. However, at other times formal agreements did not result, or at the least they have strayed from the NTA framework as originally intended. This chapter discusses two areas which are certainly of transatlantic interest, but where "New Transatlanticism" has played at most a peripheral role in the advancement of the existing regime structure in those areas.

One issue area that would seem to be the type of concern intended to be addressed by the NTA and its offshoots (TEC, TTIP) would be the mobility of individuals crossing the transatlantic space, but also the mobility of those from outside this area. Analytically, one can define "international mobility" as "movements of people across international borders for any length of time or purpose" (Koslowski, 2011). Such a regime on international mobility may encapsulate intersecting rules and norms governing various aspects of mobility, such as those on security or migration, whether these are short-term, long-term, or even indefinite. Thus, a mobility regime extends beyond simply immigration, also encapsulating the various regimes that regulate border crossings and transnational transportation. This broad perspective allows us to effectively compare the development of the formal regime on passenger name record (PNR) data, relating to airline travel, to the informal regime concerning the entry of highly skilled workers, which relates to migration, and, sometimes, immigration.

This chapter begins by considering what types of policies have traditionally been considered as more amenable to integration under a common international framework, from which we will then be able to look at our two regimes to see if they have developed as the literature predicts. The remainder of the chapter traces the development of policy for each of the two separate aspects of mobility, focusing on the political actors and institutions involved in promoting either the PNR or high skilled migration. The resulting regimes will be compared along three criteria. First, substantively, are the regimes more formal or informal in nature, and to what degree can each be considered as adequate in terms of goals and level of regulation? This also involves examining the degree to which the

New Transatlanticism was involved in advancing the regime and whether any other "new governance" types of practices have emerged within each regime. Second, what institutions within each polity are implicated, and in particular, to what degree has the less-defined catalog of competences at the EU level created mismatches and challenges? In the case of a less developed institutional structure, has this opened up the policy process to non-governmental actors? Third, how should one characterize the cooperative behavior between the US and EU in each regime? Can one speak of true partnership or have differences in institutional structure or administrative practices produced asymmetries of influence?

Theoretical Expectations Concerning a Mobility Regime

The joint declaration announcing the goals of the NTA (see Chapter 5) lays out broad areas, such as security, where cooperation would be fundamental and mentions the desire to "build bridges across the Atlantic." As is common for such international framework agreements intended to produce greater formal and informal interactions and cooperation, there is no real identification as to the what, how, and when for such further agreements. Indeed, this is one of the weaknesses of functionalist explanations of international cooperation: even with the identification of areas where cooperation would be beneficial or necessary, such regimes cannot spring forth on their own, but rather require a degree of policy entrepreneurship to advance such initial aspirations.

These obstacles parallel those that have faced European integration throughout the history of development of the European Economic Community (EEC) through to the current EU. In response to functionalists who did not offer much insight as to what impulses would drive initiatives for cooperation, and neofunctionalists such as Ernst Haas (1964), who postulated that integration, once initiated, begets the expansion of integration into other related areas, Stanley Hoffmann (1966) offered words of warning. Hoffmann argued that while the European Community (EC) had experienced continued integration after its inception, this should be viewed as far from an automatic process. There are important differences between policy areas that would determine the ease with which policy integration could proceed. Rather than reflecting the complexity of an issue, international cooperation was contingent upon whether an area of "high politics" was implicated or not. By high politics, Hoffmann was referring to those key policy areas where states would be reluctant to share competences because they were inextricably related to national sovereignty – whether that meant security or national identity – or because they were highly contested at the national level. Hence, it would be notably more difficult to pool political competences with regard to the military, immigration, or education or the welfare state than in "low politics" areas, such as international trade or transportation policy. (While security is understood to be the archetypal "high politics" area, what might constitute an area of high politics varies by country. As a crude rule of thumb, one might consider the top three issues upon which any most recent national elections hinge to constitute those which are considered high politics in that polity.)

A subsequent theoretical attempt to delineate what types of policies would be more amenable to common international policies (at least in the European setting) distinguishes between positive and negative integration (Pinder, 1968). Positive integration refers to establishing new common standards, while negative integration involves eliminating national systems of regulation to the degree that they conflict with the standards of other countries within the system. Negative integration removes national barriers, generally by forbidding or limiting certain types of regulation. This usually means that goods, services, or individuals are able to move from one polity to another as long as they meet the regulatory standards of their home country, even if this is "lower" than that of the destination country. The argument is that it is easier to come to an agreement to deregulate in this fashion than to arrive at a common standard (especially among multiple parties). (See Chapter 8 for an application of this concept to competition policy.)

Relying on these theories to derive predictions as to whether it would be easier to come to an agreement on sharing passenger data or to open up the labor market to highly skilled individuals, both theories would expect that the latter constitutes a more promising basis for agreement. While one could say that since each of these areas are part of the international mobility regime that curtails sovereignty over national borders, making them both high-politics areas, it seems clear that focusing on all airline passengers, precisely with regard to whether they pose security risks, is far closer to the traditional scope of high politics than liberalizing labor market entry for the highly skilled. Furthermore, developing a common standard for which information must be gathered on passengers is more of a positive endeavor, while opening up the labor market to non-citizens is exactly what negative integration involves.

While these two theories point toward the more economic of the two regimes as being more amenable to international cooperation, in reality we have only witnessed the development of a transatlantic regime in the area of PNRs. The chapter will therefore offer two further explanations. First, it seems that a belief in the existence of an imminent threat to national security can propel negotiations toward cooperation, even in high-politics areas. Second, and rather more basically, while high-skilled migration is an area of EU competence, in reality too much control still rests with the member states, so the prospects for any common transatlantic regime are minimal. (See Table 1.1 on p. 7 for a summary of EU competences.)

The Passenger Name Record Agreement

The PNR refers to the information that private carriers gather from their customers, which includes not only biographic information, but also financial information in the form of credit card or bank account numbers. Much of this information (for example, cell phone number) not only serves such security-related purposes as identifying potential terrorists, criminals, or immigration law violators, but it can facilitate mobility by ensuring that the bona fide passenger passage is expedited quickly (Tanaka, Bellanova, Ginsburg, & Hert, 2010).

However, the perceived importance of such information has increased exponentially in the aftermath of the 9/11 terrorist hijackings. The regime that has evolved since that time reflects a common desire between the US and Europe to prevent such acts, but its creation has been fraught with controversy due to the tension between the need to gather such information and the imperative to protect individual privacy in the form of data concerning one's person. That a transatlantic agreement concerning passenger data has been put in place is a testament as to how seriously the issue is viewed, but closer examination of its development throws into question how appropriate the use of the word "agreement" actually is in this case.

The regime concerning passenger records is not rooted in transatlantic communications on the subject, but in the unilateral reaction of the US to the vulnerability that the 9/11 attacks had exposed. Congress passed the *Aviation and Transportation Security Act of 2001* (19 C.F.R. §122.49a(b)) that November, requiring all foreign air carriers flying into *or over* the US to provide specific information on the passengers and crew (Patton, 2008). The act further empowered the US Department of Transportation (DOT) to issue additional regulations in this area, which it did, laying out the specific information that was required and mandating that it be transmitted no later than 15 minutes after take-off.

This sudden declaration caught the airlines off-guard and put those seated in Europe in a particular quandary, since they were also subject to the EU's framework concerning data protection. The 1995 Data Privacy Directive (Council Directive 95/46/EC, 1995 O.J. (L 281)) was intended to further free movement through the standardization of personal data rights and protections, particularly by creating standards and procedures for data transfers to non-EU countries. Under Article 25 of the Directive, the European Commission is tasked with examining data transfers to third countries and evaluating "the nature of the data, the purpose and duration of the proposed processing operation(s), the country of origin and country of destination, the rule of law" to evaluate the adequacy of that country's data protection standards. While the Commission offered an initial endorsement of the adequacy of the protections that the US Department of Homeland Security (DHS), Bureau of Customs and Border Protection (CBP) stated would be afforded to such data, the EU pressed the US to establish a treaty governing PNRs.

In brief, the agreement was signed in 2004, subsequently struck down by the European Court of Justice (ECJ) in 2006, revised through an interim agreement to bring it into accord with the Court's judgment, and finally a new agreement was signed in 2007. The remainder of this section outlines the circuitous path to the current framework, with particular attention to the manner in which negotiations proceeded, and what this suggests about the nature of transatlantic cooperation generally, the NTA and Transatlantic Economic Council (TEC) in particular, and about the challenges associated with crafting international agreements involving a hybrid entity such as the EU, which straddles the line between being a country and non-state actor.

The increased prominence of the EU as a security actor has been documented (Den Boer, Hillebrand, & Nölke, 2008; Guild, 2008). However, in this case we see a rather tepid response on the part of the EU, that is due in large part to the asymmetric power relations between the DHS versus those institutions within the EU that are responsible for foreign affairs and security-related matters. On the US side, the Department of State was responsible for conducting negotiations, while for the EU it was the Commission, acting upon a mandate established by the Council. See Patrick Pawlak's (2009) thorough reconstruction of the PNR negotiation process, which makes use of personal communications with those involved, and is an ideal source of information concerning the internal dynamics of the negotiations and a central guide to this analysis. (The same can be said of S. Baker, 2010, who led the US negotiations on the original agreements.) It is indicative that for the US, while the DHS also had representatives present, for the EU, beyond the central negotiators who were part of the External Relations Directorate General (Relex DG), there were also representatives from the DG Justice and DG Transport and Energy, not to mention the Council. Beyond this, the European team was also required to consult the European Parliament (EP) concerning the agreement, even if that body was excluded from the actual negotiation.

This led to some incoherence on the European side, since some of the officials privilege security while others are determined to balance such considerations with privacy, or even trade concerns. The situation was aggravated further since the cooperation between both sides took place under the framework of the NTA and TEC, which foresees bilateral meetings at various levels. This means that not only might institutions with cross-purposes be involved, but also officials in different roles. Those officials charged with homeland security were intent on rapidly achieving concrete results, and they felt impaired in this endeavor by being forced at every stage to integrate the input and sensibilities of diplomats who were more accustomed to producing broad agreements that also reflected a desire to foster further transatlantic communication and cooperation (Pawlak, 2009, pp. 565–568). This dissatisfaction led to essentially removing the PNR issue from these NTA-based negotiations into a separate security network in 2004: the High Level Political Dialogue on Border and Transportation Security.

Once NTA negotiations were abandoned, cooperation within this limited network proceeded rapidly, resulting in the 2004 agreement signed by the US and the EU (both Council and Commission). Though the 39 information items initially requested by the US had been whittled down to 34, the EP was not amused and brought an action before the ECJ to have the Act struck down (Schrader, 2006). While the EP was also irate that the legislation did little to address the question of what it saw as inadequate American standards for data storage, the only issue the Court addressed was whether there was adequate treaty authority to enter into the agreement. In 2006 the ECJ ruled that since this issue was not among those covered by the original EEC treaties, the Commission was not empowered to negotiate on the issue (Patton, 2008). Effectively, this ruling excluded not only the Commission, but also the EP, and opened the door for the Council to swiftly renegotiate an interim agreement that same year, based solely on the competence granted by the third pillar of the Treaty on European Union (TEU), which dealt with Justice and Home Affairs (Nino, 2010).

The temporary nature of that agreement necessitated passage of a new agreement the following year. The result was largely a re-write of the 2004 agreement, with a minor European victory in that fewer information items (19) would be shared, and a defeat from the European perspective in that there was no specification of which agencies within the US government could use this information, when in the 2004 agreement, the data were limited to the Department of Homeland Security (S. Baker, 2010, p. 138). Though the Commission and Council signed the agreement in 2007, only 24 of 27 member states had ratified it on December 1, 2009 when the Lisbon Treaty went into effect, altering the existing structure of the EU. This treaty largely eliminated the EU's three-pillar structure under which the Commission and EP had been largely relegated to bystander status in foreign and home affairs outside of the economic concerns of the first pillar, and this in particular necessitated that the EP now sign-off on this agreement before its passage. What followed was a two-year period during which the EP attempted to impose its conception of data privacy upon the agreement, before eventually capitulating in the face of American intransigence on these issues. In April 2012 the EP finally signed-off on the current version of the agreement, which is not open to renegotiation for the next seven years. Substantively, the agreement allows for the 19 pieces of information to be accessed by various agencies within the US for a period of six months, after which they are made anonymous and can only be accessed in cases of terrorism and "serious" crimes.

Evaluation

The resulting agreement is a functioning, binding common framework, but it would be a stretch to label this as transatlantic cooperation. This is not only due to the fact that the eventual configuration did not result through the NTA process, but due to the style of the negotiations, in which the US was a first-mover and norm-maker engaging in what has perceptively been labeled as "unilateral and forceful norm advocacy" (Argomaniz, 2009, p. 121). While the DHS may register disappointment with the reduction in information points, the most important elements of information, including credit card records, are still included. This is considerably less aggravation than US businesses express when having to deal with a myriad of protective regulations that have been set up to protect the data privacy of EU citizens generally (Pop, 2011b). On the other side of the Atlantic, most member states acknowledge the inevitability of bowing to the US demands, and certainly Ministries of the Interior stand to benefit from the collection of this data. However, beyond that, the perception of disenchantment is widespread. The Commission is upset because it could not engage in policy entrepreneurship in an area that it clearly felt it had authority to decide upon due to this being "commercial" information (Hailbronner, Papkonstantinou, & Kau, 2008), but instead has been reduced to simply mirroring the norms dictated by the Americans. The EP, with expectations of becoming a critical powerbroker in the negotiations after the passage of the Lisbon Treaty, has seen many of its members characterizing the passage of the agreement as a concession to the fact that further negotiation with Washington is "not an option" (Mahony, 2012).

That said, the DHS feels that the EP showed itself to be a formidable negotiating adversary, whose views were certainly taken into account (member of the DHS negotiating team, personal communication, 2013). While a majority of academics and European civil society decry the violation of data privacy principles and laws (Pop, 2011a), the DHS argues that the US regime for data protection is systematically misunderstood and in some respects superior to that of Europe (Callahan, 2009; Kropf, 2007; Saadet & Ballard, 2007). (At the heart, the difference in opinion rests on the European philosophy of limiting the amount of personal data that is turned over in the first place, while the American system seeks to grant individuals the ability to discover which agencies have access to, and have actually accessed, their personal data. From this perspective, the power of redress makes the American system superior to that of Europe.) In any case, these arguments will have to wait a further seven years before they can once again be raised seriously on behalf of the EU.

While the economic and military/security might of the US make it a daunting partner to negotiate with on equal terms, the EU's dissatisfaction with the final resolution must also be traced to issues related to the EU's own convoluted institutional structure. While some depictions of the negotiations – including that of the lead negotiator on the American side himself – cast the US in the role of a bully (Argomaniz, 2009; S. Baker, 2010; Schrader, 2006), the American single-mindedness is also the byproduct of US frustrations in dealing with a European partner whose undefined institutional features are sources of uncertainty. The competition between EU institutions, which saw the Commission and Council eager to exclude the EP, opened the door for the DHS to play these institutions off against one another, searching for the best deal. (Interestingly, Baker's account discloses that until shortly before the final negotiations, there was also a lack of consensus between the DHS, and the Departments of State and Justice. However, this was resolved in time for the US to project a common front contra the Europeans.)

While the three-pillar structure that obfuscated which institutions were the competent negotiation partners (between the Council and Commission) was replaced through the passage of the Lisbon treaty, there still remains the problem that the Commission Ministries, the Directorate Generals (DGs), share issue competence. This was highlighted by the fact that officials from both the Foreign Affairs and Justice DGs attempted to speak on behalf of the EU, despite possessing conflicting agendas. The existence of a transatlantic regime in the area of PNRs assures future partnership. The "success" of the Europeans in approaching some modicum of equal standing will depend on their ability to convey a clear common front and to make US officials understand the complex nature of EU policymaking.

High Skills Migration

Migration is a multifaceted phenomenon, with aspects ranging from concerns that are security, humanitarian, or economically motivated. While much of the public discourse over immigration relates to its restriction, with the case of labor migration there are a greater variety and a more politically powerful group of supporters. Still, not all types of foreign workers are equally welcome. A popular term that picks up on this is "managed migration," the idea that certain migrant populations bring substantial benefits to host societies, so that it would be wise to facilitate their entry and ability to stay permanently. In particular, it is the highly skilled who are paraded as young, dynamic, hardworking individuals who are net contributors to the social welfare system while bringing sought-after skills and innovation. Indeed, researchers and some governments have come to the realization that such specialists are valuable not only in the skills they bring, but through their ability to act as conduits between societies. Thus, there is the idea that a systems engineer from India may be even more productive if she continues to shuttle between her host and home country, such that she can establish subsidiaries for the parent organizations or identify other talented individuals from among a large pool of highly qualified and motivated compatriots. Thus, while it can be said that countries are competing for the world's best and brightest, hoping to bring them from abroad on a permanent basis, countries also understand that not all migrants need necessarily immigrate permanently for the host country to reap benefits. Indeed, especially for multinational corporations, the wellbeing of the company overrides concerns of merely "national" interest. Given the degree to which the upper global corporate echelons are interconnected, it is clear that both the US and the EU have a strong desire to enable high-skilled migration, or at least promote the circulation or mobility of this highly revered class of individuals. What is rather puzzling, then, is the failure to develop any type of transatlantic framework that reflects the mobility interests of global business concerns between the two continents.

Granted, a framework has already been laid out for the mobility of workers within the General Agreement on Trade in Services (GATS) within the WTO. However, Mode 4, which pertains to the supply of services via the presence of natural persons (read: migration), has not been actualized to a high degree by individual countries. Certain concessions have been made in terms of facilitating the entry of the highly skilled (managers, executives, and senior-level specialists), but these have largely been confined to laws dealing with intra-company transfers. Instead, in terms of multilateral migration agreements, the closest there has been are certain EU laws and NAFTA provisions. The following sections first address the regime that has developed in the US before surveying the state of policy in Europe, delineating the paths along which national policies developed, and pointing out how these individual paths have led to a dead-end in terms of supranational EU obligation.

Unilateral US Activity

Those that study international migration in advanced industrial societies often delineate different phases of postwar migration. While European and American migration trends do not coincide exactly, with guest worker programs beginning and terminating earlier in the US, one common pattern was the impact of the oil shocks of the 1970s, which slowed economic growth and spurred unemployment

(S. Castles & Miller, 2009, pp. 106–107). The result was a decline in legal labor migration from the mid-1970s through the 1980s (Winters, 2009). However, as in the case of the PNR, it was the US that reacted first, "rediscovering" the benefits of recruiting foreign workers in 1990, when it revised the existing short-term visa, known as the H-1, into the H-1B that currently exists. The major difference is that while the H-1, established as part of the Immigration and Nationality Act of 1952, required applicants to maintain foreign residence, and therefore really only facilitated the entry of those with "distinguished merit and ability" for limited periods of time, the modern H-1B reflects longer-term designs on retaining the talents of the highly skilled (Fulmer, 2009). The H-1B, as redrafted in the 1970s and again in 1990, has done away with the foreign residency requirement, since the goal, as stated by George H. Bush when passing the provision into law of the Immigration Act of 1990, has been to "encourage the immigration of exceptionally talented people, such as scientists, engineers, and educators" (Fulmer, 2009, p. 225). The vision extends beyond simply supplementing domestic workforces with the occasional technical support of foreign specialists; rather, it is to generate a constant and steady flow of top minds from abroad.

While the legislation initially set a cap of 65,000 visas, it soon became clear that the American business sector did not view this as sufficient to meet the rapidly expanding needs of the information technology sector, for which over half of the H-1B visas were being allocated in 2001 (Zavodny, 2003, p. 4). Thus, it is unsurprising that during the peak years of the hi-tech bubble, employers successfully lobbied Congress to raise the allotment to 115,000 for 1999 and 2000 (US Department of Labor, 1998), before trebling the initial allocation up to 195,000 for the fiscal years 2001–2003 (USCIS, 2000). These numbers have since been reduced, but they indicate how vast demand in this area is and how seriously governments may view the entry of the highly skilled. Even when Congress appeared unsure as to the accuracy and impartiality of the representations of employers as to the scale of the skills shortage and whether the best solution would be the recruitment of foreign specialists, it announced that it was prepared to give them the benefit of the doubt due to the heavy reliance of the American economy on computer technology (Fulmer 2009, p. 833).

The H-1B process is employer-driven, meaning that employers are the ones who must petition on behalf of an applicant, essentially through a two-stage process. First, the Department of Labor must issue a certification based upon the representations of the employer, that they could not find a candidate locally and that the wage being offered is the higher of the locally prevailing wage and that of their other employees. After the issuance of this labor certification, the application passes to the immigration service, which reviews the file and issues the visa. The process may take a few months, but it is still far quicker than the process for requesting permanent residence (the green card), which can take years before final approval, and thus it is not uncommon for both processes to be initiated simultaneously, so that the applicant can begin working based on an H-1B while the permanent residence process continues.

The visa itself is subject to frequent criticism on the grounds that the review process is not sufficiently stringent, such that employers face few difficulties in making a case for their prospective foreign workers, even if this ends up displacing local workers and suppressing wages. This has led to revisions that apply stricter scrutiny to applications from firms with a high percentage of H-1B workers in their workforce, but overall the visa remains quite employer-friendly in terms of retaining a high overall quota and a fairly predictable review process. Thus, the perception is that employers, who are more centralized and have deeper resources than those who would restrict the use of the visa, have remained the principal beneficiaries of this process (Luthra, 2009). Even legislative changes such as 2009's *Employ American Workers Act*, which expanded the pool of employers who must demonstrate having made a good-faith effort to locate American applicants, remain difficult to police and thus favor employer discretion (Beach, 2010, p. 287).

Operating in tandem with both L-visas, which permit international intra-company transfers for managers and high-level technicians, and the ability for the highly skilled to apply for permanent residence through employment, for which there are 140,000 visas allocated annually (spouses also count against this total; Zavodny, 2003), the H-1B enables the US to offer a multitude of entry avenues for the highly skilled. Indeed, in terms of volume, it is the number one destination for the world's top minds, but even that has not satiated the hunger of employers nor the reliance of industry, so there is still interest in other policy permutations that can potentially attract additional specialists. The question is whether transatlantic cooperation holds sufficient promise in this respect.

European Policy to Attract the Highly Skilled

National Responses

It would be fair to say that the size and efficacy of the American H-1B program was influential in forcing certain European countries into action. Nowhere is this clearer than in the case of the German Green Card. Though "Green Card" is not the official name for the German law intended to attract computer specialists, it is the common name for the policy, which the government itself used to discuss the program, and the fact that they retained the English language term indicates a recognition of American migration policy as a form of "best practice" worthy of emulation. The late 1990s were a time of tremendous growth within the field of information technology, and in Europe businesses were feeling the crunch of skills shortages that arose through a combination of rapidly changing technological needs, competition for those with IT skills, and an education system that had not adapted quickly enough to the needs of the new "knowledge economy" (Greifenstein, 2001). Faced with the prospects of losing business abroad and being unable to tap into online markets, the business community in Germany, spearheaded by the IT association BITKOM and Initiative D21, a pro-technology enterprise composed of several of Germany's biggest corporations, steered the administration toward introduction of the Green Card Program in 2000 (BITKON and D21, personal communication, 2003). The provisions of the regulation were to allow up to 10,000 IT workers to receive employment authorization in Germany for a period of up to three years without having to pass through an individual labor certification review. Simply being in possession of a degree in computer programming or even having work experience in the information technology industry was sufficient to allow a candidate to bypass a more lengthy scrutiny reserved for the general population of work permit applicants. While the regulation was phased out in 2005, due in good part to the bursting of the IT bubble in 2001, it has been replaced by subsequent legislation granting preferential migration opportunities to the highly skilled. Germany remains cognizant of the importance of the highly skilled, and that part of this workforce will consist of foreign nationals for whom there is a high degree of competition.

Roughly simultaneously with the announcement of Germany's Green Card, the British government announced a similar program in 2000, through which 20,000 IT specialists per year would be granted work permits without having to go through the onerous individual certification process. Though this seems roughly equivalent to the German regulation – albeit with a larger quota – there was the supposedly additional incentive that recipients of a permit in these shortage sectors would be eligible for permanent residence after four years. Not only the parallel introduction of these programs, but the apparent one-upmanship symbolizes a recognition of the global market for the highly skilled and the competition that this engendered between advanced industrialized economies. The path from employer preference to policy outcome in the British case shares its timing with the German case, but students of political economy would be somewhat surprised by the far higher degree of government leadership in the British case. While the British economy is certainly viewed as more laissez-faire than that of Germany, the absence of a similarly influential associational sector in England meant that the IT association, Intellect, was relegated to the passenger seat of this project (Intellect, personal communication, 2003), with the Department of Education and Employment and Department of Industry spearheading the initiative within the Home Office (Department for Education and Skills, 2009). As in the case of the Green Card, this initial provision is no longer in place, having been replaced by a points-based system in 2006, in which the skills requirements for entry have been raised (although there is the possibility for exemptions for certain industries – engineering is one of these, but information technology is no longer). Due also to cultural factors – the UK is an English-speaking country, which is highly attractive to IT specialists from the subcontinent who already speak English and would find a substantial expatriate Indian population – the British program can be seen as highly successful in generating inflows of the highly skilled, and for this reason, somewhat uniquely among European countries, the British government seems less convinced of the need for multilateral cooperation on this front.

The contemporaneous proliferation of such programs to attract the highly skilled in the Netherlands and Austria serves notice as to the continental dimensions of the problem of attracting highly skilled workers. In 2000 the Austrians changed their regulations to facilitate the expedited processing of key foreign workers such as IT specialists. In the same year the Netherlands also instituted a change to its work permit structure through which the process was expedited and the individual examination of credentials was greatly relaxed. Feeling threatened by the procedural changes implemented in the UK and Germany, these symmetrical responses signal a fear of being left behind. In 2004 the Dutch altered their previous provision and passed the *kenniswerker* regulation, which grants IT specialists an expedited work permit process provided that the salary being offered meets a certain pay level that is set above the industry norm. On the whole, neither of these programs have been entirely successful (the Austrian program was abandoned), mainly because these are two smaller countries with less lucrative perspectives, which often ended up losing those foreign workers that they were able to attract to larger, more competitive markets (Caviedes, 2010a). This illustrates the interconnection of the European labor market for the highly skilled, and indicates that there might be interest in establishing a common policy that could serve to coordinate European policies rather than to pit their efforts against one another.

European Union Policy

Mindful of what was transpiring at the national level, the EU was eager to provide a boost to the national economies that appeared serious in actualizing the EU's dream to become the world's "foremost knowledge-based economy" by 2010. Empowered by institutional changes in the Treaty of Amsterdam that transferred the right of initiative for immigration-related policies to the supranational level, the first cautious attempt by the European Commission was the Open Method of Coordination in Migration. The proposal submitted to the Council in 2001 foresaw a loose system of policy guidelines in the area of migration, which countries are free to adopt or not, depending on their individual comfort levels. Labor migration was just one of the different policy areas that were addressed by this initiative, and in terms of highly skilled immigration there was little indication of what type of substantive policy was being promoted (Caviedes, 2004). Since the Council never adopted the proposal, one can see this as being a moot point as well as an initial preview of the lack of interest on behalf of the EU member states to enter into a Commission-led compact on the issue of labor migration.

Perhaps the Commission learned something from the member states' reluctance, for its next concrete offering on the subject of immigration, the Green Paper of 2005 (European Commission, 2005), appears to draw from the above delineated examples of the individual member states' sectoral policies of the previous five years, in which information technology and hospitality workers in particular were the beneficiaries. It proposes that labor migration policy should be developed in particular sectors that regularly suffer from labor shortages, rather than establishing a single comprehensive visa or policy. It was not until 2007 that actual legislation on labor migration was proposed by the Commission, but unlike the Green Paper, which foresaw policy in multiple sectors, the new initiative, entitled the Blue Card, was reduced to catering only to the highly skilled. Perhaps this was a wise choice, since high-skilled migration has repeatedly proven to be the least controversial aspect of migration policy, and indeed the Blue Card has not been the subject of criticism by domestic workers or their representatives (Caviedes, 2010b). The final result has been the 2009 directive that allows third-country nationals who have resided in an EU country for a period of at least 18 months to apply for similar employment authorization in a fellow EU member state. At first glance, this may sound like a significant enhancement to the mobility of non-EU citizens, but it is subject to two caveats that substantially reduce the impact of this policy. First, the program is conditional on the applicant receiving a salary corresponding to 1.5 times the national level. Unless faced with severely urgent skills shortages, it seems unlikely that employers could offer such a salary to anyone short of truly exceptional. Second, there is no automatic guarantee of being able to work in a second EU country, since each individual member state can still deny access to foreign workers simply by stipulating that the domestic labor market is too tight to warrant entry of foreign workers. Essentially, this provision renders adherence to the overall policy largely voluntary.

While one can say that high-skilled migration policy in Europe took place in an international setting that owes a good deal to competitive pressures among European neighbors, it is also evident that policy at the international – that is, EU – level is but a shadow of national policies in terms of dimension and scope. Until labor migration policy is determined more exclusively at the EU level, there is also precious little opportunity for the development of transatlantic cooperation, be it within or under the shadow of the NTA.

Evaluation

It must be restated that in speaking of the mobility regime for the migration of the highly skilled, there is no single coherent regime, and certainly no common transatlantic regime. Instead, what can be seen are systems that operate independently and even in competition with one another. The dizzying number of highly skilled workers who were entering the US at the turn of the millennium proved worrying for European policymakers, whose businesses were clamoring for hi-tech know-how, and it is reflected in the provisions and spirit of the European sectoral policies of the early 2000s. In the aftermath of the 9/11 attacks, US immigration policy and institutions were reformed, but it was economic recession, rather than sharper migration scrutiny, that led to a slowdown in the migration of the highly skilled in the early 2000s. While supporters of high-skilled mobility, such as the advocacy group Compete America, warn that the Blue Card may draw the top minds away from the US and toward Europe, in reality it remains the Europeans who are reacting to US policy, and not vice versa.

The EU's Blue Card is considerably less expansive than the H-1B, and indeed the Commission remains disappointed at the lack of scope in EU migration policy. While firms may voice similar dissatisfaction at the absence of a seamless labor market like that of the US, in the end the member states have chosen not to pursue deeper integration. Countries with successful systems like the UK do not see the value-added of a European level of migration policy, and even those that struggle to attract the highly skilled have in large part prioritized national control when it comes to something as related to the labor market as a visa for the highly skilled (Caviedes, 2010b). Though a structure has been put in place for Commission leadership in the area of immigration policy, subsidiarity thinking prevails. Labor migration policy, whether low- or high-skilled, remains a de facto competency of the member states. Moreover, to the extent that a European policy has emerged, this Europeanization has occurred more through the roundabout pattern of "uploading" certain countries' policies than as the result of policy entrepreneurship emanating from the center.

Though this issue area is a business and mobility concern that would appear ideal for transatlantic policy initiatives, in the end, much of the targeted migration is not transatlantic, but instead there is mutual competition for highly skilled workers who arrive largely from Asia. Absent direct security implications as in the NPR case, the regime for the highly skilled is rather ad hoc, functioning in a parallel manner, but not in terms of depth or scale. Due to the separate development of the two systems and the yet unsettled delineation of EU versus national competencies in the area, it also seems unlikely that it could fruitfully become a target for transatlantic policymaking in the near future.

Conclusion

The goals of the New Transatlanticism represent the recognition by the transatlantic partners that there are many policy realms where issues are proving too far-reaching and complex to be adequately resolved by either party unilaterally. However, this has not meant that cooperation has been easy or at times even forthcoming at all. While the two aspects of mobility addressed in this chapter both constitute pressing concerns for the US and Europe, a transatlantic regime has only emerged in the area of the PNRs. In a larger sense, this seems to indicate that integration in the form of common policy can occur even in high-politics areas such as security, provided the issue is viewed as sufficiently urgent. However, it would probably be incorrect to suggest that the absence of a regime for high-skilled immigration is simply a result of less urgency. Instead, we see the struggles that exist due to the diffusion of policy competence on this issue in the European case. The creation of a common regime demands a reasonably clear demarcation of internal competences within the EU, and in the case of high-skilled migration there is very little of this, despite the nominal presence of the Blue Card. Rather than a system of cooperation, with regard to high-skilled migration there is transatlantic competition, by which the EU imitates US law, but this has occurred through the indirect method of uploading member state preferences, as opposed to EU leadership, much less direct US–EU interaction.

The same problem of indefinite and shifting policy competence within the EU has confounded the development of the PNR regime itself. The absence of clearly defined European competences in this case was damning to the continued usage of the NTA as a framework for policy creation and negotiation. The very fact that there is competition between European institutions led to an inability to provide a common front and weakened the EU's bargaining position as a whole, amplifying the asymmetries that already existed due to the US's ability to dictate the agenda from the inception. In conclusion, one must appreciate the pragmatism of the parties in being able to craft an agreement in the end, even if there was dissatisfaction on both sides with the perhaps overly inclusive nature of the NTA process. Nevertheless, the NTA certainly served to provide a common springboard for conversation of the issue in a setting in which the presumption is one of mutual benefit and transatlantic partnership. Thus, the lessons that can be taken from this example are two-fold, but interrelated. First, NTA–TEC cooperation will often be challenged by the degree to which the EU has not established a clear and somewhat exclusive policy competence at the supranational level. This is why high-skilled immigration has not even approached a common regime. Second, even when the supranational competence has been largely settled, the configuration of the EU can be awkward both to itself and its negotiation partners. The gray zones in competence and conflicts of interests that may exist in a given area would need to be properly identified and understood from the beginning, to avoid frustrations and the premature abandonment of the New Transatlanticism framework.

11 Transatlantic Financial Services Regulation

Laurie Buonanno

Introduction

Financial services cover a wide range of instruments, including debts (bonds and mortgages), equity (ownership in a company), hybrids (mixture of debt and equity features), insurance, and derivatives (futures, forwards, swaps) (Murphy, 2013, p. 5).

American and European financial institutions together account for more than three-quarters of global financial services by transaction volumes, and operate the world's largest financial markets. The extent of their dominance is wide-ranging, controlling 65% of global banking assets, accounting for 79% of the volume of interest-rate derivatives outstanding, collecting 75% of insurance premiums in global insurance markets, and accounting for 96% of the involvement in foreign exchange transactions worldwide by currency pairs (Transatlantic Business Dialogue, 2010, pp. 7, 9; 2012, p. 4). But with this dominance comes risks – vulnerability to financial market collapse and the inability, as illustrated by the 2007–2008 meltdown in the financial services industry, to prevent a contagion, originating on one side of the Atlantic, from spreading to the other. Government regulators are expected to balance their responsibility to protect the public from illegal practices of individuals and firms operating in the financial services industry while avoiding a too heavy regulatory hand that could depress industry growth.

Prior to the 2007/2008 collapse of financial markets, American and European regulators were mainly concerned with market liberalization and enforcement of existing regulations. The "Great Recession" – which was precipitated by misdeeds of the financial services industry related to innovative derivatives (collateralized debt obligations [CDOs] derived from, as it turned out, bad mortgage debt) – reoriented the public's charge to regulators. In both the EU and the US, regulators were to implement tighter regulations and intensify supervisory activities. The transatlantic dialogue in financial services, too, was reset from discussions aimed at opening each other's markets to one of building comparable transatlantic "prudential" (oversight) regimes.

Therefore, since 2008 EU and US regulators have had to face the same challenge: the task of mediating between the powerful financial services' industry lobbies (especially that of banking) and public opinion against banks, while simultaneously minimizing the chances that they (the regulators) would be drawn into a zero-sum game of regulatory arbitrage (financial services' firms playing the EU and US off against each other by offering lower regulatory burdens for businesses operating in their jurisdictions). This, then, is the contemporary conundrum transatlantic cooperation must solve: eliminating regulatory arbitrage in order to protect the transatlantic economy from reckless and avaricious decision-making in the financial services industry, while simultaneously ensuring that the Atlantic Community retains its dominance in the development and trade of financial services.

With the launching of the Transatlantic Trade and Investment Partnership (TTIP), the question became whether financial services regulation will be included in the negotiations or in a similarly tight, legally binding transatlantic framework.

The first section of this chapter lays out several possible governance scenarios for EU–US financial services regulation. The second section examines EU and US financial services regulation prior to the global financial meltdown, including a comparison of the two regulatory regimes. The third section focuses on some of the problems faced, both uniquely and commonly, by the EU and the US in the aftermath of the 2007–2008 global financial meltdown. The fourth section discusses the regulatory reforms enacted after the global financial meltdown. The fifth section compares these new regulatory regimes. The penultimate section assesses the feasibility of each of the governance models discussed in the first section. The chapter concludes with implications for the future of transatlantic regulatory cooperation in the financial services sector.

Governance Paradigms

The global financial meltdown of 2007–2008 that triggered the start of the Great Recession represents a classic example of the crisis management of a "wicked problem": "domestic" pressures on both Brussels and Washington heightened the risk of regulatory arbitrage in the absence of a hierarchical authority or binding rules.

Two factors, however, mitigate the temptation of the Atlantic partners to engage in regulatory arbitrage. First, trade figures hide the extent to which "markets are effectively interwoven [and] how easily capital can flow between them" (Transatlantic Business Dialogue, 2012, p. 4). Second, EU and US companies are both feeling increasingly threatened by China, home to three of the largest banks worldwide (Transatlantic Business Dialogue, 2012, p. 4). The implication is that if the EU and the US do not strike an acceptable balance between risk and regulation they will be handing their dominance of the financial services industry to emerging economies. Thus, bankers, insurers, brokers, and investment banks – both in the EU and the US – argue that "excessive" (such as high capital requirements for banks) and "duplicative" (EU and US dual compliance structures) will undermine the financial services industry's health. So despite the fiercely competitive nature of this industry, the "culture" among business interests in the Atlantic Community is converging. And increasingly "competitors" in one transaction turn up as "partners" or "investors" in another. This is nowhere more evident than in the fact that of the total European foreign direct investment (FDI) in the US, 21.7% is in banking and other financial services (Cooper, 2014, p. 7).

At the same time, the American and European electorate continue to demand that Brussels and Washington provide safeguards to prevent another Great Recession. Thus, EU and US policymakers are increasingly pressured to cooperate in establishing a common transatlantic regulatory regime. But which form of governance will accomplish the Atlantic Community's goals: Continued shared dominance of this sector, while minimizing – if not eliminating – a repeat of the global financial meltdown?

There are three basic choices for global governance: markets, hierarchy, and networks. According to Marsh, hierarchy is "a mode of governance characterized by a very close structural coupling between the public and private level, with central coordination, and thus control, being exercised by the government." Markets, on the other hand, lack central coordination and are "driven by the interplay between a plurality of autonomous agents drawn from the public and the private spheres" (Marsh 1998, p. 8).

When the problem is complex, information is scarce or its validity and interpretation are contested, and the parameters are constantly changing, hierarchical control will not only fail to resolve the problem, but may apply remedies which exacerbate the situation. However, when markets govern, market failure surely follows. Indeed, neither hierarchy nor markets have been able to resolve "wicked problems" such as climate change, poverty, nuclear weapon proliferation, financial regulatory arbitrage, poverty, drug and human trafficking, and terrorism (Blanco, Lowndes, & Pratchett, 2011).

Network governance has been advanced as an alternative to the traditional governance dichotomy of hierarchy and markets, and has gained currency as a governance solution to wicked problems. Slaughter (2005, p. 24) argues that network governance contributes to "world order," by "creating convergence and informed divergence, by improving compliance with international rules; and by increasing the scope, nature, and quality of international cooperation." (See Blanco et al., 2011; Börzel, 1998; Klijn & Koppenjan, 2012; Pollack & Schaffer, 2001a; Slaughter, 2005 for excellent treatments of these three basic governance forms, with special focus on the network model.)

These three "pure" forms of governance serve as our basis to advance five distinct governance "choices" for transatlantic financial services regulation. Placing these options on a continuum from market-based, no governmental intervention (Option 1) to treaty-driven, hierarchical global management (Option 5), the EU and the US can select from the following menu of options:

Option 1: Market governance (do nothing).
Option 2: Rely on existing transatlantic fora and groups to share information and agree to best practices.
Option 3: Rely on existing multilateral fora to share information and agree to best practices.

Option 4: Binding transatlantic agreement managed by an EU-US regulatory agency.
Option 5: Binding international agreements managed by an international governmental organization.

Zahariadis, in his analysis of competition policy (Chapter 8) frames transatlantic policy cooperation in the context of "negative" and "positive" integration. He finds that where positive integration is required, little action has taken place in the realm of transatlantic policy cooperation. He is also skeptical about the ability of the Atlantic Community to agree to hierarchical governance not simply because it would involve a loss in sovereignty in economic issues, but because there are just too many differences in bureaucratic organizations, norms, economic structures, and legal approaches to competition/antitrust policy between the Atlantic partners. He recommends that where the option of negative integration is available, it should be attempted as the most realistic option for transatlantic governance.

Looking at the five options available for transatlantic cooperation in financial services regulation – Options 2 and 3 involve negative integration, while Options 4 and 5 would require positive integration (tight regulatory regime with dispute settlement mechanism). Therefore, one would expect both the EU and the US to favor a combination of Options 2 and 3. However, the EU has rejected both of these "easy" options. Instead, the EU has persistently voiced its support for Option 4 – a binding transatlantic agreement. An explanation of the EU's position follows.

The Commission (2014c, p. 2) has urged that "in the post-crisis era where we have fundamentally upgraded financial regulation on both sides of the Atlantic, we should also seek to upgrade the mechanisms for regulatory co-operation." Nadia Calviño, Deputy Director General for Financial Services at the European Commission, underlined this point when she stated, "We want to set a system of mutual consultations in advance of any new financial measures that may significant affect [the other side]" and avoid a repeat of the derivatives regulation final ruling in the US

> where despite the fact that we were signaling there were problems ... there was really no attempt to address those problems in advance until it was the 11th hour, four in the morning ... and because of the enormous market pressure and political pressure.
>
> (Quoted in Monahan & Payne, 2014, p. 5)

Furthermore, the Commission seeks a comprehensive approach, beginning at the legislative level in the financial services regulation policymaking process:

> It is inevitable that regulatory difference would occur given the differences between our market structures and legislative frameworks, but we should work together, at an early stage in the legislative process to ensure that we aim for consistent rule making, and where consistency is not possible, we mitigate the unintended consequences of inconsistency.
>
> (European Commission, 2014c, p. 2)

The Obama Administration, however, has resisted inclusion of financial services regulation in the TTIP, or indeed any formal regulatory cooperation. The US position is articulated in a statement made in December 2013 by Jacob J. Lew, US Treasury Secretary:

> While finishing high standard free trade agreements presents real opportunities to drive growth and create jobs, we will not allow these agreements to serve as an opportunity to water down domestic financial regulatory standards. And let me be clear: We will press other jurisdictions to match our robust standards – including in Europe and across Asia. And we will do so by continuing to pursue our international regulatory agenda in the bilateral and multilateral forums that have been and will continue to be at the forefront of advancing global financial reforms such as the FSB and G-20.
>
> (Quoted in Monahan & Payne, 2014, p. 5)

Significantly, this issue has also been raised in the most important transatlantic forum for EU–US financial services regulation – the EU–US Financial Markets Regulatory Dialogue (FMRD). Quoting from a report from the January 2014 meeting: "EU officials also reiterated their request to include a financial regulatory cooperation framework in the Trans-Atlantic Trade and Investment Partnership. The U. S. officials reiterated that financial regulatory cooperation should continue separately in existing global and bilateral fora" (EU–US Financial Markets Regulatory Dialogue, 2014, p. 1).

Monahan and Payne (2014, p. 6) list a number of reasons informing the Obama Administration's position: the danger of reopening Dodd–Frank; increasing the chances that some of the stricter approaches to prudential regulation adopted in the US will be watered down under external pressure; undermining the connection between the American public and regulators by catering to the interests of sovereign governments or big banks; and, finally, increasing pressure on the Federal Reserve and other regulators to take account of foreign jurisdictions when making policy decisions, at the expense of the national interest.

Virtually every transatlantic lobbying group has weighed in on the controversy over whether to include financial services regulation in the TTIP. The Transatlantic Business Council (TBC; Transatlantic Business Council, 2013a, p. 2), responding to a joint EU and US call for input on regulatory issues in advance of the TTIP negotiation, wrote:

> Regulatory cooperation between the EU and the U.S. should play a significant role in the process of setting international standards and best practices related to financial markets regulation and oversight. It is essential that the EU and the U.S. continue to coordinate and collaborate on finding the best approaches to financial markets regulation in order to drive down regulatory duplication costs for companies operating on both sides of the Atlantic.

The Transatlantic Consumer Dialogue (TACD; Transatlantic Consumer Dialogue, 2013b, p. 2) expressed skepticism in its October 2013 statement:

"Unfortunately, US and European financial services firms have made clear their interest in using the TTIP to roll back financial reforms enacted in the wake of the global financial crisis."

In sum, the US favors Options 2 (transatlantic dialogue) and 3 (global dialogue) along with bilateral links as adequate mechanisms for governing financial services, whereas the EU favors Option 4 (the TTIP or, failing that, a tight regulatory regime to be negotiated in parallel to the TTIP).

Which is the "correct" position? This is a difficult question to answer because there are so many conditioning factors – threats to sovereignty; the structure of the financial industry in the US and the EU member states; disparate financing of industry (the US relies more heavily on equity financing, and the EU member states – the UK being the exception – tend to utilize debt financing); and possible linkages to other transatlantic trade issues (Monahan & Payne, 2014, p. 11).

To begin to answer this question, it may be helpful to conceptualize the problem as one of a modified "prisoner's dilemma" of transatlantic cooperation, which is depicted in Figure 11.1.

It is assumed that the broad goals of EU and US officials are identical: continued transatlantic dominance of the financial services industry and financial stability. Based on statements by public officials (see above), it can be assumed that the EU believes effective transatlantic cooperation needs to be in the form of Option 4, while the US believes transatlantic cooperation can be achieved through Options 2 and 3. Defecting from transatlantic cooperation would involve one partner abandoning transatlantic cooperation in favor of bilateral and

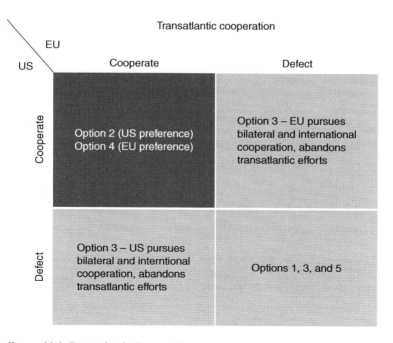

Figure 11.1 Transatlantic Cooperation.

international cooperation while the other sought continued transatlantic cooperation. Finally, both parties would defect from transatlantic cooperation if they abandoned any cooperation at all (Option 1 – anarchic markets) or pursed a binding international agreement (Option 5) to the exclusion of transatlantic cooperation.

To further explore the necessity of Option 4 – binding transatlanticism – we will need to inventory and analyze EU and US financial services regulatory policy. Specifically, we will need to assess the extent to which these regimes may have converged *without* the benefit of the tight regulatory forum (Option 4) advocated by EU leaders. This is the task of the next two sections of this chapter. The first section seeks to identify commonalities and differences in EU and US regulatory regimes prior to the global financial meltdown. The second section performs a similar analysis for the post-global meltdown regulatory regime.

Financial Services Regulation Prior to the 2007–2008 Global Financial Meltdown

Early Transnational Dialogue Centered on Accounting and Reporting

"Coordinated" efforts of EU and US regulators can be traced to the regulatory fallout from corporate accounting legerdemain in the 1990s, which hid from potential investors the rot in companies such as the giant energy trader Enron. This led the US Securities and Exchange Commission (SEC) – the federal government's regulatory body with the authority to set accounting standards – to issue a unilateral requirement for all corporations (including foreign corporations) to adopt Generally Accepted Accounting Principles (GAAP) set by the US-based Financial Accounting Standards Board (FASB), despite the fact that European corporations utilize the International Financial Reporting Standards (IFRS) set by the London-based International Accounting Standards Board (IASB) (Norris, 2012). The SEC issued this new regulation without consulting the EU.

Naturally, the EU and its member states protested that requiring their corporations to undergo the expense of accounting in both IFRS and GAAP represented an unfair trade practice (raising the cost of doing business). The EU's complaint triggered talks between the SEC, the Commission (DG Industry and Enterprise), and member states' authorities to resolve their differences. As a result of these discussions, the SEC backed down on the GAAP requirements – the 2002 Norwalk Agreement – but with the proviso that FASB and IASB work toward establishing convergence in the accounting of financial instruments.

Significantly, the EU–US FMRD was established at this time to discuss accounting standards and to prevent a repeat of the SEC incident, but then quickly moved to broaden discussion of economic liberalization in the transatlantic arena.

A Focus on Capital Flow in the EU

The EU began building its financial services policy in the 1990s as part of the larger internal market project. As has been the central feature of the policymaking process in the internal market's completion, the EU liberalized capital movements by reducing member state technical barriers to trade in financial services and cross-border mergers. (See Chapter 8 for a detailed discussion of negative integration in the context of the internal market and competition policy.) The most important EU legislation prior to the 2007–2008 meltdown is the *Markets in Financial Instruments Directive* (MiFID) 2004/39/EC adopted in 2004, implemented in 2007, and covering all financial services. MiFID instituted two major changes to the regulation of financial sources in the EU. First, it deregulated stock markets (breaking the monopolies of national exchanges and thereby encouraging "alternative trading venues to emerge" (Wishart, 2011). Second, MiFID created a rule book or "passport" that harmonized national rules for investment services, operation of exchanges, and cross-border provision of financial services (thus enabling authorized investment firms, banks, and exchanges to provide their services freely across borders) (European Commission, 2007).

MiFID is managed through "The Lamfalussy Process," which combined legislative duties (framework legislation) with technical committees. Supervision (prudential management) continued to be the responsibility of the Commission and the member states. In the EU member states, the supervisory function is carried out by public authorities rather than the quite different US approach, which relies heavily on "self-policing" through self-regulating organizations (SROs). In European regulatory ideology, national authorities believe "regulation is primarily a role for public and statutory authorities" and are concerned about the inherent conflicts of interests that can arise with self-regulation. In sum, self-regulation plays a "minor role" in the regulation of financial services in the EU (Carson, 2010, pp. 2–3, 6).

US Regulation as a Three-Legged Stool

US financial services policy in this period was quite different from the EU's because it already had a strong regulatory focus on the national level, but was in the process of "liberalizing." Prior to the post-2008 reforms, US securities regulation rested on a three-legged stool consisting of: (1) a powerful national regulatory agency in the SEC (dating from the Roosevelt-era 1934 Securities Exchange Act); (2) powers delegated to the self-regulating Financial Industry Regulatory Authority (FINRA) and Municipal Securities Rulemaking Board (MSRB) (SROs were authorized in the Securities Exchange Act so that all dealers of equity, corporate bonds, securities futures, and options must belong to one of these SROs); and (3) the SEC's Regulation National Market System (Reg NMS), which sought to promote competition among markets and individual orders, comparison shopping, and required lower access fees – mainly in an effort to protect consumers.

At the same time, the desire among US policymakers to govern through markets (in the name of "competitiveness") had begun with the 1999 passage of the Gramm–Leach–Biley Act (1999), essentially repealing the Depression-era Glass–Steagall Act, which had limited the combination of commercial and investment banking (Pan, 2008).

Comparative Analysis

In the first period of "cooperation," the EU and the US focused on market liberalization. As the EU sought to improve market competitiveness with MiFID, the US SEC issued Reg NMS, with both coming into force in 2007 (Boskovic, Cerruti, & Noel, 2009, p. 1). Although the US already had in place a mature regulatory structure at a time when the EU was mainly concerned with increasing cross-border trade in financial services among EU member states (completing the internal market), both Brussels and Washington were concerned to increase the competitiveness of their financial services industries.

Fragmentation in both regulatory systems

During this time period, EU and US financial services regulators also faced similar criticism from financial services firms, mainly over what the industry saw as excessive fragmentation in regulatory regimes, which they claimed unnecessarily added to the time and cost of conducting business. MiFID I, for example, is a directive, and therefore needed to be implemented by the legislatures of each member state, whereas regulation of financial services institutions continued to be primarily the responsibility of the member states.

While the US system may seem to have been more unified (due to the presence of a powerful regulator and the fact that, unlike the EU, it is a *bona fide* federal state), the US regulatory system, too, was highly fragmented. At the federal level, three agencies were responsible for oversight of financial instruments: the SEC for stocks and corporate bonds, the Commodity Futures Trading Commission (CFTC) for commodities and derivatives, and the Federal Reserve Board (the Fed) for the financial instruments issued by banks. As was discussed above, the US SEC relies extensively on two SROs to regulate the behavior of securities actors. There was no federal body providing overall supervision of the regulatory system. And there was no federal body whatsoever engaged in oversight of the insurance industry. Indeed, in the US the states have primary regulatory power in the insurance industry. There are numerous agencies with regulatory power – state securities regulators, state insurance regulators, state banking regulators, and state attorneys general – involved in rule-making, regulation, and enforcement when not pre-empted by federal law. State officials – especially in New York State – have been particularly active in investigating, imposing fines, and prosecuting brokers and investment advisors.

As will be discussed later in this chapter, this fragmentation – itself an inherent feature of the American federal system – continues despite far-reaching reforms since passage of the 2010 Dodd–Frank Act. As a result, regulated firms continue to complain about the high cost of compliance. The financial industry also argues that regulatory competition (turf battles among federal oversight agencies) has impeded the development of new financial instruments. (One example was the SEC's long-standing opposition to security futures, ostensibly because these would be regulated by the CFTC – see Pan, 2008.) Another common complaint has been that the many government agencies do not coordinate their activities, especially state and federal regulators, with, as Pan (2008, p. 842) suggests, costly consequences for financial services firms:

> Financial firms have found themselves in recent years being subject to civil penalties from the SEC, criminal charges from the US Department of Justice, and criminal and civil charges from state regulators in addition to private lawsuits. Because federal and state regulators and prosecutors frequently fail to coordinate their enforcement actions, financial firms face the prospect of defending themselves against multiple agencies, unable to negotiate settlements or propose remedies that would allow the firm to free itself of further liability.

In the fall of 2007, when the financial services industry began to unravel in the US and the consequences of this collapse spread to the EU the following year, the electorate and politicians alike agreed the regulatory system was considered as having been inadequate to police the financial services industry in both the EU and the US. If, at the time, the EU and the US had agreed and implemented a binding transatlantic regime (Option 4), could the Atlantic Community have escaped the financial collapse? The answer is, "probably not." Neither set of regulators had grasped the danger of overheated housing markets to their economies, which had been fueled by risky mortgage lending and novel derivative instruments (which provided the liquidity to continue to fuel lending).

Post-Financial Meltdown: Common Problems Confronting the EU and the US

Seeking answers to the cause of the global financial meltdown, EU and US officials identified a number of shortcomings in the financial services industry and the regulatory regime. And in separate analyses of their own regulatory systems – the de Larosière Report (de Larosière Group, 2009) and the US Department of Treasury (2008) – it became evident that they faced common problems. Box 11.1 summarizes problems specifically identified in these studies. One problem on this list, however, was unique to the EU – the lack of a bank supervisor. The sovereign debt and banking crises, however, soon created the conditions to alter this disparate approach, so that at the end of 2012 the EU had decided to make the ECB a bank supervisor along the same lines as the Fed (European Council – The President, 2012). This point will be taken up in further detail below.

Current Regulatory Regimes

Beginning in 2010, the EU and the US engaged in substantial overhaul of their financial services regulatory regimes. Congress passed and President Obama signed *The Wall Street Reform and Consumer Protection Act* (Dodd–Frank) in

Box 11.1 Problems EU and US Policymakers Confronted in Regulating the Financial Services Industry, Made Apparent by the Great Recession

Common Problems

1. Inadequate regulations, especially of complex/opaque instruments such as collateralized debt swaps (CDS) and other non-transparent derivatives.
2. Lack of macroprudential supervision of financial institutions.
3. Financial institutions too big to fail and too big to manage.
4. Costs to taxpayers of winding down troubled financial institutions.
5. Low transparency of over-the-counter (OTC) markets.
6. Public opinion outraged at executive compensation.
7. Cozy connections between credit rating agencies (CRAs) and financial institutions.
8. Fraud perpetrated against consumers and investors (e.g., lack of transparency in mortgage instruments, such as the balloon payments in adjustable rate mortgages (ARMs)
9. Deposit guarantees encourage risky behavior by banks.
10. Minimum capital requirements for banks and definitions of "safe" capital.
11. Debate over how much power legislatures should bestow on regulators.
12. Which governmental entity should be the bank supervisor?
13. Heavy lobbying by powerful business interests.
14. Fragmentation of regulatory oversight.

Problems Unique to the EU (prior to the 2012 establishment of a banking union)

1. Lack of uniform deposit guarantees across the member states.
2. Lack of an obvious bank supervisor.
   (Boskovic et al., 2009; de Larosière Group, 2009; European Commission, 2010d; Quaglia, 2013; US Department of Treasury, 2008)

2010, which is being implemented in phases. The EU has engaged in two phases of reforms – first in 2010 by agreeing to an EU-level regulatory structure, and in 2014 agreeing to a regulatory package addressing industry practices.

EU Reforms

In all, the Commission has published more than 30 financial proposals since the start of the Great Recession (Hirst, 2014a). The EU has undertaken reform in two distinct phases.

Phase I: European System of Financial Supervision

The first phase, agreed in 2010 and implemented in 2011, reformed the regulatory infrastructure by establishing the European System of Financial

Supervision. *Regulation 1092/2010* established a European Systemic Risk Board (ESRB Regulation), *Regulations 1093/2010, 1094/2010,* and *1095/2010* established "European Supervisory Authorities" (ESAs), and *Regulation 1096/3010* conferred specific tasks on the European Central Bank (ECB) concerning the functioning of the ESRB.

The de Larosière Report (2009) had offered 31 recommendations for reform of the financial services regulatory system. Among the recommendations were structural changes that have been put in place and now feature as the spine of the "European System of Financial Supervision" (ESFS): specifically, "bringing together the actors of financial supervision at national level and at the level of the Union, to act as a network" (European Commission, 2010c, p. 3). This new regulatory infrastructure has been in place since January 2011. The European Systemic Risk Board (ESRB) was placed at the head of the ESFS. The ESRB regulation states that:

> The ESRB shall be responsible for the macro-prudential oversight of the financial system within the Union in order to contribute to the prevention or mitigation of systemic risks to financial stability in the Union that arise from developments within the financial system and taking into account macroeconomic developments, so as to avoid periods of widespread financial distress. It shall contribute to the smooth functioning of the internal market and thereby ensure a sustainable contribution of the financial sector to economic growth.
>
> (European Commission, 2010c, Article 3 (1))

The three "micro-prudential supervisors" were upgraded from the status of technical committees (in MiFID) to supervisory authorities:

- the European Banking Authority (EBA) (formerly the Committee of European Banking Supervisors);
- the European Insurance and Occupational Pensions Authority (EIOPA) (formerly the Committee of European Insurance and Occupational Pensions Supervisors);
- the European Securities and Market Authority (ESMA) (formerly the Committee of European Security Regulators).

The main tasks of the EBA (European Banking Authority, n.d.) are to contribute to the creation of the European Single Rulebook in banking, to promote convergence of supervisory practices, and to assess risks and vulnerabilities in the EU banking system (see, for example, the EBA's risk assessment of EU and EEA banks in the first half of 2013 at European Banking Authority, 2013). While originally a more direct role in supervising national banks had been envisaged for the EBA by some individuals in the financial services regulator reforms, events – specifically the eurozone banking and debt crises – were to alter the role of the EBA in the ESFS (see Buonanno & Nugent, 2013, pp. 205–207).

Therefore, the build-up of pressures for a banking union led to, in June 2012, the establishment of the European Stability Mechanism (ESM), to be tied to the creation of a single banking supervisory agency run by the European ECB. The "Single Supervisory Mechanism" (SSM), which went into effect on November 4, 2014, was enacted through *Council Regulation (EU) No 1024/2013* of October 15, 2013 and *Regulation (EU) No 1022/2013* of the European Parliament and of the Council of October 22, 2013, amending *Regulation (EU) No 1093/2010 Establishing a European Supervisory Authority* (EBA). The SSM empowers the ECB to monitor the financial stability of banks in participating states (eurozone, required and non-eurozone EU members, voluntarily) meeting certain conditions (see below), while national authorities play a supporting role (European Central Bank, 2014; European Commission, 2014a). The ECB supervises approximately 130 credit institutions, representing almost 85% of total banking assets in the eurozone (European Central Bank, 2014). National authorities supervise those banks not meeting the requisite conditions for SSM supervision. A bank must be supervised by the ECB if it meets one of the following conditions: assets value exceeds €30 billion; assets value exceeds both €5 billion and 20% of GDP of the member state in which it is located; the bank is among the three most significant banks of the country in which it is located; the bank has large cross-border activities; or, the bank receives, or has applied for, assistance from the ESM or EFSF (European Commission, 2013h).

Decision-making in the EFSF continues to incorporate the Lamfalussy Process utilized in MiFID I, but with the ESAs engaged in supervision and the ESRB acting as the overarching supervisory body. The Lamfalussy Process operates on the premise of appropriate decision-making "levels" that combine supranational and national institutions and actors. Level 1 is legislative (drafting of legislation by the Commission and passage of directives and regulations by the Council and EP). Rules are implemented in Level 2 by the authorities. Interaction between national authorities and the ESAs takes place at Level 3. And at Level 4, the Commission monitors member state implementation and compliance.

Phase II: Regulatory Policy Regime

With a new regulatory infrastructure in place, the Commission then set out to build a tougher regulatory policy regime. The second phase of EU regulatory reform began when the European Commission (2011a) proposed MiFID II in October 2011 (*Financial Instruments Directive*). While the Commission had been able to take advantage of the policy window provided by the financial crisis to overhaul the institutional structure of the financial services regulatory regime, the policies themselves now became subject to intense contestation among member states, EU institutions, consumer groups, and financial sector actors. The Commission's controversial proposal for strong regulation of short-selling (where traders bet that the price of a security will fall) and derivatives, illustrate the nature of a highly contested environment, with the UK government – believing such regulation would damage the interests of the City of London – insisting that decisions on the regulation of such activities remain with the member states and not be transferred to the ESMA (Wishart, 2013).

The European Market Infrastructure Regulation (EMIR) 648/2012 on Over-the-Counter (OTC) derivatives, central counterparties (CCPs) and trade repositories (TRs) entered into force on August 2012. Subsequent Commission delegating regulations were published in the EU *Official Journal* in February 2013 and entered into force in March 2013 (ESMA, n.d.). EMIR established compulsory clearing requirements such as the application of risk-mitigation techniques for non-centrally cleared OTC derivatives; reporting to trade repositories; and application of requirements for trade repositories, including the duty to make certain data available to the public and relevant authorities. Because the G-20 had agreed to the provisions which are contained in EMIR (see below), disagreement in the Council was largely avoided. EMIR was subsequently amended by the Market in Financial Instruments Regime (MiFIR) in June 2014.

With MiFID up for review over the next two years (2012–2014), financial services regulatory reform was highly contest among the EU's legislative actors. For example, the European Parliament (EP) proposed 1,550 amendments to the Commission's MiFID II proposal (B. Fox, 2014a). The Council and the Parliament finally agreed to the MiFID II on January 14, 2014 after a seven-hour marathon trilogue (Hirst, 2014b). (The "trilogue" is the EU's equivalent of the "conference committee" in the US Congress whereby negotiations take place between the Council and the EP – with the Commission present – to reach a common position.) The legislation was published in the EU's *Official Journal* in June 2014 and must be transposed by the member states into national law by January 1, 2017.

Hundreds of measures are being transposed and implemented – 444 by the ESM alone (European Securities and Markets Authority, 2014). It is the sheer complexity involved with the implementation of MiFID II, MiFIR, and Dodd–Frank which has prompted the Commission to call for tighter transatlantic regulatory cooperation (Option 4).

Soon after a political agreement was reached on MiFID II, the Commission issued a proposal to ban the EU's largest banks (around 30) from engaging in proprietary trading beginning in January 2017 (Hirst, 2014a). This agreement is the EU's "Volcker Rule." (On this rule, see "US reforms," below.) In announcing the proposal, Michel Barnier (the then Commissioner for Internal Market and Services) echoed his US counterparts in stating: "too big to fail, too costly to save and too complex to resolve."

US Reforms

The Wall Street Reform and Consumer Protection Act (Dodd–Frank), which the 111th US Congress passed and President Obama signed in 2010, gave sweeping new power to federal regulators. The US financial regulatory architecture overhaul (depicted in Table 11.1) represents the most substantial reform since the system was set up by Franklin Delano Roosevelt during the Great Depression.

Table 11.1 Post-Dodd–Frank US Regulatory Framework

Financial Stability Oversight Council (FSOC)
Regulating systemically important institutions and recommending heightened prudential standards

BHCs – Banks/SLHCs – Thrifts	Securities and Securities-Based Derivatives	Commodity Futures and Derivatives	Consumer Financial Protection	Insurance
Federal Reserve	Securities and Exchange Commission	Commodity Futures Trading Commission (CFTC)	Federal Reserve/Consumer Financial Protection Bureau	US Treasury/Federal Insurance Office
• BHCs, SLHCs, and any firm designated as systematically significant by the FSOC	• Security exchanges, brokers and dealers; mutual fund (including hedge funds with assets over $150 million)	• Main mission is to prevent excessive speculation	• Writes rules to carry out the federal consumer financial protection laws	
• Lender of last resort to member banks (through discount window lending)	• Nationally recognized statistical rating organizations	• Future exchanges, brokers, commodity pool operators, and commodity trading advisors	• Nonbank mortgage-related firms, private student lenders, payday lenders, and larger consumer financial entities (to be determined by the Bureau)	
• In "unusual and exigent circumstance," the Fed may extend credit beyond member banks, to provide liquidity to the financial system, but not to aid failing financial firms	• Security-based swaps: dealers, major participants, and execution facilities	• Swaps: dealers, major swap participants, and swap execution facilities	• Consumer businesses of banks with over $10 billion in assets	
• May initiate resolution process to shut down firms that pose a grave threat to financial stability (requires concurrence of two-thirds of the FSOC)	• Corporations selling securities to the public must register and make financial disclosures	• May suspend trading, order liquidation of positions during market emergencies	• Does not supervise insurers, SECT and CFTC registrants, auto dealers, sellers of nonfinancial goods, real estate brokers and agents, and banks with assets less than $10 billion	
	• May unilaterally close markets or suspend trading strategies for limited periods	• Overseas industry SROS (futures exchanges and the National Futures Association)		
	• Authorized to set financial accounting standards which all publicly traded firms must use			
	• Oversees industry SROs (FIMA)			

Financial Institutions Regulatory Authority	State regulatory agencies	State consumer protection agencies	State insurance regulators
Office of the Comptroller of the Currency – the major prudential regulator for federally chartered banks and thrifts			State insurance regulators
Federal Deposit Insurance Corporation – federally insured depository institutions, including state banks and thrifts that are not members of the Federal Reserve System • Operates a deposit insurance fund for federally chartered and state chartered banks and thrifts. • After making a determination of systemic risk, the FDIC may invoke broad authority to use the deposit insurance funds to provide an assistance to depository institutions	State regulatory agencies	State consumer protection agencies	

continued

Table 11.1 Continued

Financial Stability Oversight Council (FSOC)
Regulating systemically important institutions and recommending heightened prudential standards

BHCs – Banks/SLHCs – Thrifts	Securities and Securities-Based Derivatives	Commodity Futures and Derivatives	Consumer Financial Protection	Insurance
National Credit Union Administration (NCUA) • Federally chartered or insured credit unions • Operates a deposit insurance fund for credit unions • Serves as a liquidity lender to credit unions experiencing liquidity shortfalls through the Central Liquidity Facility State regulatory agencies				

Sources: Murphy, 2013, p. 13; PriceWaterhouseCoopers, 2010.

Table 11.1 lists the federal regulatory bodies with respect to their areas of competence (deposit and lending; securities; commodities; and consumer protection). *The Dodd–Frank Act* established the Financial Stability Oversight Council (FSOC) as an interagency coordinating body and authorized a permanent staff to monitor systemic risk. The Secretary of the Treasury chairs the FSOC, with the other voting members consisting of the heads of the Fed, FDIC, OCC, NCUA, SEC, CFTC, Federal Housing Finance Agency (FHFA), and CFPB, and a member with insurance expertise appointed by the President. Non-voting members serve in an advisory capacity and represent various other governmental actors such as a state banking supervisor, a state insurance commissioner, and a state securities commissioner (Murphy, 2013, p. 28). Dodd–Frank also reduced from five to four the number of regulatory bodies overseeing banking (the Office of Thrift Supervision was merged into the US Department of Treasury's Office of the Comptroller of the Currency). Dodd–Frank granted the Fed and the FDIC resolution authority over the largest financial firms ("too big to fail"). Finally, Dodd–Frank consolidated consumer protection rule-making (which had been dispersed among several federal agencies) in a new agency – the Consumer Financial Protection Bureau (Murphy, 2013, p. iii).

Federal regulators are roughly divided according to whether they focus on prudence (monitoring and regulating the risks of financial services firms) or disclosure (monitoring and regulating the information that firms and exchanges provide to potential market participants). The latter represents an important policy change because prior to Dodd–Frank, federal regulators focused on disclosure rather than prudence (see Murphy, 2013, p. 1).

Similar to the EU experience, reforming the regulatory architecture proved to be the easier part of the process: developing new regulations has proven very contentious. One particularly controversial new regulation that was included in Dodd–Frank is the "Volcker Rule," intended to curb most forms of proprietary trading where commercial banks trade in securities, derivatives, or futures for their own gain, and also capped bank ownership in hedge funds and private equity funds at 3%. The Volcker Rule was approved in December 2013 and implemented April 1, 2014 with full compliance required by July 21, 2015 (*New York Times*, 2013).

In general, in exercising their rule-making power, US federal regulators have been confronted with intense opposition not just from industry actors, but sometimes from foreign regulators as well. One example of the latter is the "cross-border guidance rule" proposed by the CFTC, which under Dodd–Frank now has regulatory supervision over the annual $700 trillion market in derivatives. This rule requires overseas branches of American banks, foreign financial institutions, and hedge funds to report foreign trades if they involve US customers or are guaranteed by a financial institution with American ties (Lipton, 2013). The EU considers this rule to be an overreach of American regulatory authority and an infringement on EU sovereignty.

As has been seen with post-financial crisis EU regulatory reforms, *The Dodd–Frank Act* – which mandates 533 rules, 60 studies, and 93 reports

(PriceWaterhouseCoopers, 2010) – is still evolving. Again, one can easily grasp the rationale for the Commission' desire to establish a tighter transatlantic regulatory consultation mechanism.

Comparing Regulatory Regimes

Commonalities and Differences

Table 11.2 compares the key regulatory bodies in the EU and the US. Bodies placed on the same rows indicate that they have the same function in the US and the EU. The final column indicates the problem (identified in Box 11.1) each of the regulatory bodies is empowered to address.

Commonalities:

1. Creation of a macro-prudential oversight agency (ESRB and FSOC).
2. Substantial alignment between MiFID II and Dodd–Frank with respect to financial instruments subject to regulation, with the exception of derivatives (see below).
3. Volcker Rule as part of Dodd–Frank, implementation April 2014–July 2015; Commission adopted a similar rule in 2014, to be fully implemented by January 1, 2017.
4. The Basel Committee for Banking Supervision, G-20 agreements with respect to increasing banking capital requirements and disclosure rules, which are detailed later in this chapter.
5. Fed and ECB (EU banking union, which became operational in the fall of 2014) have powerful oversight authority over large banks (too big to fail).

Differences:

1. The continued importance of SROs in the US – particularly, FINRA (US) (a non-governmental regulator overseeing approximately 4,270 brokerage firms) – as compared to the regulation of securities dealers a responsibility of public authorities at both the national and, now, EU level (ESMA) (Financial Industry Regulatory Authority, 2013).
2. The establishment in the US of a consumer financial protection bureau (no such entity is found at the EU level).
3. Derivatives are supervised by the US CFTC, while in MiFID II derivative oversight remains the responsibility of member state national authorities.
4. The EU now has an authority (EIOPA) to oversee insurance. The US federal government has been unable to gain regulatory authority over the insurance industry. Title V of Dodd–Frank does create the Federal Insurance Office within the Department of Treasury, which has the authority to collect information and monitor all types of insurance (except health insurance); but, in the main, the federal government could not (yet) wrest control over regulation of the insurance industry from state regulators. The insurance industry is divided on whether it prefers regulation at the federal level

(decreases the costs of complying with 50 state laws) or to stay with the system that it knows (state regulation) and seems to be functioning reasonably well.

Problem #11 – debate over how much power legislatures should bestow on regulators (see Box 11.1) – has become central to the regulatory overhaul in both the EU and the US. Because MiFID II and Dodd–Frank legislation are written broadly, they require extensive rule-making by the securities regulators, prompting outrage – naturally more so from the American center-right – about onerous rules written by an unelected bureaucracy.

With respect to regulatory arbitrage, the EU's regulatory framework may actually be more reliable and stable than the US framework. This is because MiFID II was passed by a center-right dominated Council and center-right dominated Parliament. In the US, Dodd–Frank was passed when Democrats controlled both houses of Congress and the Presidency. So even if the Council (whose ideological composition changes gradually with national elections) and the Parliament (the next elections will not be held until 2019) became center-left dominated, the EU's regulatory framework would be expected to be stable (if any change, the direction would be toward a more robust regulative framework). Whereas in the US if Republicans gain control of the federal government (at the time of this writing, the federal government is "divided" with the Republicans holding the majority in the US House of Representatives and the Republicans having won control of the US Senate in the November 2014 mid-term elections), Congress will certainly attempt to weaken Dodd–Frank. There is ample evidence of this desire, if not intent: since the Republicans gained control of the House of Representatives in January 2011, the center-right has begun chipping away at Dodd–Frank. (See, for instance, US House of Representatives, 2011.) So, too, congressional Republicans tied passage of the federal budget to roll back of regulations on the ability of banks to trade in derivatives (Eavis 2014; Krugman 2014). Politics matter, and here the US mortgage industry is a particularly instructive example. The atomistic mortgage industry – consisting as it did pre-financial meltdown of hundreds of independent mortgage brokers – has been a reliable constituency for small-town and suburban Republicans. This group now decries the strict mortgage-writing rules and the squeezing out of mortgage brokers, with the "onerous" rules now favoring larger capitalized entities (big banks). (Wells Fargo and JPMorgan Chase together control one-third of the mortgage market – see Olick, 2014). But federal government regulators were "burned" in the mortgage industry collapse in the Great Recession. Therefore, they focus on balancing prudential concerns with growth: they want to be assured that when they fine mortgage lenders for the peccadilloes of rogue underwriters, the funds will be there to "pay up." Otherwise, the taxpayers get stuck with the bill.

Table 11.2 Comparison of EU and US Regulatory Regimes (Post-Great Recession)

EU Regulatory Bodies	Duties	US Regulatory Bodies	Duties	Problem Designed to Resolve (Box 11.1)
European Systemic Risk Board (ESRB) – NEW	Macro-prudential oversight	Financial Stability Oversight Council (FSOC) – New; • Office of Financial Research (OFR); • Financial Research Fund	Macro-prudential oversight; • Self-funding used to fund OFR	1–3
		Bureau of Consumer Financial Protection (BCFP) – New agency; • Data Center of BCFP; • Research and Analysis Center of BCFP	• Conducts independent analysis	
European Securities and Markets Authority (ESMA)	Securities[1] supervisor	Commodity Futures Trading Commission (CFTC)[2] – New powers	Supervisor – commodities and derivatives	5
		Securities and Exchange Commission (SEC) – New powers mainly in shareholders' rights; investors' rights; • Office of Credit Ratings (new office)	Supervisor – stocks and corporate bonds; monitors corporate governance, especially in ensuring shareholders' rights	6, 7
Committee of European Securities Regulators (CESR) – links national authorities				
European Central Bank (ECB)	Supervisor large banks	Federal Reserve (FED)	Supervisor large banks (all bank holding companies)	4, 8, 10
European Banking Authority			All nationally chartered banks must be Fed members. All state-chartered banks wishing to use Fed's lending facilities (and are then subject to Fed regulation)	4, 8, 10

ECB, member state deposit insurance schemes (required in EU law)	Federal Deposit Insurance Corporation (FDIC)	Membership required for all depository institutions in the US (other than credit unions). Primary regulator for all state-chartered banks not Fed members
European Insurance and Occupational Pensions Authority (EIOPA)		
ECB	Office of the Comptroller of the Currency	Charters, regulates, and examines national banks
	National Credit Union Administration (NCUA)	Charters, regulates, and insures federal credit unions
	Federal Insurance Office	Creates the first ever office in the federal government focused on insurance
Member state securities regulators, insurance regulators, banking regulators, home office	State agencies – state securities regulators, state insurance regulators, state banking regulators, state attorneys general	

Source: US Senate Committee on Banking Housing and Urban Affairs, 2010.

Notes

1. Derivatives in the EU are regulated by the member state national regulators. Both the EU and the US (generally) exempt non-financial entities using a swap to hedge or mitigate commercial risks.

2. The CFTC was created in 197 (Commodity Futures Trading Commission Act), mainly to oversee futures in agricultural commodities. Title VII of the Dodd–Frank Act amends the Commodity Exchange Act to establish a comprehensive new regulatory framework for swaps and security-based swaps (which covers derivatives).

The Future of Governance in Financial Services Regulation: An Analysis of Five Options

In the flurry of regulatory activity, the EU and the US have taken a similar approach to financial services regulation. With some exceptions (in the regulation of insurance – centralized body in the EU; consumer protection – centralized body in the US; continued reliance on SROs in the US for stock market regulation; and continued member state regulation of derivatives), the regulatory structures are quite similar. So, too, are regulatory rules and even the underlying philosophies driving financial market regulation.

Given these similarities that exist without a binding transatlantic regulatory approach, why would the EU think that Option 4 is necessary? The Commission's choice seems obvious – the evolving rules and their (long-term) implementation. While the analysis of the previous section indicated that broad rules have been established by legislatures, naturally there could be considerable divergences of interpretation in the writing of rules and their application by government regulators. Why, then, would the US oppose what seems a very sensible approach?

At the beginning of this chapter, five options for the governance of financial services regulation were proposed. This section attempts to analyze the optimal choice to satisfy both partners by analyzing the various options available to the EU and the US in the context of the latest reforms and past and current EU–US cooperative efforts. Our guiding question is the following: which option holds the most promise for minimizing transatlantic regulatory arbitrage? There are two conditioning factors which must be considered as well: first, conserving transatlantic dominance of the financial services industry; and second, options characterized by negative integration should be preferable to those options which require positive integration.

Option 1: Market Governance

Do nothing – let the markets decide. This is just no longer taken as a serious option. From the G-20 to the TEC's FMRD, stakeholders expect governments to act to curb the excesses of the market. Responsible financial institutions also welcome a robust regulatory regime (so long as it does not undermine their own profits!) to curb excesses among irresponsible and dishonest actors and institutions in the financial industry.

Option 2: Rely on Existing Transatlantic Fora and Groups to Share Information and Agree to Best Practices

As noted earlier in this chapter, EU–US "informal" cooperation in financial services is long-standing. The primary transatlantic forum has been that of the FMRD. The FMRD is co-chaired by the US SEC (with participation by the US Treasury and the Federal Reserve) and the European Commission DG Internal Market. The US Department of State (2009b) has characterized the FMRD as:

a key mechanism for the U.S. and EU to discuss implementation of broad strategy and focus on specific regulatory issues. By bringing together policy and regulatory officials, technical expertise can be brought to bear on broad policy decisions and translated into concrete action.

The SEC's head similarly attested to the importance of the FMRD in March 22, 2012 testimony before Congress (*Testimony Concerning "International Harmonization of Wall Street Reform: Orderly Liquidation, Derivatives, and the Volcker Rule" by Commissioner Elisse B. Walter, US Securities and Exchange Commission*, 2012):

> [FMRD] has evolved into a vehicle for in-depth discussion of regulatory issues of mutual concern, enhancement of understanding of each other's regulatory systems, and exploration of areas of regulatory cooperation and convergence in the development of high-quality regulation.

Table 11.3 summarizes some of the activity that has taken place within the FMRD before and after the EU and the US reformed their financial services regulatory regimes, where it can be seen that the principals discussed a number of matters, including bank stress tests and proposals for restructuring financial supervisory architecture.

This option involves maintaining the status quo, but could involve additional linkages that are currently underdeveloped or non-existent. This would consist of three actions: building on the FMRD, encouraging more meaningful interaction between the EP and the US Congress, and encouraging stakeholder participation in FMRD.

Officials from the relevant "ministries" and regulatory agencies attend FMRD meetings – from the EU side, representatives from the ESAs (EBA, EIOPA, ESMA) and on the US side, from the Federal Reserve, CFTC, FDIC, and SEC participate in the FMRD (EU–US Financial Markets Regulatory Dialogue, 2014). It is expected that the ECB, with its new powers of bank supervision, will begin participating as well.

This option could be strengthened with more frequent scheduling and coordination of meetings. One piece of evidence supporting the feasibility of this option is suggested by Steven Lofchie (2014) from the Center for Financial Stability, who observed in his commentary on the January 2014 FMRD meeting that, "U.S. regulators seem to be striking a far more cooperative tone with non-U.S. regulators lately."

A second course of action to strengthen transatlantic ties is through building effective linkages between the EP and the US Congress, especially among oversight committees. The wrinkle here is that legislation is meant to be broad, with rule-making the responsibility of government officials in the executive branch. Furthermore, in the unlikely scenario that the EP and Congress are willing to work together closely, legislatures are by definition highly politicized arenas and one would expect the very last forum the EU and the US should want to discuss regulatory convergence. At any rate, in a study conducted by the Congressional

Table 11.3 Financial Markets Regulatory Dialogue: Sample Meetings and Actions

Date	Action
June 2004	First meeting of the EU–US FMRD (EU–US Financial Markets Regulatory Dialogue, 2004)
April 2007	The SEC and the European Commission have had a first exchange of views in the FMRD on their respective considerations of how and in which areas to establish mutual recognition of comparable regulatory regimes in the field of securities (Transatlantic Economic Council, 2007)
February and December 2008	Proposals for restructuring financial services supervisory architecture: account standards, securities regulatory regimes; insurance/ reinsurance, SEC and European Commission agreed to undertake a comparability assessment of US and EU securities regimes
June 2009	• The US shared its experience with bank stress testing as the EU prepared for its EU-wide stress testing exercise • Significant interactions between the technical experts on both sides working on stress testing • Credit rating agencies: agreed on "equivalency" • Derivatives: agreed critical to make progress on derivatives, agreed reporting all OTC derivative contracts to trade repositories, clearing all standardized contracts through central counterparties and shifting trading of standardized contracts onto exchanges/ electronic platforms where appropriate, will significantly reduce risk and improve transparency within the financial system • Hedge funds: agreed to increased supervision • Insurance: Both sides discussed developments in insurance, including the approval of Solvency II in the EU and its provisions on the treatment of third-country insurers and reinsurers, proposals in the US to create a national insurance office within the Treasury Department and to reform reinsurance collateral rules applicable to third-country reinsurers not licensed in the US (US Department of State, 2009b)
January 2014	• G-20 commitments, including implementation of Basel III capital and liquidity rules • Status of implementation of derivatives reforms (including cross-border issues) • Development of resolution regimes and strategies • Structural proposals in banking systems • Insurance, rating agencies, benchmarks, audit, accounting, money market funds, and data transfers and information sharing for supervisory and enforcement purposes (EU–US Financial Markets Regulatory Dialogue, 2014; Lofchie, 2014)

July 2014

- G-20 commitments, including implementation of Basel III capital, liquidity, and leverage rules
- Implementation of OTC derivatives reforms (including cross-border issues)
- Orderly resolution of global banks
- Reiterated intention to take into account each other's regulatory systems and strive to work together in implementation of OTC reforms
- Noted entry into force of MiFID II and ESMA's publication of its consultation and discussion papers are of MiFID II implementation
- SEC staff describe finalized rules for security-based swaps that focus on certain cross-border rules
- Commission and CFTC staff intend to continue to discuss the technical aspects of any rule proposals
- Commission and CFTC and SEC staffs will continue to engage on determinations of equivalence for US central counterparties and risk-mitigation techniques
- EU and US staff discuss the need to minimize divergences from international margin standards for non-cleared derivates once implemented, and the need to align on timing
- EU staff explain the rule in MiFID II addressing high-frequency trading, while SEC staff outline initiatives to evaluate and enhance US equity market structure, including those related to high-frequency trading
- Participants agree to continue cooperation on the regulation of algorithmic trading
- Participants welcome the deep cooperation between the EC, EBA, FDIC, and Federal Reserve on technical aspects of resolution.
- Participants decide to continue the necessary work toward a covered agreement on reinsurance collateral and engage all stakeholders in a transparent manner
- Participants commended the concrete steps made on cross-border cooperation and commit to continue work to further develop a stable framework for cooperation on audit oversight
- On accounting, participants reiterate their commitment to convergence on high-quality accounting standards. They welcome the completion of the International Accounting Standards Board's and US Financial Accounting Standards Board's joint project on revenue recognition. Participants encourage continued work to complete the remaining key outstanding convergence projects, while also recognizing the need to adopt high-quality standards in a timely manner. Participants commit to continue their efforts to ensure consistent application of high-quality accounting standards
- Participants discuss the ongoing international review of benchmarks and the draft legislation currently under negotiation in the EU. Participants reiterate their support for the recently agreed July 2013 final report on IOSCO principles for administrators of interest rate, foreign exchange, and other financial benchmarks, and are committed to fight market abuse, including benchmark manipulation. Both sides commit to discussing benchmarks at the next FMRD meeting in January 2015

(US Department of Treasury, 2014)

Research Service to explore the potential for more cooperation between Congress and the EP, the authors make two critical points: Transatlantic Legislators' Dialogue (TLD) participation is limited to the House and that Congress does not "regularly inject itself into regulatory matters" (Archick & Morelli, 2010, p. 6).

It is hard to imagine a scenario in which Congress would consult with the EP on financial services regulation (or any policy, for that matter – see the concluding chapter of this volume with respect to counter-terrorism cooperation between Congress and the EP). While certainly MEPs and congresspersons do meet both informally and in the TLD, "mandated" consultation and joint resolutions may be resisted.

To date, the attempt to forge links has been mainly one-sided. Archick and Morelli (2010) document the EP's attempts to reach out to Congress, including its opening of a liaison office in Washington, and the seemingly lower interest among Congress (for example, difficulty in maintaining continuity in TLD membership). Perhaps the most convincing argument against the viability of the TLD as a governance vehicle is that reported by Archick and Morelli (2010, p. 16):

> In the view of many experts, it continues to be a real stretch to expect the Foreign Affairs Committee staff who are responsible for following issues and events in places ranging from Russia to Kosovo to Eurasia can somehow also find the time to become proficient on cloud computing, internet freedom, automobile crash testing, container screening, toy safety, and hedge fund transparency.

The third option is for the EU and the US to actively promote the participation of stakeholders in transatlantic dialogues around financial services regulation. (See Harcourt, 2012 on the role of non-governmental actors with respect to international regulatory policy.) Financial services regulation involves a veritable who's who of non-governmental actors weighing in with opinions. But if the case of the situation with *accounting standards boards* (see introduction to this chapter) is any guide, there had been a decided lack of leadership among transatlantic regulators in dealing with the FASB and IASB. EU and US regulators have repeatedly expressed to the FASB and IASB the importance of agreeing to a set of standards, but in the more than 10 years since these NGOs began "cooperating" to produce standards, they had yet to agree to common standards for financial instruments. Without a common standard, it will be very difficult for EU and US regulators to undertake meaningful comparative outcomes in the regulations of their financial services industries (Norris, 2012). In early 2014 the FASB and IASB were engaged in a three-phase joint project on "accounting for financial instruments" (Financial Accounting Standards Board, n.d.). Indeed, the FMRD (2014, p. 2) commented on this long-running inability of the FASB and IASB to reach agreement in a joint statement issued after its January 2014 meeting:

> On accounting, participants noted with concern delays on the convergence of accounting standards and reiterated their commitment to convergence on high quality accounting standards. In this regard, they will take stock of

progress made on convergence at the next FMRD in July 2014. Participants also will continue their efforts to ensure consistent application of accounting standards.

With EU and US regulators pressurizing these NGOs, however, they eventually did complete their joint project on revenue recognition, as reported in the July 2014 FMRD meeting (US Department of Treasury, 2014).

An analysis of FMRD reports since its inception in 2002 suggests an increase in formal meetings (averaging every six months) supported by an increasingly ambitious agenda and frequent interactions among regulators. Thus, from the its origins – to discuss accounting standards – at the most recent FMRD meeting (July 8, 2014) at the time of this writing (fall 2014), the participants reported on and discussed a comprehensive list of common regulatory concerns – derivatives, resolution, insurance, auditing, accounting, banking, and benchmarks (US Department of Treasury, 2014). So, for example, at the July 2014 meeting:

> The EU staff explained the rules in MIFID II, which addressed high-frequency trading (HFT), while the SEC staff outlined a series of initiatives to evaluate and enhance U.S. equity market structure, including those related to HFT issues, that SEC staff was currently undertaking. Participants agreed to continue cooperation on the regulation of algorithmic trading in order to ensure market integrity and promote market stability.

Option 3: Rely on Existing Multilateral Fora to Share Information and Agree to Best Practices

Box 11.2 contains a list of the multilateral fora in which both the EU and the US are represented. The G-20 and the Bank for International Settlements (BIS) have served as the two especially active fora for establishing international standards for financial services reform.

Agreements on banking rules are made through the BIS's "Basel Committee on Banking Supervision," a forum for cooperation on banking supervisory matters (Bank for International Settlements, 2013). There are two categories of bank capital: Tier 1 and Tier 2. Tier 1 capital is considered "core capital." Core capital is primarily common stock and retained earnings (cash). US banks, however, resist issuing more equity because debt is cheaper – it does not require the payment of dividends and does not offer the same tax advantages associated with debt issuance. Tier 2 capital is "supplementary capital," consisting of revaluation reserves, undisclosed reserves, hybrid instruments, and subordinated term debt. Subordinated, sometimes called "junior" debt, are those debts that are paid after other debts are cleared in liquidation or bankruptcy. Basel III was agreed in 2010–2011 by the Basel Committee on Banking Supervision and is being implemented in member states in the period 2013–2019 (extended from the original agreement of 2015). The principal purpose of Basel III is to increase bank equity to 4.5% (Basel II is 2%) and Tier 1 capital to 6% (4% in Basel II) of "risk-weighted" assets.

Box 11.2 IGOs and INGOs for Financial Services Regulatory Coordination

G-20's Financial Stability Board – coordinates work of national financial authorities and international standard setting (IGO).
Bank for International Settlements – Basel Committee for Banking Supervision – forum for cooperation on bank supervisory matters (IGO).
International Organization of Securities Commissions – brings together the world's securities regulators and is recognized as the global standard setter for the securities sector (INGO).
International Accounting Standards Board – the international counterpart of the American-based Financial Accounting Standards Board, which sets accounting standards for European companies (INGO).
International Association of Insurance Supervisors – composed of insurance supervisors and regulators and is the international standards-setting body for developing and assisting in the implementation of principles and standards for the supervision of the insurance sector (INGO).

(International Association of Insurance Supervisors, 2014;
Monahan & Payne, 2014, p. 7; OICU-IOSCO, 2014)

In 2008, the G-20 converted the G-8's Financial Stability Forum to the Financial Stability Board (FSB), with a mandate "to coordinate at the international level the work of national financial authorities and international standard setting bodies and to develop and promote the implementation of effective regulatory supervisory and other financial sector policies" (Financial Stability Board, 2013). US participants are the Fed, SEC, and Department of Treasury. In addition to EU member state participation, the EU is represented by the ECB and the European Commission. The FSB has discussed and reached agreement on a number of standards, including the regulation of derivatives and cross-border issues.

While IGOs have contributed to transatlantic policy convergence, especially through committees operating under the auspices of the G-20 and BIS, the structure of the G-20 is too diverse, and the importance of the financial services sector to the members' respective economies widely varies. The BIS (Basel III) has been very effective in agreeing best practices, especially in prudential requirements in banking. It is not, however, equipped to deal on a comprehensive basis with the many other instruments in the financial services industry. Furthermore, not all EU member states are represented in multilateral fora.

The Obama Administration prefers a combination of Options 2 and 3, believing that international bodies "ensure mutual consultation in advance of new financial regulations" (Monahan & Payne, 2014, p. 7).

Option 4: Binding Transatlantic Agreement Managed by an EU–US Regulatory Agency

This is the EU's preferred option. The European Commission (2014c, p. 2) has argued that the FMRD and other meetings between EU and US officials are too "ad hoc," "informal," or "at the very last minute" to provide the institutionalized framework needed to ensure that regulatory "outcomes" converge. Nevertheless, the US has reiterated its position repeatedly – the US will not include financial services regulation in the TTIP negotiations.

In response to the US position, the European Commission (2014c) proposed upgrading the FMRD to a high-level permanent financial services regulatory dialogue, and has put forward a compromise in which consultations be included as part of the overall TTIP process. These negotiations would take place outside of the formal TTIP negotiations:

> The aim of the EU proposal is not to negotiate within the TTIP on the substance of the international standards, on the on-going implementation of these standards or on other elements of on-going regulatory reforms (e.g., the Volcker rule, or rules on foreign banking organisations) that are being currently implemented. Discussions on these subjects may continue in parallel with, but outside of, the TTIP negotiations.
>
> (European Commission, 2014c, p. 4)

Option 4, however, is simply unrealistic in light of continued US opposition. This sentiment was expressed by US Ambassador to the EU Anthony L. Gardner in a rather definitive way in an interview conducted by an EU affairs news site in July 2014 (EurActiv, 2014b):

> We keep on getting asked about this and we keep on giving the same answer. Somehow, that does not seem to be sufficient as the Commission keeps on pushing for this issue when they know what the answer is. So, I will give you the same answer that they have heard many times. We have a bilateral dialogue (in fact we had a large delegation here last week anticipating the financial markets regulatory dialogue with the EU) which we have used for some time now to address important issues about financial regulatory reform. That dialogue, in our view, has been working and has resulted in important and greater convergence between our two sides. On top of the bilateral dialogue, we have a multilateral dialogue in the G20, which in our view has been working. So, for those reasons we do not see what would be achieved by having a formal mechanism about a financial regulatory dialogue in a trade agreement. We still have not heard articulated from the EU what that would achieve in addition to what is already taking place. Having said that, there is going to be a chapter on financial market access.

A key concern for the Obama Administration is that if financial services regulation were to be addressed in the TTIP (or any international agreement), it could re-open Dodd–Frank to congressional scrutiny (Hakim, 2013). (See earlier discussion with respect to Option 4.) Thus, the view that the US position is "short-sighted since most of the Dodd–Frank regulations will be adopted before TTIP is completed" (Lannoo, 2013, p. 8) underestimates the stark ideological divide between Democrats and Republicans, which is far wider than center-left and center-right parties in Europe. The European center-right long acculturated to the European Social Model, but the Republicans worked to undo *The Afford-able Care Act* (in the US Supreme Court and in the House of Representatives). Republicans would have a "field day" with Dodd–Frank if the federal courts (which most surely would be brought into the picture) ruled that Dodd–Frank needed to be reconsidered in light of treaty obligations.

In sum, it is difficult to envisage any scenario where financial services regulation *could* be included in the TTIP or even on a parallel track that leads to more than the "informal" consultations available through the FMRD. Much of Dodd–Frank is not yet implemented, inserting an unacceptable level of unpredictability into the political process. So, for example, a Republican president will be under enormous pressure from banks and mortgage brokers to undo elements of Dodd–Frank. A future Democratic president will not wish to re-open Dodd–Frank, knowing that his/her party won on Dodd–Frank from a combination of Democratic control of both Houses of Congress and the presidency (coupled with an extra-ordinary window of opportunity in the Great Recession, which enabled legislators to overcome the opposition of America's extremely powerful bank lobby).

Yet leaving domestic politics aside, there is another important reason that the US is unlikely to agree to binding rule-making. The reason is grounded in the differences in the US system (a federal state) and the EU (a mix of quasi-federal features and intergovernmentalism). As various studies have shown – and, this point is particularly brought out in Dudek's institutional analysis of GMO policymaking in this volume – the EU governance project is constantly evolving. So, too, the eurozone crisis demonstrated the inadequacy of EU governance, particularly in its failure to agree to a fiscal union when it established its monetary union. The ability to make fiscal transfers is an important feature of fiscal unions, which enables the central government to assist parts of the country that are distressed by economic downturns, especially under conditions of low labor mobility such as exist in the EU. The US, therefore, has the fiscal and governance structures in place to collect sizeable taxes (the EU's budget is minuscule compared to the budgets of *bona fide* federal states) to transfer revenues from high-growth regions to economically distressed regions (see Buonanno & Nugent, 2013, pp. 222–223, 322–324).

The fiscal union is one important reason why the US emerged from the Great Recession faster than did many EU member states, particularly those countries' economies that were most weakened by the eurozone sovereign debt and banking crises. Thus, the EU has a greater incentive to try to impose "external" controls on financial services regulation, because it is less able to ameliorate the effects of economic downturns through "internal" measures.

Finally, Option 4 fails the test of simplicity. Option 2 does not require positive integration, but Option 4 does. Yet Option 2 seems to have facilitated transatlantic dialogue that contributed to policy convergence. The increasingly ambitious program since the FMRD was created in 2002 (see Table 11.3) is evidence of increased "formal" dialogue, and the similar regulatory policy outcomes evidence of policy convergence.

Option 5: Binding International Agreements Managed by an International Governmental Organization

There are four aspects of this scenario that make it a highly unlikely course of action for the foreseeable future. First, there is a multilateral forum in place in which trade and services is subject to binding rules (treaties) and binding dispute settlement (the WTO's Dispute Settlement Body and panel system). However, the WTO is not a forum for regulation (positive integration), but rather deregulation (negative integration) as illustrated by its GATS agreements on liberalization of financial services in the 1990s Uruguay Round (World Trade Organization, 1997) – a liberalization which the EU and the US very much wanted at the time. Second, the US is already concerned over potential complaints lodged by other WTO members on the basis of Dodd–Frank – particularly the Volcker Rule – with respect to liberalization of the financial services industry (see Morgenson, 2012). Therefore, the US is unlikely to subject itself to any more risk of challenges to its financial services regulatory regime from WTO parties. Third, accords on financial services have been stalled as part of the general malaise of the Doha Round, undermining the attractiveness of the WTO as a body to advance regulatory agreements. Fourth, the other relevant international bodies or multilateral fora – such as the BIS, G-20, OECD, or IMF – either are not set-up for or envisaged to produce binding agreements with dispute and policing mechanisms – and/or they are exclusive rather than inclusive in their membership.

Conclusions

Financial services regulation has been and will continue to be a particularly difficult field in which to build a more tightly integrated and even binding transatlantic approach to transatlantic regulatory cooperation for at least four reasons.

First, this policy area has been unusually salient on both sides of the Atlantic due to the Great Recession, which most observers agree was caused by lax regulation and oversight of the financial services industry in both the EU and the US (although the most spectacular collapses – AIG, Bears Stearns, and Lehman Brothers – started in the US, and the popular storyline in Europe is that the US is mostly, if not wholly, at fault).

Second, the financial services industry is complex, comprising a number of very different kinds of financial instruments including insurance, home and commercial mortgages, bank lending, corporate and government bonds, equity, currency trades, commodity trading, and the many complex instruments that have been developed to hedge or profit from risk.

Third, the EU and the US virtually invented the financial services industry, and dominate the field; thus, together they hold a great deal of collective power in setting global standards, both for today and the future. However, they are also aware of the very fine line between over-regulation and under-regulation – mistakes in either direction threaten to chip away at their global dominance over Japan and the BRICs (especially China). Mandated consultation (rather than voluntary cooperation) would reduce the "nimbleness" and latitude of regulators on both sides of the Atlantic.

Fourth, despite the intertwined nature of transatlantic financial services, the basic structure of financing businesses differs between the US and most of the EU's member states.

The difference is especially stark when eliminating the UK from the analysis and comparing the US with the continent. France, Italy, and Germany combine commercial and investment banking, activities and functions historically separated in the UK and US. Another difference is the tendency for European companies to rely more on debt than equity financing where "total stock market capitalization is the EU is almost half of what it is in the US" (Lannoo, 2013, p. 2). Furthermore, bank lending (debt) supplies nearly 70% of all EU corporate funding, but just 18% in the US (Rolet, 2012). Americans – whether Democrats or Republicans – believe the availability of equity financing is critical to the dynamic SME/start-up success in the US, and that dislike as one might the incomprehensible investment vehicles in innumerable types of derivatives, equity and all of its related instruments, these seem to fuel US economic growth. Thus, it stands to reason that Americans are *less* likely to agree with Europeans about regulation of equity markets, and particularly act so as to dampen the creation of novel investment instruments.

Further undermining the cohesiveness of the EU is that the UK and the US are more alike in this respect than is the UK to its EU partners. So, for example, the UK is not a member of the eurozone not just because the UK is the "awkward partner," but for reasons having to do with the structure and composition of the UK's economic activities. In comparison to the other "Big Four" EU member states, the UK enjoys a stronger services sector (concentrated in financial services and media); a higher degree of technology exports; a large energy sector (both the technology and energy sectors price their products in US dollars); a relatively smaller agricultural sector; low savings rates among British consumers; and higher home ownership rates than on the continent (Buonanno & Nugent, 2013, p. 69). The ability of the City of London to maintain its competitive advantage rests at least partly on the policy freedom to be able to create innovative financial instruments (Baimbridge & Whyman, 2008, p. 87). Thus, the UK will likely continue to "side" with the US in agreeing that Options 2 (FMRD) and 3 (multilateral fora) are the most effective and realistic choices for transatlantic governance.

What does the future hold? The Commission will continue to emphasize the need for a transatlantic approach to regulation of financial services. This is so because the EU, in one important respect, has more to lose than the US in global economic disturbances. The EU's higher vulnerability can be traced to the incompatibility of the operation of a currency union without two features found in full-fledged federal states: labor mobility and fiscal unions. Without an EU finance ministry with independent taxing and spending authority, there is no EU-wide capability (cohesion funds are woefully inadequate) to assist parts of the union that are distressed by economic downturns. The integration project may have "dodged the bullet" in the Great Recession, but writing in the autumn of 2014, there continues to be a great deal of worry about the rise of protest parties in Europe (as seen in the May 2014 EP elections), the public support for which is fueled by stubbornly high unemployment rates. Furthermore, ECB actions to fuel growth were not taking hold in several member states and there were fears that parts of Europe could be heading back into recession, a concern exacerbated by the crisis in Ukraine (and sanctions on Russia that negatively impacted some European companies).

Nevertheless, for a number of reasons advanced throughout this chapter, barring another financial global meltdown in the near future, the US is likely to continue to favor Options 2 (current transatlantic informal cooperation) and 3 (voluntary participation in multilateral fora) to the exclusion of Option 4 (institutionalization of binding transatlantic regulatory cooperation).

Naturally, the American stance pressurizes the EU to strengthen efforts to build its fledgling banking union and the fiscal federalism which is needed to bring long-term stability to the eurozone. As discussed in other parts of this book (particularly Chapter 2), a more integrated (and federal) Europe has been the persistent goal of US Administrations since the end of World War II. It is unlikely that the US will agree to any policy (barring negative consequences for the US itself) that takes the pressure off EU member states to establish a *bona fide* federal state.

12 GMO Food Regulatory Frameworks in the US and the EU

Carolyn Marie Dudek

Introduction

Genetic modification is a bio-technological process that "allows selected individual genes to be transferred from one organism into another, and also between non-related species" (World Health Organization, 2010). This chapter focuses on one aspect of food safety – governmental regulatory policy concerning the cultivation and sale of GMO plant products.

Genetically modified organism (GMO) policymaking in the EU and the US is important for the study of transatlantic public administration and policy for two reasons.

First, GMOs have been a major point of contention in trade relations in the Atlantic community. Accordingly, David Vogel (2012, p. 73) argues that "policies toward GM foods, crops, and seed represent the most economically significant – and undoubtedly the most contentious – divergence between European and American food and agriculture regulations and policies."

The disparity in treatment of GMOs in the Atlantic Community has led to considerable trade tension, including a 2003 WTO trade complaint the US (along with other countries utilizing GMO crops) filed against the EU. A WTO panel was convened to examine the dispute and on November 21, 2006 three panel reports ruled that the EU lacked sufficient scientific evidence for its GMO moratorium and, therefore, was in violation of the WTO Sanitary and Phytosanitary (SPS) Agreement (World Trade Organization, 2008). While the EU has reached agreements with both Argentina and Canada (Europa, 2010b), the EU and US have yet to reach a settlement, and this remains a sticking point in EU–US trade relations.

With the announcement to create the Transatlantic Trade and Investment Partnership (TTIP), speculation has emerged that GMO crops would not be easy to negotiate. Alluding to GMOs and other concerns, Robert Zoellick, former US trade representative, stated: "Agriculture ... is going to be one of the most difficult issues." Moreover, US Senator Max Baucus, chairman of the Senate Finance Committee asserted: "There has to be significant market access before it [the agreement] gets through – we care deeply about that ... I think we should base it on science" (Politi & Chaffin, 2013). On the EU side, Commission President José Manuel Barroso has stated the EU will not change its position on GMOs and that the European public supports the EU's cautious approach (Politi & Chaffin, 2013). Similarly, former Agriculture Commissioner Franz Fischler stated "It would be a mistake simply to use these free-trade negotiations to put pressure on the European side that they should agree to get rid of GMO restrictions ... I think this will fail" (Politi & Chaffin, 2013). Thus, the political rhetoric at the start of the TTIP negotiations reflects how perceptions of GMO regulations differ between EU and US policymakers, and could be problematic for the conclusion of an agreement.

The second reason an understanding of GMO policymaking in the EU and the US is important for transatlantic policy studies is because the divergence in regulatory policy offers a guide to the regulatory outcomes (and points of disagreement) in transatlantic cooperation or lack thereof. Specifically, is there something about the characteristics of GMO regulation that can explain regulatory divergence that is not evident from other case studies of market failure policies? (See chapters covering competition policy, trade policy, and financial services regulation policy in this volume.)

From the earliest introduction of GMOs in the late 1980s, the EU has been skeptical and cautious, whereas the US federal government has been more accepting and used a less risk-averse approach to regulating such products. The difference in regulatory outcomes is astounding: since 1992, the EU has only approved 39 GM products importable for food and feed uses (mainly for animal feed and industrial uses) and only one for cultivation (maize MON 810 – for animal feed), which itself faces authorization review (EuropaBio, 2011; European Parliament, 2014a). In December 2013, the EU's General Court annulled the 2010 authorization of the cultivation of Amflora, a GM potato created by German company BASF to make glossy paper coatings, clothing finishes, and adhesive cement, and the only other GMO variety that had been authorized for cultivation. (BASF stopped growing Amflora potato in Europe in 2012, see Dunmore, 2013.) The case was brought by Hungary, supported by Austria, France, Luxembourg, and Poland, on the grounds that the authorization procedure was not properly followed (Keating, 2013b). Furthermore, nine EU member states ban the cultivation of MON 810 – Austria, Bulgaria, France, Germany, Greece, Hungary, Italy, Luxembourg, and Poland.

The EU's authorization record for GMOs contrasts sharply with that of the US, which has approved over 100 varieties (D. Vogel, 2012, p. 1).

This stark difference in the acceptance of GMOs (especially GMO cultivation) is even more startling in light of Vogel's comprehensive analysis of a precautionary tendency in risk regulation in the transatlantic community, finding that, "if new risk regulation was enacted on either side of the Atlantic in the three decades prior to 1990, then it is *more likely* (emphasis in original) that the American standard was initially, and in some cases remained, more risk averse" (D. Vogel, 2012, p. 2). Indeed, this shift in the stringency of transatlantic regulation occurred at precisely the time GMOs were entering the market.

In order to address these two points of contention with respect to trade protectionism and divergent regulatory approaches, this chapter is divided into four sections. The first section reviews the evolution of GMO policy in the EU and the US and details the current regulatory regimes. The second section of the chapter identifies and evaluates the major exogenous variables shaping GMO policy in the EU and the US – specifically, institutions, economic interests, multi-level governance (MLG), and public opinion. The chapter closes with an interpretation of the findings with respect to policy cooperation and the likelihood of the Atlantic Community reaching agreement on the trade and cultivation in GMO products within the TTIP negotiations.

GMO Policymaking in the US and the EU

American geneticists Stanley Norman Cohen and Herbert Boyer created the first genetically engineered organism in 1975 (Powell, 1999, p. 3). Two key meetings – one in 1973 sponsored by the US National Science Foundation and the US National Institutes of Health (NIH) discussed the concerns surrounding lab safety and fears of untested GMOs entering the environment. This conversation continued in the 1975 International Congress on Recombinant DNA Molecules (the Asilomar Conference) (Pew Trust, 2001, pp. 4–5) where the scientific community agreed to a self-imposed moratorium until guidelines could be developed. Because the vast majority of scientific research conducted in the academy is funded by federal agencies under NIH ethics rules, the federal government's decision would be decisive. Consequently, the moratorium on GMO research was lifted in 1976 when the NIH established the US NIH Recombinant DNA Advisory Committee (NIHRAC) and issued the first set of guidelines for experimentation with GMOs (Cantley, 2007, p. 26; Powell, 1999, p. 3). The European Commission issued similar guidelines in COM (1986) 573 as did other national authorities, the Organization for Economic Cooperation and Development's *Recombinant DNA Safety Considerations* ("Blue Book"), and the World Health Organization (WHO).

However, as the following discussion illustrates, as GMO bio-technology left the lab for field tests, the market, and cultivation, regulatory policy development within the US, and the EU and its member states, began to diverge.

United States

Background

As GMO technology progressed from lab to field (mid-1980s), it was unclear which federal departments or agencies would have responsibility for regulating GMOs (Pew Trust, 2001, p. 5). The US Department of Agriculture's (USDA) Animal and Plant Inspection Service (APHIS) and the USDA Economic Research Service (ERS) were early government actors in GMO field testing. The US Environmental Protection Agency (EPA), however, soon became concerned about the environmental effects of GMOs, announcing in 1983 that it planned to regulate GMOs using existing legislation (the Toxic Substances Control Act). The EPA's announcement created two opposing camps in the federal bureaucracy, which was further complicated by unclear and overlapping regulatory authority among three principal actors charged with regulating food and feed and protecting human health in the US – the USDA; the US Department of Health and Human Services (HHS) – Food and Drug Administration (FDA); and the EPA.

The USDA and the White House Office of Science and Technology Policy (OSTP) focused on the economic potential of GMOs, and thus advocated regulating the end *product* of agricultural bio-technology; in effect, GMOs would be held to the same standards ("substantial equivalence") as products that were not the result of bio-engineering. This contrasted with the more cautious *process* approach advocated by the EPA (see Lynch & Vogel, 2001, p. 4; Patterson & Josling, 2002, p. 5). This came to a head during the Reagan Administration, when in 1984 the OSTP convened an interagency "Domestic Policy Council Working Group on Biotechnology," composed of personnel drawn from the FDA, the EPA, the USDA, the Occupational Safety and Health Administration, the National Science Foundation, and the NIH (US Office of Science and Technology Policy, 1986). In the end the interest in the market potential of GMOs won out over the EPA's concern for the process of creating GMOs, which meant the adoption of a guiding principle of product regulation rather than process regulation. The outcome was that the group proposed the *Coordinated Framework for the Regulation of Biotechnology*, setting out the regulatory framework for GMO approval in the US (discussed in more detail, below), which has served as the regulatory framework for GMO approval since 1986.

Current Regulatory Framework

The Coordinated Framework (see above) established the product approach in GMO approval; specifically, no new legislation is needed for the regulation of GMOs. Instead, GMOs would be treated no differently than non-genetically engineered products (US Office of Science and Technology Policy, 1986, p. 3). Moreover, because GMOs are dealt with the same as any other new food or feed product, no special labeling is required. Significantly, the US Congress has never enacted legislation governing GMOs and "American policies toward GM varieties have essentially been formulated and implemented by regulatory and administrative agencies that have consistently supported their commercial application" (D. Vogel, 2012, p. 74).

Jurisdiction over GMOs is determined by their use (as with traditional products) as laid out in the Coordinated Framework (US Office of Science and Technology Policy, 1986, p. 8):

> Foods, food additives, human drugs, biologics and devices, and animal drugs are reviewed or licensed by the FDA. Food products prepared from domestic livestock and poultry are under the jurisdiction of the USDA's Food Safety Inspection Service (FSIS). Animal biologics are reviewed by the Animal and Plant Health Inspection Service (APHIS). APHIS, also reviews plants, seeds, animal biologics, plant pests, animal pathogens and "regulated articles", i.e., contain genetically engineered organisms

containing genetic material from a plant pest. An APHIS permit is required prior to the shipment (movement) or release into the environmental of regulated articles, or the shipment of a plant pest or animal pathogen.

The Coordinated Framework also establishes jurisdiction with respect to experiments, whether federally or commercially funded and whether there is release into the environment (US Office of Science and Technology Policy, 1986, pp. 10–11).

This sometimes confusing array of overlapping jurisdictions with respect to GMOs is an entrenched feature of the US federal government (see Landau, 1969 for a discussion of redundancy in the federal bureaucracy), and coordinating bodies are often employed to remedy this problem. Thus, inter-agency coordination for GMO policy is provided by the Office of Science Coordination and Policy Biotechnology Team, which is housed in the EPA (Office of Science Coordination and Policy Biotechnology Team, n.d.).

What has been the impact of the US regulatory regime for GMOs? Vogel (2012, p. 74) concludes that the

> Coordinated Framework developed by the Reagan Administration thus created a pattern of regulatory path dependence. More than two decades later, the Framework remains the basic administrative structure for the regulation of agricultural biotechnology in the United States. It has enabled American agricultural biotechnology firms to retain a privileged position in the policy process and effectively relegated non-business constituencies to a marginal role in this policy area.

European Union

Background

Morris and Spillane (2010) identify five phases of EU GMO regulatory policy: (1) non-legislation period (1973–1983); (2) reorganization period (1983–1986); (3) first legislation period (1986–1991); (4) second legislation period (1992–2001); and (5) third legislation period (2001 to present). In many respects – certainly in terms of legislative activity – the EU's GMO regulatory regime is much more complex than that of the US and has been characterized by highly contested politics. It has also involved a de facto moratorium on the approval of the sale of GMO varieties from 1998 (when two GM varieties of carnations were approved for importation) to May 2004 (Pollack & Schaffer, 2010, p. 342).

The first period (see the general discussion above) was not very different from that of the US early period, except for an important difference in the locale of regulatory authority, which rested with the member states rather than in the US, at one level of government (i.e., with the federal government). This situation concerned the Commission, which sought harmonized regulations, principally to be able to compete with the US (which by now had a lead in agricultural biotechnology) (D. Vogel, 2012, p. 74).

During the "Reorganization" period (1983–1986) the Commission Vice-President Étienne Davignon and DGs Agriculture and Internal Markets formed the "Biotechnology Steering Committee" (1983) chaired by DG Science, Research and Development (Morris & Spillane, 2010, p. 360), originally excluding DG XI Environment, Nuclear Safety and Protection. During this period, the Commission experienced a recognizable pattern of bureaucratic disagreement – with "ministries" charged with promoting innovation, trade, and competitiveness (DG Agriculture and DG Innovation) favoring GMOs, and those charged with protecting the public (at the time, DG XI Environment, Nuclear Safety and Protection), taking a more cautious approach (see Cantley, 1995; 2007, p. 8). DG XI became the responsible authority shaping the Biotechnology Regulation Inter-Service Committee created in 1986, chaired jointly by DGs Internal Market and Environment, Nuclear Safety and Protection. The Biotechnology Regulation Inter-Service Committee completed an inventory report of member states' biotechnology regulations, with the Commission's aim of establishing an EU-wide framework (Morris & Spillane, 2010, p. 360). DG XI, like its US counterpart, the EPA, also sought to regulate the process rather than the product of GMOs. Since in the US the EPA did not take the lead in regulating GMOs, an explanation of "disparate bureaucratic-policy cultures" is likely a viable explanation as to policy divergence: an environmentally focused department took the lead in Europe, while a market focused one led in the US.

The first legislation period (1986–1991) began the same year that the US adopted the Coordinated Framework, when the European Commission's Biotechnology Regulation Inter-Service Committee published "A Community Framework for the Regulation of Biotechnology" (European Commission, 1986), which Cantley (2007, p. 27) identifies as "the starting point for subsequent EU technology-specific legislation." This phase also coincided with the jumpstarting of the EU's internal market with ratification of the *Single European Act of 1986* (SEA). The SEA provided the treaty basis for EU regulation of GMOs (as an internal market necessity).

With respect to GMOs, unlike in the US where there are no separate laws dealing with GMOs (see above), in 1988 the European Commission proposed two Council directives for the regulation of GMOs, and which departed from the "scientific advice of the time" (for example, the European Molecular Biology Organisation), which recommended the same regulatory approach as the US (product rather than process) (Morris & Spillane, 2010, p. 361). This was the beginning of EU regulatory authority over GMOs, but as Vogel (2012, p. 75) points out, "it came at a price."

The two directives were 90/219/EEC (contained use of GMO microorganisms, dealing with laboratory procedures) and 90/220/EEC (the deliberate release of GMOs into the environment – GMO cultivation), the latter being the more controversial of the two directives. "The price" of EU authority was this – European Parliament (EP) amendments to the directives became more restrictive than the Commission had envisaged. Whether this was the EP flexing new powers under the SEA (see Buonanno & Nugent, 2002 on institutional opportunism) or the rise of the Green Party in Europe (see Morris & Spillane, 2010,

p. 361), the fact is the legislation was more restrictive than the Commission had proposed. Indeed, "an amendment to the deliberate release directive proposing a five-year moratorium on GMO field releases" (Morris & Spillane, 2010, p. 361) nearly gained enough EP support, an early indication of mistrust of GMOs among a large number of Members of the European Parliament (MEPs) and a signal that agricultural bio-technology was not going to have an easy time of it in the EU.

The 90/220/EEC (*Deliberate Release*) set up a complex, multi-step system involving member states, the Commission, and the Council (see Pollack & Schaffer, 2010, pp. 337, 339) and included a "safeguard" clause. The safeguard clause enables member states to temporarily stop the production or sale of a GMO if they have additional information determining a GMO to be a hazard to humans or the environment

The second legislation period (1992–2001) was shaped by several factors – food safety scares, public opinion, continued power struggles among EU institutions, dissatisfaction of the agricultural bio-technology community, and pressure from the international community (mainly the US) over the moratorium on the approval of GMO varieties, the latter of which had taken effect in 1998 at the insistence of 12 of 15 member state governments. At the same time, agro-business interests and the Commission were increasingly discouraged by the de facto moratorium (Morris & Spillane, 2010, p. 361).

Food scares and environmental concerns were important factors affecting GMO regulation in this period. Europeans had endured a spate of food crises (see Buonanno, Zablotney, & Keefer, 2001, pp. 4–5) and consumer and environmental advocates began to express concern regarding the safety of GMOs. Distrust over the EU's ability to protect the food safety supply in the greatly expanded internal market came to a head in the BSE (mad cow disease) crisis, where two general suspicions were voiced at the EP's 1996 BSE hearings and the subsequent "Medina Report" (European Parliament, 1997): that DG Agriculture had experienced regulatory capture and that it was overly managed by member states (in this case the UK) rather than on behalf of the general welfare of European citizens (see Buonanno, 2006, pp. 263–264). Environmentalists gained traction on the issue when *Nature* magazine published research by scientists suggesting that pollen dust from GMO *Bt* corn plants was interfering with monarch butterfly larvae development (Losey, Rayor, & Carter, 1999).

Under orders from the European Council to remedy the perceived lapse in food safety regulation, pressure from agro-business to break the logjam, the EP's calls for the EU to protect the food chain, and public hostility toward GMOs, the Commission was tasked with revising the GMO regulatory structure and to reform its DGs and reassign portfolios.

The Commission's first response was to reorganize its ministries: DG XI became DG Environment and a new DG was formed that would focus on consumer safety – DG Health and Consumers (often referred to by its French acronym DG SANCO). Food and feed regulation (including GMO regulation) was moved to DG SANCO (from DG Agriculture). However, this reform was deemed unsatisfactory by the EP, with this body calling for further reform, especially an "arm's length" regulatory body (see Buonanno, 2006; Buonanno et al., 2001). Thus, at the behest of the European Council, the Commission (European Commission, 2000b) published a White Paper proposing regulatory reform of food and feed, which included GMOs. After wide consultation and two years of debate, the EP and the Council agreed to a new regulation on food safety (European Commission, 2002).

Among the major changes brought about by this legislation was the establishment of an independent Community agency – the European Food Safety Authority (EFSA) – and the current regulatory framework. New legislation regarding GMOs was also approved. These reforms constitute the basis of the EU's current regulatory framework.

Current Regulatory Framework

In the EU the regulatory function is separated from risk assessment and communication. Regulation is carried out through the Commission's DG SANCO through its Standing Committee on the Food Chain and Animal Health (SCFCH) (see European Commission – Standing Committee on the Food Chain and Animal Health, 2013b for information about DG SANCO's standing committees and their regulatory functions), and the relevant SCFCH Section – Genetically Modified Food and Feed and Environmental Risk (European Commission – Standing Committee on the Food Chain and Animal Health, 2013a).

This regulatory structure contrasts sharply with the US model, specifically in the centrality of the Department of Agriculture in US regulatory policy on GMOs and the housing of risk assessment, risk management, and risk communication within single agencies. As a consequence, EFSA, unlike the HHS's FDA, the USDA's APHIS, and the EPA, is not a regulatory body, but instead is a risk-assessment agency composed of scientific experts. While an early wiseman's paper had proposed a powerful independent regulatory agency that would resemble a combined EPA and FDA (see James, Kemper, & Pascal, 1999), in the regulation (referenced above), EFSA was established to offer independent scientific advice (risk assessment) and communication of risks to the Commission and the member states (European Food Safety Authority, n.d.). Indeed, the Commission argued that under the "Meroni Doctrine" (the delegating authority can only delegate to an agency powers that it possesses itself under the EC Treaty) the regulatory function needed to stay within the Commission's regulatory committees barring a change to the Treaties (see UK Parliament, 2009 for a discussion of the Meroni Doctrine).

The current EU GMO regulatory framework rests on three main pieces of legislation. One is the *Directive on the Deliberate Release into the Environment of Genetically Modified Organisms* (2001/18), which replaced 90/220 (European Parliament and Council, 2001). This piece of legislation was created to ensure human health and environmental safety with the deliberate introduction of GMOs. In particular, the document lays out the use of the precautionary principle in order to ensure safety as well as the option of a "safeguard clause," which is Article 23 of the legislation. The directive consists of six main elements: first, "to make the procedure for granting consent for the deliberate release and placing on the market of GMOs more efficient and more transparent; second, to limit such consent to a period of ten years (renewable); third, to introduce compulsory monitoring after GMOs have been placed on the market; fourth, to provide a common methodology to assess case-by-case the risks for the environment associated with the release of GMOs; fifth, mandatory public consultation; and sixth, compulsory GMO labeling.

The second important piece of legislation shaping GMO regulations is the *Regulation on Genetically Modified Food and Feed* (1829/2003) (European Parliament and Council, 2003a). The food and feed regulation focuses on the need for "safety assessment through a Community procedure," in part to ensure the free movement of goods across countries with varying regulations; in particular, highlighting the need for Community authorization of GMO feed. In addition, the regulation seeks to improve the 1997 regulation 258/97 to make the procedure "streamlined and more transparent," and to give greater centrality to EFSA in the scientific evaluation of GMO safety (European Parliament and Council, 2003a).

The third piece of legislation is *Regulation 1803/2003 on Traceability and Labelling of GMOs*. In the EU any product "produced from GMOs, *meaning* derived whole or in part, from GMOs, but not containing or consisting of GMOs" must be labeled (European Parliament and Council, 2003b, Art 3.2). In the late 1990s it became clear to GMO lobbying groups such as Europabio that the majority of member states as well as MEPs would only allow GMOs if labeling was part of the deal (Grant & Stocker, 2009). Thus, labeling requirements in the EU were introduced early, with the introduction of GMOs.

Since its establishment in 2002, EFSA has become the recognized body of experts providing the Commission and member states with its findings on GMO products. Since January 1, 2005 purveyors of GMO products must submit applications to market their products to member state governments which (following Regulation 1829/2003) the member state must immediately forward to the EFSA. The EFSA must endeavor to give an opinion to the Commission within six months (EFSA, 2012). The Commission will then issue a ruling with respect to the application. Thus, the 2001 institutional reforms shifted regulatory authority (risk management) for GMOs (and food and feed safety in general) from the national to the EU level (Buonanno, 2006, p. 275).

Nevertheless, because the EU adopted a "precautionary approach" to regulating GMOs, it has had the effect of creating bureaucratic slowdowns (Patterson & Josling, 2002). (See European Commission, 2000a; Lynch & Vogel, 2001 for the Commission's interpretation of the precautionary principle.) Furthermore, GMO regulation takes place through the complex comitology procedure (see Joerges, 1999b for a discussion of comitology in terms of "supranational deliberation") and which will be elaborated in the next section of this chapter. In addition, while regulation of GMOs for food and feed was streamlined in the 2001–2003 legislative reforms, to win approval in the Commission all DGs must be consulted and cabinet heads must agree as part of inter-service consultation (Official with DG Sanco, personal communication, 2013).

Factors Shaping GMO Policy

The previous section reviewed the evolution of GMO governance in the EU and the US and the current regulatory frameworks. This section explores four explanatory variables that will condition GMO regulatory policy convergence in the Atlantic Community. These are the policy process, economic interests, MLG, and public opinion.

Policy Processes

Comitology System

The EU's unique governance structure has played a part in the development of GMO regulation. Unlike in *bona fide* federal systems, the EU utilizes a confederal arrangement for GMO approval where a qualified majority (QM) of member states must agree for GMO approval. And, because member states count on one another's support on issues which are of important national concern, it is unusual for member states to take a decision – even under QM – when a substantial minority of member states oppose the measure.

GMO regulation is governed by the "comitology procedure," which Jorges and Neyer (1997) fashion "deliberative supranationalism." In essence, comitology is a confederal compromise between the two regulatory possibilities in an internal market: mutual recognition (supported by adjudication and case law, distasteful to continental Europeans accustomed to statutory law) and an independent regulatory agency – the supranational/federal solution, which "requires the renunciation of power by politically accountable actors" (Joerges, 1999a, p. 7).

Undoubtedly, comitology is a difficult construction both to operate and to understand. In the realm of GMO regulation, comitology can involve two or more stages, depending upon a number of circumstances and previous actions: (1) whether a GMO regulation or directive is being considered; (2) a new GMO is being considered for import or cultivation; (3) the comitology committee cannot achieve consensus; or (4) the Council cannot achieve a QM.

In the first stage of the GMO regulatory process, EFSA undertakes its scientific review and submits its report to the Commission. In the second stage, the Commission submits a draft (technical) regulation to the standing committee composed of national experts (the comitology committee) or the EFSA report in the case of GMO licensure. If the national experts unanimously agree, the proposal passes; however, if the experts fail to achieve consensus, they must approve or reject the proposal by a two-thirds majority (which is difficult to achieve). If unable to attain QM, the decision then goes to the relevant Council configuration, which must reach its decision through qualified majority voting (QMV). If QMV is not met, the Commission can make the final decision. In the case of *all* GM issues since 1998 the Commission has taken the final decision.

The most recent such controversial cases involving the Commission occurred in March 2010 and February 2014. In the 2010 case the Commission approved

Amflora for cultivation (see introduction to this chapter). The approval of Amflora was controversial because it broke the 12-year de facto moratorium on *cultivating* of GMO varieties in Europe, which as this chapter's discussion has shown, has been far more controversial than the importation of GMO products. There is speculation that DG SANCO pushed for approval due to the inexperience of the new DG SANCO Commissioner John Dalli, who may not have understood the political implications of Commission approval (Contiero, Greenpeace Member, personal communication, 2012; Member of DG SANCO, personal communication, 2013). The political storm that followed made the political situation very clear. Indeed, Hungary and supporting countries successfully challenged the Commission in the Court of Justice of the European Union (CJEU) based on the Commission's failure to follow this procedure, as laid out earlier in this chapter. The second case, approval of Monsanto Pioneer 1507 maize, is in some ways even more complicated than the 2010 case, involving all EU actors – the EFSA, the Commission, the comitology committee, the CJEU, and the EP in a decade-long struggle by Monsanto Pioneer to win authorization for Pioneer 1507 cultivation. The Commission had originally proposed authorization in 2009, but then did nothing, triggering Monsanto Pioneer to take its case to the CJEU. Authorization of 1507 was still being debated at the time of this writing (July 2014) after the General Affairs Council deadlocked on authorization in mid-February 2014, with the Commission indicating it had no recourse but to stand by the 2009 decision. (See the concluding chapter of this volume for an examination of the 1507 authorization controversy in the context of institutional power and member state disagreements.)

Because comitology is intended to assure national interests are represented when the Commission exercises its regulatory powers, it has been described as "the Council within the Commission" (Chambers, 1999, p. 100). One can immediately recognize that no such regulatory arrangement confers such status on US states, which must rely on their congressional representatives and lobbyists to insert themselves into the regulatory process. Yet the emphasis on "national" representation should not be taken too far. This is because there is some evidence to suggest that member state representation in comitology committees is overstated. Hooghe and Marks (2001) argue that national governments often select individuals outside of the central government to serve on the committees. In many instances, sub-national officials, technical experts, interest group representatives, scientists, and academics ended up serving on committees, thus lessening the central government's participation in comitology. Along these lines, Dogan (1997) suggests that the discussion of which institutions gain more power or competency over certain policy areas within the comitology procedure is a misleading way to view how the comitology procedure works. Rather, the policy itself dictates whether the supranational or national levels will have greater competency. But undoubtedly, as the GMO cases cited above demonstrate, when the decision is sent up to the relevant Council configuration for decision-taking, intergovernmentalism holds and the member states are the "deciders."

European Citizens' Initiative

Public influence is also a factor that impacts the policy process. One way that public opinion and citizen action can influence EU decisions is through the European Citizens' Initiative (ECI) introduced in the Lisbon Treaty. The ECI allows EU citizens to ask the Commission to bring forward a legislative proposal if the signatories of an initiative number at least one million, originate in at least 25% of the member states, and the required minimum numbers of signatures from each member state amounts to the number of members of Parliament elected in each member state multiplied by 750. The ECI gives citizens the ability to call on the European Commission to make a legislative proposal (European Commission, 2013c). In the US, citizen initiatives are provided for in the constitutions of a number of states (mainly in the West), but there is no such formal citizen input in federal government.

Significantly, the first ECI concerned GMOs, which was spearheaded by Greenpeace and Avaaz on December 9, 2010 in response to the Amflora potato decision. The ECI "calls for a moratorium on all new GM crop production in Europe until a proper safety regime has been put in place" (EurActiv, 2010). The impact of this ECI prompted then Commissioner of DG SANCO, John Dalli, to hold conferences regarding the risk assessment of GMOs (although this had little immediate policy impact).

Economic Interests

As detailed in the introduction to this chapter, the US is the leading global producer of GMO crops, with 69.5 million hectares (International Service for the Acquisition of Agri-Biotech Applications, 2012). Furthermore, as Frankel (2005) points out, more US companies have developed the technology and produce GMOs than European companies and, as a result, US producers have more to lose if there are stricter regulations and slower government approval rates. For instance, US industrial giants such as DuPont, Syngenta, Monsanto, and Dow hold several patents on GMOs and have been able to influence both the executive and legislative branches of the US government to protect their interests (Knowles, 2013). Thus, since Europe was not an early innovator in commercial applications of GMOs, EU member state governments faced little pressure from this sector, while environmental and consumer groups heavily mobilized against the introduction of GMO products, and especially varieties for cultivation.

As a consequence, Monsanto – the world's largest seed company – has "permanently stepped out of Europe's application line" for cultivation of GMOs, instead focusing on the cultivation of conventional seed (News Desk, 2013). So while Monsanto will continue to export GMO products, it has decided that its applications for six types of corn, a soybean variety, and a modified sugar beet had little chance of approval (RT Question More, 2013).

In addition to there being a greater number of GMO products produced in the US, there is also a greater occurrence and less aversion to revolving-door practices between bio-tech firms and government regulating bodies than in the EU

(J. M. Smith, 2007), where the EFSA has been subject to criticisms of conflict of interest and revolving-door concerns. In May 2012 the EP delayed approval of three agencies' budgets for 2010, one of which was the EFSA due to MEPs' concern over potential conflict of interests. One of the most notable cases was that of Diana Banati, the head of EFSA's board. Banati took a position with the International Life Sciences Institute, a powerful industry lobby group based in Washington, DC that was seen as incompatible with her post with the EFSA. As a result, the EFSA requested her resignation and she complied. Also, as a result of the EP's actions, the EFSA also changed members of its panel and management board (European Parliament Green Party staff member, personal communication, 2013). Likewise, a 2012 Court of Auditors' (EU's internal watchdog) report called for greater independence and transparency of the EFSA.

Thus, within the EU there are increased pressures against revolving-door actions, whereas in the US there has been little government action or attention paid to the more pervasive revolving-door activity regarding GMOs. For instance, some of the more notable occurrences in the US have been Michael Taylor, Ann Veneman, and Roger Beachy, among others (J. M. Smith, 2007).

Michael Taylor was a staff lawyer at the FDA in the mid-1970s and then practiced law during the 1980s at a law firm that represented Monsanto. In 1991 he returned to the FDA as Deputy Commissioner for Policy. He then led the USDA's Food Safety Inspection Service in 1994–1996. In the late 1990s he was employed at Monsanto for 16 months, and beginning in 2000 he spent almost a decade in academia; in 2009 he returned to lead the food side of the FDA. Taylor has been candid, however, regarding "revolving door" concerns, and explains that "to guard against such conflicts, the government has clear rules about what a person can and cannot work on under those circumstances, and he follows those rules very carefully" (Marler, 2013).

Ann Veneman served as Deputy Secretary of the USDA (1991–1993). Following this position she joined the Board of Directors of Calgene, Inc., which became the first company to market genetically engineered produce, the Flavr Savr tomato. While on Calgene's Board, she was a lawyer at Patton Boggs and Blow, where one of her clients was Dole Foods, the world's largest producer of fruit and vegetables. Between 1999 and 2001, Veneman was an attorney with Nossaman, Guthner, Knox and Elliott, where she focused her attention on food, agriculture, environment, technology, and trade related issues. From 2001 to 2005 under the George W. Bush Administration she returned to the national public scene and served as Secretary of Agriculture.

Roger Beachy was appointed as the first Director of the National Institute of Food and Agriculture in October 2009, serving until May 2011. He also served as Chief Scientist of USDA from January 2010 till October 2010. Prior to his government post he was the founding president of the Danforth Center, serving from 1999–2009. Yet the Danforth Center was founded in 1998 through a $60 million gift from the Danforth Foundation, a $50 million gift from the Monsanto Fund, the donation of 40 acres of land from Monsanto Company, and $25 million in tax credits from the State of Missouri (Donald Danforth Plant Science Center, 2013). From 1991 to 1998, Dr. Beachy also headed the Division of Plant

Biology at the Scripps Research Institute, a biomedical research center in La Jolla, California. He was also Professor and Scripps Family Chair in Cell Biology and Co-Director of the International Laboratory for Tropical Agricultural Biotechnology. Thus, his work at the Danforth Center and Scripps Research Institute were both positions heavily supported by the bio-tech industry. For all three of these cases, individuals served in very high-ranking regulatory positions at the national level after working for bio-tech industries in some capacity and some even returned to bio-tech after public office.

Multi-Level Governance

At the heart of GMO regulatory policy in Europe is the question of subsidiarity. Subsidiarity is an important goal of the EU codified in treaties, which tries to ensure the handling of policies at the lowest, most appropriate government level possible. It seems that with regulating GMOs what we are witnessing are pressures to centralize regulatory power in the European Commission and at the same time pressures to decentralize (giving member states some influence as well), but only in certain areas such as coexistence (cultivation rules stopping the spread of GMOs to traditional or organic crops).

One example of the EU's attempt to preserve subsidiarity is the safeguard clause, a key component of the EU's regulatory regime. Since other member states are unwilling to vote against the invocation of the safeguard clause by another state (Member of DG Sanco, personal communication, 2013), the only recourse is for the aggrieved importer or producer to bring a case before a national court, which can then rule or refer the case to the CJEU. Thus, for example, the CJEU ruled in September 2013 that the EU had "unreasonably delayed decisions on GM authorisation applications" in the case of DuPont's 2001 application for its Pioneer 1507 maize variety (Keating, 2013b), despite both Spain and the EFSA approving its cultivation (Keating, 2013a).

As the case of Spain's support for the cultivation of Pioneer maize demonstrates, not all EU states oppose GMO cultivation. So, for example, UK Prime Minister David Cameron's government has gone on the offensive in favor of GMO cultivation, with Environment Minister Owen Paterson stating that "Europe risks becoming the museum of world farming as innovative companies make decisions to invest and develop technologies in other markets" (Harvey, 2014). Indeed, Keating (2013b) reports the Council of Ministers is evenly divided between pro- and anti-GMO states. And while nine EU member states have banned the cultivation of MON 810 maize (see introduction), it is now cultivated in five member states – Spain, Portugal, the Czech Republic, Slovakia, and Romania. Furthermore, national courts are not always willing to support their country's ban. For example, in August 2013 France's highest court found that the French ban on MON 810 violated EU law (Keating, 2013c).

The EU situation contrasts with that of the US, where agricultural states are highly dependent on agricultural exports and crops grown from GMO seed varieties, including corn, cotton, soybeans (the three main crops), canola, squash, and papaya. This further entrenches GMO supporters in Congress, where each state has equal representation in the US Senate regardless of population size (in 14 states, well over 75% of their soybeans are GMOs – translating into 28 US senators who control House and Senate agriculture committees and the numbers to filibuster anti-GMO legislation in the Senate). Some states are heavily dependent upon GMOs. For example, in South Dakota 79% of all corn and 95% of all soybeans are genetically modified; in Mississippi, 97% of all cotton under cultivation are GMO varieties; and in Hawaii, 50% of papayas are genetically modified (Pew Initiative on Food and Biotechnology, 2007, p. 4). Furthermore, the US accounts for 63% of the global land area planted in biotechnology varieties (Pew Initiative on Food and Biotechnology, 2007, p. 2).

Although some states in the US have attempted to pass legislation requiring the labeling of GMOs in food, earlier efforts were not successful. At the federal level on May 21, 2013, US Senator Bernie Sanders from Vermont introduced an amendment to Farm Bill S. 954 permitting states to require GMO labeling, but the amendment was voted down. Environmental, consumer health, and slow food/locally produced groups have all lobbied the federal level to require labeling, but such attempts have failed thus far. The tide, however, may be beginning to change with passage of GMO labeling laws in 2013–2014 in Connecticut, Maine, and Vermont and ballot initiatives gaining strength in some states (Kardish, 2014).

A significant development occurred at the end of 2013 in Hawaii, where GMO cultivation has been challenged on two islands as follows. New GMO plantings have been banned on Hawaii Island (the Big Island) except in papaya industry (see Harmon, 2014). While the US Supreme Court has ruled on GMO patents, it has not been involved in any ruling regarding state regulation of GMOs. This could change now that DuPont, Syngenta, and Dow, which have test fields on the Hawaiian island of Kauai, filed a joint action suit in US District Court in Honolulu on January 10, 2014 seeking an injunction of implementation against a local law requiring disclosure of chemical use and GMO cultivation and banning the growing of GMO crops near schools and nursing homes (Warren, 2014). As environmental and consumer activists begin to make significant inroads at the local and state level, we will likely see a broader basis for EU–US policy understanding, especially with respect to the necessity of politicians who will increasingly need to address GMO concerns among the American public.

Public Opinion

Public opinion is another factor that has shaped European and US regulations on GMOs (Frankel, 2005). It is generally thought that Europeans have expressed more suspicions and concern about the safety of GMOs than Americans. This was perhaps true in the past when Pew public opinion polls reported that one-quarter of Americans (2001) and later, 29% (2006) of Americans felt that GMOs were "basically unsafe" (Melman Group Research Based Strategy, 2006). If we look at European public opinion today regarding GMOs it is clear that, overall, Europeans have a very negative view of them. A recent Eurobarometer

(European Commission 2010e) opinion poll publication asserts that 66% of Europeans in the EU-27 are worried about having GMOs in their foods and drinks. Recent public opinion polls in the US, however, are beginning to reveal widespread mistrust of GMOs. In a late winter 2013 poll conducted by the Huffington Report, 35% of the respondents said they think GMOs are unsafe to eat (Swanson, 2013). In a January 2013 *New York Times* poll, 26% said GMO foods were unsafe to eat and 75% expressed concern about GMOs in their food, with most of those worried about health risks (Kopicki, 2013). (The Huffington poll was a YouGov Poll web-based poll open to all readers who visited the website, while the *New York Times* conducted telephone surveys using scientific sampling techniques; the margin of sampling error is plus or minus three percentage points.)

On the question of food labeling, the late winter 2013 YouGov poll reported that 82% of Americans think GMO foods should be labeled, with broad-based agreement across political parties and demographic groups (Swanson, 2013). Similarly, the *New York Times* poll found that 93% of respondents said that GMO foods should be labeled accordingly. Interestingly, while few vegetables and fruits available in the US market are GMO varieties, 40% of the respondents in the *New York Times* poll thought most of the produce they consume are GMOs and 50% indicated they were aware that a "large amount of the processed and packaged foods they now buy at the grocery store contain GMO ingredients." Finally, about one-half of all Americans said they would not eat GMO vegetables, fruits, and grains.

This shift in American opinion follows popular media figures who have voiced skepticism of GMOs. At the same time, voluntary labeling has increased in the US market among GMO-free products.

These polls suggest a game changer in the US with respect to GMOs. Significantly, it also indicates that with converging public opinion among Europeans and American, EU and US policymakers are now going to be facing similar pressure from the voting public regarding GMOs.

Conclusions

Examining the evolution of the regulatory framework, there are clear differences, which continue to shape GMO regulatory policy in the EU and the US. First, the US adopted the preventative approach, taking into consideration actual risk; whereas the EU adopted the precautionary approach focusing on possible risk. Second, the US does not have separate legislation guiding the regulation of GMOs, whereas the EU has developed a considerable body of regulatory law in this area. Third, the lead administrative locus of regulation is in the USDA (rather than in the HHS), whereas in the Commission it is in DG SANCO (rather than in DG Agriculture). Fourth, the EU established a new agency – the EFSA – to carry out risk assessments, while the US was able to utilize existing risk-assessment capacity in several federal agencies/services, including within the FDA, USDA, and NIH. Fifth, GMO regulation in the EU operates through MLG, with member state and EU engaged in co-governance, while US state governments have not involved themselves in GMO regulation.

A number of factors account for the disparate approach in the US and the EU to GMO regulatory policy. One was a "perfect storm" – the completion of the EU's internal market and food scares occurred at about the same time GMOs were leaving the laboratory for field trials. Second is the obvious difference between the US and the EU with respect to far greater importance of agri-business in the US as compared to the EU, which in no small part contributed to the commercialization of GMOs. Since the US is a large innovator, cultivator, and exporter of GMOs, the US has more to lose economically with slow regulatory approval and also with European markets blocking GMO varieties for cultivation in the EU. The US turned to the international system (WTO) to break the EU's logjam, and, while the market is now fairly open with respect to the importation of GMO products (which are mainly used for industrial purposes), cultivation is at a standstill. As a result, US corporations have tended to abandon cultivation approval and are focused mostly on importation or the cultivation of traditional seed crops (Member of DG Sanco, personal communication, 2013; Member of Europabio, personal communication, 2013; News Desk, 2013).

One obvious marker of the difference in the latitude policymakers have had in the US with respect to GMO policy is that in the past public opinion polls have reported that Americans are less concerned about GMOs than Europeans. Nevertheless, recently there has been "push back" from sectors of the US public (and no doubt aided by the transnational nature of INGOs such as Greenpeace), including the calling for mandatory labeling of GMO products and field crops under cultivation and outright bans on GMO cultivation.

Regarding the TTIP, it seems that the Commission is not willing to change the fundamentals of its regulatory framework, since there are strong political pressures from member states (Member of DG SANCO, personal communication, 2013; Member of European External Action Service, DC Delegation, personal communication, 2013). As a member of the bio-tech lobby Europabio points out, the Commission has not kept to the requisite timeline, a point to which members of the Commission concede; however, the Commission explains that there is also a requirement for public input and investigation after public input, which makes the imposed deadlines impossible to follow (Member of DG Sanco, personal communication, 2013; Member of Europabio, personal communication, 2013).

In terms of interest intermediation, a new chapter in transatlantic GMO policy may be opening, one that intensely involves all three levels of transatlantic cooperation – intergovernmental, transgovernmental, and transnational. And, unlike other policy areas explored in this book (competition, trade, and financial services regulation) – all of which affect consumers' choices and prices – GMO regulation attracts two important transnational interests – environmental and consumer protection – which are well entrenched in advanced industrialized democracies and have become highly sophisticated actors through the standard strategies of public interest groups (lobbying, astroturfing, campaign donations, etc.) and/or through political party affiliation (e.g., the Green Party).

In the meantime, agricultural technology has not stood still. Indeed, scientists have been actively working to find a way around the GMO dilemma, not only due to the EU's resistance to GMOs, but because of increased hostility to GMOs in various countries and regions (for example, Mexico's GMO ban and the controversy in Southeast Asia over Golden Rice, which has involved the destruction of a test field in the Philippines). Intensive efforts are underway, for example, to improve plant resistance to droughts, pests, pesticides, and any number of the many characteristics bred into plant crops, through alternative biogenetic processes that will not carry the same stigma as GMOs (that is, as transgenetic). So, for instance, the ability to improve drought resistance through DNA transference within the *same* plant variety would not be classified as a GMO.

Cultivation of GMOs in Europe may be off the table, but the US federal government may demand shorter time frames for approving imported GMOs, especially ones for animal feed. But to speculate on the fate of GMOs in the TTIP negotiations would be hazardous, especially as the sleeping giant – the American public – has been awakened to the "unknowns" of GMOs, which may or may not counter the influence of the revolving door between regulatory agencies and corporations and the influence of GMO producers in the legislative process.

The history of policymaking in American federalism suggests that states and localities often lead (witness the recent executive orders and federal court rulings upholding same sex marriage) and the federal government follows. With bills proposed in some 20 states to require GMO labels on foods with ingredients made from genetically engineered crops (Harmon, 2014), American politicians and bureaucrats will likely get a "taste" of the highly contested politics of GMOs that their European counterparts have been experiencing for over two decades. This development, in and of itself, may lead to greater transatlantic understanding about the regulation of GMOs, if not policy convergence.

Part IV

The Transatlantic Trade and Investment Partnership

Prospects and Challenges

13 The TTIP Arrives

Politics and Processes

Laurie Buonanno

Introduction

The Transatlantic Trade and Investment Partnership (TTIP) negotiations opened to much fanfare in July 2013. In the preface to this book, the editors listed some of the tantalizing economic benefits this "economic NATO" is projected to deliver. The preceding chapters of this book, however, suggest a more cautious interpretation. While the EU and the US have been cooperating in a number of areas (see the discussion of transatlantic governance in Chapter 5), this book has shown that in some key economic sectors (agriculture – particularly, with respect to GMOs and American farm practices; government procurement; aircraft) as well as in overall policy areas (for example, competition/antitrust policy and trade) the transatlantic partners have been unable to reach agreement, despite sometimes years of negotiations in bilateral and multilateral fora.

The TTIP is the next "phase" of transatlantic governance and, therefore, must be understood in the larger context of the Atlantic alliance outlined in Part I of this volume. Such a "holistic" view is expressed in remarks by transatlantic policymakers; for example Robert Hormats (2013), Under Secretary for Economic Growth, Energy, and the Environment, US Department of State has commented on the need for "periodic strengthening" of US–European ties "to ensure that current and future generations of Americans and Europeans recognize not only the important legacies we share, but also that at present and in the future our common economic benefits and security relationships are intertwined."

The TTIP merits study also for the attributes of its partners. In an era when preferential trade agreements (PTAs) have re-emerged (not least due to Doha's failure to satisfy the EU's and US's trade and investment concerns), the TTIP is unlike any other PTA. Along these lines, Akhtar and Jones (2014, p. 6) observe:

> In terms of how the United States and EU negotiate, the comparable economic size of the two trading partners means that neither side will be able to dominate the negotiations. To reach consensus, they may need to be more flexible than they have been in other FTA negotiations, which generally have been with countries of lower levels of development and economic clout.

The purpose of this chapter is threefold: first, to connect the TTIP negotiations to our knowledge of transatlantic economic governance explored in Parts I and II of this volume; second, to present and discuss the projected economic benefits of the TTIP; and third, to examine the politics engendered by a TTIP Agreement.

The idea for a transatlantic trade agreement or association was not completely novel when in early 2013 the EU and the US announced their intent to begin negotiations. The first section of this chapter offers an explanation of "why now?" The second section begins where Chapters 2 and 5 end – with a discussion of the EU–US High-Level Working Group on Jobs and Growth (HLWG), which recommended the TTIP in its final report. This section also lists some of the projected benefits of the TTIP. The third section focuses on TTIP's mechanics – the negotiating process, the timelines, and the negotiating rounds. The fourth section discusses the politic of the TTIP. The fifth section examines the controversy involving claims of lack of transparency in the TTIP negotiations leveled by TTIP opponents. The last section summarizes the findings of this chapter.

A Policy Window Opens

As earlier chapters in this book have noted, the path to the TTIP has been incremental, and without these earlier steps beginning with the Transatlantic Declaration (TAD) and the policy learning that has taken place at the intergovernmental, transgovernmental, and transnational levels, the TTIP would not now be possible. The *idea* of a transatlantic trade area is neither new nor unique to the current time period. Indeed, trade liberalization was an objective of the New Transatlantic Agenda (1995) and was formally proposed by the European Commission in March 1998 as the New Transatlantic Marketplace (NTM). The EU and the US had reason to be optimistic at the time, not least because of the perceived success of the GATT/WTO's Uruguay Round (Schott & Oegg, 2001, p. 745). The NTM proposed removing technical barriers to trade (TBTs) and liberalizing investment, government procurement, and intellectual property (Frost, 1998; International Centre for Trade and Sustainable Development, 1998). Businesses were complaining about "duplicative test and certification procedures – over $1 billion a year for the US information technology industry alone" (Frost, 1998). Very early into consultations, however, EU and US officials began to realize that significant differences in EU and US regulatory policies and farm price supports would make a wide-ranging bilateral agreement exceedingly difficult to negotiate. Nor had the European Commission considered the possibility that the NTM could well undermine the very success the EU and US had recently achieved in establishing the WTO by diverting trade to the EU and US (Schott & Oegg, 2001, p. 745). The "net worth" of a PTA, after all, must always be measured by the foundational principles of the GATT/WTO – it should create rather than divert trade.

France led EU member state opposition to the NTM, particularly over the communications, agriculture, and audiovisual sectors, but other member states, too, opposed the bilateral nature of the NTM on several grounds: that the EU–US bilateral dispute mechanism envisaged in the agreement would undermine the WTO dispute settlement process; would weaken the GATS initiative to liberalize trade in services; and, in general, that a bilateral agreement would amount to the West turning its back on the multilateral system they themselves championed and founded in the postwar era (Frost, 1998; International Centre for Trade and Sustainable Development, 1998). As Baldwin and Francois (1997, p. 8) wrote at the time:

> In the case of a transatlantic free trade agreement, the gains by transatlantic exporters will be mild (since these sectors have already been substantially liberalized) but the short-term loss of – and therefore political opposition from – agriculture, textiles and clothing sector (and U.S. steel) will be great.

International politics acted against the NTM as well. There was the familiar Anglo-Franco-American triangle, with France less than pleased upon learning that the NTM's main spokesman and champion, Trade Commissioner Leon Brittan, discussed the proposal with the US prior to approaching the EU member states. Simultaneously, EU member states were still very annoyed by US unilateral action (the Helms-Burton Act of 1986) intended to isolate Cuba and force regime change by starving the island of foreign investment (International Centre for Trade and Sustainable Development, 1998), but which if faithfully implemented interfered with European investment. As a consequence, the Transatlantic Economic Partnership (TEP), agreed in May 1998 (detailed in Chapter 5), adopted an incremental approach, and by so doing, was a pale version of the transatlantic FTA Brittan and others had hoped to negotiate.

What, then, changed in the intervening years for the TTIP to land on the transatlantic policy agenda?

John Kingdon's (2011) policy streams approach is helpful in understanding the origins of the decision to launch the TTIP negotiations. As the NTM proposal illustrates, there has long been a *"policy stream"* with the European Commission taking the role of policy entrepreneur, but also politicians in some member states (and most particularly Germany and the UK) also trumpeting the mutual economic advantages of an Atlantic FTA. So, for example, in January 2007 – prior to the onset of the Great Recession – Chancellor Angela Merkel gave a speech at the Davos Economic Forum in which she promoted greater dialogue toward opening up transatlantic trade (*Speigel Online*, 2007):

> I feel it is very important that trans-Atlantic economic relations are intensified.... History shows that close trans-Atlantic economic integration is always the impetus for boosting economic growth ... I see the need and possibilities for negotiations about non-tariff barriers, like for example technical standards, rules for financial markets, energy, environmental questions and intellectual property. The different approaches to regulation on the two sides of the Atlantic create unnecessary transaction costs. We can reduce these costs. Our goal should be the creation of structures similar to those of an internal market.

Despite the supposed winding down of the Great Recession, persistent low growth and high unemployment continued in the 2011–2012 period, which together fed the "*problem stream.*" Meanwhile, budget deficits and high national debt in the US and many European countries restricted the ability of national leaders to implement (costly) short-term social programs and longer-term solutions (e.g., more funds allocated to vocational training and post-secondary education). In 2010, government debt as a percentage of GDP stood at 233% in the US, 118% in Italy, 145% in Greece, and 83% in Germany. Budget deficits in eurozone member states climbed to well above the 1997 Stability and Growth Pact's (SGP) ceiling of 3% of GDP. Indeed, Ireland reported a 31.3% deficit to GDP ratio after bailing out its failed banks, which had teetered on the edge of bankruptcy from bad mortgages. Even Germany exceeded the SGP's ceiling with a budget deficit 4.3% above GDP (Buonanno & Nugent, 2013, p. 210). With adoption of the Fiscal Compact in December 2011 followed by the ratification of the Treaty on Stability, Coordination and Governance (TSCG) in 2012, the ability of eurozone member states to continue racking up debt was even more severely circumscribed. Furthermore, the pre-euro device of depreciating the national currency was no longer an option for eurozone member states as it had been in 1998 when the NTM had been proposed.

The problem stream was further exacerbated by the failure of the Doha Round to achieve breakthroughs in trade and investment liberalization. As a result, the EU and the US were increasingly turning to preferential trade agreements, notably with South Korea (US–South Korea; EU–South Korea), Japan (EU–Japan), and the US participation in TransPacific Partnership (TPP; Australia, Brunei, Chile, Canada, Japan, Malaysia, Mexico, New Zealand, Peru, Singapore, Vietnam). The TPP was particularly worrisome to the EU because the North American Free Trade Agreement (NAFTA) and the TPP involve a higher volume of trade in goods and services than EU–US trade (Akhtar & Jones, 2014, p. 8).

As Akhtar and Jones (2014, p. 6) observe, the EU and the US "run the risk of being disadvantaged in each other's market in the absence of their own bilateral FTA," and that negotiations that were underway for the EU–Canada Comprehensive Economic and Trade Agreement (CETA) "makes the absence of a U.S.–EU FTA all the more notable." Connected to this, and discussed in Chapter 2 of this volume, the so-called "Asian pivot" (of which the TPP negotiations seemed to provide ample proof) was interpreted by Atlanticists as strong evidence of a weakening transatlantic alliance (Choblet & Hager, 2013, p. 9).

A new concern, one that did not weigh heavily in the 1990s during NTM discussions, entered the problem stream: the BRICS's (Brazil, Russia, India, China, and South Africa) challenge to EU and US competitiveness. The failure to reach agreement in Doha with the BRICS on areas of key concerns to the EU and the US (e.g., protection of intellectual property rights, trade in services) increased the incentive for the EU and the US to undertake bilateral negotiations.

The "*politics stream,*" too, favored the free trade solution to the continued economic malaise. Center-right and center-left EU member state governments and the center-right holding the plurality in the European Parliament (EP) and the Council of Ministers looked to overseas markets as a business-favorable solution to the obstinately high unemployment rates. This is nowhere more evident than in British Prime Minister David Cameron's and German Chancellor Angela Merkel's suggestion to US President Barack Obama after his re-election to make a commitment to pursue a transatlantic FTA (Schmitz, 2013). So, too, divided government at the federal level created a situation where Obama needed to work with a Republican-controlled House of Representatives and a US Senate where the Democratic Party held a slim majority of seats. Republicans (with the exception of its populist Tea Party faction) tend to favor free trade agreements (FTAs) and international cooperation on regulatory matters. The realities of party control and ideology in Europe and the US, thus, closed the option of a "soak the rich" solution (which center-left President François Hollande had all but promised in his 2012 presidential campaign).

Within EU institutions, pressures for export-led growth were quite intense. For example, on the occasion of a TEP conference in May 2012 the governing German CDU/CSU parliamentary group issued a discussion paper that was permeated with calls for the creation of a transatlantic FTA. Among specific demands addressed by the parliamentary group to the German government was

> pursuing a comprehensive approach in negotiating on a free trade agreement between the EU and the USA, which in addition to dismantling customs duties and non-tariff barriers also encompasses, *inter alia*, the liberalization of services and the protection of intellectual property.
> (CDU/CSU Parliamentary Group, 2012)

So, too, a resolution put to a vote in October 2012 to open up EU–US trade negotiations easily won in the EP (526 for, 94 opposed, and 7 abstentions) (European Commission, 2013a, pp. 5 – footnote 2).

The public mood, which was one of such intense frustration, proved to be another factor driving the politics stream. Politicians needed to be seen to be trying to *do something*, anything, to grow their economies. Interest groups, too, played an important role in the political stream, where American and European business interests worked together to declare that duplicative governmental regulatory standards were undermining growth in a wide range of sectors, from automobiles to chemicals. Such sentiments were voiced in the many comments contributed by industries and trade associations to the European Commission, the US Department of Commerce, and the US Trade Representative in response to a request for information about transatlantic barriers to trade and investment. (See, for example, American Chemistry Council/European Chemical Industry Council, 2012; Blunt, 2012; European Commission and US Government, 2012; Office of the United States Trade Representative, 2012; US Department of Commerce – International Trade Administration, 2011; US Department of State, n.d.) Furthermore, those groups suspicious or even hostile to an "economic NATO" are precisely those interests that have had little ability to forge transatlantic alliances (see Chapter 5 on the role of stakeholders in transatlantic governance). Therefore, minimal serious oppositional pressure countered the movement of the political stream toward convergence with the problem and policy streams. With the convergence of these three streams, a "policy window" began to open in

November 2012 at the EU–US summit and was fully opened when President Obama delivered his State of the Union address on February 12, 2013 calling for negotiations to begin on the TTIP. This was then followed by a joint statement from Obama, European Council President Herman Van Rompuy, and European Commission President José Manuel Barroso announcing the EU–US joint decision to pursue TTIP negotiations (White House – Office of the Press Secretary, 2013; White House, 2013).

The High Level Working Group on Jobs and Growth

At the 2011 EU–US summit leaders had directed the Transatlantic Economic Council (TEC) – see Chapter 5 for background on both the summits and the TEC – to establish the HLWG chaired by US Trade Representative Ron Kirk and EU Trade Commissioner Karel de Gucht. The summit leaders charged the HLWG "to identify policies and measures to increase U.S.–EU trade and investment to support mutually beneficial job creation, economic growth, and international competitiveness" (EU–US, 2011). To accomplish this task, the HLWG was to undertake a number of discussions as outlined in Box 13.1 and to draw up an interim and final report covering these mandates.

In its final report issued in February 2013, the HLWG recommended that the EU and the US "initiate as soon as possible the formal domestic procedures necessary to launch negotiations on a comprehensive trade and investment agreement," which should not only address a "broad range of bilateral trade and investment issues, including regulatory issues," but also contribute "to the development of global rules" (High Level Working Group in Growth and Jobs, 2013, p. 1).

The Economic Projections

The Models

Naturally in a geographic area which trades \$2.7 billion/€2.0 billion on a daily basis (US–EU High Level Working Group on Jobs and Growth, 2013, p. 1), one would expect there to be unrealized economic opportunities if barriers to trade could be eliminated. This had long been the position advanced by proponents in the years prior to agreement to begin negotiations on a transatlantic FTA. Absent from the discussion, however, were comprehensive economic analyses, including the costs and benefits of a transatlantic FTA. Two such studies published in 2013 closed this gap: one was conducted by the Centre for Economic and Policy Research (CEPR) (Francois, Manchin, Norberg, Pindyuk, & Tomberger, 2013) and the other by the Bertlesmann Stiftung (Bertlesmann Foundation) (Felbermayr, Heid, & Lewhwald, 2013). Both studies employ computable general equilibrium models (CGE), a technique that is not without its detractors (see, for example, L. Taylor & Von Arnim, 2007); however, both models arrive at similar conclusions with respect to GDP growth, job growth, and welfare benefits.

Box 13.1 Heads of Government Charge to the High-Level Working Group on Jobs and Growth

Options to consider:

- Conventional barriers to trade in goods (tariffs and tariff-rate quotas).
- Reduction, elimination, or prevention of barriers to trade in goods, services, and investment.
- Opportunities for enhancing the compatibility of regulations and standards.
- Reduction, elimination, or prevention of unnecessary "behind the border" non-tariff barriers to trade in all categories.
- Enhanced cooperation for development of rules and principles on global issues of common concern and also for the achievement of shared economic goals relating to third countries.

In terms of:

- short- and medium-term impact on economic growth, job creation, and competitiveness;
- the feasibility of each option;
- the implications for, and consistency with, bilateral and multilateral trade obligations.

Recommendations:

- Consider and recommend the practical means necessary to implement any policy measures identified such as regulatory cooperation or negotiations of bilateral trade agreements.

(EU–US, 2011)

The CEPR study (Francois et al., 2013), conducted under contract with the European Commission (2013k), created various models to analyze different policy options – from partial agreements (98% of tariffs eliminated; "services only" with 10% reduction in non-tariff barriers (NTBs); or "procurement only" with 25% of procurement NTBs eliminated) to comprehensive liberalization – the latter analyzed using a "less ambitious" and "ambitious" scenario (Francois et al., 2013, p. 28). The CEPR study also drew on data from the Ecorys study (2009), the most comprehensive study of NTBs in EU–US trade and investment.

Not surprisingly, given already low average tariff rates between the EU and the US (see discussion, below), the predicted gains were not impressive under either a 98% reduction (CEPR study) or zero tariff scenario (Bertlesmann Foundation study). However, in the most "ambitious" comprehensive scenario, which assumes tariffs are reduced to zero, NTBs in goods and services are reduced by 25%, and public procurement barriers are reduced by 50%, the CEPR reported that a TTIP agreement would increase the size of the EU economy by approximately €119 billion (0.5% of GDP) and the US by €95 billion (0.4% of

GDP) per annum, by 2027 or €545 extra disposable income for a family of four per annum in the EU and €655 per family in the US (European Commission, 2013k, p. 6; Francois et al., 2013, p. vii, 2). Similar positive results were found by the Bertlesmann Foundation study in its "deep" liberalization scenario.

From where would these gains be realized? The CEPR study reveals that "as much as 80% of the total potential gains could come from cutting costs imposed by duplicative bureaucracy" (European Commission, 2013k, p. 7) – in other words, in the messy intersection where domestic politics meets international trade.

Trade Diversion or Creation?

In the Bertlesmann Foundation study (see Felbermayr et al., 2013, pp. 5–8 for a detailed explanation of the model utilized), the data analysis leads the authors to make similar conclusions to those of the CEPR study: namely, that lowering tariffs, alone, will not produce significant "trade-creating effects," but that "a comprehensive and deep agreement has much stronger effects" (Felbermayr et al., 2013, p. 14). The implications of these findings follow.

Transatlantic Trade with Third Countries

Naturally, bilateral and regional trade agreements concern supporters of the multilateral system on the grounds that such agreements will divert trade to the exclusive benefit of the regional/bilateral partners. The CEPR analysis, however, found that other countries – both OECD and low-income economies – would gain from the TTIP because global income would increase by almost €100 billion per year (Francois et al., 2013, p. vii). The idea is this: because American and European consumers are projected to have more disposable income (see projections, above), there will be an increase in demand by American and European companies for components and services from suppliers in other countries. Furthermore, third countries will benefit from transatlantic regulatory compatibility by having to comply with just one (TTIP) rather than two standards (EU and US). (For more on the harmonization assumption, see below.)

The Bertlesmann Foundation study, focusing primarily on the impact of German imports and exports, projects substantial trade diversion with third countries. Some of the highlights follow.

Germany's exports will increase to Japan with both zero tariffs and comprehensive liberalization (zero tariffs and elimination of duplicative regulations), but Japan's exports will increase to Germany only if comprehensive (deep) liberalization is achieved (Felbermayr et al., 2013, p. 14).

Turning to the BRICS, considerable trade diversion is predicted (Felbermayr et al., 2013, pp. 15–16):

> If a deep liberalization scenario is assumed, both exports and imports undergo increased trade diversion: German exports that previously went to the BRICS now go to the USA; and Germany replaces imports from the

BRICS with imports from the USA. This occurs even though the trade barriers with the BRICS have not changed nominally. Trade diversion is driven solely by the change in relative trade costs.

There are also impacts among North American countries, with exports and imports declining among NAFTA members (Canada, Mexico, and the US). The study predicts increased trade between Canada and Mexico due to the TTIP's effect of a "less attractive" US market due to intensified competition from European manufacturers, at least in part enabled by NAFTA trade liberalization (Felbermayr et al., 2013, p. 19).

Trade diversion in the current Germany–BRICS and US–BRICS relationship is also likely in the comprehensive liberalization scenario. Sometimes this percentage decline will be quite substantial, with an average decrease on both sides of 33% in China–US trade. Similarly, India–US, Russia–US, and Brazil–US trade will decrease in both directions, on average by 30% (Felbermayr et al., 2013, p. 20).

Comprehensive liberalization as a result of the TTIP would also decrease EU trade with its neighbors (the Maghreb, Egypt, Russia, Belarus) (Felbermayr et al., 2013, pp. 16–17). It also appears that real per capita income would decline in developing countries. In a zero-tariff scenario, relative tariffs faced by developing countries become "on average" higher, and would seem particularly troubling for the countries of North and West Africa which carry on intensive trade with Europe (Felbermayr et al., 2013, p. 28).

A consideration of the impact of the TTIP on Turkey is important for a number of reasons – Turkey's candidacy for EU membership, the EU–Turkey customs union, and Turkey's geostrategic importance to the Western alliance, particularly NATO. With 40% of Turkey's foreign trade with the EU and the US and two-thirds of Turkish capital invested in the EU and the US, Turkey has been particularly concerned about the negative impact of the TTIP with respect to its customs union with Europe and has been making this concern known through a number of channels, including at the highest levels (see Kirişci, 2014, p. 5). So, for example, Turkey's foreign minister, Egeman Bagîs, commented shortly after the TTIP was announced: "Every time a trade deal is signed, the balance of mutual interest between Turkey and the EU achieved by the customs union creates a new deficit" (A. Gardner, 2014c). Turkey also points to the idea that the TTIP is not simply a trade and investment agreement, but also has geopolitical implications, and that Turkey has been an important geopolitical partner with the EU and the US through NATO and the OECD (Kirişci, 2014, p. 8). While Turkey has requested observer status to the TTIP negotiations, this request has not been granted, at least in part because of complications a formal role played by Turkey might portend for the TTIP when the agreement is sent to the EP for consent (ratification), a body where the question of Turkish accession to the EU is very controversial (A. Gardner, 2014c).

Intra-EU Trade

The Bertlesmann study suggests that trade creation between the EU and the US would come about through "significantly" altering the "trade diversion effects" now operating among EU member states as a result of the EU's customs union. Furthermore, the effects will not be uniform across the EU, where the UK is expected to benefit the most from a comprehensive TTIP agreement because of "relatively low natural trade barriers (language, culture)" with the US (Felbermayr et al., 2013, p. 14).

The TTIP would most certainly upset those trade patterns that arise from the EU's customs union. France, for example, would experience a share decline in its trade with Germany (a decrease of 23% in both directions) (Felbermayr et al., 2013, p. 42). The impact of comprehensive (deep) liberalization is significant, not just on the face of it, but for what it may portend for the UK's perceived benefit of EU membership and France's support for the TTIP. The study predicts an increase of 60.56% in the UK's exports to the US and an increase of 60.61% in US exports to the UK. But, exports from the UK to Germany decrease by 40.93% and German exports to the UK decrease by 40.91%. Similar percentage decreases are forecast for the UK's trade with France, Italy, Spain, and even Ireland (Felbermayr et al., 2013, p. 18). These predictions lead the authors to conclude:

> In other words, through the transatlantic agreement, having Great Britain remain in the European Customs Union would be less valuable for both Great Britain and the other EU member states. Given this background, the discussion of Great Britain's exit from the EU could take on additional energy.
>
> (Felbermayr et al., 2013, p. 18)

Counterbalancing the decrease in trade among EU member states is the very large percentage increases in EU–US trade predicted among those eurozone members that have been struggling with high unemployment and high budget deficits since the Great Recession – Greece, Ireland, Italy, Portugal, and Spain (GIIPS). These countries do very well with comprehensive liberalization. Predictions for increased trade flows between the US and the GIIPS is very high in both directions – Greece, 90%; Ireland, 77%; Italy, 92%; Portugal, 91%; and Spain, 80% (Felbermayr et al., 2013, p. 18).

Per Capita Income

Change in real per capita income in the EU would also be realized by comprehensive liberalization. The European average increase is 4.95% and all EU member states benefit. But the different effects are quite pronounced – with France at the lowest end of the spectrum benefiting at only 2.64% (France–US trade is currently low) to a 9.70% gain for the UK. Importantly, the real per capita income gain of the GIIPS is substantial: Greece at 5.13, Ireland at 6.93, Italy at 4.92, Portugal at 5.03, and Spain at 6.55% (Felbermayr et al., 2013, p. 24).

In the zero-tariff scenario, the world "becomes richer by some 0.1 percent," although this gain is mainly due to EU and US gains (because together they account for 40% of world GDP measured as purchasing price parity and account for 30% of world trade). Some countries left out of the agreement will experience slight declines (with the exception of North and West Africa, mentioned above, which may experience greater decreases in trade with the EU) (Felbermayr et al., 2013, pp. 28–30).

But in the deep liberalization scenario, projected decreases in real per capita income are quite pronounced across the board – rich, BRICS, and developing countries. So, for example, Australia's real per capita income would decline by 7.4%, Canada by 9.5%, Mexico by 7.2%, Chile by 5.6%, Iceland and Norway by 3.9%, and Japan by 5.9% (Felbermayr et al., 2013, p. 30). These percentage decreases are very significant, because it is this effect that the EU and the US expect will be the basis for a new era of transatlantic global standard setting. The real loss of income will propel other countries to adopt worldwide standards (set by the EU and the US) that have heretofore eluded global standard-setting bodies. It may be a naked bilateral exercise of market power, but if the model's predictions are correct it will be a powerful inducement for the world to conform to EU and US regulatory standards.

Employment

American and European politicians have also advanced the TTIP as an initiative that will increase employment on both sides of the Atlantic. While the zero-tariff scenario effects are small – in the range of increased employment by 0.11% and 0.20% in the EU and the US, respectively – with comprehensive liberalization, employment in the EU and the US rises by 0.78%. Significantly, employment rises in all of the GIIPS – sometimes quite substantially (0.97% in Ireland). The UK does especially well, with an increase of 1.38%. OECD member countries – Australia, Canada, Iceland, Japan, New Zealand, Norway, South Korea, Turkey, and Switzerland – all log decreases in employment, and as with income loss, would increase the pressure on them to adopt EU–US regulatory standards (Felbermayr et al., 2013, p. 39).

The EU and US also would gain jobs in both the tariff and deep liberalization scenarios – again, with the distance between zero tariffs and deep liberalization quite substantial. The US would gain 276,623 jobs with zero tariffs, but 1,095,501 with deep liberalization. The UK gains 106,134 and 400,203, respectively. Germany gains 44,831 and 181,092. Italy gains 35,538 and 140,979 jobs (Felbermayr et al., 2013, p. 41). There would be inevitable labor displacement, but the CEPR study projects "a relatively small number of people would have to change jobs and move from one sector to another – 0.2 to 0.5 percent of the EU labor force" (Francois et al., 2013, p. vii).

In conclusion, while overall the EU and the US both win in a TTIP agreement (to a small extent with zero tariffs and to a very large extent with deep liberalization), the results will have significant effects in terms of upsetting the status quo (reducing the trade diversion caused by the EU customs union). Nor are the benefits the same for all EU member states – with the UK, the GIIPs, the EU's Scandinavian members, and the Baltic countries – doing substantially better under the TTIP than other EU member states.

The current scenario on the table is not unlike that faced in the 1950s when six European nations (Benelux, France, Italy, and West Germany) agreed to form the European Economic Community as a customs union rather than an FTA (the main reason the UK refused to join). As discussed in Chapter 2 of this volume, the US favored the formation of the EEC, not only seeing the economic advantages for the US of a unified market, but also for political and security reasons grounded in Cold War politics. So, too, France stood to gain enormously from a customs union with West Germany. But the former EEC has now grown to a 28-member state entity that covers most of the European continent. It faces competitive pressure not just from Japan (the economic challenge of the 1970s and 1980s that helped drive the impetus for completing the single market), but from the BRICS. The eurozone crisis has also changed the dynamics of economic decision-making among the eurozone's members. The large EU economies – France, Germany, and the UK – have failed to "jumpstart" the economies of the GIIPS. Given the projected benefits of deep liberalization to these post-2008 beleaguered economies, the obvious benefits to the UK and various other EU members, one can anticipate a larger reservoir of political will among many EU politicians to complete a successful transatlantic trade and investment agreement.

Yet the "devil is in the details." How can the EU and the US hope to negotiate successfully such a wide-ranging agreement? The next section of this chapter begins to address this question with an overview of the negotiation process.

Negotiations

The EU Process

Due to its customs union, the EU enjoys exclusive competence in the conduct of trade policy. What follows is a brief description of the process. (See Buonanno & Nugent, 2013, pp. 256–261 for a general discussion of the policy actors and policy processes involved in EU trade policy.) The negotiation process begins with the Commission making a recommendation to the Council (Foreign Affairs Council – FAC) that the EU should seek to conclude a trade agreement with a third country or international organization. The Council takes a decision as to whether negotiations should proceed and issues a negotiating "mandate." With respect to the TTIP, the Council's negotiating mandate was issued as a restricted (confidential) document (Council of the European Union, 2013); high-ranking MEPs from Germany's Green Party leaked the mandate on March 7, 2014, but the European Council agreed to "officially" publish the negotiating mandate in October 2014, only after being called upon to do so by some MEPs, the Trade Commissioner Karel de Gucht, the European Ombudsman, and civil society organizations (EurActiv, 2014c).

The Commission's team, led by an official from DG Trade, then negotiates the prospective trade agreement on behalf of the EU, but must report regularly to the Council's Trade Committee (a unit of the Committee of Permanent Representatives – COREPER – a body composed of member state senior officials, which meets weekly) as well as a special committee set up for the TTIP, throughout the course of the negotiations. For the TTIP, these officials are the EU Commissioner for Trade (Karel de Gucht in the first year of the talks, followed by Cecilia Malmström in the Juncker 2014–2019 Commission) and Ignacio Garcia Bercero (chief negotiator) from the Directorate General for Trade of the Commission. However, because the TTIP also involves negotiations dealing with agriculture and fisheries, environment, and consumer protection (shared competences with the member states), the member states need to be regularly consulted. At the conclusion of the negotiations, the Commission may "initial" a negotiated settlement, but the treaty must be approved by unanimity in the FAC and in the EP through the consent procedure (up or down vote, majority). The EP has been following the TTIP negotiations carefully, which have included briefings by the European Commissioner for Trade as to the progress of the talks (see, for example, European Parliament, 2014c, 2014d).

The US Process

US trade policy is the responsibility of the Office of the US Trade Representative (USTR), which is part of the executive office of the president. The USTR is the president's principal trade advisor, negotiator, and spokesperson on all trade issues. The USTR is Michael Froman and the TTIP's Chief US negotiator is Dan Mullaney.

Congress, however, has the constitutional authority to "regulate commerce with foreign nations," and therefore, will be the final decision-making authority on the TTIP Agreement. Congress gave power to the executive branch to negotiate trade agreements through the Trade Promotion Authority (TPA), which was last amended in 2002 and expired at the time of this writing. A critically important aspect of the TPA is its "fast track" feature where Congress guarantees accelerated voting by requiring an "up-or-down" vote without amendments, which would be comparable to the EP's consent procedure that will be used for the TTIP.

Despite the TPA's expiration, the president and congress have acted in accordance with its provisions with respect to the TTIP (see Table 13.1). Congress has been actively involved in monitoring the TTIP through both informal and formal mechanisms; for example, several congressional committees have held oversight hearings on the TTIP (the House Ways and Means Committee, the Senate Foreign Relations Committee, the House Energy and Commerce Subcommittee on Commerce, Manufacturing, and Trade, and the Senate Finance Committee) (Akhtar & Jones, 2014, p. 4).

Table 13.1 Transatlantic Trade and Investment Partnership Timeline

Date	Event
February 11, 2013	HLWG releases final report
February 12, 2013	President Obama announces the launch of TTIP in State of the Union Address
February 13, 2013	Obama, Van Rompuy, and Barroso issue joint statement announcing decision to launch TTIP negotiations
March 12, 2013	European Commission agrees to a draft mandate for TTIP negotiations
March 20, 2013	Obama Administration notifies Congress it will negotiate the TTIP under the Trade Promotion Act (TPA), 90-day consultation period begins for congressional comment before negotiations can begin
June 2013	USTR holds requested public comments and held a public hearing on the TTIP
July 8–12, 2013 (Washington, DC)	Round 1 – Focused on the structure of negotiations, including the possible chapters and specific issues to be included
November 11–15, 2013 (Brussels)	Round 2 – Examination of approaches to trade and investment; discussion of potential convergence in services, investment, regulatory, energy, and raw materials
December 16–20, 2013 (Washington, DC)	Round 3 – Identification of areas of convergence and divergence in approaches to negotiating issues, with discussion beginning of specific negotiating proposals
March 10–14, 2014 (Brussels)	Round 4 – Tariff elimination proposals; regulatory cooperation in medical devices, automobiles, and chemicals
May 19–23, 2014 (Washington, DC)	Round 5 – Exchanged specific ideas for addressing the majority of the negotiating areas
July 18, 2014	Round 6 – Clarifying technical issues in nine sectors – including automobiles, pharmaceuticals, information technology
September 29–October 3, 2014	Round 7 – Focuses on regulatory pillar in terms of standards, the strategic dimension (setting global standards), and compatibility; specific areas discussed – energy and raw materials; customs and trade facilitation; intellectual property rights; SMEs; and services
December 2015	Anticipated conclusion of negotiations

Sources: Akhtar & Jones, 2013, 2014; European Commission, 2014h; A. Gardner, 2014a; Office of the United States Trade Representative, 2013a, 2013b; Sutton, 2014.

TTIP Rounds

The TTIP negotiations opened on July 8, 2013 (see Table 13.1). There are several "chapters" under negotiation (discussed in Chapter 14), but the heart of the FTA will be establishing an FTA and deep liberalization.

The inclusion of NTBs in the negotiations places the TTIP in a different category than other FTA negotiations.

What are the negotiations like? They are not nearly as exciting, it would seem, as the politics that negotiations have engendered: Fox (2014b) reports that "boring," tedious," and "technical" are the three "most commonly used words to describe" negotiations. So while the elimination of tariffs and harmonizing and/ or mutual recognition of regulatory standards are creating great consternation among some groups (particularly consumer, environmental, and labor), the negotiations themselves are carried on at a very technical level by civil servants rather than politicians.

Negotiations take place in "rounds," which consists of 24 negotiating groups totaling approximately 100 people meeting for one to two days during each round (B. Fox, 2014b; A. Gardner, 2014b). The negotiations are held in events centers and universities because there are too many actors to be accommodated in Commission offices in Brussels and those of federal agencies in Washington, DC. About mid-way through each of the rounds, US and EU negotiators hold an open public forum during which stakeholder groups (business, consumer, labor, and environmental) have the opportunity to make formal presentations.

During the first year of talks, the EU and the US were able to agree to five consolidated texts (B. Fox, 2014b), which then served as the basis for horse-trading and deal-making.

Policy Exclusions

There are several areas the EU and/or the US have indicated that they will not include in the TTIP: financial services regulation, GMOs, energy, cultural (audiovisual), and defense/security issues. The reader is referred to Chapter 11 (financial services regulation) and Chapter 12 (GMOs) for a discussion of EU opposition to the inclusion of GMOs and US opposition to the inclusion of financial services regulation. The exclusion of defense/security issues is standard operating procedure in FTAs for a number of reasons, such as the nation's fundamental right of self-defense and to protect industries directly involved in this effort. The exclusion of the energy and audiovisual sectors will require some explanation.

As Kirschschalger (2013, p. 80) points out, the "culture and trade debate," has long been controversial – with the quest to liberalize trade, on one hand, but also facilitation of "self-reflection and discourse within society." He suggests that the audiovisual sector is characterized by three features: first, they are culture-specific and, therefore, "non-substitutable." Second, due to low marginal costs, producers with large markets have larger production budgets. Specifically, the English language market is large enough to offer audiovisual products that can take advantage of economies of scale. This is why the US can produce high-budget films with special effects, which are popular with viewers in smaller markets (thus putting the audiovisual industry of the importing country at a severe disadvantage). Because of the large number of languages spoken in Europe, the EU cannot compete with these English scale advantages. Third, the consumption of audiovisual products can "affect the attitude or behavior of consumers" (Kirchschlager, 2013, p. 81). The rationale for subsidies of the audiovisual industry in smaller markets is that to survive economically, local producers will mimic the dominant culture's product; therefore the state must provide support for those producers who are contributing indigenous products that reflect the local culture.

France has been the driving force in excluding the audiovisual sector from bilateral and multilateral trade pacts, but in debating the TTIP negotiating mandates France was joined by 13 cultural ministers of other EU member states, a move that had been opposed by the UK's Prime Minister David Cameron (the British audiovisual sector benefits from the English language dominance) who believed "everything should be on the table" (Vandystadt & d'Imécourt, 2013). Consequently, in June 2013 the European trade ministers agreed to exclude the audiovisual sector from the mandate for TTIP negotiations.

However, the cultural exception debate is hardly over. This is because while audiovisual products comprise just 2% of the trade volume between the EU and the US (Kirchschlager, 2013, p. 82), the delivery of audiovisual products (via online services) and intellectual property protections are key issues for other stakeholders. Consumer groups want uncensored and unrestricted access on online services, but they also want lower intellectual property restrictions. So while Europe will doubtless continue to subsidize its audiovisual industry to resist Gramscian Hollywoodization, the long-standing issue of protection for a country's cultural identity is now complicated by issues of delivery, ownership, and data privacy.

The other policy exclusion to consider in this section is energy, which the US has resisted inclusion as a separate chapter. Naturally, domestic politics is driving the exclusion – specifically, the US gas boom brought about by advances in the technology of hydraulic fracturing or "fracking" to release gas from shale, from which US consumers are benefiting in the form of lower prices. Fracking is highly contentious in some parts of the US, particularly in New York State, whose governor in December 2014 banned fracking due to health considerations (despite extensive fracking in its southern neighbor, Pennsylvania). Thus, to be able to supply European demand, the price of gas would have to increase for US consumers. (The US maintains a licensing system to export gas and bans the exports of crude oil – European Commission, 2014g, p. 4.) Furthermore, many regions in Europe are sitting on very rich shale deposits, but concern over environmental impacts is making governments hesitant to drill. France, for example, outlawed fracking in 2011 (de Saint Jacob, 2011).

Politics and the TTIP

European Parliament and US Congress

Both the EP and the US Congress must approve the TTIP. The TTIP enjoys strong support among center-right parties, weaker support among the center-left, and opposition by the "protest parties." Elections to the EP are on a five-year cycle, with the latest having taken place in May 2014. Thus, the current political configuration, reproduced in Table 13.2, will be in effect when the TTIP Agreement is presented for "consent" to the EP. Protest parties, naturally, matter in the EP and not in the US Congress, especially if large numbers of the center-left Progressive Alliance of Socialists & Democrats (S&D) group vote against the TTIP. (See discussion in Chapter 1 of parties and ideology in the context of comparative public policy.)

The European People's Party (EPP) and European Conservative and Reformists (ECR) groups are the TTIP's stronger supporters in the EP. However, looking ahead to the EP's vote, S&D support will be needed, and possibly the Alliance of Liberals and Democrats for Europe (ALDE) group as well, to win 376 of the 751 available votes. (Fueling some concern over the eventual fate of the TTIP in the EP is that approximately 25% of MEPs come from national "protest parties.")

But given the Commission's constant taking of the temperature of the S&D group, it is unlikely that a TTIP agreement would be signed that does not satisfy the concern of the majority of S&D. Furthermore, while the EP groups generally tend to vote along ideological lines, member state does matter. As shown in the analysis earlier in this chapter, several member states are predicted to benefit considerably from the TTIP, including two countries with a large number of MEPS – Italy and the UK.

The American political climate indicates that the TTIP will not necessarily benefit from deep bipartisan support, and is by no means assured "smooth sailing" in the US Congress. The first clue to difficulty for the TTIP is that Congress has not acted on President Obama's request for the TPA (fast-track authority) to negotiate both the TTIP and the TPP agreements (Hughes, 2014). Many US Senate Democrats – including the (then) Senate Majority Leader, Harry Reid – indicated they would not give the President this authority prior to the mid-term elections (November 2014) in an effort to keep from alienating its political base. In January 2014, 12 of the more progressive US senators wrote a letter to Harry Reid opposing renewal of the TPA for the TPP and the TTIP – neither a groundswell of Democratic opposition (all are Democrats with the exception of Socialist Bernie Sanders of Vermont) nor enough to derail renewal of the TPA. As a greater percentage of Republicans turn out to vote, especially in mid-term elections, the Democratic leadership had to be especially cautious about upsetting its base (which could have jeopardized turn-out). The political base of Democrats – environmentalists, consumer protection advocates, and labor unions (which are suspicious of trade pacts – see more on this point below) – are able to energize their members to vote in mid-term elections. Therefore,

Table 13.2 Political Groups in the European Parliament, 2014–2019

Political Group	Seats	Ideology	Type	TTIP Position
European People's Party (EPP)	221	Center-right	Mainstream	Pro – support ambitious agenda
Progressive Alliance of Socialists & Democrats (S & D)	191	Center-left	Mainstream	Conditional support – concern over SPS, ISDS, GIs
European Conservatives and Reformists (ECR)	70	Center-right	Mainstream	Pro – support ambitious agenda
Alliance of Liberals and Democrats for Europe (ALDE)	67	Center/Center-left	Mainstream	Pro, but data privacy a special concern for European liberals
Non-attached members (NI)	52			
European United Left/Nordic Greens (GUE/NGL)	52	Far left	Protest	Con
The Greens/European Free Alliance (Greens/EFA)	50		Protest	Con
Europe of Freedom and Direct Democracy (EFDD)	48	Far right	Protest	Con
Total MEPs	751			
Total needed to pass the TTIP agreement	376			

Sources: Alliance of Liberals and Democrats for Europe Group, 2013; European Parliament, 2014c.

with Democrats fighting to retain control of the Senate in the 2014 elections (a battle they lost), it was not a fortuitous time for the Obama Administration to request renewal of fast-track authority. In sum, a Republican-controlled Congress at the conclusion of TTIP's negotiations indicated "smoother sailing" for the agreement.

Republicans, on the other hand, support fast-track authority for the US President because the wishes of the corporate lobbies trump party politics. (But Tea Party groups – the populist wing of the Republican Party – oppose fast-track as well, somewhat complicating the issue for Republicans.)

The EU's insistence on opening public procurement, and demands that "Buy American" provisions be removed from congressional legislation (see Chapter 14 for details), however, will also be very sensitive in Congress and within the states and municipalities (many of which have local content requirements).

Winning over the congressional representatives of the states will be important if the TTIP Agreement is to be passed by Congress. This fact is not lost on TTIP supporters. A joint effort to convince the 50 states of the potential gains of the TTIP was made in a report circulated by the British Embassy, the Bertlesmann Foundation, and the Atlantic Council, in which a factsheet for each state is prepared with state exports of goods and service to the EU and estimated impact of full TTIP implementation on key sectors of the state (British Embassy, Bertlesmann Foundation, & Atlantic Council, 2013).

Public Stakeholders, Civil Society Organizations

Institutionalized Consultation

If there is a single characteristic of the "New Transatlanticism," discussed in Parts I and II of this volume, that distinguishes it from the "Old Transatlanticism" revolving around security issues, it is the extensive involvement of civil society actors seeking to engage Brussels and Washington on matters of mainly economic and social policy. The pattern of institutionalized consultations (sometimes even resembling corporatist patterns) had been established in the TEC (see Chapter 5). The HLWG (2013, p. 2) engaged "intensively" with key stakeholders – including business, environmental, consumer, labor, and other representatives – which included formal consultations in both the EU and the US as well as joint solicitation with respect to transatlantic regulations (Office of the United States Trade Representative, 2012; US Department of Commerce – International Trade Administration, 2011). So, too, consultations have continued throughout the TTIP negotiation process, where societal interests are consulted in each round. Furthermore, the Commission held a public consultation (March–July 2014) on the Investor–State Dispute Settlement (ISDS) (which will be discussed in Chapter 14) after TTIP negotiations were underway.

The public debate and stakeholder involvement has clearly influenced the nature and scope of the TTIP negotiations in many respects – policy exclusions (American consumers and the exportation of natural gas; the audiovisual industry in Europe; the American Left opposing the re-opening of Dodd–Frank), the

TTIP chapters dealing with market access (tariff rates, public procurement), regulatory measures (NTBs, SPS measures), and rules (ISDS, geographical indications).

Civil society organizations are formally represented in the EU's TTIP Advisory Group, which is composed of individuals representing trades unions (ETUC, T&E, Indutriall European Trade Union), consumer organizations (BEUC), trade associations (agriculture, automobile, chemicals, food and beverage, financial services, services, Association of German Chambers of Commerce, Business Europe), environmental (European Environmental Bureau), health organizations, as well as independent experts (European Commission, 2014f). The group meets regularly (typically monthly during TTIP negotiations), discussing relevant TTIP chapters (European Commission, 2014g). Likewise, the US has been engaging in extensive consultation prior to and during TTIP negotiations, including fora established during TTIP rounds and the extensive pre-existing advisory groups associated with the USTR (Office of the United States Trade Representative, 2014b, 2014c). When negotiating trade agreements, USTR works with a series of advisory committees that were established by Congress to provide fora for stakeholder views. Tier I is the President's Advisory Committee on Trade Policy Negotiations. Tier II consists of five committees (agriculture, labor, environment, intergovernmental, and Africa) (Office of the United States Trade Representative, 2014c).

Opponents of the TTIP Agreement

Those European NGOs opposing the TTIP do so on several grounds – lack of transparency in the TTIP negotiation process, a perception that the US has lower consumer protection for data privacy, concerns over losing what is thought to be higher environmental, health, and safety protections in Europe, and that the Agreement will open up Europe to America's lower labor standards. These issues will be taken up in detail in Chapter 14, when each of these negotiation chapters is discussed. The reader is also referred to Chapter 4 of this volume, in which the "cultural" questions were explored. In general, an apt description of the sentiment among opponents of the TTIP in both Europe and the US is that the TTIP is "a new bill of rights for multinational corporations" (Hilary, 2014) and that MNCs have "captured the TTIP talks" (The Greens-European Free Alliance of the European Parliament, 2014).

In both the EU and the US, the most vociferous opponents of the TTIP are Greens/environmentalists, consumer protection advocates, and the radical left in Europe and what would be called the "progressive left" in the US. Opposition among some Europeans to the TTIP was further expressed through an attempt to use the European Citizens' Initiative (ECI) called "STOP TTIP" to end the TTIP negotiations, which the European Commission blocked as falling "outside the framework of the Commission's power to submit a proposal for a legal action of the Union"; specifically that, "the preparatory Council decisions authorizing the opening of international negotiations or repealing such authorization do not fall within the scope of the ECI Regulation" (EurActiv, 2014a).

While the American groups opposing the TTIP mirror those in Europe, at least three points explain their weaker ability to mobilize the public. First, the NSA spying scandal was a direct affront to Europeans, while many Americans took it as "business as usual" for a superpower. For them, Edward Snowden was a misguided whistleblower, at best, and a traitor, at worst (the latter view reinforced by his "defection" to Russia). Second, Americans do not have the same level of concern for data privacy as do Europeans. Even in light of multiple credit card hacking scandals, Americans are not any less inclined to use their credit cards, addicted as they are to not only the credit and convenience, but the points, discounts, and cash-back offers. Third, Americans have only one target on which they need to focus – Congress – whereas the anti-TTIP forces in the EU need to rally support in all 28 member states. Under the Lisbon Treaty the Commission has the power to negotiate trade agreements which then must be approved by the EP's consent procedure, but in July 2014, 16 member state parliaments signed and submitted a letter to the European Commission suggesting that the TTIP should be considered a "mixed agreement" because they deal with both EU and national competences, and therefore should be presented for approval by the national parliaments (Fox, 2014c). Not only has this development injected a degree of uncertainty to the approval process, it most certainly has established the idea that member state parliaments needed to be consulted and informed throughout negotiations.

The Special Case of Labor

Trades union attitudes about the TTIP are more nuanced. European trades unions have traditionally supported trade deals because trade liberalization was seen as a way to import growth, and therefore create jobs; so, for example, the European Trade Union Confederation (ETUC) has suggested the TTIP could have "positive impacts on jobs and investment flows" (A. Gardner, 2014b). The TTIP, however, could prove to be different because of privatization fears, which have been fueled by uncertainty as to the nature of the TTIP negotiations (see below for a discussion of transparency). Examples driving opposition are German trades union concerns that water utilities could be privatized and for British trades unions that services provided through the National Health Service (NHS) could be contracted out to American companies. The issue is connected to the ISDS mechanism (see Chapter 14 for details), and specifically fear that if currently contracted out services were then brought back into state control, American companies could sue the UK for loss in profitability. UK unionists, supported by the Labour Shadow Health Minister, have been calling for the exclusion of the NHS from the TTIP (A. Gardner, 2014b; M. Taylor, 2014). This position is in direct conflict with David Cameron and his Conservative Party, which have taken the position that all subjects should be on the TTIP agenda. And it is part of a larger conflict brewing between Labour and Tories in the UK over ISDS, where it has been reported that the UK was the only EU member state in the EU–Canada FTA talks to provide "unconditional support" for the ISDS (Hilary, 2014).

The peak labor organization in the US – the AFL-CIO – has also taken a cautious approach, stating that "increasing trade ties with the EU *could* [italics in original] be beneficial for both American and European workers, but as with all trade agreements, the rules matter" (AFL-CIO, 2013). The AFL-CIO points out that worker protections lag in Bulgaria, Cyprus, Romania, and Slovakia, and that in Hungary and Poland worker protections have been attacked. The AFL-CIO warns American workers

> should be aware that some multinational corporations could be intending to use a U.S.–EU trade agreement to move jobs from the U.S. to these countries whose wages and worker protections do not reach the level of the rest of the EU.

Furthermore, the AFL-CIO warns of overly optimistic predictions of job gains (equally optimistic – but unrealized – predictions bought union support for NAFTA and permanent normal relations with China). And, specifically, the AFL-CIO opposes "efforts to undermine job creation policies like Buy America."

Of particular concern to unions is the "labor" chapter anticipated in the TTIP agreement. Interestingly, American labor unions are looking to gain the stronger protections afforded by European labor afforded by EU directives on workplace safety and health and on temporary agency work. Specifically, the AFL-CIO suggests that the TTIP "presents an opportunity for the U.S. government to go beyond the 'lowest common denominator' approach to labor rights." This point is important, because Congressional Democrats will be looking for American labor's support to extend TPA, and for guidance in their decision to vote for the TTIP agreement. To win this support, American labor wants a "race to the top" – for an extension of Europe's more favorable labor practices (including perhaps, but unrealistically in the short term, labor representation on corporate boards) – to the US. These, of course, are the labor market rules which are currently under attack in Europe by the center-right, and blamed for continued high unemployment in many member states. Finally, the EU faces an uphill battle in persuading the US to eliminate Buy American provisions in federal legislation. It would be hard to imagine any "deal" that the labor chapter could offer which would persuade American labor to drop its opposition to ending local content laws in the US.

Transparency and Trust

The European Commission is keeping a wary eye on the anti-TTIP forces, not least because of the unexpected success opponents logged in their 2012 online campaign against the Anti-Counterfeiting Trade Agreement (ACTA), which at the time has been ratified by some EU member states! The anti-ACTA forces used lack of transparency to bring the public behind them, and are now using what proved to be a successful tactic with ACTA in their campaign against the TTIP. US opponents have joined their EU allies in trying to build public support against the TTIP by equating "secret" talks to "backroom deals" favoring MNCs at the expense of the environment, the consumer, and the worker.

The EU and the US have attempted to respond to the transparency complaint in several ways. First, within days of a round's closing, the EU "draws up a report of around 60 pages for the EU's member states and EP, which the member states dissect and discuss in twice per week meetings" (A. Gardner, 2014b). These reports are restricted, but have been the subject of much speculation and complaints by opponents that the negotiations are not properly transparent. The typical pattern is to

> move from a position paper (setting out the EU's aims in a particular area), via an outline of a chapter, setting out the EU's proposed structure and ideas for language, to textual proposals and a consolidated text, which includes both sides' positions in legal language.
>
> (European Commission, 2014g, p. 2)

All papers the Commission sends to the EU have been discussed with member states and shared with the EP. On the other hand, the US does "not allow its papers to be made available to member states or the EP, as current practice in the US is not to share negotiating partners' documents with Congress or its own advisors" (European Commission, 2014g, p. 2). For the US part, public officials have been meeting with member state officials to try to allay some of the public's concerns (A. Gardner, 2014a).

Furthermore, the chief negotiators engage in a post-round joint press conference, which is posted to EU and US official websites. There is also a wealth of information available on these websites. So while the intricate details are unknown to the public, the subjects being discussed are in the public record.

Naturally, the necessity of secrecy in diplomacy has long been debated – it served as the basis for de Tocqueville's assumption that because secrecy is counter to democracy, only authoritarian governments could be skillful at international diplomacy. Yet when it comes to international negotiations, the majority of the electorate tends to tolerate secrecy – understanding, perhaps, that "public" bargaining can prevent a country's leaders from obtaining policy objectives deemed to be in the national interest – regardless of whether these interests are primarily of an economic or security nature. Indeed, this point is demonstrated by Leventoğlu and Tarar (2005, p. 420) in their use of game theory to study the negotiation of trade agreements or treaties:

> when the two negotiators face fairly similar costs for violating a public commitment, a prisoner's dilemma is created in which both sides make high public demands which cannot be satisfied, and both negotiators would be better off if they could commit to not making public demands. However, making a public demand is a dominant strategy for each negotiator, and this leads to a suboptimal outcome. Escaping this prisoner's dilemma provides a rationale for secret negotiations.
>
> (Leventoğlu & Tarar, 2005, p. 419)

In the meantime, the American and European Left claim that regardless of any agreement produced, massive protests will ensure. The basis of this "warning" is extrapolated from the mass protests against the US in free trade negotiations with Ecuador, South Korea, and Thailand (Janusch, 2013); however, the parallel is likely much overblown and should be tempered by the recognition that unlike in the EU and the US, civil society in those countries has limited access to the levers of power. Nevertheless, as Robert Putnam (1988) explained, international negotiations are "two-level" games when ratification is required. So while the executive negotiates the agreement at the international level, domestic politics kicks in when the agreement faces ratification in legislatures. Thus, while opponents have not succeeded in derailing the TTIP on "secrecy" grounds, once the TTIP is agreed, it will be open to public scrutiny. This is why it has been so important for the EU and the US to continue to take the temperature of stakeholders throughout the negotiation process.

A major victory for the "pro-transparency" forces was won in November 2014 when the European Commission announced its "fresh start" for the TTIP, which includes more extensive access to TTIP documents, a review of the classification status of information, broad access to all MEPs, and a series of other measures such as publishing and updating a list of TTIP documents shared with the EP and the Council and increasing engagement with civil society and the general public both in Brussels and within the member states (European Commission, 2014h).

The transparency issue is also a proxy for "trust." Chapters 1 and 4 of this volume discussed recent concerns involving a breach of trust between the EU and the US with respect to the NSA spying scandal, which at the time seemed to threaten the TTIP talks before they had begun. Obviously trust is a key factor in any negotiation, and as Anthony Gardner, the US Ambassador to Brussels noted, "trust – or rather the lack of it – is 'the elephant in the room, particularly when it comes to perceptions about privacy of data' " (B. Fox, 2014b).

Conclusions

As Akhtar and Jones (2014) observed, the TTIP represents the first time that equal economic powers have sat at opposite sides of the table to negotiate a bilateral FTA. A similar point was made by Markus Beyrer, Director-General of the business lobby BusinessEurope, who noted that TTIP is an agreement between "equals who are normally able to impose their wills" (A. Gardner, 2014b). Gardner (2014b) observes that "the TTIP talks have become much like any other negotiation, abiding by the traditional mantra that 'nothing is agreed until everything is agreed.' "

This idea of "nothing is agreed until everything is agreed," along with the fact that two economic behemoths are sitting at opposite sides of the negotiating table, is what makes the TTIP such a complicated project to dissect. Yet we do know enough about the EU and US "positions," from the many studies of transatlantic policymaking in the past several decades, a discussion to which the preceding chapters of this volume have contributed. We also know the areas or "chapters" which the TTIP will cover. The task of the next chapter is to examine those chapters where the EU and the US need to reach agreement if the TTIP is to achieve it potential as an "economic NATO."

14 The TTIP Agreement

Market Access, Regulations, and Rules

Laurie Buonanno

Introduction

The TTIP can be distinguished from the earlier transatlantic cooperation agreements inventoried in Chapter 5 for its ambitious objectives, which will cover a wide range of issues divided into three categories – market access, regulations, and rules (Akhtar & Jones, 2014, p. 11). Market access covers tariffs on goods and services, government procurement practices, government practices regarding service providers, and the presence and perceived advantages of state-owned enterprises. Regulations focus on non-tariff barriers (NTBs). Finally, a wide range of rules are being negotiated such as a provision for Investment–State Dispute Settlement (ISDS) to intellectual property rights. The next sections of this chapter are devoted to a discussion and analysis of several issues/chapters which are noted for long-running transatlantic disputes and/or are being characterized as especially difficult to reach agreement.

Market Access

Market access involves a number of areas such as advantages for state-owned enterprises and tariffs. This section focuses on the three areas of market access that are the most important in terms of impact on transatlantic trade and investment, both in terms of projected benefits and as indicated by the partners as being key areas of concern. These are tariffs, government practices regarding service providers, and government procurement.

Tariffs

The TTIP seeks to eliminate all tariffs and other duties on trade in agricultural, industrial, and consumer products between the EU and the US (Office of the United States Trade Representative, 2014a). Trade in goods accounts for approximately 65% of EU–US trade, which suggests that a zero tariff should increase goods more than services (Francois et al., 2013, p. 9). (See Chapter 7 for statistics on EU–US trade.) The most important sector is trade in machinery and transport equipment, with the second trade in chemicals, while the third is fuels and mining products, and the fourth is agriculture products and raw materials (Francois et al., 2013, p. 9).

A substantial share of transatlantic trade is considered intra-firm or related-party trade – such as when BMW of Germany sends parts to BMW of South Carolina or when 3M ships components for its office produces from St. Paul to affiliates in Germany or the UK (Hamilton & Quinlan, 2014, p. 27). The EU and the US are each other's largest investment partners (see data provided in "investment" section of this chapter) and this has generated highly complex "cross-border value chains." Foreign investment and affiliate sales are crucial to the trade relationship; in 2011, approximately 62% of US imports from the EU consisted of intrafirm trade. Intrafirm trade accounted for 32.3% of US exports to Europe and nearly half of total US exports to Belgium and the Netherlands, 34.9% of exports to Germany, and 27.9% of exports to the UK (Hamilton & Quinlan, 2014, p. 27). Thus, it is difficult to separate out the negative impact of tariffs on transatlantic investment decisions. As Hamilton and Quinlan (2014, p. 4) also point out, although tariff averages are low, "since the volume of US–EU trade is so huge, eliminating even relatively low tariffs could boost trade significantly."

Sector Analysis

Tariffs between the EU and the US are, on average, approximately 3.5% (Felbermayr et al., 2013, p. 9), but this average masks higher tariffs in some sectors. In general, EU tariffs are "slightly higher" than US-imposed tariffs on imports from the EU (Francois et al., 2013, p. 9). The EU and the US also display "heterogeneity" in applying tariffs; for example, EU average tariffs are "substantially higher" than US tariffs for motor vehicles and processed food. The EU's tariff of 8% on motor vehicles is nearly eight times higher than that of the US, while the EU's tariff of 14.6% on processed food is more than four times higher than that of the US (Francois et al., 2013, p. 14).

Two sectors account for over three-fifths of EU export of goods to the US and over half of EU imports of goods from the US: machinery and other equipment (40% of EU exports of goods to the US, 38.5% of EU imports of goods from the US); and chemicals (23.7% of EU exports of goods to the US, and 21.8% of EU imports of goods from the US). Therefore, lowering tariffs will impact industries differently and will involve politically unpopular decisions in the EU and the US. It would seem that for tariffs to be lowered, businesses will need relief in other areas. The obvious place is in the reduction of NTBs. Thus, it may be that the zero-tariff option is politically unfeasible without a companion reduction in NTBs for sectors that will lose tariff protections.

The Special Case of Agricultural Tariffs

Agriculture has been central to EU–US tariff disputes for decades. US farmers are particularly eager for further opening of EU markets to their produce, not least because 20% of US farm income is derived from exports (Office of the United States Trade Representative, 2014a). Domestic politics plays a key role in both the EU and the US because crops are associated with particular regions of the US and the EU, which in turn shapes farm lobbying in both Brussels and Washington. In the US, for example, because agricultural exports tend to originate in specific regions of the country, this places pressure on congressional representatives to ensure farming interests are well represented in the TTIP negotiations. So, for example, in 2013 out of a record-setting export amount of $145 billion, the EU imported just over $10 billion of US agricultural exports, which the Office of the US Trade Representative (2014a) argues is "a figure that can and should be much higher."

The nature of transatlantic trade in agricultural produce is as follows. The annual value (2012) of total EU agricultural exports (includes forest and fish products) is $17.8 billion, of which two-thirds is composed of "consumer-oriented" foods, mainly beverages and snack foods, with only 2% being bulk commodities. Intermediate products (mainly oils) comprise 27% of the total. The composition of US agricultural exports to the EU $12.1 billion (2012) differs, with 40% consumer-oriented products and 20% bulk commodities. Intermediate products (25%) are primarily animal feed and oils (Grueff, 2013, p. 5). The expectation is that transatlantic trade in the agricultural sector could be considerably higher, not least due to similar (Western) tastes and consumers with high disposable incomes. Yet as Grueff (2013, p. 8) argues, considerable challenges face EU and US negotiators because they bring "substantially different mindsets" to the TTIP negotiating table with "diverging approaches" to trade negotiations, sanitary and phytosanitary (SPS) regulatory policy, and domestic agricultural policy and market access.

According to Grueff (2013, p. 4), the key issues for EU agriculture are geographical indications (discussed below under "Intellectual Property") and better access to the US market for European dairy products. The US side expects the TTIP to not only address outstanding SPS issues, but to establish a structural mechanism to discuss and resolve future problems. This section focuses on agricultural tariffs. A discussion of SPS issues is included in the section on "Regulations."

Table 14.1 lists the applied rates on EU and US agricultural imports. One can see that, on balance, the EU's tariffs are higher than those fixed in the US.

Table 14.1 US and EU Average Applied Tariff Rates for Agricultural Products (2012)

Products	US	EU
Animal products	2.2	20.4
Dairy products	19.9	52.9
Fruits, vegetables, plants	4.7	10.7
Coffee, tea	3.3	6.2
Cereals and preparations	3.1	17.1
Oilseeds, fats, and oils	4.8	5.6
Sugars and confectionery	14.4	32.1
Beverages and tobacco	14.0	19.9
Cotton	4.1	0.0
Other agricultural products	1.1	4.3
Fish and fish products	0.8	11.8

Source: World Trade Organization, 2013b.

Furthermore, these figures are the "average" rates within product groups. When one drills down to the actual product, the figures can be considerably higher. So, for example, EU apple growers pay no duties on apple shipments to the US, while US growers face a 7% duty. Similarly, US olive oil must pay a $1,680/ton tariff in the EU, while EU shippers pay $34/ton on shipments into the US (Office of the United States Trade Representative, 2014a).

The CEPR study, cited above, found that when combining agriculture, forestry, and fisheries, the TTIP could bring about an increase of 0.06% in the EU economy, but that there will be a likely negative impact in some sectors (European Commission, 2013k, p. 8).

Grueff (2013, pp. 5–6) points out that in multilateral negotiations – including in the Doha Round – the EU and the US "clearly had the objective, although generally not publicly stated, of reaching an agreement that would not require any fundamental and immediate structural changes to their programs for domestic agricultural subsidies." However, the Doha Round illustrated that the US was willing to take a "no exceptions approach" even for sugar and dairy (heavily subsidized sectors), while the EU "focused almost entirely on limiting new access to its own markets" – this, despite, the fact that the EU is the world's largest agricultural exporter – and has excluded beef, dairy products, and some fruits and vegetables from its other FTAs (Grueff, 2013, pp. 8–9).

So, too, EU and US farm policy has evolved. Whereas in the mid-1960s close to 80% of the EU budget was earmarked for the CAP, today this remains just over 40%. The Commission, particularly, has advocated freeing-up the EU budget from CAP spending for new policy initiatives. Thus, the system from the 1960s of price support for agricultural products has been largely replaced by direct payments to farmers (Buonanno & Nugent, 2013, pp. 173–174). A similar pattern of market-oriented policies also evolved in the US. And although in recent years the US had returned to granting farm subsidies (Alons, 2013, p. 65), the 2014 farm bill eliminates direct payments (paying producers regardless of whether they incurred losses), relying instead on crop insurance (US Department of Agriculture, 2014). Indeed, now only about 37% of all US farms receive government payments (Grueff, 2013, p. 14).

Nevertheless, there are some sectors that will be protected regardless of the extent of liberalization in the TTIP agreement. The US government is committed to its dairy and sugar price support program; specifically, the US government sets the price for dairy and sugar by the obligation to intervene in the market and acquire stocks if the domestic price falls below the support level, an action it has taken "many times" over the past several decades (Grueff, 2013, p. 14). Grueff (2013, p. 14) concludes that "import protection for dairy and sugar products is an essential element of US agricultural policy" and is underpinned by "two of the most influential players (dairy and sugar) among the agriculture lobbies, and they are traditionally quite effective in pursuing their policy objectives with Congress and the administration." This will play out in the TTIP because the EU feels that the US's dairy supports disadvantages European cheese exporters, whose quality is perceived as higher, in general, than American cheese, and as such should be able to increase its market share.

The end result is likely to come down to whether US agricultural interests believe that they have a deal that promises resolution and an ongoing (effective) forum to resolve new disputes arising from NTBs (mainly SPS measures, discussed under "Regulations"). Grueff (2013, p. 19) argues that the treatment of agricultural issues will be crucial to congressional approval of the TTIP:

> At the end, the U.S. Congress will listen to the views of the agricultural interests before it votes to accept the FTA or not. Given the long history of agricultural disputes with the EU, Congress will have high expectations that the FTA addresses these and provides a way for a more compatible trade relationship in the future.

Liberalization of Services

The HLWG (2013, p. 3) final report recommended that in services "the goal should be to bind the highest level of liberalization that each side has achieved in trade agreements to date, while seeking to achieve new market access by addressing long-standing market access barriers." The report also recommends "transparency, impartiality, and due process" in licensing and qualification requirements and procedures. However, the issue of professional qualifications and licensing is complex and involves numerous actors. The latter characteristic arises from the fact that in the EU licensing is regulated by the 28 member states and in the US by the 50 states (Akhtar & Jones, 2014, p. 16). Therefore, one difficulty for advancement of the transatlantic partnership is that just as the EU cannot always speak with one voice (see Chapter 2), neither can the US!

In addition to professional services, states are also heavily involved in regulating insurance, banking, and private pension funds – all areas EU businesses see as lucrative markets (Ahearn, 2009, pp. 9–10). So, too, states have a great deal of authority in setting environmental standards and other market failure policies with which EU businesses have to contend (see P. Baldwin, 2009 on the differences among and between US states and EU member states; and D. Vogel & Swinnen, 2011 with respect to regulatory requirements in the state of California). States and local public authorities, each with their own independent taxing and revenue bases, control state and local government procurement as well – which can be very significant in the transport sector (see discussion below).

While not insurmountable, it is certainly the case that the TTIP agreement will not be able to settle the issue of professional licensing. This means that the EU and the US will be looking at the TTIP as a means to establish a long-term institutional mechanism in which the stakeholders can work through their differences.

Hamilton and Quinlan (2014, p. 4) refer to services as the "sleeping giant" of the transatlantic economy. The US and Europe are the two leading service economies in the world and about 70% of their GDP is derived from the service sector (European Services Forum, 2011, p. 4; Hamilton & Quinlan, 2014). Their service sectors are intertwined to a greater extent than ever before, especially in financial services, telecommunications, utilities, insurance, advertising, computer services, and related activities (Hamilton & Quinlan, 2014, p. 16)

The EU dominates in commercial services, accounting for 24.8% of world exports and 21% of imports, compared to 18.2% and 12.9%, respectively, for the US (Buonanno & Nugent, 2013, p. 254). In terms of transatlantic trade, Europe accounted for 38.1% of total US service exports and for 41.6% of total US service imports in 2012 (Hamilton & Quinlan, 2014, p. xi). While the US merchandise trade deficit with the EU was $125 billion in 2013, it ran surpluses in the services trade ($67 billion in 2012) (Hamilton & Quinlan, 2014, pp. x–xi).

The growth area in services has been in the sales of services by US and EU foreign affiliates operating in each other's markets, which now stands at more than $1 trillion: $645 billion for US affiliates operating in Europe and $467 billion for European affiliates operating in the US. These totals mask individual member state success – French and German affiliates sold more services in the US than US affiliates sold in France and Germany (Hamilton & Quinlan, 2014, p. xi). Clearly, there is a good deal of money to be made in services, both delivered from abroad and through affiliates. Business leaders, however, suggest that the EU and US service markets can be further liberalized.

The CEPR study (Francois et al., 2013, pp. 19–20) reported barriers in the services sectors to be higher on the EU side for the business and ICT sector, communications sector, construction, and personal, cultural, and other services. On the other hand, the US barriers for EU exporters in the services sectors are higher than in the EU in the finance and insurance sectors. Hamilton and Quinlan (2014, p. 4) report that electricity, transport, distribution, and business services "suffer from particularly high levels of protection." Meanwhile, the European Commission argues the "tariff equivalent" of US service barriers can amount to 73% in the construction industry, 41% in finance, and 29% in telecommunications (European Commission, 2010a, p. 21).

Schott and Cimino (2013, pp. 6–7) suggest that the basis for agreement should be grounded in the "hybrid framework" of the WTO's International Services Agreement (ISA). The ISA utilizes a "negative list" approach for nationally sensitive services and a positive list approach to market access commitments. Even so, some service areas will "likely require protracted negotiations."

Government Procurement

Multilateral efforts to liberalize government procurement can be traced to the 1979 "Tokyo Round Code on Government Procurement," which became the Government Procurement Agreement (GPA) in 1994 when the WTO was established. The EU and the US are parties to the Revised Agreement on Government Procurement, which entered into force on April 6, 2014 (World Trade Organization, 2014a). As with the 1994 agreement, three years after entering into force and "periodically thereafter," the parties agreed to "undertake further negotiations to progressively reduce and eliminate discriminatory measures" (World Trade Organization, 2014a). The Council's (2013, Item #24) negotiating mandate states the TTIP agreement "shall aim for the maximum ambition, completing the outcome of the negotiations of the revised GPA in terms of coverage (procurement entities, sectors, thresholds and service contracts, including in particular public construction)." The mandate particularly takes aims at "local content or local production requirement in particular Buy America(n) provisions."

What is at stake for the EU? The US federal government spending totals around $500 billion annually on goods and services (Urbina, 2014), thus making it a very desirable market for EU vendors. The EU argues that it has opened up much of its own domestic public procurement to international tendering; however, it is an area that continues to be heavily protected in the US. The Commission estimates that while €312 billion of the EU's public procurement market is open to international bidders, only about €34 billion is open in the US (European Commission, 2011c, p. 26). The EU is particularly concerned about the exclusion of railway equipment and construction, where EU businesses are very competitive (European Commission, 2013a, p. 21). The EU is also concerned because 13 states are not covered under the GPA and, significantly, the GPA does not cover the procurement of cities and municipalities (which impacts utility procurement). Ignacio Garcia Bercero, the EU's Chief Negotiator, says that, on public procurement, the EU is aiming "for a level of ambition that is at the level of tariffs" and is an area Gardner (2014b) suggests "where the EU is likely to fight particularly strongly."

Unlike the US, the EU has more recent experience with opening up government procurement because member state procurement practices had been a significant obstacle in establishing the single market. The Commission thinks that it can use these same arguments – interconnectivity, efficiency – to further pry open government procurement in the US.

There are two very difficult obstacles the United State Trade Representative (USTR) faces in negotiating government procurement liberalization: Buy American provisions and persuading the states and municipalities to open up their procurement to EU member states.

The Buy American "movement" has a long and "venerated" history in US politics. The *Buy American Act of 1933* (BAA), the *Berry Amendment of 1941*, and the *Fly America Act of 1995*. The BAA requires federal agencies and contractors to purchase goods manufactured in the US and services provided by US companies. The BAA requires that "substantially all" of the costs of foreign components not exceed 50%. The *Berry Amendment* prohibits the US Department of Defense (DOD) from acquiring food, clothing (including military uniforms), fabrics, stainless steel, and hand or measuring tools from sources not grown or produced in the US, with 100% domestic content required (Grasso, 2014, p. 14). The *Fly America Act* restricts federal procurement of transportation services to US flag airlines. The *Small Business Act of 1953* requires set-asides for minority and small businesses, which accounts for almost one-quarter of federal procurement. Congress has prohibited the waiver of set-asides (thus its exclusion in the GPA) (Grier, 2014). Congress included Buy American provisions in the *Clean Water Act of 1979* as a condition of state and local funding. The US Department of Transportation (DOT) "applies the most extensive domestic content requirements to non-federal procurement," with Buy American provisions on all state and local highway, railway, and transit projects (Grier, 2014). Buy America was incorporated in The *American Recovery and Reinvestment Act of 2009*, extending the domestic content provision to a wider range of projects. Most recently, in 2014 The *Water Resources Reform and Development Act of 2014* imposes new Buy America restrictions on iron and steel used in large water infrastructure projects receiving federal funding (Grier, 2014). The GROW America Act, a $302 billion, four-year program to rebuild America's transportation infrastructure which the Obama Administration sent to Congress in the spring of 2014, contains Buy American provisions (US Department of Transportation, 2014).

Despite the prevalence of Buy American provisions in Congressional bills, Hufbauer and Scott (2009) make the case that local content requirements do not provide enough jobs to make up for the negative consequences – violating US trade obligations, especially G-20 commitments "not to implement new protectionist measures," and the risk of retaliatory measures that, on balance, decrease American jobs.

The second difficulty – persuading states to drop advantages for local content providers – can be traced to the federal system. Annex I (World Trade Organization, 2014b) of the GPA specifies the access provided by each party of the central government and Annex II of sub-central government agencies (World Trade Organization, 2014b). These lists include thresholds and exceptions. So, for example, only executive branch agencies in Florida and California agreed to procure according to the GPA requirements. In New York, all state agencies, the state university system, public authorities and public benefit corporations (except those with multi-state mandates) procure in accordance with GPA provisions, but New York specifically exempts transit cars, buses, and related equipment. In addition, there are a number of exemptions found in most states, including California, Florida, and New York, for procuring construction-grade steel; programs promoting the development of distressed areas and businesses owned by minorities, disabled veterans, and women; environmental considerations; as well as federal funds for mass transit and highway projects (World Trade Organization, 2014c, p. 6).

But there is an increasingly large US lobby opposed to Buy American and local content provisions. American MNCs with foreign production facilities do not benefit from Buy American clauses. So, too, state economic development officials are concerned about retaliation against their exporters. The AFL-CIO, however, adamantly supports Buy American provisions.

What is the likely outcome? The TTIP agreement would likely empower the Administration to waive Buy American requirements for those partners with "reciprocal" procurement agreements. This would leave Buy American clauses in place, but EU member states would be exempted from its restrictions.

Regulations

The HLWG's Final Report recommended a TBT-plus chapter (referring to the WTO Agreement on Technical Barriers to Trade, which would include a permanent mechanism for addressing TBTs). Such an institutional mechanism would address any number of issues from transparency to early consultations; best practices; promoting regulatory compatibility; as well as promoting harmonization, equivalence, or mutual recognition. The leaked Council (2013, Item #25) negotiating directive, too, emphasizes the need to achieve cooperation with respect to NTBs, "including early consultations on significant regulations, use of impact assessments, evaluations, periodic review of existing regulatory measures, and application of good regulatory practices."

Schott and Cimino (2013, p. 1) blame "strong resistance from independent regulatory agencies pressing their own agendas in response to political pressure" for the lack of significant progress in achieving mutual recognition. Furthermore, the "piecemeal" approach (Schott & Cimino, 2013, p. 1), which was covered in detail in Chapter 5 of this volume, is thought inadequate to effect widespread regulatory cooperation. Therefore, the TTIP aims for a comprehensive and ongoing approach to achieving regulatory cooperation.

Why does the reduction/elimination of NTBs figure so prominently in the TTIP? The next section reviews economic analyses of NTB effects in transatlantic trade.

Effects

NTBs and TBTs can have two main effects: increase the cost of doing business (typically a regulation that has the effect of reconfiguring the product to comply with the export market) or restrict market access (the typical example being an import quota) (Francois et al., 2013, p. 16). So, for example, a motor vehicle manufacturer may need to run two assembly lines – one for cars to be sold in Europe and a separate line for cars manufactured for the US market.

Multinational corporations (MNCs) and their trade associations make the argument that disparate standards in the EU and the US are unnecessarily duplicative and simply increase the costs of American and European products for the consumer. A statement by the Transatlantic Business Council (TBC) (2013c, p. 2), a trade association representing American and European business (see Chapter 5 of this volume), encapsulates this point of view: "it would be surprising, given broadly comparable stages of development, if consumers on one side of the Atlantic were more tolerant of unsafe products than the other." And, indeed, it is thought that a commonality in advanced industrialized democracies is a lower tolerance for risk (Wildavsky, 1988; Wilson, 1985).

The CEPR (Francois et al., 2013, pp. 15–17) utilized "perceived NTBs" derived from mixed method data collection, including literature reviews, business surveys, econometric analyses, and consultations with regulators, businesses, and sector experts as the basis for their analysis. This process found NTBs highest for food and beverage products (US imports to the EU facing a 56.8% tariff equivalent; EU exports to the US facing a 73.3% tariff equivalent) (Francois et al., 2013, p. 19). The effects of comprehensive liberalization are also quite profound for motor vehicles (especially parts and components) (Francois et al., 2013, p. 70).

These gains do, however, effect employment in ways that will generate concern among EU and US politicians. The CEPR study predicts that in the EU, employment will increase by 1.28% for skilled labor and 1.27% for less skilled labor in the motor vehicles sector, but these increases are accompanied by "a significant contraction" in the electrical machinery and metals sector. Employment will fall in the US motor vehicles sector, while employment will increase in the metals and metal products sector (Francois et al., 2013, p. 72).

Despite obstacles to eliminating duplicative regulations, corporate stakeholders see the TTIP as an avenue or path that can facilitate policy convergence. Much of the EU–US consultation with stakeholders that took place prior to the launch of, and continued during the TTIP negotiations, has centered on this issue as illustrated by a US Department of Commerce request for comments:

> The U.S. Government recognizes that economic recovery and job creation will depend significantly on its ability to work collaboratively with key trading partners to promote free and open trade and investment while also protecting public health and safety, the environment, intellectual property, and consumers' rights. In our trade and investment relationship with the European Union, the main impediments to greater trade and investment – and more open foreign markets for U.S. exporters and investors – are not tariffs or quotas, but rather differences in regulatory measures. These regulatory measures – which include standards developed by a government and used in regulation, standards developed by other bodies at the request or direction of a regulator for use in regulation, or proposals to provide a presumption of compliance to technical requirements developed by a government – may be unnecessary and may increase costs for producers and consumers.
>
> (US Department of Commerce – International Trade Administration, 2011)

As explained in Chapter 9's discussion of automobile agreements, EU and US automobile manufacturers complain that international fora (the main one being the World Forum for Harmonization of Vehicle Regulations under the auspices of the UN) are inadequate to facilitate transatlantic trade in autos and auto parts. They have called for the EU and the US to include "mutual recognition or functional equivalence of existing regulations and standards" in the TTIP negotiations (European Commission, 2013j). There are a number of examples of duplicative testing. If the EU and the US would recognize each other's crash tests and related standards, for example, the price savings on cars and trucks could average 7% (Hamilton & Quinlan, 2014, p. 4).

Harmonization or Mutual Recognition?

Naturally there will always be regulatory differences between the EU and the US for all sorts of reasons arising from culture, language, geography, history, and preferences (Francois et al., 2013, p. 7). There are essentially three ways to reduce NTBs impeding the free movement of goods: liberalization, approximation (harmonization), or mutual recognition. The HLWG's (2013) final report as well as the Council's (2013) leaked negotiating directive refer both to mutual recognition and harmonization as options to lower NTBs.

Liberalization applies to products that are not considered "risky" and which normally would not be subject to national regulation (Buonanno & Nugent, 2013, p. 150). Naturally, "liberalization" – which assumes that goods and services have an "automatic right to enter markets" (Buonanno & Nugent, 2013, p. 147) is unrealistic and undesirable. Even among EU member states, the CJEU has ruled that free trade is not a perfect right among EU member states in such cases when a member state raises concerns about human health or public safety.

The quest to complete the internal market through elimination, or at least drastic reduction of NTBs with the Single European Act (1986) has provided EU regulators with a great deal of experience with the challenge of "approximation." The difficulty was never in interpretation of the "law," because Article 3 of the EEC Treaty states: "the activities of the Community shall include … (h) the approximation of the laws of the Member States to the extent required for the proper functioning of the common market." Approximation, however, is fraught with difficulties, mainly owing to the fact that it is just too complicated to reach agreement to approximate (harmonize is a synonym for approximation) standards on a wide array of products from chocolate to lawnmowers. For one, it takes a very long time, and, if achieved, will most likely be the result of compromises that have invariably weakened the standards. The process also cannot keep up with those products and services which are evolving rapidly. This failure to approximate standards in the internal market led to what has been called the "new approach," which has been described as a "lighter touch" than traditional approximation "in which the EU stipulates essential requirements, but the specification of technical standards is undertaken by European Standards Organizations (Buonanno & Nugent, 2013, pp. 147–148). The "new approach" is guided by multi-year action plans for standardization, which single-out diverse product types which the EU will focus on achieving approximation during the time period covered by the plan. To give the reader a sense of the task the EU and its member states have been confronted with, in 2012 approximately half of all goods traded within the EU were subject to approximation directives (European Commission, 2012b). Approximation, rather than mutual recognition or liberalization, tends to be used in "high-risk" products such as chemicals, pharmaceuticals, construction goods, automobiles, and some foodstuffs. The automobile sector, alone, is governed by 100 approximation and 300 implementing directives (European Commission, 2008, p. 2, 7).

The EU experience with approximation is important for the TTIP for three reasons. First, a study of the EU's struggle with agreeing standards should put to rest any notion that a single negotiated agreement would be capable of achieving approximation. Approximation requires continuous dialogue among government regulators – in this case US federal bureaucrats and the European Commission. This is, of course, the reason the EU anticipated a permanent body to discuss such regulatory issues. Second, "old" approximation (vertical and/or specific) is very difficult to achieve, and has given way to the "new approach" (broad and/or horizontal laws) (see Pelkmans, 2005 for a detailed discussion). Thus, the EU and the US will need to be prepared to cede some control to standardization agencies – a move that will expose the partners to further assaults as the minions of big business (opposition to the TTIP is discussed in Chapter 13). Third, the very high-risk products which the EU has had to "approximate" make up a great deal of the trade between the EU and the US (see the figures above). This suggests the partners will find it difficult to achieve approximation without "vertical" agreements specifying the standards goods must meet to be sold both in the EU and the US.

Mutual recognition, which would involve the EU and the US recognizing and accepting each other's regulations, is the "middle" solution between liberalization and approximation. Mutual recognition has been utilized by the EU since the 1974 *Dassonville* and 1979 *Cassis de Dijon* CJEU rulings, which struck down NTBs except under the "safeguard clause" (then Article 30 of the EEC Treaty, now Article 36 TFEU). As Buonanno and Nugent explain (2013, p. 148):

> Under the mutual recognition principle established by the Court, member states must mutually recognize and accept each other's standards where national regulatory objectives are similar. Where regulatory objectives differ, member states must attempt to agree on the objectives. The point of mutual recognition is that member states are obliged, without exception, to work together to find ways of ensuring free movement.

Mutual recognition tends to be used for lower-risk goods – examples include pasta and office equipment (European Commission, 2012b). The key to mutual recognition is the concept of "proportionality" – if, for example, the aim is to protect citizen health, food labeling should be utilized rather than banning the product.

The Atlantic Community is therefore tasked with the prospect of four different decision-making processes with respect to eliminating duplicative regulatory standards: liberalization, old approximation, new approximation, and mutual recognition. And as Gardner (2014b) points out, in some sectors (such as chemicals), the level of protection is seen to differ and, therefore, "will not find that TTIP creates a (near-)single market." The negotiations, in such cases, are likely, then, "to focus on ways to make the bureaucratic process faster – and, therefore, cheaper."

Opposition to Negotiating Reduction in Non-Tariff Barriers

In Chapter 7 of this volume, Jarman suggests that the "operationalizing of regulatory harmonization" has been particularly difficult because

> the EU and US genuinely have very different ideas about how to regulate things like food (including GMOs), cars, chemicals, and pharmaceuticals. Both have well-developed existing standards and industrialized economies, so there is no "natural" underdog, no trade-dependent state that can be induced to adopt the standards of the hegemonic power.

While US risk regulation is often a more *"ex post facto* litigation risk"* (Transatlantic Business Council, 2013c), since the late 1990s the EU has adopted a decidedly more precautionary approach to risk assessment, especially with respect to SPS. (See D. Vogel, 2012 for a comparative study of "precaution" in EU and US health, safety, and environmental regulations.) Furthermore, there is a perception that American exceptionalism (see Chapter 4's discussion of culture) may extend to risk (see Jassanoff, 1990). And there is some evidence suggesting disparate risk tolerance informing regulatory practices between the EU and the US. Carolyn Dudek's analysis of GMO policy demonstrates the importance of public opinion and national culture in the shaping of what has become a long-standing dispute between the EU and the US over authorization of GMO cultivation, a dispute which has been carried over into the TTIP. (See, for example, US Ambassador to the EU's comments about GMO and the TTIP in Vieuws, 2014.)

Cries of regulatory capture have been raised since the TTIP's objectives were announced. Joseph Stiglitz (2013a), for example, writes that:

> the USTR's office, representing corporate interests, will almost surely push for the lowest common standard, leveling *downward* rather than upward. For example, many countries have tax and regulatory provisions that discourage large automobiles – not because they are trying to discriminate against US goods, but because they worry about pollution and energy efficiency.

De Ville (2013) offers a rather devastating assessment of the TTIP with respect to both harmonization and mutual recognition. Noting the previous failed attempts by the partners to achieve harmonization in regulatory standards (see Chapter 5 of this volume for a detailed look at transatlantic governance), he argues that the partners will fall back on mutual recognition. The problem with eliminating transatlantic NTBs through mutual recognition is that "no transatlantic standard is established" (De Ville, 2013, p. 15). Instead, the EU and the US have simply agreed to mutually recognize each other's standards (see discussion above with respect to mutual recognition and the completion of the EU's internal market), thus disadvantaging third countries. In effect, the goal of international standards-setting will not be achieved, and, worse yet, an exclusive trade zone would have been established between the EU and the US. Furthermore, De Ville (2013, p. 15) argues that (pure) mutual recognition "tends to lead to a race-to-the-bottom" because firms will try to devise the economically cheapest way to achieve the minimum standards.

The Way Forward for Reducing NTBs?

Given the opposition to reducing NTBs, how can the EU and the US achieve agreement?

One place to start is to compare and contrast EU and US "legislative and regulatory systems," a task undertaken in a paper by Parker and Alemanno (2014), written specifically to inform TTIP negotiations. (See Chapters 8, 11, and 12 in this volume for comparative policy studies in the areas of competition, financial services, and GMOs, each of which discusses legislative and regulatory processes.) These studies show that while legislative and regulatory processes differ in the US and the EU, they share two important commonalities – active public consultation and transparency.

In light of the current "state of play," it is likely that the solution will involve several interconnected protocols for reducing regulatory barriers: a permanent institutional body; incremental measures; identification of best practices; public participation; and notification.

Permanent Institution

The permanent institutional body as anticipated in the Council's negotiating mandate, discussed above, will be in the establishment of a Regulatory Cooperation Council (RCC) (the name is not important at this point, but its function is), an idea and name formally endorsed by the EU's Trade Commissioner in October 2013 (CorporateEurope, 2013, p. 4; European Commission, 2013i). An RCC would be composed of senior-level representatives from the regulatory agencies as well as trade representatives, meeting at least twice per year to device and monitor an agreed annual Regulatory Program. The RCC would be assisted by sector-level ad hoc working groups. Furthermore, "specific modalities" will be established for RCC interaction with the US Congress and the EP. Finally, a "multi-stakeholder" advisory committee would regularly meet with EU and US regulators in "crafting regulatory measures or taking decisions how to further compatibility of existing regulations."

Mutual Recognition

In cases where mutual recognition will not be possible in the final TTIP Agreement, an incremental approach is likely. So, for example, there will be a focus on "test cases." In the auto sector, this would translate into a "methodology that would allow assessment of the real impact of a particular technical regulation on safety on each side, and to compare results" (European Commission, 2014g, p. 2). Mutual recognition will be taken forward as much as possible through recourse to currently accepted standards such as "Good Manufacturing Practices" in the pharmaceutical industry (European Commission, 2014g, p. 2).

Notification

The EU and the US, through the WTO and practices established under the NTA framework (see Chapter 5's discussion of transatlantic governance) along with informal networks between EU and US civil and public servants, now notify one another to a very large extent – but as was illustrated in Chapter 11, financial services regulation, notification does not always take place. The establishment of an RCC with sector-level working groups would provide a forum in which early notification could be required before legislation and regulations were adopted.

Stakeholder Participation

Stakeholder participation would be ensured through the institutionalization of an advisory group composed of stakeholders' representatives and sector-level working groups. The key here is to budget for stakeholder participation to ensure both online and face-to-face participation on a regular basis.

The Special Case of Sanitary and Phytosanitary Measures

Perhaps the most publicized disagreement in the Atlantic Community (other than the "banana wars") have been with Sanitary and Phytosanitary (SPS) measures, specifically practices on the US side (antibiotics, growth hormones, and GM crops) that the EU considers detrimental to human and animal health. The HLWG's (US–EU High Level Working Group on Jobs and Growth, 2013, p. 4) report recommended:

> an ambitious "SPS-plus" chapter, including establishment of an on-going mechanism for improved dialogue and cooperating on addressing bilateral SPS issues ... including the requirements that each side's SPS measures be based on science and on international standards or scientific risk assessments, applied only to the extent necessary to protect human, animal, or plant life or health, and developed in a transparent manner, without undue delay.

Since 1 January 1989, when an EU ban on importation of meat containing hormones for animal growth production when into effect, the US has been trying to force the EU to accept US imports of beef raised with growth hormones. In response to the entrenched dispute (and the inability of GATT to resolve it), the WTO's SPS Agreement (World Trade Organization, 1995a) was negotiated during the GATT's Uruguay Round, establishing the WTO, and applies the WTO's dispute settlement understanding (Article 11) to the SPS Agreement. Article 2(2) of the SPS Agreement states that "Members shall ensure that any sanitary or phytosanitary measure is applied only to the extent necessary to protect human, animal or plant life or health, is based on scientific principles and is not maintained without sufficient scientific evidence."

While the EU and the US are both parties to the SPS Agreement, neither party has been able to agree on growth hormones in pork and beef cattle (which are used in the later stages to accelerate growth and improve feeding efficiency) (Grueff, 2013, p. 11); antibiotic use in animals; and GM crops (see Chapter 12 for a comprehensive treatment of the EU–US GMO dispute). In 1998 the WTO issued a ruling that the EU was not in compliance with the SPS Agreement in that the ban on hormones in meat was not based on a risk assessment (European Commission, 2001), which then prompted the US to apply retaliatory duties on a range of EU imports.

At the heart of the dispute is the long-running disparity between the EU and the US in the methodology of risk assessment, particularly in SPS, where the USDA insists that the EU produce studies based on "hard science" and the EU utilizes the precautionary principle. (See Chapter 12 for more on the precautionary principle.) The US has since dropped its retaliatory tariffs in exchange for the EU's opening up its market to hormone-free beef (Grueff, 2013, p. 11). But the fact is that the EU and the US just have very different philosophies about how to ensure safe meat:

> A clear example is the differing approaches to the use of pathogen reduction treatments (PRTs) during the slaughter process for meats. In the U.S., it is regular practice to apply PRTs as antimicrobial agents in the slaughter houses as part of a science-based approach to food safety. The EU perspective, on the other hand, is that with careful application of the total food chain concept there is no need for PRTs, and that PRTs are likely to be used to cover up inadequate hygienic practices.
>
> (Grueff, 2013, p. 11)

The EU is not the only "culprit," however, as it should be noted that the US continued it 1989 ban on the importation of live ruminants, beef, and products from Europe due to continued concerns over BSE, despite scientific evidence deeming European beef BSE free (Grueff, 2013, p. 12; US Department of Agriculture – APHIS, 2013). This ban was (partially) lifted in the fall of 2013 (see below).

A great deal of the opposition in Europe to the TTIP has come about due to fear that the US will use the negotiations to achieve its long-standing objectives of opening up the EU to hormone beef and even GMOs. This is not an unfounded concern because US policymakers have been quite explicit about including SPS in the TTIP. For example, Robert Hormats (2013), the US State Department's Under Secretary for Economic Growth, Energy and the Environment remarked in a speech delivered in the spring of 2013:

> We aim to address entrenched obstacles to U.S.–EU trade liberalization ... while SPS issues remain highly contentious, TTIP negotiations provide a real opportunity to break down some of the barriers that have kept us from taking full advantage of trade opportunities in the past. Our aim is for commitments to base SPS standards on science and international standards with an emphasis on scientific risk assessments.
>
> (Hormats, 2013)

Americans sometimes underestimate the depth of the European polity's concern over SPS issues. It was for a reason that Jean-Claude Juncker, the successful candidate for European Commission president (whose EPP group is pro-TTIP), quipped during one of the election's presidential debates that "the chicken does not want to be chlorinated either" (B. Fox, 2014b). Naturally, opponents of US slaughterhouse practices would be suspicious of the Commission because it had sought in 2009 (based on the EFSA's evaluation of chlorine's use as a PRT to be safe) for the Council to approve chlorine-washed poultry (which in any case, it denied) (Grueff, 2013, p. 12).

In the first parliamentary debate on the TTIP after the seating of the new EP after May 2014 elections, Trade Commissioner de Gucht addressed the SPS issues specifically, stating: "We won't import any meat with hormones. We won't give blanket approval of GMOs" (European Parliament, 2014c). At these debates, David Martin, MEP (European Parliament, 2014c) representing the S&D group (whose votes will be needed for the EP to approve the TTIP), stated:

> The Socialists were proud to be at the birth of TTIP. We don't want to be the TTIP's assassins. If we have to be, we will be. The Commission must listen to us about issues such as food safety. Regulatory convergence must not lead to chlorinated chickens, hormone treated beef, or GMOs getting access to the EU market. We've had assurances from the commission on this, and we want to remind you that we're going to continue to watch you.

Can the EU and the US Agree on SPS Measures?

With such entrenched EU and US positions in food safety evaluations (specifically, the EU's use of the precautionary principle for SPS and "other legitimate factors" – mainly European public opinion and member state opposition) (Grueff, 2013, p. 4), what is the likelihood the partners can ever reach agreement?

James Grueff (2013, p. 13) suggests that there is "reason for some optimism" even in the SPS area. He cites several examples such as the EU Food Hygiene Package (2004), which is a risk-based and transparent approach to the approval of US slaughter plants; approved lactic acid as used in US beef plants; and revised animal health requirements to allow the US to ship live swine into Europe. On the US side, in November 2013 the USDA-APHIS (2013) announced a "BSE Comprehensive Rule" allowing the import of some products, such as boneless beef, even if there has been a case of BSE in that region because "scientific knowledge and international guidelines show that boneless beef presents a negligible risk of BSE transmission." The USDA-APHIS, in announcing this new policy, stated: "These actions will further demonstrate to our trading partners our commitment to international standards and sound science, and we are hopeful it will help open up markets and remove remaining restrictions on U.S. cattle and cattle products." Cooperation is also evident in the US and EU development of a Veterinary Equivalency Agreement (VEA) (Grueff, 2013, p. 13), based on mutual recognition (United States Mission to the European Union – Foreign Agricultural Service, 2014), permitting "veterinary inspection requirements to differ between the U.S. and the EU while safeguarding both parties' right to establish its own level of public health inspection."

Another area where EU–US cooperation has been achieved is the 2012 "equivalence agreement" on organic produce, which eliminated the requirement of organic producers to obtain separate certifications, inspections, etc., and in 2006 Agreement on Trade in Wine (working towards mutual recognition of winemaking practices) (Grueff, 2013, p. 13).

Finally, in Item #25 (Regulatory Issues and Non-tariff Barriers) of the Council TTIP negotiating mandate, the Council (2013) states:

> The Parties shall establish provisions that build upon the WTO SPS Agreement and on the provisions of the existing veterinary agreement, introduce disciplines as regards plant health and set up a bilateral forum for improved dialogue and cooperation on SPS issues,

which suggests that the Atlantic Community is serious about minimizing, if not ending, SPS disputes.

Rules

Because the TTIP is meant to be a comprehensive agreement, there is a long list of "rules" to be negotiated. These include investment; customs and trade facilitation; labor; environment; intellectual property rights; transparency; anti-corruption; competition; and the ISDS. This discussion will focus on three of these areas: geographical indications (an intellectual property right), investment, and the ISDS.

Geographical Indications

Intellectual property rights (IPRs) encompass four main areas: patents, copyrights, trade secrets, and geographical indications (GI). Schott and Cimino (2013, p. 10) point out that "US and EU officials have used FTAs to expand the scope of IPRs beyond the baseline level of protection provided by the 1995 WTO and its Agreement on Trade-Related Aspects of Intellectual Property Rights (TRIPS)" or "TRIPS Plus" (Akhtar & Jones, 2014, p. 31). While there are differences between the EU and the US in IPRs, they are quite minor in comparison to the BRICs and developing countries. The readers is referred to Akhtar and Jones' report to the US Congress (Akhtar & Jones, 2014, pp. 30–35) for a detailed discussion of IPRs.

TRIPs defines GIs in the following manner: "indications which identify a good as originating in the territory of a Member, or a region or locality in that territory, where a given quality, reputation or other characteristic of the good is essentially attributable to its geographic origin" (World Trade Organization, 1995b, Article 22 (1)).

Technically, under the TRIPS (Article 23) the EU and US have agreed to the principal of providing a "minimum" standard of protection for GIs (to prevent unfair competition and misleading the public as to the product's quality) and a "higher or enhanced" level of protection for GIs for wines and spirits ("cognac" for example, is certified as a GI by the US Patent and Trademark Office (USPTO). Furthermore, in 2006 the US and EU signed a bilateral Agreement on Trade in Wine. The agreement was an attempt to address difficult issues such as limiting US wine's use of certain semi-generic names (Grueff, 2013, p. 13).

Nevertheless, the EU and US take fundamentally different approaches to GIs. The USPTO, which has been providing protections for domestic and foreign GIs since at least 1946, states that GIs "can be viewed as a subset of trademarks, because they source-identify, guarantee quality, and are a valuable business interest." Therefore, the US position has been to protect GIs through the trademark system (typically as certification or collective marks), and in so doing, believes it is providing a TRIPS-plus level of protections for GIs (US Patent and Trademark Office, n.d., p. 1) GIs can even be protected through common law – such was the case with "cognac": in 1998 it was affirmed "cognac" is protected as a "common-law (unregistered) certification mark in the United States"; thus, "cognac" is "a valid common law regional certification mark, rather than a generic term, since purchasers in the US primarily understand the 'Cognac' designation to refer to brandy originating in the Cognac region of France, and not to brandy produced elsewhere" (US Patent and Trademark Office, n.d., p. 6). Examples of geographical indications in the United States include: "FLORIDA" for oranges; "IDAHO" for potatoes; and "WASHINGTON STATE" for apples (US Patent and Trademark Office, n.d., p. 1).

While "Roquefort" and "Cognac" are designated as GIs under US law, the EU and the US are quite far apart on GIs for many other products, covering a wide range from "salami" meat to "feta" cheese – both protected GIs under EU law – but which the US considers "generic". The EU's protection for GIs is quite extensive – about 3,000 products are so certified.

The EU maintains three levels of protection: Protected Designation of Origin, Protected Geographical Indication, and Traditional Specialty Guaranteed. As of 2010 there were 2,768 GIs registered in the EU-27, covering agricultural products and foodstuffs, wines, aromatized wines, and spirits (European Commission, 2012d, p. 4). The worldwide sales value of GI products (2010) registered in the EU-27 (Croatian figures not available in this study) was €54.3 billion and represents 5.7% of the total food and drink sector in the EU-27 (European Commission, 2012d, p. 4). Furthermore, GI registrations are heavily weighted to particular member states, as illustrated in Table 14.2, suggesting these governments have a bigger stake in persuading the US to modify its stance on GIs.

The US position follows the USPTO guidelines that a "generic" term cannot be protected. The US and the EU, however, disagree on whether terms are "generic" or so unique as to afford trademark-like protection. And sometimes the US provides certification for more than one manufacturer. An example of this practice can be seen in the treatment of "Roquefort (US Registration No. 571,798) which "is used to indicate that the cheese has been manufactured from sheep's milk and cured in the caves of the Community of Roquefort (France) in accordance with their long established methods and processes" (US Patent and Trademark Office, n.d., p. 2). The USPTO has refused to provide certification to some cheeses – such as Fontina – as a GI (1986 case).

More telling for the prospect of reaching agreement is that the EU and the US have been taking fundamentally different approaches to GIs in their free trade agreements (FTAs) with other countries where it has negotiated GIs in KOREU, EU–Singapore FTA, EU, Columbia, and Peru FTA, EU and the Central America

Table 14.2 Geographic Indications in the EU (2010) (Top 15)

Member State	Wine	Agriculture Products and Foodstuffs	Spirits	Aromatized Wine	Total
Italy	521	193	39	1	754
France	432	168	75	1	676
Spain	131	126	28	0	285
Greece	147	86	19	0	252
Portugal	40	111	19	0	170
Germany	39	68	35	2	144
Romania	50	0	19	0	69
Bulgaria	54	0	13	0	67
Austria	29	13	13	0	55
Hungary	35	4	6	0	45
UK	4	32	3	0	39
Czech Republic	13	22	1	0	36
Belgium	9	7	10	0	26
Slovenia	17	1	7	0	25
Netherlands	12	6	5	0	23

Source: European Commission, 2012d, p. 8.

FTA. This point can be illustrated by the FTAs negotiated with South Korea (KORUS and KOREU), where KOREU "specifies a GI registrar for foodstuffs, wines, and spirits and designates GI protection for more than 160 products covered by the EU (cheeses, hams, and wines) and 64 products covered for Korea (teas, spices, vegetables, and fruits)" (Schott & Cimino, 2013, p. 12). KORUS, however, while confirming that GIs are "eligible for protection as trademarks … the agreement does not separately distinguish and expand on the terms of protection" (Schott & Cimino, 2013, p. 12).

But the US is not South Korea. Many of the "generics" established themselves with European emigrants to the US. This can be seen particularly among Italian-Americans who brought mozzarella, bologna, and prosciutto-making to the US. Cheese is a concern to both parties: the EU is the world's largest cheese producer, followed by the US. US demand for specialty and artisan cheese has been growing (Agricultural Marketing Resource Center, 2012), which has increased the interest of European producers in gaining greater access to the US market, and the ability to use GIs to increase the marketability of their products.

The dispute has become particularly messy due to the inclusion of GIs in EU FTAs. In a letter signed by 45 US Senators addressed to the USTR and the USDA Secretary, the senators stated, "In country after country, the EU has been using its FTAs to persuade trade partners to impose barriers to U.S. exports under the guise of protecting GIs" (US Senator Pat Roberts, 2014).

Thus, the GI dispute is not limited to transatlantic trade, but also has spilled over into global trade. Is there any space for compromise in this situation? There apparently is. Schott and Cimino (2013, p. 8) suggest that the TTIP agreement should provide for three GI lists: one would agree to compound terms for GI protection (e.g., Parma ham), a second would be an exceptions list for generic terms, and the third would be a list of GIs subject to future negotiations under the TTIP structure.

Investment

The EU and the US have a great deal of experience in transatlantic investment. The US accounts for 56% of total foreign direct investment (FDI) in the EU and the EU accounts for 71% of total FDI in the US, and are each other's major foreign investors (Hamilton & Quinlan, 2014, pp. vi, ix). These facts are indicative of relatively open investment climates. The CEPR study concluded that "with a few exceptions, both the US and EU are shown to be relatively open by the standard of third countries." However, there are sector-specific exceptions to openness to FDI – aerospace (the US and EU), motor vehicles (the EU), cosmetics (the EU), information, communications, and technology (the EU), and transport (the US) (Francois et al., 2013, pp. 88–89).

The "breakthrough" for the EU and the US, however, would be to fashion a common set of investment rules through the TTIP that would then serve as the basis for global standards. At the present time there is an "incomplete" network of bilateral investment treaties (BITs). So, for example, the US has 40 BITs in force (seven with EU member states), while EU member states together have approximately 1,200 BITs in force with non-EU countries (Akhtar & Jones, 2014, p. 30). In 2012 the EU and the US issued a joint statement laying out "shared principles for international investment," which included: open and non-discriminatory investment climates; a level playing field; strong protection for investors and investments; fair and binding dispute settlement (an issue to be discussed below); robust transparency and public participation rules; responsible business conduct; and narrowly tailored reviews of national security considerations (European Union and the United States, 2012).

Investor–State Dispute Settlement

The ISDS is a procedure which allows investors to bring claims against a foreign government instead of requiring their government (state-to-state) to put forth claims on their behalf when the state has acted inconsistently with an investment protection agreement (Akhtar & Jones, 2014, p. 31; Group of the Progressive Alliance of Socialists & Democrats in the European Parliament, 2014). ISDS agreements are mainly negotiated to protect foreign corporations against discrimination and to protect against unlawful expropriation.

Arbitration is typically conducted under the auspices of the United Nations Commission on International Trade Law (UNCITL). An international ISDS arbitration panel is composed of three judges (one each selected by the state, the corporation, and the UNCITL. Companies have used ISDS around 600 times to seek compensation from governments (de Pous, Dings, Goyens, & Kosinska, 2014).

ISDS clauses, which can be traced to the German government, which began using them in the late 1950s, are routinely inserted by the EU and the US in FTAs (B. Fox, 2014b). Indeed, the EU and the US have fully anticipated including an ISDS in the TTIP agreement (Council of the European Union, 2013, Item 23; de Pous et al., 2014).

There are several reasons why foreign companies favor ISDS, including: courts may be biased or lack independence; investors may not have access to local courts in the host country (e.g., countries have expropriated foreign investment and denied access to local courts); and countries do not always incorporate into local laws the rules made in an investment agreement (European Commission, 2013f, p. 1).

In line with the overall goals of the TTIP for setting global standards, the EU and the US expect that with an agreed ISDS, this system could then be used as a standard in third countries where foreign investment protections are weaker. Other goals drive ISDS inclusion as well. Starting with the US perspective – first, the US is seeking efficiency for its MNCs with a single rule and the easing of one agreement, which would then replace the current ISDS agreements the US has with nine of the EU's member states; and second, the US argues that legal protections for investors in the 28 member states are uneven (Vieuws, 2014). From the EU perspective, the TTIP is an opportunity to drive uniformity in internal market rules, a long-established pattern of using international pressures as a lever to consolidate the single market.

Opposition to ISDS

Within months of the start of TTIP negotiations, opposition began to emerge throughout Europe to inclusion of an ISDS chapter. The opposition in Germany, in particular, could not be ignored. The leader of Germany's Social Democrats wrote a letter to Karel de Gucht warning that Germany might not agree to a TTIP agreement should an ISDS chapter be included (Pardo, 2014, p. 4). Opposition in the EU to an ISDS chapter in the TTIP became so intense that the Commission postponed negotiation on this chapter in order to carry out an online public consultation, which took place between March 27 and July 13, 2014 and returned 149,399 contributions. A complete analysis of the commentaries was expected in November 2014 (European Commission, 2014d).

EU policymakers were taken by surprise by the depth of opposition to the ISDS, once it became known that the Council had included ISDS in its June 2013 negotiating mandate to the Commission. And it is understandable that the Commission would not have anticipated the depth of the opposition, given that the EU and all but one of the 28 member states is party to agreements with ISDS (European Commission, 2013f, p. 1), and EU investors have been involved in 53% of ISDS cases (Pardo, 2014, p. 1).

Driving European opposition to the ISDS have been several high-profile cases in recent years: the Swedish Energy Company Vattenfall case in Germany challenging that country's law to phase out nuclear power plants, the Philip Morris case in Australia, brought under the Australia–Hong Kong ISDS agreement, and Lone Pine Resources challenging Quebec's moratorium on hydraulic fracturing. The Philip Morris case has been circulated as a "cautionary tale" of the unexpected consequences an EU ISDS with the US might entail (Panichi, 2014). The background is that Australia passed legislation in 2011, the first of such in the world, requiring plain packaging of cigarettes (Attorney General – Australian

Government, 2014). At the time of this writing, and based on preliminary rulings of the international tribunal hearing the case, it seems unlikely that Philip Morris will prevail (on the grounds that it invested in a cigarette manufacturing operation in Australia in order to challenge Australia's anticipated plain packaging legislation). Importantly, when Australia passed its plain packaging legislation, the EU had been considering the *Tobacco Products Directive* (TBD), a directive that aimed to not only harmonize tobacco legislation in the member states, but toughened regulations (which it did accomplish for those member states with weaker public health protections) – but, significantly for this discussion, public health officials wanted the TBD to include plain packaging (Panichi, 2013). However, it should be noted that the TBD does allow member states to introduce further measures relating to standardization of packaging, including plain packaging, when these are justified on public health grounds (European Commission, 2014e). Therefore, it would seem perfectly reasonable that consumer protection advocates would be alarmed by the Philip Morris suit and possible future action an American corporation might take that would undermine the EU's or its member states' latitude in enacting legislation aimed at protecting consumers.

Michael O'Neill's, in this volume (Chapter 4), examines the cultural question, providing important perspective for the ISDS controversy. The European public perceptions – whether true and fair or not is quite immaterial – are driving opposition to ISDS. Europeans think Americans are more litigious than Europeans (a perception of American legal culture that much of the world shares), and that an ISDS chapter in the TTIP agreement would expose EU member states (and European taxpayers) to multiple lawsuits. As discussed above (Regulations), Europeans tend to perceive America through the "Wild West" lens of "anything goes" – sacrificing European consumer and worker protections for profit. The fear is that US corporations will sue EU member states that pass laws to protect consumers and workers after the ISDS is in effect, on the grounds that such regulations reduce company profits.

The Greens, naturally, opposed the ISDS (one of the items prompting the Greens to leak the negotiating mandate in March 2014), but especially troubling for EU negotiators has been the EP's S&D group's announcement (whose votes are needed for passage of the TTIP) that it will oppose the introduction of an ISDS in the TTIP negotiations on the grounds that ISDS "would mean opening the door for big corporations to enforce their interests against EU legislation. This would deprive states of crucial policy space in important fields such as health or environment" (Group of the Progressive Alliance of Socialists & Democrats in the European Parliament, 2014).

Environmentalists and consumer protection organizations oppose the ISDS as well, fearing that loopholes in ISDS will jeopardize the EU's and member states' rights to enact environmental and consumer protections. In an opinion piece several members of the EU's TTIP Advisory Group explained their opposition to ISDS on the following grounds: it undermines member states' legal systems; it provides privileged treatment for foreign investors over domestic ones; governments might defer or abandon regulation to avoid litigation; and the cost to the state if a company wins its suit (de Pous et al., 2014).

A Way Forward for ISDS

ISDS can be reformed to satisfy the concerns of its opponents. The Commission has recommended, for example, that arbitrators be selected by both disputing parties and, if the parties cannot agree, arbitrators would be appointed from lists established by parties to the agreement. The ISDS chapter would also include a "far-reaching" code of conduct. Furthermore, litigation costs could be borne by the losing party (diminishing the incentive for lawyers to file frivolous cases) (European Commission, 2013f, p. 4).

Conclusions

This analysis of the principal objectives around which the TTIP negotiations have been fashioned suggests that it is quite unrealistic to expect the TTIP agreement to be a full-fledged transatlantic FTA, let alone a transatlantic common market. There will be some immediate successes with the low-hanging fruit, but achieving the TTIP agreement's objectives will require sustained interaction and a determined will from the partners for the foreseeable future. Therefore, despite a number of conditions and "ifs" which could undermine achievement of some of the more entrenched differences between the EU and the US, there is reason for (long-run) optimism that the TTIP, in the future, could become the West's "economic NATO."

15 The New and Changing Transatlanticism

Lessons Learned and Future Challenges

Laurie Buonanno

The transatlantic relationship is unusual for its cordiality (even if, at times, this characteristic is tested), intricate web of relationships, and resilience. There are innumerable examples of comity between bordering countries, such as the extraordinarily close relationship between Canada and the US despite sharing such a long border. Yet unlike the Canadian–American relationship – one that can be attributed to sharing the world's largest repository of fresh water, breathing the same air, hundreds of citizens crossing their borders on a daily basis for work and leisure, speaking the same language, and sharing the bond of being the two former large British colonies of the Americas – the EU and the US have no such shared interests tied to propinquity and a colonial past. So it is all the more unusual, and thus, remarkable, that two entities – one a federal state, the other a quasi-federal *sui generis* construction – would expend so much time, energy, and human resources in building and maintaining the transatlantic partnership.

This book has explored many factors that, together, help to explain the enduring transatlantic partnership – security, economic growth, and a shared vision of how to live and govern, in a globalized world.

What conclusions can we draw about transatlantic policy processes and policy outcomes? In this chapter we return to the questions posed in Chapter 1 to draw conclusions about the "new" and "changing" transatlanticism:

1. How can we characterize the policy outcomes associated with the new transatlanticism? Which variables best explain policy outcomes? Are policies converging or diverging?
2. What is the nature of the EU–US relationship? Is the transatlantic relationship conflictual, cooperative, or neither (little interaction)?
3. Are transatlantic agreements arrived at by mutual agreement or "imposed" by either the EU or the US?
4. To what extent are the EU and the US currently seeking to build deeper cooperation or integration? Specifically, has transatlantic policymaking been primarily concerned with breaking down existing barriers to trade and investment (negative integration such as reducing tariff barriers) or intended to create new systems of agreement (such as mutual recognition or harmonized/approximated standards to reduce non-tariff barriers and technical barriers to trade (NTBs/TBTs)?

The next four sections of this chapter will address these questions.

Policy Outcomes

Economics

The studies in this book have found that both short- and long-term economic trends contribute to our explanation of the shape and direction of transatlantic policymaking. Undoubtedly the most impactful short-term economic factor has been the recession that set in after the fall of 2007 (the "Great Recession"). Our contributors – particularly in Chapters 2, 3, and 11 – explain that political leaders in both the EU and the US were desperate to be seen to be "doing something" to promote growth to counteract the extreme suffering experienced by many citizens as tax revenues declined and governments implemented austerity budgets. As argued in Chapter 13, the idea of a transatlantic free trade area (FTA) has been circulating for years, the long recession coupled with austerity measures required of eurozone countries opened a policy window for the TTIP to the extent that European and American policymakers were now incentivized to work toward the extremely difficult objective of reducing NTBs, the TTIP's core objective. But one should not confuse the desire for politicians to be seen to be "doing something," with their ability, or even willingness, to "do something."

The intensive cooperation in the area of financial services regulation (Chapter 11) illustrates the critical importance of short-term economic factors in transatlantic policymaking. This is because the Great Recession began with a collapse in financial services. Its cause was traced to poor regulatory oversight of the mortgage industry and the derivatives tied to mortgage lending, repackaging, and insuring. However, as Chapter 11 shows, transatlantic regulatory convergence depends upon two factors: first, which partner stands to benefit most from transatlantic cooperation (the EU, in this case, because of the vulnerability of eurozone countries that can no longer resort to currency depreciation as an anti-recessionary strategy), and second, variability between and among the partners (the US and the UK lead in the invention and marketing of innovative financial services investment instruments). As Zahariadis argues in Chapter 8, European leaders must also contend with the polity's integration fatigue. If high unemployment rates persist in those member states most adversely affected by the eurozone and sovereign debt crises, the European public may very well oppose the greater market liberalization the TTIP is meant to achieve. The gain of the Far Right in the 2014 European Parliament (EP) elections was interpreted as a backlash against austerity and the European integration project. Conversely, many Europeans may see the EU as the solution to the inability of Europe's larger economies to absorb their goods and services at rates needed to fuel domestic economic growth.

Long-term economic factors, too, have exerted influence in transatlantic policymaking. The increased interconnectedness of the EU and US at many levels – particularly the dense networks of multinational corporations (MNCs) and, increasingly, of international non-governmental organizations (INGOs) and non-governmental organizations (NGOs) as well as the competitive challenge from BRICs – have been driving the "New Transatlanticism," a term Egan and Nugent introduced in Chapter 2 to describe an increasingly networked relationship between EU and US officials. So, too, long-term economic trends have encouraged EU–US cooperation. As has been noted by scholars of welfare capitalism (see, for example, Esping-Andersen, 1990; Hall & Soskice, 2001), the UK's socio-economic system differs from the continental varieties of more corporatist and statist approaches. The UK has long acted as a bridge between the EU and the US – drawing on the "special relationship" – within transatlantic dialogues. The UK's policy priorities also influence EU policymaking *prior* to a problem landing on the transatlantic policy agenda. Thus, some policy convergence may be taking place within the EU (the UK has been influential, for example, in continual opening up of the internal market, access to which is an important incentive for the US to engage in transatlantic policymaking), which then makes it more likely the EU and the US can find common ground in their negotiations. Nevertheless, the EU and the US are structured differently, with the European Social Model enshrined in EU treaties and the engrained notion of "individual responsibility" in America's "pragmatic" political ideology. Therefore, the EU will be more resistant to any agreements in the TTIP which imply a "race to the bottom" because of a perceived disadvantage when competing with US firms (whose "social costs" are thought to be lower).

Culture

Political culture and public opinion impact, sometimes significantly, transatlantic policymaking. Dudek (Chapter 12) finds that European public opinion opposing genetically modified organisms (GMOs) has had a significant impact on the authorization of their importation and, especially, cultivation. Her GMO case study has also found that public opinion can cross the Atlantic – in this case, European requirements for GMO labeling and bans of GMO cultivation are now influencing the American public's perceptions of GMOs. While the US Department of Agriculture has remained an impenetrable fortress supporting GMO cultivation and the genetic engineering of still more GMO crops, federalism has facilitated GMO opposition where activists in several states are attempting to limit, and even ban, GMO cultivation and to impose product labeling in their states. Thus, the controversy over GMOs has long "upset" the EU's internal market; it is also now (admittedly still in its infancy) beginning to challenge America's single market as well (where Congress has never legislated on GMOs).

Broadening this discussion to all policy areas where consumer protection (whether pertaining to consumer health or finances) is key, it can be argued that what passes as culturally bound notions of risk assessment – precautionary (the oft-stated philosophical underpinning of EU regulation) or *ex post facto* litigation (again, the presumed US approach) – is a far deeper concern policymakers must confront in postindustrial societies: the public's justifiable distrust of government regulators and the activities of those industries they are charged with regulating. "Transparency and accountability" has become a mantra of a (admittedly, loose) coalition of American and European consumer protection advocates, environmentalists, and, in general, "the Left." Their concerns cannot be easily dismissed. Two highly salient cases illustrate this point. The spread of BSE (mad cow disease) among cattle, and horrifically, the suspected fatal human disease vCJD contracted from eating BSE-contaminated meat (World Health Organization, 2012) could have been minimized if EU regulators had acted more swiftly to investigate abattoir culling and feed practices among British cattle farmers. Similarly, an ignition switch flaw sold by General Motors (GM) that shut off the ignition and disabled air bags (thereby preventing their deployment in automobile crashes), had been brought to the attention of the US auto safety regulator – the National Highway Traffic Safety Administration (NHTSA) – at least a decade before GM acknowledged the flaw and recalled nearly 2.6 million cars in 2014 (Wald, 2014). And while the problem is not widespread in Europe (a combined total of fewer than 10,000 vehicles of the recalled models Chevrolet HHR and the Opel GT), the lesson is there – neither GM nor the NHTSA seemed to act in the best interests of the public. In the financial services industry, too, banks on both sides of the Atlantic engaged in reckless lending, which fueled the housing bubbles in some regions of the EU and the US.

These two cases suggest that the dilemma for the reduction of NTBs based on the principle of mutual recognition may be less one of disparate cultural risk tolerance, but about accountability and trust – a subject O'Neill introduces to our study in Chapter 4. As citizens living in postindustrial societies, Americans and Europeans *should* present similar risk tolerances (or, more accurately, intolerance), but corporate and governmental accountability are crucial in consumer protection policy. There simply is no transatlantic oversight mechanism for the 2014 congressional (GM recall) and 1997 parliamentary hearings (BSE) where elected officials take corporations and regulatory agencies to task. TTIP opponents find it difficult to understand how accountability can be forged in a partnership of two sovereign entities. Therefore, the most realistic basis for short-term cooperation under the TTIP may be "business as usual" – the cooperative dialogues inventoried in Chapter 5. It will take time for a "Regulatory Cooperation Council" (RCC) to adjust to the "accountability" issue.

Institutional Structures

Federalism

Because the US and the EU are federalist (US) and multi-level governance (EU) systems, achieving consensus is far more difficult than if the partners were unitary political systems. Nevertheless, of the two, the EU is probably the more "squishy" partner because even in spheres where the US federal government must share policy leadership with its states (such as transport), these policy areas are characterized by tightly linked cooperative federalism and the federal government's power of the purse. So, for example, a key difference between the EU and the US is the presence of federal government officials working in district offices throughout the US in a wide range of regulatory functions, including environmental protection (EPA), infrastructure (US Army Corps of Engineers), and agriculture (US Department of Agriculture). The EU, on the other hand, must rely on member state bureaucrats to correctly interpret and implement EU directives and regulations. The EU's dependence on member states to implement EU law continues to be of great concern to Washington bureaucrats and politicians, especially with respect to regulatory law. Further complicating policy implementation is the nature of bureaucracy in the Central and Eastern European countries (CEECs), some of which continue to struggle with widespread corruption.

Although throughout this volume contributors have emphasized a positive correlation between European integration and transatlantic policy convergence, it is a question of degree: The US is a federal system with well-established institutional structures and political processes, while the EU is a *sui generis* federal/intergovernmental hydra in a state of near continuous evolution. While it is true that since the signing of the Transatlantic Declaration (TAD), the EU is increasingly a more reliable partner for US policymakers in a wide range of policy areas, European integration is never "quite enough" for the Americans. This "structural tension" between a partner with a multiplicity of voices and the US with one person (the US President) empowered to make decisions is no better illustrated than in a leaked telephone conversation between Victoria Nuland, Assistant Secretary of State for European and Eurasian Affairs (and former US Ambassador to NATO) and the US Ambassador to Ukraine in which she "profanely dismissed European efforts in Ukraine as weak and inadequate to the challenge posed by the Kremlin" (Smale, 2014). That the EU has only limited policy competence in home affairs, foreign affairs, and external security (defense) is particularly frustrating for American policymakers because it is these areas where an executive authority (president or prime minister) is needed so as to act with "energy and dispatch."

Federalism also affects transatlantic agreement in another important way. State aid, which cannot be used in the EU except under exceptional circumstances – such as economic recession (member states must receive permission from the Commission) – is a common practice among the 50 states and local authorities through the activities of hundreds of economic development agencies and local content laws. This complicates efforts to establish a level playing field when the US federal government has no authority to control local and state behavior in this area.

Another problem related to federalism/multi-level governance (MLG) has been the persistent power struggles between EU member states and Brussels. While this is a classic and recurrent problem in federal systems (witness the recent laws, executive orders, and local/state policing in several US states encroaching on the federal government's exclusive competence to manage immigration and protect external borders – attempts, however, largely rebuffed by federal courts), the regular occurrence of such disagreements in the EU undermines its ability to act as a reliable partner in transatlantic policymaking. A particularly salient area for transatlantic trade where such conflict and confusion negatively impacts the ability to reach agreement is in GMO authorization. The convoluted system that has been agreed for GMO authorization (for background, see Dudek's discussion in Chapter 12) was created because member states are taking up positions that do not leave room for compromise. The UK, Sweden, Finland, Spain, and Sweden favor GMO cultivation; 20 member states absolutely oppose. In a few abstaining states, their citizens tend to oppose GMO use, but the political leadership wishes neither to alienate agribusiness nor the US (Germany, Belgium, the Czech Republic). A 10-year-old failure of the Commission to take a decision on the DuPont's Pioneer application in 2001 for approval of its insect-resistant 1507 maize (to be used as animal feed and biogas production) led the (exasperated) company to take the case to the CJEU, which ruled in September 2013 that the Commission had a duty to send the authorization proposal to the Council of Ministers within three months. Prior to the deadline for a Council vote, the EP passed a non-binding resolution (336/201, 30 abstentions) on January 16, 2014 specifying that Pioneer 1507 should not be placed on the market for cultivation, because its insect-resistant pollen might harm non-target butterflies and moths (European Parliament, 2014a). When the vote was put to the Council of Ministers on February 11, 2014, the voting configuration under qualified majority produced neither a vote for authorization nor rejection, which then triggered authorization to "revert" back to the Commission, which had originally proposed authorization in 2009. More debate and stalemate followed, with the Commission stating it must authorize, opponents calling for more studies, and the Commission reminding the member states that the European Food and Safety Authority (EFSA) had issued two more scientific studies since the 2009 authorization indicating no harmful effects of Pioneer 1507. Opponents argued that with both a supermajority of states in the Council opposing and the EP's resolution, it was simply undemocratic to allow Pioneer 1507 to go forward (Keating, 2014). In June 2014 the Council (environmental ministers) reached a political agreement amending *Directive 2001/18/EC* on new rules for growing GMOs providing a legal basis for member states to restrict or prohibit the cultivation of GMOs on their territory for reasons other than health or environmental considerations, adding socio-economic, land use and town planning, agricultural policy objectives, and public policy issues to the list of legitimate reasons. (GMO authorization falls under the ordinary legislative procedure and, therefore, the Council agreement – "First Reading" – must be negotiated in the "Second Reading" phase with the EP, which was expected to commence in early autumn 2014.) But the point here is not to offer a detailed discussion of GMO sale and cultivation, but to offer a sense of the highly contested debate on the rules of democratic decision-making (after all EU member states *agreed* both to qualified majority for food safety issues and to respect the impartial scientific standing of the EFSA). If the internal market is to mean anything at all, then the rules establishing it have to, above all, be clear and adhered to by all parties, even when a member state does not agree with the outcome. One might reasonably ask how the US can build a transatlantic regulatory regime with a partner whose agents do not agree to fundamental rules of their own political system?

Bureaucracies

Another important issue is the organization of and role of the bureaucratic actors – namely, the US executive branch and the EU Commission.

Administrative culture can represent an obstacle to achieving agreement. Take again the case of GMOs, where regulatory authority in the US is housed in agriculture (USDA) but in the EU in consumer protection (DG SANCO). As explained in Chapter 12, the EU shifted its regulatory authority from DG Agriculture in the wake of several food crises that rocked Europe in the 1980s and 1990s. This decision to move regulation from an administrative culture more inclined to be favorable to GMOs (sympathetic to the agricultural lobby) to one that is more risk averse (consumer protection) set into motion a clash between two disparate sets of regulatory authorities on opposite sides of the Atlantic with quite different missions and constituencies.

Zahariadis, in his study of competition policy, too finds important "institutional divergence" between regulatory authorities in the EU and the US. The US regulatory system is very complex and more litigious, while the EU system is more "bureaucratic, broader, and regulatory in nature." He also explains that the US system employs more legal experts and economists, while the EU system is "thin on human resources, relying far more on national experts seconded to the Commission for specific tasks."

Yet another difference is found in the patterns and authority of "enforcement" where in competition policy "90 percent of enforcement in the US still depends on private civil action. In Europe, enforcement is very much the task of European or national regulators." Zahariadis concludes that the EU regulatory authority is more predictable than the US antitrust policymaking system. Achieving convergence will be particularly difficult because US antitrust policy is based on "century-old litigation" in the courts, while the EU's competition policy is treaty-based and in many respects has been subject to interpretation of the European Commission.

On the other hand, Henderson (Chapter 6) suggests a common administrative culture among American and European regulators who are increasingly acculturated away from the traditional Wilsonian emphasis on hierarchical governing and a rather clear distinction between politician (policymaker) and civil servant (implementer), to New Public Management (NPM) (entrepreneurial and business-like) and New Public Governance (NPG) (network managers and leaders). Similarly, Buonanno (Chapter 11) suggests policy actors from both sides of the Atlantic working in the transatlantic Financial Market Regulatory Dialogue (FMRD), as well as key international fora, seem to be operating from the same regulatory philosophy and have adopted remarkably similar regulatory reforms since the Great Recession.

Another issue connected to bureaucratic participation and power harkens back to a running theme of this volume – the many actors who are authorized to "speak" on behalf of the EU. So, for example, Caviedes finds that in negotiations over the Passenger Name Record (PNR), the US sent representatives from the State Department (lead negotiator) and the Department of Homeland Security,

while on the EU side, not only the DG Relex (lead negotiator prior to the establishment of the EEAS in the Lisbon Treaty) and DG Justice participated (before
this DG was divided into two DGs), but also DG Transport and Energy and the
Council of Ministers (rotating presidency). This constellation of actors tended to
handicap the European negotiating team because with the inclusion of actors
with portfolios outside of foreign affairs and internal security (home affairs), the
European negotiating position was diluted by attempting to balance the agreement with privacy and even trade concerns.

Executive–legislative power

The disparate executive and legislative structures between the EU and the US do
appear to shape, at least to some degree, the outcome of transatlantic agreements.
In his analysis of PNR negotiations, Caviedes documents the EP's dissatisfaction with Congress' unilateral passage of legislation requiring all foreign air
carriers flying into or over the US to provide specific information on the passengers and crew, and the EP's insistence that the original deal be treated as provi-
sional. The European Commission, after many false starts and delays, reached
agreement with the US over a PNR, but the EP brought an action before the
European Court of Justice (ECJ) to have it struck down over data protection and
privacy concerns. Instead, the ECJ ruled that the Commission did not have the
treaty authority to enter into the PNR – effectively cutting out the Commission
and the EP from the process! Thus, the Council of Ministers swooped in and
"swiftly" negotiated an interim agreement based on the competence granted by
the Treaty on European Union's (TEU) third pillar. Indeed, the much-
commented on institutional opportunism among EU actors (in this case, the
Commission and the Council seeking to exclude the EP from involvement in the
PNR Agreement) epitomizes, as Caviedes writes, "US frustrations in dealing
with a European partner whose undefined institutional features are sources of
uncertainty." The drawn out PNR Agreement negotiations hardly endeared the
EU to the US as a reliable partner with which to negotiate over issues of significant concern to the American public. Before the member states had ratified the
new PNR Agreement, the Lisbon Treaty came into effect (2009), eliminating the
third-pillar structure "under which the Commission and EP had been largely relegated to bystander status in foreign and home affairs." The result? Now a PNR
Agreement was further delayed until 2012 when a "permanent" agreement which
took due account of the EP's new power in home affairs and "what followed was
a two-year period during which the EP attempted to impose its conception of
data privacy on the agreement, before eventually capitulating in the face of
American intransigence on these issues." At the end of the process, the EP's vote
was hardly reassuring to Americans with 409 in favor, 226 against, and 33
abstentions (European Parliament, 2012b).

The case studies also reveal some disparity in the powers enjoyed by the
executive and legislatures in the EU and the US. In the PNR case, Congress was
not involved in the negotiations to the same extent as the EP (although it should
be noted that congressional legislation is what propelled PNR into a transatlantic

issue). On the other hand, Congress played a much more central role than the EP in financial services regulatory overhaul, where in the EU the Commission was the central actor because of its treaty-based power as the sole originator of EU legislation. Thus, the PNR and financial services regulation cases illustrate that executive–legislative relations differ in the EU and the US, and sometimes in ways which do not follow any pre-established pattern.

Politics

Differences among the polity with respect to striking the proper balance in fundamental values – freedom (individual liberties) versus order (the government's police powers) and equality versus freedom (the extent to which governments should intervene in the economy) – form the basis of the "politics of policymaking." Competition, trade, financial service regulation, and GMO food and feed involve a complex mix of freedom, order, and equality in the relationship between governors and governed. As with domestic policymaking, negotiations can never "close" in highly contested policy areas, but will be a continual source of consultations and new agreements.

Various approaches to regulatory activity are also shaped by ideological differences. This can be seen in the disparate approach to competition policy among the Atlantic partners, where according to Zahariadis (Chapter 8), US competition law is influenced by the center-right Chicago School where "potential harm and economic power are seen as short-term effects on price and output," while the Commission is much more likely to take account of "industrial, regional, social and environmental polices" in its decision-making.

MEPs are elected through proportional representation, and the EP operates through coalitional politics. Congress, especially the House of Representatives, is organized as a body in which two sides constantly maneuver for advantage over the other in a partisan environment contested by two political parties. The result is that, especially with well-publicized initiatives such as the TTIP and financial services regulation, the EU must operate within the parameters set by a sometimes hostile and very partisan Congress – a legislative body to which the EU has little access and enjoys even less influence. (See Chapter 11's discussion of interaction – or lack thereof – between the EP and Congress.)

As J. H. H. Weiler (2014) wrote on the eve of the 2014 EP elections, there is a "weak connection between voter preference as expressed in European elections and the EU's political orientation and legislative programme. In essence, the two primordial features of any functioning democracy are missing – the great principles of accountability and representation." The democratic deficit likely impacts on transatlantic policymaking because, unlike in the US, EU actors (MEPs and the Council of Ministers) are more insulated from the public than their counterparts in the US Congress. Especially in taking stands European business favors, the EU can be far more accommodating. But this point should not be taken too far. In issues of high salience to the European public, such as food safety and data privacy, the EP has been highly sensitive to public opinion.

As laid out in Chapter 5 and touched on throughout this volume, Brussels and Washington increasingly have sought a transatlantic perspective in a number of ways: through establishment of the Transatlantic Business Dialogue (TABD; in the TAD); stakeholder participation in high-level fora; seeking of joint comments by EU and US trade associations prior the opening of TTIP talks; and stakeholder consultation sessions during the TTIP negotiations (Office of the United States Trade Representative, 2012, 2014b; Transatlantic Business Council, 2013a; US–EU High Level Working Group on Jobs and Growth, 2013; US Department of Commerce – International Trade Administration, 2011).

Converging or Diverging?

The policy chapters in this book have found some levels of transatlantic cooperation and even convergence, but this observation has to be immediately qualified with direct references to policy areas and events where the EU and the US do not agree. No single model or pattern emerges from our case studies of transatlantic policies in competition, financial services regulation, transportation, GMO regulation, mobility regimes, and foreign policy. There are, however, two conditions where convergence is more likely to occur.

The first condition is a policy that can be agreed through negative rather than positive integration, a process through which advancements have been made in competition and trade policy. The other condition is a crisis that impacts both partners and therefore opens a policy window, as has been the case in financial services regulation and the decision to open up negotiations on the TTIP.

Where the objective can be achieved only through positive integration – the adoption of common regulatory standards, for example – it is very difficult to achieve policy convergence without a policy window being opened by a shared crisis. So, for example, the EU has been more sympathetic than the US to market regulation, partly for reasons linked to the European Social Model and partly because it places a greater reliance on the precautionary principle, as can be seen by the analysis of the transatlantic disputes concerning the sale and cultivation of GMOs in Chapter 12 and more generally in trade disputes, discussed in Chapter 7.

An internal security crisis precipitated by terrorist attacks (9/11, London, Madrid) paved the way for transatlantic counter-terrorism agreements. Crises, however, do not necessarily impact the EU and the US equally. Thus, the US had been more determined to reach counter-terrorism agreements (where the US experienced more harrowing attacks) and the EU likewise has had more at stake than the US in attempting to build a transatlantic financial services regulatory regime tied to the TTIP (because the EU has been less resilient than the US in recovering from the Great Recession).

Despite the "narcissism of minor differences" thesis, disparities in values, norms, cultures, markets, and political institutions are substantial enough to undermine mutual recognition efforts. The stakes are especially high in the service industry, where the EU sees enormous potential if the US would be willing to address mutual recognition in areas such as construction licensing and professional services. The importance of mutual recognition of regulatory standards cannot be overemphasized because up to 80% of the gains from the TTIP would come from mutual recognition in health, safety, environment, financial services, and data security (European Commission, 2013b).

Nature of the EU–US Relationship: Conflictual, Cooperative, or Neither?

The case studies in this book have uncovered evidence of conflict – sometimes long and seemingly intractable – but also instances of hard won and ultimately very satisfying cooperation. Conflict, sometimes reaching a very intense pitch, has broken out at various times in several key policy arenas, including, trade, bio-technology, competition, and counter-terrorism, and at intergovernmental, transgovernmental, and transnational levels. The long-running conflict over the trade in and cultivation of GMOs – a dispute in which an exasperated US government resorted to moving outside of the normal transatlantic diplomatic channels to an international body (the WTO) – is an example of a case where conflict has occurred among actors at both the intergovernmental and transgovernmental levels, but also has involved transnational actors – bioagricultural corporations on one side, and consumer protection and environmental advocates lining up on the other. The transatlantic GMO dispute also illustrates the understudied role of the transatlantic diffusion of ideas on transatlantic public policymaking. It has long been understood that Americans equate French and Italian cuisine and couture with the very best. Americans flock to Paris and to Tuscany to eat, drink, and shop – and if the French and the Italians (cultures that produced the *Slow Food Movement*) reject GMOs, then just perhaps, it is the Americans, not the Europeans, who have taken a wrong turn on GMOs. Thus, as can be seen in Chapter 12, American public opinion is now converging with the decidedly and long-held anti-GMO attitudes among the European public. And, it may be that the battle over GMOs is now just beginning in the US. Transnational actors – whether American celebrities or civil society organizations – have been pointing to the European public's opposition to GMOs as an important reason to question the American government's embrace of bioengineered plant varieties. Perhaps when EU and US leaders advocated "people-to-people" links in the New Transatlantic Agenda (NTA), this is not quite what they envisaged – but it's what they got, and it is possible to shape transatlantic public opinion in such a way as to make it very difficult for American negotiators to bargain hard on behalf of its enormously powerful agribusiness sector to include GMOs in the TTIP negotiations. Chapter 14 also documented the long-running disputes in the sanitary and phytosanitary (SPS) sector in general.

Home affairs – or the internal dimension of external security – has since the 9/11 terrorist attacks on the US arguably been the area with the most active transatlantic policy agenda. In Chapter 5's inventory of transatlantic agreements it can be seen that there are no fewer than eight concluded agreements and a ninth under negotiation. These agreements range from container shipping to personal data privacy protection. But as demonstrated in analyses in Chapters 9 and

10 of the PNR and Container Agreements, objections to the content of these agreements emerged from a number of quarters among EU stakeholders and policymakers. Privacy advocates in Europe – often with MEPs leading the charge – have objected to all agreements involving data transfers – from the SWIFT accord, PNR, and the ongoing conflict between the EU and the US over personal data privacy and protection. European shipping interests and national customs officials have objected to the US demands for the Container Agreement, particularly the requirement for 100% screening of containers leaving EU ports. Despite EU protests, however, transatlantic agreements *have* been concluded in this policy area.

There have been major rifts over foreign policy – such as with the US-led invasion of Iraq that divided not only the transatlantic community, but EU member states as well. However, as is pointed out in Chapters 2 and 3, there have been foreign policy successes as well. Libya, to an extent, and sanctions on Iran (uranium enrichment) and Russia (the Ukraine crisis), too, represent guarded successes. But the sometimes painfully slow and arduous business of foreign policy is not so easily measured in the short run. Looking back over the past several years, what stands out is the very effective "public diplomacy" practiced by Secretary of State Hillary Clinton and EU High Representative Catherine Ashton during the three years they were conterminously in office during the first Obama Administration, when they seemed to appear together at every conceivable global hotspot conducting joint press conferences and interviews. These two foreign policy chiefs conducted public diplomacy at its best – and it sent a message to the American and European publics that the US and the EU were acting in concert. Perhaps there still is not "one phone," but the EU in the Lisbon Treaty produced a face and a voice in time to share the stage with her US counterpart, a woman who, conveniently, happened to be an international celebrity.

Enduring even longer than the GMO dispute and showing no sign of diminishing, the Boeing–Airbus dispute is offered in Chapter 8 as an example of the intractability of governmental support for the lucrative and prestigious business of commercial aircraft production. It is perhaps an understatement to observe that subsidization of the commercial aircraft industry will be a difficult topic in the TTIP negotiations given that together Airbus and Boeing account for combined annual revenues of $100 billion (European Commission, 2013g). However, the Open Skies Agreement (discussed in Chapter 9) represented an important step as a transatlantic basis for not only competition but also for how the EU and the US approach standards-setting in global aviation safety. EU negotiators will certainly wish to discuss "regulatory convergence, free flow of investment, a bilateral reciprocal basis between the US and the EU to own and control each side's airlines, and no restrictions on air services" in TTIP negotiations (European Commission, 2013g, p. 3). A potential wrinkle, however, is the fervent opposition of American labor to including aviation services in the TTIP: see, for example, commentary by Wytkind (2013), of the Transportation Trades Department, AFL-CIO, which represents 33 unions in the transportation sector.

Chapter 14 documented the extent to which disagreement over regulation of goods has prevented transatlantic trade from reaching its full potential. As we discussed elsewhere, the European perception that the US has lower regulatory standards has driven opposition to approximation of standards. While some of this perception is certainly correct, US standards are sometimes higher than those in the EU. This point was made in remarks by Trade Commissioner Karel de Gucht in testimony before the EP (European Parliament, 2014c):

> The argument is that the protection is better in Europe than US ... and threaten EU's way of life. The Commission doesn't agree with this line of reasoning. Sometimes the protection in the US is higher than in the EU. US courts are more likely to award higher damages than EU courts. We share the same objectives – and our values are more similar than any other part of the world. Why would President Obama agree to any deal that lowered standards? It's a wrong logic – there are plenty of ways to do this. Look at the internal market – we lowered barriers to trade and increased protection.

Finally, there are also policy areas where there has been neither conflict nor cooperation – this is illustrated in Caviedes' analysis of mobility regimes (Chapter 10), in which he finds that despite the critical importance (and relevance) of high-skilled immigration to the Atlantic Community, this issue has not made it to the transatlantic agenda. The reason? A common transatlantic regime is predicated on a "reasonably clear demarcation of internal competences within the EU."

The studies in this volume suggest that the levels of activity now associated with the new and changing transatlanticism are a function of the EU's increased policy competences. In the 1970s, all, or virtually all, major policy decisions were taken at the *national level* in several policy areas, including: the free movement of capital; monetary policy; transport policy; monitoring and controlling movements across internal borders; foreign policy; and police and judicial cooperation (see Buonanno & Nugent, 2013, p. 7). As a consequence, the EU had no competence to negotiate on the behalf of its member states in transatlantic dialogues. What has changed since the 1970s is that in each of these policy areas, policy competence is either *shared* between the EU and national level (foreign policy, transport policy, police and judicial cooperation) or most major policy decisions are *taken* at the EU level (monitoring and controlling movements across internal borders – especially for Schengen members; free movement of capital; and monetary policy – for eurozone members). The new reality for the Atlantic Community is that because the EU has more and deeper policy competences than in the past, a more vigorous transatlanticism was made possible, and the EU's ability to negotiate on a wide variety of policies has only deepened (rather than reversed) since the launch of the NTA.

Power, Resources, and Bargaining

Our third question – are the observed outcomes arrived at by mutual agreement or imposed by either the EU or the US? – asks us to examine power and resources. Clearly the EU and the US do not have equivalent resources with which to undertake negotiations, reach agreements, monitor implementation, and measure outcomes. As we learned in Chapter 6, the European Commission has 26,000 employees and the US federal bureaucracy (executive branch) has 2,697,000 employees. And while it is undeniable that a great many of the US executive branch federal employees are involved with policies such as defense, immigration, border control (the US border patrol has nearly as many agents as Commission employees), social welfare (Social Security), housing (Housing and Urban Development), the human resources among those departments and bureaus in the US involved with transatlantic issues overwhelm the European Commission's Directorate Generals (DGs). In the foreign policy bureaucracies, as can be seen from Table 15.1, the EU employs 3,417 staff (one-third from the EEAS and two-thirds from the Commission) (EEAS, 2013), compared to the Department of State's 20,000 employees.

At first glance, a compilation as is found in Table 15.1 might seem to be so obvious as to be a pointless exercise: the US is a federal state and should have a more well-developed executive bureaucracy, while the EU is a "regulatory" state relying on its member states for the implementation of its laws. Yet the lopsided staffing *must* be factored into any hypothesis predicting a more vibrant, networked transatlanticism driven by transgovernmental actors. Such a vision of the future rests on human resources to lead and manage these transatlantic networks.

Table 15.1 Comparison of Human Resources, EU and US Public Administrators

European Commission (2013)	US Federal Bureaucracy – Executive Branch (2013)
DG SANCO – 730	US Department of Health and Human Services – 62,999
DG Trade – 544	US Department of Commerce, International Trade Administration – 1433 Office of the US Trade Representative – 200
DG Justice – 311 DG Home Affairs – 260	Department of Justice – 113,000
DG Economic & Financial Affairs – 651	US Department of the Treasury – 162,119
DG Competition – 724	Federal Trade Commission – 1,131 (Justice Department also has competence in antitrust policy)
DG Mobility and Transport – 430	Department of Transportation – 100,000
DG Energy – 484	Department of Energy – 14,000
DG Agriculture and Rural Development – 922	US Department of Agriculture – 100,000
DG Taxation and Customs Unions – 433	US Department of Homeland Security – 240,000

Sources: EU – European Commission, 2013e, US – OPM and agency websites and reports.

The EU may wish to develop a more equal partnership, but is simply not resourced to engage fully with the US federal executive branch.

Finally, with respect to the whole panoply of counter-terrorism measures agreed between the EU and the US in the past several years, the evidence points to the US "getting its way." While the EP was able to extract some minor concessions (particularly in the SWIFT accord), in all of these security-based agreements the US obtained its objectives, with the EU ultimately acquiescing to US demands. An important test comes with the *EU–US Data Privacy Framework* currently on the table at the time of this writing, which since the Edward Snowden leaks began on June 2013, has complicated negotiations for the Americans. But then Ukraine imploded – and, once again, the EU found itself in the position of needing US help to manage the politics and security of its own backyard. Furthermore, the terrorism concerns brought about by European citizens joining ISIS has brought the Atlantic Community's homeland security goals into closer alignment.

Deeper Cooperation

Much of this book has been devoted to exploring the extent to which deeper cooperation has been taking place between the EU and the US in a wide range of policy areas. The most recent and highly publicized attempt to foster and cement cooperation is in the ongoing and ambitious TTIP negotiations which was the subject of Chapters 13 and 14 of this volume. Because the TTIP negotiations had been taking place for just 18 months at the time of this writing, it is too early to draw any definitive conclusions. Nevertheless, the early results, and extrapolations of future directions based on the studies in this book, do point to potential for cooperation in the three broad areas – market access, regulations, and rules. Within each of these areas, however, are controversial chapters such as geographical indications, investor–state dispute settlement (ISDS), SPS measures, and mutual recognition and harmonization in products and services in a number of sectors which are significant to transatlantic trade, and will not all be settled within a "static" TTIP agreement. Furthermore, those policies that have been subject to long-running disputes or are of special concern to one of the partners – Buy American, cabotage in American domestic flights, financial services regulation, GMOs, energy supplies, and audiovisual products – have been excluded from the TTIP negotiations.

Our investigations suggest (see Chapter 14 for the TTIP dimension) that achieving meaningful and lasting cooperation over the long run will require institutionalization of an unprecedented nature between the EU and the US and regular, even intensive, interaction among American and European civil servants. This will likely be in the form of a "Regulation Cooperation Council," a body whose challenge will be to build a permanent network of consultation based on "early warning." American and European regulators will need to work toward harmonization and mutual recognition in a "race to the top" rather than in a "race to the bottom" – or as David Vogel (1995) has put it, "trading up."

Conclusions

Because of the technical nature of the TTIP, it is principally an activity for bureaucrats. But with the increasingly powerful EP, American legislators would be missing an opportunity to engage directly with their European counterparts. Therefore, one avenue for reform could be the institutionalizing of links between MEPs and US congresspersons (see TLD discussions, Chapter 3 and 11). While Congress is not going to insert itself in regulatory matters (the Wilsonian distinction between "politicians" and "bureaucrats" is alive and well in American national politics) beyond their constitutional budgetary and oversight responsibilities (grounded in accountability and transparency), counterterrorism policy and trade policy are both salient issues with the public and with which Congress will remain highly engaged.

One interesting development is an emerging friction between the EP and Congress over data privacy protections. Inter-legislative disagreement may be beneficial for transatlantic cooperation to the extent that they could point to a pathway toward legislative engagement. MEPs have been critical of the *US–EU Framework Agreement for Data Privacy and Protection*, still under negotiation at the time of this writing (see Chapter 5). Thus, when in late 2013 an MEP invited NSA leaker Edward Snowden to testify about data privacy as part of the EP's broader inquiry about the data privacy treaty, Mike Rogers, Chair of the US House of Representatives Intelligence Committee, warned it "would be beneath the dignity of the European Parliament to deal with someone who was wanted by the US government for stealing secrets" (T. Vogel, 2013). Rogers also intimated that if the EP went ahead with the testimony, the body might imperil the TTIP. Nevertheless, some MEPs, too, seized on possible linkages between the TTIP and US reluctance to agree to the EU's negotiating demands with respect to the framework data privacy and protection agreement. So, for example, at the Munich Security Conference (January 31–February 2, 2014), Elmar Brok, Chair of the EP's Foreign Affairs Committee, linked US progress on joint data protection standards to EP support for the TTIP (Ermert, 2014).

Significantly, this is not the first time MEPs have used their post-Lisbon legislative power in home affairs to question whether US counter-terrorism measures undermine the privacy rights of European citizens. The original PNR agreement was annulled after the EP formally lodged a case with the ECJ, which then forced the US to reduce the numbers of "shareable information it requested from 34 to 19" (McNamara, 2011). So, too, the EP objected to the EU–US TFTP (SWIFT) Agreement (the main objections being a lack of reciprocity), which eventually resulted in a revised agreement (TFTP II), approved in 2010.

Beginning with the postwar Marshall Plan, American presidents have advocated and, at times, avidly supported European integration. And, as European integration has widened and deepened, so has transatlantic cooperation. Most Americans simply do not understand why Europe is not more integrated, mainly because theirs is a history grounded in the teaching of *The Federalist Papers*, not the *Antifederalist Papers*. Even US Nobel Prize winners preach of the advantages, if not the necessity, of forming a more perfect European Union (Sargent, 2011).

This widely held American understanding of the proper construction of federal systems translates into a situation where European negotiators cannot expect a great amount of sympathy over member state differences: Americans want the EU to "get on already" with integration. So, too, the US executive bureaucracy is stretched thin with an ever-expanding portfolio and shrinking human resources. As was argued in several places in this book, American presidents (generally) are becoming more reluctant to deal with EU member states on a bilateral basis, especially when they see differences among member states as "minor."

American impatience with what is seen as the slow pace of European integration – in many ways an impatience that has been building since the EEC's establishment in 1957 – is no more evident than in Bindi's analysis of transatlantic foreign policy cooperation in which the Obama Administration had expected a "more unified actor in foreign policy than the EU could be." The EU and the US are good partners and competitors. But the US can have trade partners in other parts of the world as well – particularly as is illustrated by the Asian pivot (discussed in Chapters 2 and 3), manifested particularly in the US-led TPP negotiations. Thus, the transatlantic governance documented throughout this book (particularly in Chapters 5 and 13) should not be seen as motivated purely by economic interests, but rather as inextricably connected to American and European security needs. And if one doubted the connection between trade associations and the security objectives of sovereign states, one need only look to the reaction of Russia when Western Ukrainians chose the EU's Eastern Partnership over Russia's Eurasian common market for stark affirmation of this observation.

The studies in this volume have endeavored to assist future and current policymakers in coming to terms with both the opportunities and obstacles attendant with such a complex undertaking as closer transatlantic economic relations, in general, and the TTIP, in particular.

The studies in this volume illustrate that, at a minimum, policymakers need to understand the policy thinking and activities of their Atlantic partners. One need not work on the "European/Eurasian" or "American" desk to be confronted with a situation where cross-national understanding and cooperation is expected, or, at least helpful in carrying out one's duties. It is also increasingly clear that there is a role for legislative staff in the "new and changing" transatlanticism, especially with respect to two current sets of policy initiatives that likely will occupy staff at member state parliaments, Congress, and the EP: counter-terrorism and the TTIP. This necessity will be especially the case with such agreements requiring ratification by EU member state legislatures.

Public administrators in advanced democracies are expected to undertake training in leadership, entrepreneurial public management, and network management (increasingly to manage public–private partnerships). These skills are directly transferable to the new and changing transatlanticism, which is a network-based form of governance and dovetails with work being produced by scholars who advocate moving away from an overdependence on the market model of NPM toward NPG. NPG, grounded as it is in a "cluster of principles, such as process focus, co-ordination, participation, and co-production" (Torfing & Triantafillou, 2012, p. 5), seems more suitable to the needs of transatlantic cooperation. While NPG cannot match hierarchy on dispatch and efficiency, it does seem to be the only realistic option for conducting transatlantic policy on the governance continuum anchored by world government (hierarchy) and regulatory arbitrage (markets).

The new public manager will need to combine NPM management skills such as outcomes assessment and performance-based measurements with NPG skills, not just in domestic policymaking, but in the transatlantic arena as well. Public managers will also need to have a better understanding of their partners on the other side of the Atlantic – their markets, political institutions, language, and culture – because as Ann Marie Slaughter reminds us: diplomats are no longer confined to the State Department or Foreign Ministry. The "new" diplomat is just as likely to work at the US Bureau of the Census and EuroStat, exchanging best practices in data collection techniques to support their government's efforts to advance transatlanticism.

References

Aberbach, J. D., Putnam, R. D., & Rockman, B. (1981). *Bureaucrats & politicians in western democracies*. Cambridge, MA: Harvard University Press.

Adler, E. (1997). Imagined (security) communities: cognitive regions in international relations. *Millennium, 26*, 249–277.

Adolino, J. R., & Blake, C. H. (2011). *Comparing public policies: Issues and choices in industrialized countries* (2nd ed.). Washington, DC: CQ Press.

AFL-CIO. (2013). U.S.–E.U. free trade agreement. Retrieved from www.aflcio.org/Issues/Trade/U.S.-EU-Free-Trade-Agreement-TTIP.

Agricultural Marketing Resource Center. (2012). Cheese industry profile. Retrieved from www.agmrc.org/commodities__products/livestock/dairy/cheese-industry-profile.

Ahearn, R. J. (2009). *Transatlantic regulatory cooperation: Background and analysis.* Washington, DC: Congressional Research Service.

Ahearn, R. J. (2012). *US–EU trade and economic relations: Key policy issues for the 112th Congress*. Washington, DC: Congressional Research Service.

Akhtar, S. I., & Jones, V. C. (2013). *Proposed transatlantic trade and investment partnership (TTIP): In brief R43158*. Washington, DC: Congressional Research Service.

Akhtar, S. I., & Jones, V. C. (2014). *Transatlantic trade and investment partnership (TTIP) negotiations R43387*. Washington, DC: Congressional Research Service.

Alliance of Liberals and Democrats for Europe Group. (2013). The Parliamentary Committee on International Trade welcomes the prospect of free trade with the United States of America – March 25 [Press release]. Retrieved from www.alde.eu/nc//press/press-and-release-news/press-release/article/the-parliamentary-committee-on-international-trade-welcomes-the-prospect-of-free-trade-with-the-unit/.

Alons, G. (2013). The TAFTA/TTIP and agriculture: Making or breaking the tackling of global food and environmental challenges? In D. Cardoso, P. Mthembu, M. Venhaus, & G. M. Verde (Eds.), *The transatlantic colossus: Global contributions to broaden the debate on the EU–US free trade agreement* (pp. 63–66). Berlin: Berlin Forum on Global Politics.

Amato, G. (1997). *Antitrust and the bounds of power*. Oxford: Hart.

American Chemistry Council & European Chemical Industry Council. (2012). CEFIC-ACC response to EU and U.S. call of 7 September 2012 for input on regulatory issues for possible future trade agreement.

Amitin, K. (2010). Making job satisfaction surveys more useful. *Public Manager, 29*(1), 5–9.

Anderson, R. D., & Kovacic, W. E. (2009). Competition policy and international trade liberalization: Essential Complements to ensure good performance in public procurement markets. *Public Procurement Law Review, 19*, 67–101.

Archick, K. (2013a). *EU–US cooperation against terrorism*. Washington, DC: Congressional Research Service.

Archick, K. (2013b). *The European Parliament: Congressional Research Service RS21998 CRS Report for Congress*. Washington, DC: Congressional Research Service.

Archick, K., & Mix, D. (2014). *U.S.–EU cooperation on Ukraine and Russia IN10129*. Washington, DC: Congressional Research Service.

Archick, K., & Morelli, V. (2010). *The U.S. Congress and the European Parliament: Evolving transatlantic legislative cooperation CRS 41552*. Washington, DC: Congressional Research Service.

Argomaniz, J. (2009). When the EU is the "norm-taker": The Passenger Name Records Agreement and the EU's internationalization of US border security norms. *Journal of European Integration, 31*(1), 119–136.

Arujo, B. A. M. (2013). Intellectual property and the EU's deep trade agenda. *Journal of International Economic Law, 16*(2), 439–474.

Ash, T. G. (2004). *Free world: America, Europe, and the surprising future of the West.* New York: Random House.

Attorney General – Australian Government. (2014). Tobacco plain packaging: Investor–State arbitration. Retrieved from www.ag.gov.au/tobaccoplainpackaging.

Baimbridge, M., & Whyman, P. (2008). *Britain, the Euro and beyond.* Abingdon: Ashgate Publishing Group.

Baker, J. (1989). A new Europe, a new Atlanticism, speech delivered by US Secretary of State, James Baker, to the Berlin Press Club on December 13.

Baker, S. (2010). *Skating on stilts: Why we aren't stopping tomorrow's terrorism* Stanford, CA: Hoover Institution Press.

Baldwin, P. (2009). *The narcissism of minor differences: How America and Europe are alike.* Oxford: Oxford University Press.

Baldwin, R., & Francois, J. (1997). Preferential trade liberalization in the North Atlantic. London: Centre for Economic Policy Research.

Ban, C. (2013). *Management and culture in an enlarged European Commission: From diversity to unity?* Basingstoke: Palgrave Macmillan.

Bank for International Settlements. (2013). About the Basel Committee. Retrieved from www.bis.org/bcbs/about.htm.

Bank, R. K., Craig, A. W., & Sheppard IV, E. J. (2005). Shifting seas: A survey of US and European linear shipping regulatory developments affecting the trans-Atlantic trades. *Maritime Economics and Logistics, 7*, 56–73.

Barker, T. (2012). *A second Obama Administration and Europe*. Washington, DC: Bertelsmann Foundation.

Baumgärtner, M., Gebauer, M., Gude, H., Medick, V., Schmid, F., & Schindler, J. (2014, July 9). Spiraling spying: Suspected double agent further strains German–US ties. *Speigel Online*. Retrieved from www.spiegel.de/international/germany/arrest-of-bnd-employee-strains-ties-between-germany-and-us-a-979738.html.

BBC News. (2008). Open Skies deal comes into effect. *World News*. Retrieved from http://news.bbc.co.uk/2/hi/business/7318455.stm.

Beach, A. (2010). H-1B Visa legislation: Legal deficiencies and the need for reform. *South Carolina Journal of International Law and Business, 6*(2), 273–297.

Benhke, A. (2007). *Re-Presenting the West: NATO's security discourse after the end of the Cold War.* Stockholm: Stockholm Political Studies in Politics.

Berden, K. G., Francois, J., Thelle, M., Wymenga, P., & Tamminen, S. (2009). *Non-tariff measures in EU–U.S. trade and investment: An economic analysis* Rotterdam: Ecorys.

Bhagwati, J. (1988). *Protectionism*. Cambridge: Cambridge University Press.

Bindi, F. (2011). One year on: Assessing the European foreign policy and the European external action service. *The Brown Journal of World Affairs, 17*(2): 125–138.

Blais, A. (1986). *A political sociology of public aid to industry*. Toronto: University of Toronto.

Blanco, I., Lowndes, V., & Pratchett, L. (2011). Policy networks and governance networks: Towards greater conceptual clarity. *Political Studies Review, 9*(3), 297–308.

Blunt, M. (2012). Comment from Matt Blunt, AAPC/ACEA on USTR notice, promoting US EU regulatory compatibility: Requests for comments. Retrieved from www.regulations.gov/#!documentDetail;D=USTR-2012-0028-0057.

Blyth, M., & Matthijs, M. (2012). The world waits for Germany. *Foreign Affairs*. www.foreignaffairs.com/articles/137697/mark-blyth-and-matthias-matthijs/the-world-waits-for-germany?page=show.

Boon, V., & Delanty, G. (2006). Europe and its histories: A cosmopolitan perspective. In H.-A. Perrson & B. Strath (Eds.), *Reflections of Europe: Defining political order in time and space*. Brussels: Peter Land Verlag.

Börzel, T. A. (1998). Organizing Babylon: On the different conceptions of policy networks. *Public Administration, 76*(2), 253–273.

Börzel, T. A. (2005). Pace-setting, foot-dragging and fence-sitting: member state responses to Europeanization. In A. Jordan (Ed.), *Environmental policy in the European Union: actors, institutions, and processes* (pp. 162–182). London: Earthscan.

Boskovic, T., Cerruti, C., & Noel, M. (2009). *World Bank working papers: Comparison between the European and United States securities regulations: MiFID versus corresponding U.S. regulations*. Herndon, VA: World Bank Publications.

Brinkley, A. (1998). *Liberalism and its discontents*. Cambridge, MA: Harvard University Press.

British Embassy, Bertlesmann Foundation, & Atlantic Council. (2013). TTIP and the fifty states: Jobs and growth from coast to coast. www.atlanticcouncil.org/images/publications/TTIP_and_the_50_States_WEB.pdf.

Buonanno, L. (2006). The European food safety authority. In C. Ansell & D. Vogel (Eds.), *What's the beef: The contested governance of food safety* (pp. 259–278). Cambridge: MIT Press.

Buonanno, L., & Nugent, N. (2002). *Institutional opportunism: The case of the European Parliament with regard to food safety policy*. Paper presented at the ECSA Canada Conference May 30–June 1, Toronto, Canada.

Buonanno, L., & Nugent, N. (2013). *Policies and policy processes of the European Union*. Basingstoke: Palgrave Macmillan.

Buonanno, L., Zablotney, S., & Keefer, R. (2001). Politics versus science in the making of a new regulatory regime for food in Europe. *European Integration Online Papers (EIOP), 5*(12).

Bush, G. W. (2010). *Decision points*. New York: Crown.

Callahan, M. E. (2009). Finding relief for privacy infringements in the New World. *Data Protection Law and Policy, 6*(June), 4–7.

Camps, M. (1956). *The European common market and American policy*. Princeton, NJ: Center of International Studies, Princeton University.

Cantley, M. (1995). The regulation of modern biotechnology: A historical and European perspective. A case study of how societies cope with new knowledge in the last quarter of the twentieth century. In D. Brauer (Ed.), *Biotechnology: Legal and ethical dimensions* (pp. 506–681). Weinheim: VCH Verlag.

Cantley, M. (2007). *An overview of regulatory tools and frameworks for modern biotechnology: A focus on agro-Food.* Retrieved from www.oecd.org/futures/long-termtechnologicalsocietalchallenges/40926623.pdf.

Carson, J. (2010). *Self-regulation in securities markets.* Washington, DC: World Bank.

Castle, S. (1999, November 22). Clinton, Blair & Co hold a progressives' board meeting. *Independent.* Retrieved from www.independent.co.uk/news/world/clinton-blair-co-hold-a-progressives-board-meeting-1127967.html.

Castle, S. (2013, June 30). Report of U.S. spying angers European allies. *New York Times.* Retrieved from www.nytimes.com/2013/07/01/world/europe/europeans-angered-by-report-of-us-spying.html?hp&_r=0.

Castle, S., & Calmes, J. (2013, June 17). U.S. and Europe to start ambitious but delicate trade talks. *New York Times.* Retrieved from www.nytimes.com/2013/06/18/business/global/us-europe-trade-talks-to-start-in-july.html?_r=0.

Castles, F. G. (Ed.). (1993). *Families of nations: Patterns of public policy in western democracies.* Aldershot: Dartmouth Publishing.

Castles, S., & Miller, M. J. (2009). *The age of migration: International population movements in the modern world* (4th ed.). Basingstoke: Palgrave Macmillan.

Caviedes, A. (2004). The open method of co-ordination in immigration policy: A tool for prying open Fortress Europe? *Journal of European Public Policy, 11*(2), 289–310.

Caviedes, A. (2010a). *Prying open Fortress Europe: The turn to sectoral labor migration.* Lanham, MD: Lexington Books.

Caviedes, A. (2010b). Towards a European model for high skilled labor migration? In A. Luedtke (Ed.), *Migrants and minorities: The European response* (pp. 61–81). Newcastle upon Tyne: Cambridge Scholars Press.

CDU/CSU Parliamentary Group. (2012). *Shaping the future of the transatlantic economic partnership now.* Discussion paper on the occasion of the conference of the transatlantic economic partnership, May 9.

Centre for Aviation. (2013). The North Atlantic: The State of the market five years on from EU–US Open Skies. *Aviation Analysis.* Retrieved from http://centreforaviation. com/analysis/the-north-atlantic-the-state-of-the-market-five-years-on-from-eu-us-open-skies-100315.

Chalmers, A. W. (2011). Interests, influence and information: Comparing the influence of interest groups in the European Union. *Journal of European Integration, 33*(4), 471–486.

Chambers, G. (1999). The BSE crisis and the European Parliament. In C. Joerges & E. Vos (Eds.), *EU committees: Social regulation, law and politics* (pp. 95–106). Oxford: Hart Publishing.

Charlemagne Column. (2014, May 25). The Globish-speaking Union. *The Economist.*

Choblet, M., & Hager, W. (2013). TAFTA/TTIP: New dawn for Atlanticists, sunset for old Europe? In D. Cardoso, P. Mthembu, M. Venhaus, & G. M. Verde (Eds.), *The transatlantic colossus: Global contributions to broaden the debate on the EU–US free trade agreement* (pp. 8–11). Berlin: Berlin Forum on Global Politics.

Cini, M. (2000). Administrative culture in the European Commission: The cases of competition and environment. In N. Nugent (Ed.), *At the heart of the union* (2nd ed.). London: Macmillan.

Cini, M. (2009). *Competition policy in the European Union* (2nd ed.). Basingstoke: Palgrave Macmillan.

Cini, M., & McGowan, L. (1998). *Competition policy in the European Union* Basingstoke: Macmillan.

Clark, N. (2012, September 27). Europe to seek sanctions against U.S. over Boeing subsidies. *New York Times.* Retrieved from www.nytimes.com/2012/09/28/business/global/europe-to-seek-sanctions-against-us-over-boeing-subsidies.html?_r=1&.

Clinton, H. (2012a). Secretary Clinton remarks at Euro-Atlantic Community initiative, Munich, February 4.

Clinton, H. (2012b). U.S. and Europe: A revitalized global partnership, Speech at Brookings Institution, November 29.

Coeuré, B., & Pisani-Ferry, J. (2007). The governance of the European Union's international economic relations: How many voices? In A. Sapir (Ed.), *Fragmented Power: Europe and the Global Economy* (pp. 21–60). Brussels: Bruegel.

Combs, J. (2012). *The History of American Foreign Policy from 1895*. Lexington, MA: M. E. Sharpe.

Committee for Economic Development – Research and Policy Committee. (1959). *The European common market & its meaning to the United States*. Washington, DC: Committee for Economic Development.

Compa, L. A., & Meyer, H. (2010). A social dimension for Transatlantic economic relations. Cornell University, ILR School Digital Commons.

Cooper, W. H. (2014). *EU–US economic ties: Framework, scope, and magnitude*. Washington, DC: Congressional Research Service.

CorporateEurope. (2013). TTIP: Cross-cutting disciplines and institutional provisions. Position Paper – Chapter on Regulatory Coherence.

Coultrap, J. (1999). From parliamentarianism to pluralism: Models of democracy and the European Union's "democratic deficit". *Journal of Theoretical Politics, 11*(1), 107–133.

Council of Ministers. (n.d.). Transport, telecommunications and energy. Retrieved from www.consilium.europa.eu/policies/council-configurations/transport,-telecommunications-and-energy?lang=en.

Council of the European Union. (2003). *A secure Europe in a better world: European security strategy*. Retrieved from http://ue.eu.int/ueDocs/cms_Data/docs/pressdata/en/reports/76255.pdf.

Council of the European Union. (2008). *EU US Summit, 12 June 2009, Final Report by EU–US High Level Contact Group on information sharing and privacy and personal data protection 9831/08*. Retrieved from www.dhs.gov/xlibrary/assets/privacy/privacy_intl_hlcg_report_02_07_08_en.pdf.

Council of the European Union. (2009). The EU–U.S. Energy Council, Annex 2. http://eeas.europa.eu/us/sum11_09/docs/energy_en.pdf.

Council of the European Union. (2010). EU–U.S. and member states 2010 declaration on Counterterrorism. Retrieved from www.consilium.europa.eu/uedocs/cms_Data/docs/pressdata/en/jha/114874.pdf.

Council of the European Union. (2013). *Directives for the Negotiation on the Transatlantic Trade and Investment Partnership between the European Union and the United States of America – EU Restricted*. Retrieved from www.laquadrature.net/files/TAFTA%20_%20Mandate%20_%2020130617.pdf.

Council of the European Union. (2014). *EU–US Summit Joint Statement*. (8228/14). Retrieved from www.consilium.europa.eu/uedocs/cms_Data/docs/pressdata/en/ec/141920.pdf.

Council on Foreign Relations. (2009). Council on Foreign Relations discussion with Assistant Secretary of State Phil Gordon.

Cowles, M. G., & Eagan, M. (2012). *The evolution of the transatlantic partnership: The Transatlantic relationship and the future of global governance*. Retrieved from www.transworld-fp7.eu/?p=665.

Cox, M. (2004). Empire? The Bush doctrine and the lessons of history. In D. Held & M. Koenig-Archibugi (Eds.), *American Power in the 21st Century* (pp. 21–51). Cambridge: Cambridge University Press.

Craig, P. (2012). *EU Administrative Law*. Oxford: Oxford University Press.

Cross, M. K. D. (2015). Transatlantic cultural diplomacy. In R. Henze & G. Wolfram (Eds.), *Exporting culture in a global world*. New York: Springer VS.

Daalder, I. (2003). The end of atlanticism. *Survival, 45*(2): 147–166.

Damro, C. (2005). Sole of discretion: Competition relations in the transatlantic marketplace. In M. Egan (Ed.), *Creating a Transatlantic Marketplace* (pp. 62–81). Manchester: Manchester University Press.

Damro, C. (2006). Transatlantic competition policy: Domestic and international sources of EU–US cooperation. *European Journal of International Relations, 12*(2), 171–196.

Damro, C. (2012). Market power Europe. *Journal of European Public Policy, 19*(5), 682–699. doi: 10.1080/13501763.2011.646779.

De Bièvre, D. (2006). The EU regulatory trade agenda and the quest for WTO enforcement. *Journal of European Public Policy, 13*(6), 851–866.

de Grazia, V. (2005). *Irresistible empire: America's advance through twentieth century Europe*. Cambridge, MA: Harvard University Press.

de Gucht, K. (2013). Speech: A European perspective on transatlantic free trade. March 2, 2013. Retrieved from http://europa.eu/rapid/press-release_SPEECH-13-178_en.htm.

de Larosière Group. (2009). The High-Level Group on Financial Supervision in the EU. Retrieved from http://ec.europa.eu/internal_market/finances/docs/de_larosiere_report_en.pdf.

de Pous, P., Dings, J., Goyens, M., & Kosinska, M. (2014, May 21). An election to determine the future of EU–US trade. *European Voice*. Retrieved from www.europeanvoice.com/other-voices/an-election-to-determine-the-future-of-eu-us-trade.

de Saint Jacob, Y. (2011, July 21). France's "GreenVote" kills shale gas – and targets nuclear power as well. *European Energy Review*. Retrieved from www.europeanenergyreview.eu/site/pagina.php?id=3154.

De Ville, F. (2013). Why the TAFTA/TTIP will not live up to its promises. In D. Cardoso, P. Mthembu, M. Venhaus, & G. M. Verde (Eds.), *The Transatlantic colossus: Global contributions to broaden the debate on the EU–US free trade agreement* (pp. 13–16). Berlin: Berlin Forum on Global Politics.

Dehghan, S. K. (2014, January 20). US hails "unprecedented opportunity" as Iran halts enriching high-level uranium. *Guardian*. Retrieved from www.theguardian.com/world/2014/jan/20/iran-halt-enrichment-uranium-iaea-confirms-eu-sanctions.

Delreux, T. (2011). The relation between the European Commission and EU member states in the transatlantic Open Skies negotiations: An analysis of their opportunities and constraints. *Journal of Transatlantic Studies, 9*(2), 113–135.

Den Boer, M., Hillebrand, C., & Nölke, A. (2008). Legitimacy under pressure: The European web of counter-terrorism networks. *Journal of Common Market Studies, 46*(1), 101–124.

Department for Education and Skills. (2009). *Skills for the information age. Final Report from the Information Technology, Communications, and Electronics Skills Strategy Group*. Nottingham: DfEE Publications.

Destler, I. M. (2005). *American trade politics*. Washington, DC: Institute for International Economics.

Devuyst, Y. (2001). Transatlantic competition relations. In M. Pollack & G. Schaffer (Eds.), *Transatlantic governance in the global economy* (pp. 127–151). Latham, MD: Rowman & Littlefield.

Dewatripont, M., & Legros, P. (2009). EU competition policy in a global world. In M. Telò (Ed.), *The European Union and global governance* (pp. 87–103). London: Routledge.

Dobbins, J. (2004). The effect of terrorist attacks in Spain on transatlantic cooperation in the war on terror. Testimony before the Senate Committee on Foreign Relations – Subcommittee on European Affairs (March 31). www.rand.org/content/dam/rand/pubs/testimonies/2005/RAND_CT225.pdf.

Dogan, R. (1997). Comitology: Little procedures with big implications. *West European Politics, 20*(3), 31–60.

Donald Danforth Plant Science Center. (2013). Donald Danforth Plant Science Center: History. Retrieved from www.danforthcenter.org/the_center/about_us/history.asp.

Duchêne, F. (1973). The European Community and the uncertainties of interdependence. In M. Kohnstamm & W. Hager (Eds.), *A nation writ large? Foreign policy problems before the European Communities* (pp. 1–21). London: Macmillan.

Dunmore, C. (2013). Update 1: EU court annuls approval of BASF's Amflora GMO potato. *Reuters.* Retrieved from www.reuters.com/article/2013/12/13/eu-gmo-potato-idUSL6N0JS22W20131213.

Eavis, P. (2014, December 12). Wall St. Wins a Round in a Dodd–Frank Fight. *New York Times.* Retrieved from http://dealbook.nytimes.com/2014/12/12/wall-st-wins-a-round-in-a-dodd-frank-fight.

Eckes, Alfred, E. (1995). *Opening America's market: US foreign trade policy since 1776.* Chapel Hill, NC: University of North Carolina Press.

The Economist. (2013, December 9). The World Trade Organization: Doha delivers.

Ecorys. (2009). Non-tariff measures in EU–US trade and investment: An Economic analysis. Report prepared by K. Berden, J. F. Francois, S. Tamminen, M. Thelle, and P. Wymenga for the European Commission, Reference OJ 2007/S180-219493.

EEAS. (2013). *EEAS review.* Retrieved from http://eeas.europa.eu/library/publications/2013/3/2013_eeas_review_en.pdf.

EFSA. (2012, December 19). European Food Safety Authority: Genetically Modified Organisms. Retrieved February 12, 2012, from www.efsa.europa.eu/en/topics/topic/gmo.htm.

Eftestøl-Wilhelmsson, E. (2010). Regulating European multimodal transport: European Union competence under the Lisbon Treaty. *University of Helsinki Legal Studies Research Papers, 16,* 29–45. Retrieved from http://papers.ssrn.com/sol3/papers.cfm?abstract_id=2001906.

Eichner, M. (2006). The role of identity in European–US relations. In G. Gustenau, G. Holl, & T. Nowotny (Eds.), *Europe–USA: Diverging partners* (pp. 245–268). Nomos: Baden Baden.

Eising, R. (2004). Multilevel governance and business interests in the European Union. *Governance: An International Journal of Policy Administration, and Institutions, 17*(2), 211–245.

Ellinas, A. A., & Suleiman, E. (2012). *The European Commission and bureaucratic autonomy: Europe's custodians.* Cambridge: Cambridge University Press.

Elliott, L. (2013). Bali Summit invigorated World Trade Organisation, says Roberto Azevêdo. *Guardian.* Retrieved from www.theguardian.com/business/2013/dec/18/roberto-azevedo-wto-bali-global-trading.

Elliott, K. A., & Freeman, R. (2003). *Labor standards and trade agreements: can labor standards improve under globalization?* Washington, DC: International Institute for Economics.

Erlanger, S. (2011, September). What the war in Libya tells Europe. *Carnegie Europe.* Retrieved from http://carnegieeurope.eu/publications/?fa=45569.

Ermert, M. (2014). Move on data protection or fail on TTIP, EU Parliament Chair says. *Intellectual Property Watch.* www.ip-watch.org/2014/02/02/move-on-data-protection-or-fail-on-ttip-eu-parliament-chair-says.

ESMA. (n.d.). European Market Infrastructure Regulation (EMIR). Retrieved from www. esma.europa.eu/page/European-Market-Infrastructure-Regulation-EMIR.

Esping-Andersen, G. (1990). *The three worlds of welfare capitalism*: Princeton, NJ: Princeton University Press.

EU–US. (2011). Press release: EU–US Summit. Fact sheet on High-Level Working Group on Jobs and Growth. Retrieved from http://europa.eu/rapid/press-release_ MEMO-11-843_en.htm.

EU–US Financial Markets Regulatory Dialogue. (2004). EU–US Financial Markets Regulatory Dialogue: State-of-play. Retrieved from http://ec.europa.eu/internal_market/ finances/docs/general/eu-us-dialogue-report-state-of-play_en.pdf.

EU–US Financial Markets Regulatory Dialogue. (2014). Financial Markets Regulatory Dialogue – Joint statement, January 30.

EU, & US. (2001). *Agreement between the United States of America and the European Police Office*. Retrieved from www.europol.europa.eu/sites/default/files/flags/united_ states_of_america.pdf.

EU, & US. (1995). *The New Transatlantic Agenda*. Retrieved from http://eeas.europa.eu/ us/docs/new_transatlantic_agenda_en.pdf.

EU, & US. (2004). *Agreement between the United States of America and the European Community on the Mutual Recognition of Certificates of Conformity for Marine Equipment*. Retrieved from www.uscg.mil/hq/cg5/cg5214/docs/US%20-%20EC%20MRA. pdf.

EurActiv. (2010). First "citizens' initiative" to call for GM crop freeze. *EurActiv.com*. Retrieved from www.euractiv.com/cap/citizens-initiative-call-gm-crop-news-498524.

EurActiv. (2013). Germany, France demand "no spying" agreement with US. *EurActiv. com*. Retrieved from www.euractiv.com/global-europe/germany-france-demand-spying-agr-news-531309.

EurActiv. (2014a). Commission opposes European citizens' initiative against TTIP. *EurActiv.com*. Retrieved from www.euractiv.com/sections/trade-industry/commission-opposes-european-citizens-initiative-against-ttip-308406.

EurActiv. (2014b). TTIP will not include financial services, says Ambassador: Interview with EurActiv. *EurActiv*. Retrieved from www.euractiv.com/sections/euro-finance/ttip-will-not-include-financial-services-says-us-ambassador-303536.

EurActiv. (2014c). TTIP negotiating mandate finally declassified. *EurActiv*. Retrieved from www.euractiv.com/sections/trade-industry/ttip-negotiating-mandate-finally-declassified-309073.

Europa. (2007, August 22). "Open Skies" Agreement between Europe and the United States. Retrieved from http://europa.eu/legislation_summaries/external_relations/relations_with_third_countries/industrialised_countries/l24483_en.htm.

Europa. (2010a). Division of competences within the European Union. Retrieved from http://europa.eu/legislation_summaries/institutional_affairs/treaties/lisbon_treaty/ ai0020_en.htm.

Europa. (2010b). EU and Argentina settle WTO case on genetically modified organisms. *Europa Rapid Press Release*. Retrieved from http://europa.eu/rapid/press-release_IP-10-325_en.htm#PR_metaPressRelease_bottom.

Europa. (2014). Summaries of EU legislation: Transport. Retrieved from http://europa.eu/ legislation_summaries/transport/index_en.htm.

Europa Press Release. (2010). EU–US Summit: Joint statement MEMO 10-597. Retrieved from http://europa.eu/rapid/press-release_MEMO-10-597_en.htm.

EuropaBio. (2011). Approvals of GMOs in the European Union. Retrieved from www. europabio.org/positions/approvals-gm-crops-eu-january-2014-update.

European Banking Authority. (n.d.). About us. Retrieved from www.eba.europa.eu/about-us;jsessionid=E1131A0C24C7E3085BB878FC6FFFABB2.

European Banking Authority. (2013). EU-wide transparency exercise. Retrieved from www.eba.europa.eu/risk-analysis-and-data/eu-wide-transparency-exercise.

European Central Bank. (2014). Banking supervision. Retrieved from www.ecb.europa.eu/ssm/html/index.en.html.

European Commission – Standing Committee on the Food Chain and Animal Health. (2013a). Genetically modified food and feed and environmental risk. Retrieved from http://ec.europa.eu/food/plant/standing_committees/sc_modif_genet/index_en.htm.

European Commission – Standing Committee on the Food Chain and Animal Health. (2013b). Standing committees. Retrieved from http://ec.europa.eu/dgs/health_consumer/dgs_consultations/regulatory_committees_en.htm.

European Commission. (1986). *Communication from the Commission: A community framework for the regulation of biotechnology COM(1986) 573.*

European Commission. (2000a). *Communication from the Commission on the Precautionary Principle COM(2000) 1.* Retrieved from http://ec.europa.eu/dgs/health_consumer/library/pub/pub07_en.pdf.

European Commission. (2000b). White Paper on food safety COM 1999 719 final. Retrieved from http://europa.eu.int/comm/dgs/health_consumer/library/pub/pub06_en.pdf.

European Commission. (2001). Hormones in bovine meat: Background and history of WTO dispute. Press release. Retrieved from http://ec.europa.eu/dgs/health_consumer/library/press/press57_en.pdf.

European Commission. (2002). Regulation (EC) No 178/2002 of the European Parliament and the European Council of 28 January 2002 laying down the general principles and requirements of food law, establishing the European Food Safety Authority and laying down procedures in matters of food safety. Retrieved from http://eur-lex.europa.eu/LexUriServ/LexUriServ.do?uri=OJ:L:2002:031:0001:0024:EN:PDF.

European Commission. (2003). *Report from the Commission to the Council and the European Parliament on the application of the agreements between the European Communities and the Government of the United States of America and the Government of Canada regarding the application of their competition laws.* Retrieved from http://eur-lex.europa.eu/LexUriServ/LexUriServ.do?uri=COM:2003:0500:FIN:EN:PDF.

European Commission. (2004a). *Review of the framework for relations between the European Union and the United States.* Brussels: European Commission.

European Commission. (2004b). *Taking Europe to the world: 50 years of the European Commission's external action service.* Retrieved from http://ue.eu.int/ueDocs/cms_Data/docs/pressdata/en/reports/76255.pdf.

European Commission. (2005). Green Paper: On an EU approach to managing economic migration COM(2004) 811 final. Retrieved from http://eur-lex.europa.eu/LexUriServ/site/en/com/2004/com2004_0811en01.pdf.

European Commission. (2007). Investment services: Entry into force of MiFID a boon for financial markets and investor protection. *Europa Press Release.* Retrieved from http://europa.eu/rapid/pressReleasesAction.do?reference=IP/07/1625&format=HTML&aged=0&language=EN.

European Commission. (2008). *The single market for goods: Information pack.* Retrieved from http://ec.europa.eu/enterprise/newsroom/cf/itemdetail.cfm?&item_id=1351.

European Commission. (2010a). *Communication from the Commission to the European Parliament, the Council, the European Economic and Social Committee and the Committee of the Regions: Trade, growth and world affairs: Trade Policy as a core component of the EU's 2020 Strategy.*

European Commission. (2010b). *European Commission Staff Working Paper: Secure trade and 100% scanning of containers SEC(2010) 131 final*. Retrieved from http://ec.europa.eu/taxation_customs/resources/documents/common/whats_new/sec_2010_131_en.pdf.

European Commission. (2010c). *Regulation No 1092/2010 of the European Parliament and the Council on European Union macro-prudential oversight of the financial system and establishing a European Systemic Risk Board*. Retrieved from www.esma.europa.eu/system/files/Reg_1092_2010_ESRB.pdf.

European Commission. (2010d). *Towards more responsibility and competitiveness in the European Financial Sector*. Retrieved from http://ec.europa.eu/internal_market/finances/docs/leaflet/financial_services_en.pdf.

European Commission. (2010e). *Special Eurobarometer 354 Food-related risks report*. Retrieved from www.efsa.europa.eu/en/riskcommunication/riskperception.htm.

European Commission. (2011a). *Directive of the European Parliament and of the Council on Markets in Financial Instruments Repealing Directive 2004/39/EC of the European Parliament and Council COM (2011) 656 final*. Retrieved from http://ec.europa.eu/internal_market/securities/docs/isd/mifid/COM_2011_656_en.pdf.

European Commission. (2011b). *EU–US joint statement on supply-chain security*. Retrieved from Ec.europa.eu/taxation_customs/resources/documents/common/whats_new/eu_us_joint_statement_protocol_en.pdf.

European Commission. (2011c). *The European Union trade policy 2011*. Retrieved from http://trade.ec.europa.eu/doclib/docs/2011/april/tradoc_147773.pdf.

European Commission. (2011d). *Face to face with transatlantic research*. Retrieved from http://ec.europa.eu/research/biotechnology/eu-us-task-force/index_en.cfm?pg=tf_who.

European Commission. (2011e). *White Paper: Roadmap to a Single European Transport Area. Towards a competitive and resource efficient transport system* COM(2011) 144 final. Retrieved from http://eur-lex.europa.eu/LexUriServ/LexUriServ.do?uri=COM:2011:0144:FIN:EN:PDF.

European Commission. (2012a, August 24). Civil Service Index. Retrieved from http://ec.europa.eu/civil_service/index_en.htm.

European Commission. (2012b). A single market for goods. Retrieved from http://ec.europa.eu/internal_market/top_layer/index_18_en.htm.

European Commission. (2012c). Single market governance: FAQs. Retrieved from http://ec.europa.eu/enterprise/newsroom/cf/itemdetail.cfm?item_id=5798&lang=en.

European Commission. (2012d). *Value of production of agricultural products and foodstuffs, wines, aromatised wines and spirits protected by a geographical indication (GI)*. Retrieved from http://ec.europa.eu/agriculture/external-studies/2012/value-gi/final-report_en.pdf.

European Commission. (2013a). *Commission staff working document – Impact assessment report on the future of EU–US trade relations accompanying the document recommendation for a Council Decision authorizing the opening of negotiations on a comprehensive trade and investment agreement, called the Transatlantic Trade and Investment Partnership, between the European Union and the United States of America SWD(2013) 68 final*. Retrieved from http://trade.ec.europa.eu/doclib/docs/2013/march/tradoc_150759.pdf.

European Commission. (2013b, December 20). EU Chief Negotiator says EU–US trade deal not about deregulation, as third round of talks end in Washington. Retrieved from http://trade.ec.europa.eu/doclib/press/index.cfm?id=1007.

European Commission. (2013c). The European Citizens' Initiative. Retrieved from http://ec.europa.eu/citizens-initiative/public/welcome.

European Commission. (2013d, February 13). European Union and United States to launch negotiations for a Transatlantic Trade and Investment Partnership. Press release. Retrieved from http://trade.ec.europa.eu/doclib/press/index.cfm?id=869.

European Commission. (2013e). *HR key figures card.* Retrieved from http://ec.europa.eu/civil_service/docs/hr_key_figures_en.pdf.

European Commission. (2013f, October 3). *Incorrect claims about Investor-state Dispute Settlement.* Retrieved from http://trade.ec.europa.eu/doclib/docs/2013/october/tradoc_151790.pdf.

European Commission. (2013g, May 28). *Liberalisation of air transport in the context of the Transatlantic Trade and Investment Partnership (TTIP).* Retrieved from http://ec.europa.eu/commission_2010-2014/kallas/headlines/speeches/2013/05/speech_liberalisation_of_air_transport_in_the_context_of_the_transatlantic_trade_and_investment_partnership_(ttip).pdf.

European Commission. (2013h). Memo: Legislative package for banking supervision in the Eurozone – frequently asked questions. Press release. Retrieved from http://europa.eu/rapid/press-release_MEMO-13-780_en.htm?locale=en.

European Commission. (2013i). Speech by Karel de Gucht, European Trade Commissioner – Transatlantic Trade and Investment Partnership: Solving the regulatory puzzle – Speech/13/801 10/10/2013. Press release. Retrieved from http://europa.eu/rapid/press-release_SPEECH-13-801_en.htm.

European Commission. (2013j). *Transatlantic Trade and Investment Partnership: The regulatory part.* Retrieved from http://trade.ec.europa.eu/doclib/docs/2013/july/tradoc_151605.pdf.

European Commission. (2013k). *Transatlantic Trade and Investment: An economic analysis.* Retrieved from http://trade.ec.europa.eu/doclib/docs/2013/september/tradoc_151787.pdf.

European Commission. (2013l). *FAQ on the EU–US Transatlantic Trade and Investment Partnership.* Retrieved from http://eeas.europa.eu/delegations/china/documents/news/20130619_02_tradoc_151351.pdf.

European Commission. (2014a). A comprehensive EU response to the financial crisis: Substantial progress towards a strong financial framework for Europe and a banking union for the Eurozone MEMO/14/244 28/03/2014.

European Commission. (2014b). EU–US Energy Council: joint press statement IP/14/365 02/04/2014.

European Commission. (2014c). *EU-US Transatlantic Trade and Investment Partnership: cooperation on financial services regulation (January 27).* Retrieved from http://trade.ec.europa.eu/doclib/docs/2014/january/tradoc_152101.pdf.

European Commission. (2014d). *Preliminary report: Online public consultation on investment protection and Investor-to-State Dispute Settlement (ISDS) in the Transatlantic Trade and Investment Partnership Agreement (TTIP).* Retrieved from http://trade.ec.europa.eu/doclib/docs/2014/july/tradoc_152693.pdf.

European Commission. (2014e). Questions & answers: New rules for tobacco products MEMO/14/134 26/02/2014. Press release. Retrieved from http://europa.eu/rapid/press-release_MEMO-14-134_en.htm.

European Commission. (2014f). Transatlantic Trade & Investment Partnership Advisory Group. Retrieved from http://trade.ec.europa.eu/doclib/docs/2014/january/tradoc_152102.pdf.

European Commission. (2014g). Transatlantic Trade & Investment Partnership Advisory Group: Meeting Report, 24 July 2014. Retrieved from http://trade.ec.europa.eu/doclib/docs/2014/july/tradoc_152667.pdf.

European Commission. (2014h). EU–US Trade – 7th round of talks on Transatlantic

Trade Pact ends in the US. Retrieved from http://trade.ec.europa.eu/doclib/press/index. cfm?id=1158.

European Commission and US Government. (2012). *Solicitation to EU & US stakeholders.* Retrieved from http://trade.ec.europa.eu/doclib/docs/2012/september/tradoc_149893.pdf.

European Commission DG Mobility and Transport. (2010). Mission of the Directorate-General for Mobility and Transport. Retrieved from http://ec.europa.eu/dgs/transport/doc/2010_05_move_mission_statements.pdf.

European Council – the President. (2012). Towards a genuine economic and monetary union. Retrieved from www.consilium.europa.eu/uedocs/cms_Data/docs/pressdata/en/ec/134069.pdf.

European External Action Service. (1990). *Transatlantic Declaration on EC-US Relations.* Retrieved from http://eeas.europa.eu/us/docs/trans_declaration_90_en.pdf.

European External Action Service. (2014a). Eastern partnership. Retrieved from http://eeas.europa.eu/eastern/index_en.htm.

European External Action Service. (2014b). United States of America. Retrieved from http://eeas.europa.eu/us/sum03_14/dialogues_en.htm.

European Food Safety Authority. (n.d.). About EFSA. Retrieved from www.efsa.europa.eu/en/aboutefsa.htm.

European Maritime Safety Agency. (2012). EU–USA Mutual Recognition Agreement. Retrieved from www.emsa.europa.eu/implementation-tasks/marine-equipment/items/id/514.html?cid=31.

European Maritime Safety Agency. (2013). About us. Retrieved from http://emsa.europa.eu/about/who-we-are/administrative-board.html.

European Parliament. (1997, February 7). *Report on the alleged contraventions or maladministration in the implementation of community law in relation to BSE, without prejudice to the jurisdiction of the community and national courts (the Medina Report).* Retrieved from www.europarl.europa.eu/conferences/19981130/bse/a4002097_en.htm.

European Parliament. (2010). Hearings in the European Parliament, High Representative for EU Foreign Affairs and Security Policy. Retrieved from www.europarl.europa.eu/ep-live/en/other-events/video?event=20100111-1531-SPECIAL.

European Parliament. (2012a, July 4). European Parliament rejects ACTA. Press release. Retrieved from www.europarl.europa.eu/news/en/pressroom/content/20120703IPR48247/html/European-Parliament-rejects-ACTA.

European Parliament. (2012b). Parliament gives green light to air passenger data deal with the US. *European Parliament News.* Retrieved from www.europarl.europa.eu/news/en/news-room/content/20120419IPR43404/html/Parliament-gives-green-light-to-air-passenger-data-deal-with-the-US.

European Parliament. (2014a). Food safety: MEPs oppose authorising new genetically modified maize. *Plenary Session Press Release.* Retrieved from www.europarl.europa.eu/news/en/news-room/content/20140110IPR32334/html/Food-safety-MEPs-oppose-authorising-new-genetically-modified-maize.

European Parliament. (2014b). Results of the 2014 European election/turnout. Retrieved from www.results-elections2014.eu/en/turnout.html.

European Parliament. (2014c, July 15). Transatlantic Trade and Investment Partnership debate, commission briefing. Retrieved from www.europarl.europa.eu/ep-live/en/plenary/video?debate=1405436531874.

European Parliament. (2014d). TTIP "fresh start"" means more clarity, debate, and realism, Malmström Tells MEPs. [Press release]. Retrieved from www.europarl.europa.eu/sides/getDoc.do?pubRef=-%2f%2fEP%2f%2fTEXT%2bIM-PRESS%2b20141201IPR81714%2b0%2bDOC%2bXML%2bV0%2f%2fEN&language=EN.

European Parliament and Council. (2001). *Directive 2001/18/EC on the deliberate release into the environment of genetically modified organisms 90/220/EEC.* Retrieved from http://eur-lex.europa.eu/LexUriServ/LexUriServ.do?uri=OJ:L:2001:106:0001:0038:EN:PDF.

European Parliament and Council. (2003a). *Regulation (EC) No 1829/2003 of the European Parliament and of the Council of 22 September 2003 on genetically modified food and feed.* Retrieved from http://ec.europa.eu/food/food/animalnutrition/labelling/Reg_1829_2003_en.pdf.

European Parliament and Council. (2003b). *Regulation (EC) No 1830/2003 of the European Parliament and Council of 22 September 2003 concerning the traceability and labelling of genetically modified organisms and the traceability of food and feed products produced from genetically modified organisms and amending Directive 2001/18/EC.* Retrieved from http://eur-lex.europa.eu/LexUriServ/LexUriServ.do?uri=OJ:L:2003:268:0024:0028:EN:PDF.

European Securities and Markets Authority. (2014). Speech by Verena Ross – Liquidity and new financial market regulation ESMA/2014/224.

European Services Forum. (2011). Facts and figures. Retrieved from www.esf.be/new/statistics.

European Union and the United States. (2007). *Framework for advancing transatlantic economic integration between the European Union and the United States of America.* Retrieved from http://ec.europa.eu/enterprise/policies/international/files/tec_framework_en.pdf.

European Union and the United States. (2012). *Statement of the European Union and the United States on shared principles for international investment.* Retrieved from http://trade.ec.europa.eu/doclib/docs/2012/april/tradoc_149331.pdf.

European Union and United States. (2007). Framework for advancing transatlantic economic integration between the European Union and the United States.

Eurostat. (2013). *News release: Euroindicators.* Retrieved from http://epp.eurostat.ec.europa.eu/cache/ITY_PUBLIC/3-02042013-AP/EN/3-02042013-AP-EN.PDF.

Evans, P. B., Jacobson, H. K., & Putnam, R. D. (Eds.). (1993). *Double-edged diplomacy.* Berkeley, CA: University of California Press.

Evenett, S. J., Lehmann, A., & Steil, B. (2000). Antitrust policy in an evolving global marketplace. In S. J. Evenett, A. Lehmann, & B. Steil (Eds.), *Antitrust goes global* (pp. 1–28). Washington, DC: Brookings Institution.

Felbermayr, G., Heid, B., & Lehwald, S. (2013). *Transatlantic Trade and Investment Partnership (TTIP): Who benefits from a free trade deal?* Gütersloh: Bertelsmann Stiftung.

Financial Accounting Standards Board. (n.d.). International convergence of accounting standards – overview. Retrieved from www.fasb.org/jsp/FASB/Page/SectionPage&cid=1176156245663.

Financial Industry Regulatory Authority. (2013). About FINRA. Retrieved from www.finra.org/AboutFINRA.

Financial Stability Board. (2013). Mandate. Retrieved from www.financialstabilityboard.org/about/mandate.htm.

Fox, B. (2014a, January 15). EU lawmakers agree deal on commodity trading. *EUobserver.* Retrieved from http://euobserver.com/economic/122723.

Fox, B. (2014b, July 28). From trade tariffs to trust: TTIP a year on. *EUobserver.* Retrieved from http://euobserver.com/economic/125070.

Fox, B. (2014c, July 2). EU–US trade deal must have national approval, say MPs. *EUobserver.com.* Retrieved from http://euobserver.com/institutional/124833.

Fox, E. M. (1997). US and EU competition law: a comparison. In E. M. Graham & J. D. Richardson (Eds.), *Global competition policy* (pp. 339–354). Washington, DC: Peterson Institute for International Economics.

France24. (2013). US–EU free trade talks to open Monday amid spying rancor. Retrieved from www.france24.com/en/20130707-us-eu-trade-talks-open-monday-amid-spying-rancor.

Francois, J., Manchin, M., Norberg, H., Pindyuk, O., & Tomberger, P. (2013). *Reducing transatlantic barriers to trade and investment: An economic assessment.* London: Centre for Economic Policy Research.

Frankel, J. (2005). The environment and economic globalization. In *Globalization: What's new*. New York: Council on Foreign Relations.

Friends of Europe. (2010). New transatlantic trends in competition policy, report of the High-Level Roundtable. Retrieved from www.friendsofeurope.org/Portals/13/Documents/Reports/2010_FoE_RT_EU-US_Competition_web.pdf.

Friends of Europe. (2011). Taming the turmoil: New rules of global finance. Report of the High-Level Roundtable. (Spring). Retrieved from www.friendsofeurope.org/Portals/13/Events/Roundtables/2011/Taming_the_turmoil/2011_Report_Taming_turmoil_web.pdf.

Frost, E. L. (1998). *The Transatlantic Economic Partnership*. Washington, DC: Peterson Institute for International Economics.

Fuchs, D., & Klingemann, H.-D. (2008). American exceptionalism or western civilization? In J. Anderson, J. G. Ikenberry, & T. Risse (Eds.), *The end of the west? Crisis and change in the Atlantic order* (pp. 263–290). Ithaca, NY: Cornell University Press.

Fulmer, C. (2009). A critical look at the H-1B visa program and its effects on U.S. and foreign workers – a controversial program unhinged from its original intent. *Lewis & Clark Law Review, 13*(3), 823–860.

Gardner, A. (2014a, July 18). Sixth round of TTIP talks end. *European Voice*. Retrieved from www.europeanvoice.com/article/sixth-round-of-ttip-talks-end.

Gardner, A. (2014b, July 24). TTIP tries to weather the mid-way squalls. *European Voice*. Retrieved from www.europeanvoice.com/article/ttip-tries-to-weather-the-mid-way-squalls.

Gardner, A. (2014c, July 3). Turkey presses for TTIP role. *European Voice*. www.europeanvoice.com/article/turkey-presses-for-ttip-role.

Gardner, A. L. (1997). *A new era in US–EU relations? The Clinton Administration and the new transatlantic agenda*. Aldershot: Avebury.

Gates, R. M. (2011). *The security and defense agenda (future of NATO)*. Brussels.

Gaus, A., & Hoxtell, W. (2013). The EU–US development dialogue: Past, present and future. GPPI Working Paper (July).

Gerber, D. J. (2001). *Law and competition in twentieth-century Europe: Protecting Prometheus*. Oxford: Clarendon Press.

German Marshall Fund. (2011). *Transatlantic trends 2011*. Retrieved from www.gmfus.org/publications_/TT/TT2011_final_web.pdf.

Gibson Dunn. (2012). 2012 Antitrust merger enforcement update and outlook. Retrieved from www.gibsondunn.com/publications/pages/2012AntitrustMergerEnforcementUpdate-Outlook.aspx.

Gladstone, R. (2014, January 23). U.S. warns against business with Iran. *New York Times*. Retrieved from www.nytimes.com/2014/01/24/world/middleeast/us-warns-against-business-with-iran.html.

Goodsell, C. (2003). *The case for bureaucracy* (5th ed.). Chatham, NJ: Chatham House.

Gordon, M. R. (2014, January 24). Kerry presses Iranians to prove nuclear work is for peaceful purposes. *New York Times*. Retrieved from www.nytimes.com/2014/01/25/world/middleeast/kerry-presses-iranians-to-prove-nuclear-work-is-for-peaceful-purposes.html.

Gordon, P. (2003). Bridging the Atlantic divide. *Foreign Affairs, 82*(1), 70–83.

Grant, W., & Stocker, T. (2009). Politics of food: Agro-industry lobbying in Brussels. In D. Coen & J. Richardson (Eds.), *Lobbying the European Union: Institutions, actors, and issues*. Oxford: Oxford University Press.

Grasso, V. B. (2014). *The Berry amendment: Requiring defense procurement to come from domestic sources*. Congressional Research Service. Retrieved from http://fas.org/sgp/crs/natsec/RL31236.pdf.

The Greens–European Free Alliance of the European Parliament. (2014). Lobbyland: Corporate-capture of TTIP talks revealed. Retrieved from http://ttip2014.eu/blog-detail/blog/lobbying%20TTIP.html.

Greenwood, J. (2003). *Interest representation in the European Union* Basingstoke: Palgrave Macmillan.

Greer, S. L. (2013). (Why) did we forget about history? Lessons for the eurozone from the failed conditionality debates in the 80s. *OSE Paper Series*, 11.

Greifenstein, R. (2001). *Die green card: Ambitionen, Fakten und Zukunftsaussichten des deutschen Modelversuchs*. Bonn: Friedrich Ebert Stiftung.

Gress, D. (1998). *From Plato to NATO: The idea of the west and its opponents*. New York: The Free Press.

Grier, J. H. (2014). Guest blog: Opening foreign procurement markets amid domestic preferences. *American's Trade Policy: Towards a 21st Century Policy*. Retrieved from http://americastradepolicy.com/guest-blog-opening-foreign-procurement-markets-amid-domestic-preferences/#.VBNUDvldUuc.

Group of the Progressive Alliance of Socialists & Democrats in the European Parliament. (2014). S&Ds want the Investor–State Dispute Mechanism out of the EU–US trade and investment agreement. Retrieved from www.socialistsanddemocrats.eu/newsroom/sds-want-investor-state-dispute-mechanism-out-eu-us-trade-and-investment-agreement-ttip.

Grueff, J. (2013). *Achieving a successful outcome for agriculture in the EU–U.S. Transatlantic Trade and Investment Partnership Agreement*. Washington, DC: International Food & Agricultural Trade Policy Council.

Guild, E. (2008). The uses and abuses of counter-terrorism policies in Europe: The case of the "terrorist lists." *Journal of Common Market Studies, 46*(1), 173–193.

Haas, E. (1964). *Beyond the nation state: Functionalism and international organization*. Stanford, CA: Stanford University Press.

Hailbronner, K., Papkonstantinou, V., & Kau, M. (2008). The agreement on passenger-data transfer (PNR) and the EU–US cooperation in data communication. *International Migration, 46*(2), 187–197.

Hakim, D. (2013, September 12). U.S. trade officials try to curb Europe's expectations. *New York Times*. Retrieved from www.nytimes.com/2013/09/13/world/europe/us-trade-officials-try-to-curb-europes-expectations.html.

Hall, P., & Soskice, D. (2001). An introduction to varieties of capitalism. In P. Hall & D. Soskice (Eds.), *Varieties of capitalism: The institutional foundations of comparative capitalism* (pp. 1–68). Oxford: Oxford University Press.

Hamilton, D., & Quinlan, J. (Eds.). (2013). *Transatlantic economy 2013: Annual survey of jobs, trade and investment between the United States and Europe*. Washington, DC: Centre for Transatlantic Relations, American Consortium on EU Studies, The Johns Hopkins University, Paul H. Nitze School of Advanced International Studies.

Hamilton, D., & Quinlan, J. (Eds.). (2014). *Transatlantic economy 2014: Annual survey of jobs, trade and investment between the United States and Europe* (Vol. 1). Washington, DC: Centre for Transatlantic Relations, American Consortium on EU Studies, The Johns Hopkins University, Paul H. Nitze School of Advanced International Studies.

Hamilton, D., & Rhinard, M. (2011). All for one and one for all: Towards a transatlantic solidarity pledge. In P. Pawlak (Ed.), *The EU–US security and justice agenda in action*. Paris: EU-ISS Chaillot Papers.

Hänggi, H., & Roloff, R. (2006). *Interregionalism and international relations*. London: Routledge.

Hanhimäki, J. M., Schoenborn, B., & Zanchetta, B. (2012). *Transatlantic relations since 1945*. New York: Routledge.

Harcourt, A. (2012). "Cultural coalitions" and international regulatory co-operation. *Journal of Common Market Studies, 50*(5), 709–725.

Harding, J. (2010, July 15). Interview with José Manuel Barroso. *London Times*.

Harmon, A. (2014, January 4). A lonely quest for facts on genetically modified crops. *New York Times*. Retrieved from www.nytimes.com/2014/01/05/us/on-hawaii-a-lonely-quest-for-facts-about-gmos.html?_r=0.

Harvey, F. (2014, January 7). Owen Paterson: Embrace GM or risk becoming "museum of world farming". *Guardian*. Retrieved from www.theguardian.com/environment/2014/jan/07/owen-paterson-gm-crops-farming.

Hay, G. A., & McMahon, K. (2012). The diverging approach to price squeezes in the United States and Europe. *Journal of Competition Law and Economics, 8*(2), 259–296.

Heclo, H. (1978). Issue networks and the executive establishment. In A. King (Ed.), *The New American Political System* (pp. 87–123). Washington, DC: American Enterprise Institute.

Heisbourg, F. (2011, August 29). Libya: a small war with big consequences. *New York Times*. Retrieved from www.nytimes.com/2011/08/30/opinion/30iht-edheisbourg30.html.

Hellmann, G. (2008). Inevitable decline versus predestined stability: Disciplinary explanations of the evolving transatlantic order. In J. Anderson, J. G. Ikenberry, & T. Risse (Eds.), *The end of the west? Crisis and change in the Atlantic order* (pp. 28–52). Ithaca, NY: Cornell University Press.

Henderson, K. (2004). Characterizing American public administration: The concept of administrative culture. *International Journal of Public Sector Management, 17*, 234–250.

Henderson, K. (2005). American administrative culture: An evolutionary perspective. In O. P. Dwivedi & J. Jabbra (Eds.), *Administrative culture in a borderless world*. Whitby: deSitter.

Herd, G. (2010). *Great powers and strategic stability in the 21st century: Competing visions of world order*. London: Routledge.

Herszenhorn, D. M. (2013, December 2). Amid unrest, Ukrainian President defends choice on accords. *New York Times*. Retrieved from www.nytimes.com/2013/12/03/world/europe/ukraine-unrest.html?hpw&rref=world&_r=0.

Hewitt, G. (2011, May 26). Obama develops mid-east strategy with Europeans. *BBC News Europe*. Retrieved from www.bbc.co.uk/news/world-europe-13562109.

High Level Working Group in Growth and Jobs. (2013). Final Report, February 11. Retrieved from http://trade.ec.europa.eu/doclib/docs/2013/february/tradoc_150519.pdf.

Hilary, J. (2014). Comment: Outrage as EU blocks democratic challenge to US trade deal. Retrieved from www.politics.co.uk/comment-analysis/2014/09/12/comment-outrage-as-eu-blocks-democratic-challenge-to-us-trad.

Hillman, J., & Kleinmann, D. (2010). Trading places: the new dynamics of EU trade policy under the Treaty of Lisbon. *German Marshall Fund Policy Paper Series*.

Hirst, N. (2014a, January 30). Commission proposes ban on proprietary trading. *European Voice*. Retrieved from www.europeanvoice.com/CWS/Index.aspx?PageID=134&articleID=79451.

Hirst, N. (2014b, January 16). Deal clinched on reform of financial systems. *European Voice*. Retrieved from www.europeanvoice.com/article/imported/deal-clinched-on-reform-of-financial-systems-/79284.aspx.

Hix, S. (2005). *The political system of the European Union* (2nd ed.). Basingstoke: Palgrave Macmillan.

Hix, S., Noury, A. G., & Roland, G. (2007). *Democratic politics in the European Parliament*. Cambridge: Cambridge University Press.

Hodgson, G. (2009). *The myth of American exceptionalism* New Haven, CT: Yale University Press.

Hoese, A., & Opermann, K. (2007). Transatlantic conflict and cooperation: What role for public opinion? *Journal of Transatlantic Studies, 5*(1), 43–61.

Hoffmann, S. (1966). Obstinate or obsolete: The fate of the nation state and the case of western Europe. *Daedelus, 95*, 862–915.

Hofstadter, R. (1955). *The age of reform*. New York: W. W. Norton.

Hogan, M. H. (Ed.). (1992). *The end of the Cold War: its meaning and implications*. Cambridge: Cambridge University Press.

Hooghe, L., & Marks, G. (2001). *Multilevel governance and European integration*. Lanham, MD: Rowman & Littlefield.

Hooghe, L., & Marks, G. (2003). Unraveling the central state, but how? Types of multi-level governance. *American Political Science Review, 97*(2), 233–243.

Hopf, T. (2005). Dissipating hegemony: US unilateralism and European counter-hegemony. In M. Evangelista & V. H. Parsi (Eds.), *Partners or rivals? European–American relations after Iraq* (pp. 39–60). Milan: Vita e Pensiero.

Hormats, R. D. (2013). The Transatlantic Trade and Investment Partnership: America's new opportunity to benefit from, and revitalize its leadership of the global economy – remarks by Under Secretary for Economic Growth, Energy, and the Environment, US Department of State – April 23. Retrieved from www.state.gov/e/rls/rmk/207997.htm.

Howorth, J. (2009). A new institutional architecture for the transatlantic relationship? In *European Visions* (Vol. 5). Brussels: Eur-IFRI.

Hufbauer, G. C., & Schott, J. J. (2009). *Buy American: Bad for jobs, worse for reputation. Policy Brief*. Washington, DC: Peterson Institute for International Economics.

Hufbauer, G. C., Schott, J. J., Adler, M., Brunel, C., & Foong, W. (2010). Figuring out the Doha Round. Retrieved from www.wto.org/english/res_e/reser_e/dialogue_paper_schott_e.pdf.

Hughes, K. (2014). Analysis: Obama's nod to trade leaves tough work ahead in Congress. *MSN Money*. Retrieved from http://money.msn.com/business-news/article.aspx?feed=OBR&date=20140129&id=17302763.

Hummel, R. (2008). *The Bureaucratic experience* (5th ed.). New York: St. Martin's Press.

Huntington, S. P. (1993). The clash of civilizations? *Foreign Affairs, 72*(3), 22–49.

Ikenberry, J. G. (1996). Myth of Post-Cold-War. *Foreign Affairs, 75*(3). Retrieved from www.foreignaffairs.com/articles/52040/g-john-ikenberry/the-myth-of-post-cold-war-chaos.

Ikenberry, J. G. (2000). *After victory: Institutions, strategic restraint, and the rebuilding of order after major wars*. Princeton, NJ: Princeton University Press.

Indyk, M., Lieberthal, K., & O'Hanlon, M. (2012). *Bending history. Barack Obama's foreign policy.* Washington, DC: Brookings Institution Press.

Inglehart, R. (1977). *The silent revolution.* Princeton, NJ: Princeton University Press.

Inglehart, R. (1990). *Culture shift in advanced industrialized societies.* Princeton, NJ: Princeton University Press.

Inglehart, R. (1997). *Modernization and postmodernization.* Princeton, NJ: Princeton University Press.

Ingraham, P. (2006). Building bridges over troubled waters: Merit as a guide. *Public Administration Review, 66*(4), 486–495.

Insurance Institute for Highway Safety. (2014). Motorcycles. Retrieved from www.iihs.org/iihs/topics/laws/helmetuse?topicName=motorcycles

International Association of Insurance Supervisors. (2014). About the IAIS. Retrieved from www.iaisweb.org/About-the-IAIS-28.

International Centre for Trade and Sustainable Development. (1998). New transatlantic marketplace: France keeps Brittan's ship at bay. *Bridges: Trade News from a Sustainable Development Perspective, 2*(6). Retrieved from www.ictsd.org/bridges-news/bridges/news/new-transatlantic-marketplace-france-keeps-brittans-ship-at-bay.

International Maritime Organization. (2012). *International shipping facts and figures: Information resources on trade, safety, security, environment.* Retrieved from www.imo.org/KnowledgeCentre/ShipsAndShippingFactsAndFigures/TheRoleandImportanceofInternationalShipping/Documents/International%20Shipping%20-%20Facts%20and%20Figures.pdf.

International Road Assessment Program. (n.d.). About us. Retrieved from www.irap.net/about-irap/about-us.

International Service for the Acquisition of Agri-Biotech Applications. (2012). Top ten facts about Biotech/GM crops in 2012. Retrieved from www.isaaa.org/resources/publications/briefs/44/toptenfacts/default.asp.

Irwin, D. (2011). *Peddling protectionism: Smoot–Hawley and the Great Depression.* Princeton, NJ: Princeton University Press.

Jaffe, G. (2012). 2 army brigades to leave Europe in cost-cutting move. *Washington Post.* Retrieved from www.washingtonpost.com/world/national-security/army-brigades-to-leave-europe/2012/01/12/gIQArZqluP_story.html.

James, P., Kemper, F., & Pascal, G. (1999). *A European food and public health authority: The future of scientific advice in the EU.* http://ec.europa.eu/food/fs/sc/future_food_en.pdf.

Jamil, I., Askvik, S., & Hossain, F. (2013). Understanding administrative culture: Some theoretical and methodological remarks. *International Journal of Public Administration, 36*(13), 900–909.

Janusch, H. (2013). Public protests and FTA negotiations with the United States: Lessons for the TAFTA/TTIP. In D. Cardoso, P. Mthembu, M. Venhaus, & G. M. Verde (Eds.), *The transatlantic colossus: Global contributions to broaden the debate on the EU–US free trade agreement* (pp. 24–27). Berlin: Berlin Forum on Global Politics.

Jassanoff, S. (1990). American exceptionalism and the political acknowledgment of risk. In E. J. Burger (Ed.), *Risk.* Ann Arbor, MI: University of Michigan Press.

Joenniemi, P. (2009). Transatlantic relations as a "community of neighbours." Danish Institute for International Studies Working Paper.

Joerges, C. (1999a). EU committees: Social regulation, law and politics. In C. Joerges & E. Vos (Eds.), *EU committees: Social regulation, law and politics* (pp. 3–17). Oxford: Hart Publishing.

Joerges, C. (1999b). "Good governance" through comitology. In C. Joerges & E. Vos

(Eds.), *EU committees: Social regulation, law and politics* (pp. 310–338). Oxford: Hart Publishing.

Jorges, C., & Neyer, J. (1997). From intergovernmental bargaining to deliberative political processes: The constitutionalization of comitology. *European Law Journal, 3*, 273–299.

Kagan, R. (2003). *Of paradise and power: America vs. Europe in the New World Order.* New York: Alfred Knopf.

Kahneman, D., & Tversky, A. (1979). Prospect theory: An analysis of decision under risk. *Econometrica, 47*(2), 263–292.

Kanter, J., & Clark, N. (2010, March 25). U.S. and E.U. agree to expand Open Skies accord. *New York Times.* Retrieved from www.nytimes.com/2010/03/26/business/global/26skies.html.

Kardish, C. (2014). What Vermont's GMO law means for the labeling movement. Retrieved from www.governing.com/news/headlines/gov-what-vermonts-gmo-law-means-for-the-labeling-movement.html.

Kassim, H., & Stevens, H. (2010). *Air transport and the European Union.* Basingstoke: Palgrave Macmillan.

Kassim, H., Peterson, J., Bauer, M. W., Connolly, S., Dehousee, R., Hooghe, L., & Thompson, A. (2013). *The European Commission of the twenty-first century.* Oxford: Oxford University Press.

Kaufman, H. (1960). *The forest ranger: A study in administrative behavior.* Baltimore, MD: Johns Hopkins University Press.

Keating, D. (2013a, October 13). Commission to give response to GM ruling. *European Voice.* Retrieved from www.europeanvoice.com/article/imported/commission-to-give-response-to-gm-ruling/78577.aspx.

Keating, D. (2013b, December 13). EU court blocks GM potato cultivation. *European Voice.* Retrieved from www.europeanvoice.com/article/2013/december/eu-court-blocks-gm-potato-cultivation/79086.aspx.

Keating, D. (2013c, August 2). French court annuls GMO ban. *European Voice.* Retrieved from www.europeanvoice.com/article/2013/august/french-court-annuls-gmo-ban/78025.aspx.

Keating, D. (2014, February 13). Legal fight looms on GM crops. *European Voice.* Retrieved from www.europeanvoice.com/article/imported/legal-fights-loom-on-gm-crops/79681.aspx.

Keene, K. H., & Ladd, E. C. (1990). America: "A unique outlook?". *The American Enterprise*, March/April.

Kennedy, J. F. (1962a). Remarks upon signing the Trade Expansion Act. *The American Presidency Project.* Retrieved from www.presidency.ucsb.edu/ws/?pid=8946.

Kennedy, J. F. (1962b). Speech delivered at Independence Hall, Philadelphia, July 4. www.jfklibrary.org/Asset-Viewer/RrjaDhW5B0OYm2zaJbyPgg.aspx.

Keohane, R., & Nye, J. (1977). *Power and interdependence: World politics in transition.* Boston, MA: Little, Brown & Co.

Kienstra, J. D. (2012). Cleared for landing: Airbus, Boeing, and the WTO dispute over subsidies to large civil aircraft. *Northwestern Journal of International Law & Business, 32*(3), 569–606.

King, A. (1973). Ideas, institutions and the policies of government: A comparative analysis: parts I and II. *British Journal of Political Science, 3*(July), 409–423.

Kingdon, J. (2011). *Agendas, alternatives and public policies* (2nd ed.). New York: Longman.

Kingston, S. (2012). *Greening EU competition law and policy.* Cambridge: Cambridge University Press.

Kirchschlager, M. (2013). In between curious economics and l'exception cuturelle: Implications of TAFTA/TTIP for the cultural sector. In D. Cardoso, P. Mthembu, M. Venhaus, & G. M. Verde (Eds.), *The transatlantic colossus: Global contributions to broaden the debate on the EU–US free trade agreement* (pp. 80–83). Berlin: Berlin Forum on Global Politics.

Kirişci, K. (2014). Turkey and the Transatlantic Trade and Investment Partnership: Boosting the model partnership with the United States. Turkey Project Policy Paper, September (2). Retrieved from www.brookings.edu/~/media/research/files/papers/2013/09/turkey%20transatlantic%20trade%20investment%20partnership%20kirisci/turkey%20and%20the%20transatlantic%20trade%20and%20investment%20partnership.pdf.

Kirkpatrick, D. D., Erlanger, S., & Bumiller, E. (2011). Allies open air assault on Qaddafi's forces in Libya. *New York Times*. Retrieved from www.nytimes.com/2011/03/20/world/africa/20libya.html?hp&_r=1&.

Klijn, E.-H., & Koppenjan, J. (2012). Governance network theory: Past, present and future. *Policy & Politics, 40*(4), 687–606.

Klüver, H. (2013). *Lobbying in the European Union: Interest groups, lobbying coalitions and policy change*. Oxford: Oxford University Press.

Knauss, J., & Trubek, D. (2001). The transatlantic labour dialogue: Minimal action in a weak structure. In M. Pollack & G. Schaffer (Eds.), *Transatlantic governance in the global economy* (pp. 235–254). Latham, MD: Rowman & Littlefield.

Knowles, D. (2013, May 22). Senator seeks to overturn so-called Monsanto Protection Act. *NY Daily News*. Retrieved from www.nydailynews.com/news/politics/push-overturn-monsanto-protection-act-article-1.1352178.

Kohler-Koch, B. (2010). Civil society and EU democracy: "Astroturf" representation? *Journal of European Public Policy, 17*(1), 100–116.

Kopicki, A. (2013, July 27). Strong support for labeling modified foods. *New York Times*. Retrieved from www.nytimes.com/2013/07/28/science/strong-support-for-labeling-modified-foods.html?_r=0.

Koslowski, R. (Ed.). (2011). *Global mobility regimes* New York: Palgrave Macmillan.

Kovacic, W. A. (2008). Competition Policy in the European Union and the United States: Convergence or divergence in the future treatment of dominant firms? *Competition Law International*(October), 8–18.

Kropf, J. (2007). Networked and layered: Understanding the U.S. framework for Protecting Personally Identifiable Information. *World Data Protection Report, 7*(6), 3–7.

Kudrle, R., & Marmor, T. (1984). Development of welfare states in North America. In P. Flora & A. J. Heidenheimer (Eds.), *The Development of Welfare States in Europe and North America*. New Brunswick: Rutgers University Press.

Kupchan, C. (2010). The potential twilight of the European Union. Working Paper, Council on Foreign Relations, September.

Kurzer, P. (2013). European health crises and the "voice of the European People" (the European Parliament). Paper presented at the Council for European Studies, University of Amsterdam, Amsterdam, the Netherlands, June 25–27.

Landau, M. (1969). Redundancy, rationality, and the problem of duplication and overlap. *Public Administration Review, 29*, 346–358.

Lannoo, K. (2013). Financial services and the Transatlantic Trade and Investment Partnership. *CEPS Policy Brief* 302.

Leventoğlu, B., & Tarar, A. (2005). Prenegotiation public commitment in domestic and international bargaining. *American Political Science Review, 99*(3), 419–433.

Lewis, M. (2012). Obama's way. *Vanity Fair*. Retrieved from www.vanityfair.com/politics/2012/10/michael-lewis-profile-barack-obama.

Liefferink, D., Arts, B., Kamstra, J., & Ooijevaar, J. (2009). Leaders and laggards in environmental policy: A quantitative analysis of domestic policy outputs. *Journal of European Public Policy, 16*(5), 677–700.

Lieven, A. (2004). *America right or wrong: An Anatomy of American nationalism*. London: Harper Perennial.

Lindblom, C. E. (1977). *Politics and markets: The World's political-economic systems*. New York: Basic Books.

Lipset, S. M. (1996). *American exceptionalism: A double edged sword*. New York: W. W. Norton.

Lipset, S. M. (1999). American society in European perspective. In J. Janning, C. Kupchan, & D. Rumberg (Eds.), *Civic engagement in the Atlantic community* (pp. 23–54). Gutersloh: Bertelsmann Foundation Publishers.

Lipton, E. (2013, April 30). Banks rally against strict controls of foreign bets. *New York Times*. Retrieved from www.nytimes.com/2013/05/01/business/banks-criticize-strict-controls-for-foreign-bets.html?pagewanted=all.

Lofchie, S. (2014). U.S. and EU hold financial markets regulatory dialogue. *Center for Financial Stability*. http://centerforfinancialstability.org/wp/?p=3812.

Losey, J., Rayor, L., & Carter, M. (1999, May 20). Transgenic pollen harms monarch larvae. *Nature, 399*, 214.

LRP Publications. (2014). *2014 Federal Manager's Guide*. Palm Beach Gardens, FL: LRP Publications.

Lucas, E. (2013). Screwed up: Hammers, nails and the Eastern Partnership. Retrieved from www.cepolicy.org/publications/screwed-hammers-nails-and-eastern-partnership.

Ludlow, N. P. (2010). Transatlantic relations in the Johnson and Nixon eras: The crisis that didn't happen – and what it suggests about the one that did. *Journal of Transatlantic Studies, 8*(1), 44–55.

Lundestad, G. (Ed.). (2003). *Just another major crisis? The United States and Europe since 2000*. Oxford: Oxford University Press.

Luthra, R. R. (2009). Temporary immigrants in a high-skilled labour market: A study of H-1Bs. *Journal of Ethnic and Migration Studies, 35*(2), 227–250.

Lynch, D., & Vogel, D. (2001). The regulation of GMOs in Europe and the United States: a case-study of contemporary European regulatory politics. *Council on Foreign Relations*. Retrieved from www.cfr.org/genetically-modified-organisms/regulation-gmos-europe-united-states-case-study-contemporary-european-regulatory-politics/p8688.

Mahony, H. (2012, March 19). Parliament gives "half-hearted" support for US data deal. *EUobserver*. Retrieved from http://euobserver.com/justice/115947.

Majone, G. (1996). *Regulating Europe*. New York: Routledge.

Majone, G. (2005). *Dilemmas of European integration: The ambiguities and pitfalls of integration by stealth*. Oxford: Oxford University Press.

Marks, G. (1993). Structural policy and multilevel governance in the EC. In A. Cafruny & G. Rosenthal (Eds.), *The state of the European Community* (pp. 391–410). Boulder, CO: Lynne Rienner.

Marler, B. (2013, March 25). Publisher's platform: Mike Taylor and the myth of Monsanto's man. *Food Safety News*. Retrieved from www.foodsafetynews.com/2013/03/publishers-platform-mike-taylor-and-the-myth-of-monsantos-man.

Marsh, D. (1998). The development of the policy network approach. In D. Marsh (Ed.), *Comparing policy networks*. Buckingham: Open University Press.

McGuire, S., & Lindeque, J. P. (2010). The diminishing returns to trade policy in the European Union. *Journal of Common Market Studies, 48*(5), 1329–1349.

McGuire, S., & Smith, M. (2008). *The European Union and the United States: Competition and convergence in the global arena.* Basingstoke: Palgrave Macmillan.

McNamara, S. (2011). European Parliament should back EU–U.S. Passenger Name Record Agreement. *WebMemo #3353.* Retrieved from www.heritage.org/research/reports/2011/09/eu-us-passenger-name-records-and-the-european-parliament.

Melman Group Research Based Strategy. (2006). The Pew initiative on food and biotechnology. Retrieved from www.pewtrusts.org/uploadedFiles/wwwpewtrustsorg/Public_Opinion/Food_and_Biotechnology/2006summary.pdf.

Meunier, S. (2005). *Trading voices: The European Union in international commercial negotiations.* Princeton, NJ: Princeton University Press.

Meunier, S., & Nicolaidis, K. (2000). EU trade policy: The exclusive versus shared competence debate. In M. Smith & M. G. Cowles (Eds.), *The state of the European Union: Risks, reform, resistance and revival* (pp. 325–346). Oxford: Oxford University Press.

Meyer, H. (2008). *The framework for advancing transatlantic economic integration: Structural shortcomings in an experimental form of international governance.* London: Global Policy Institute.

Meyer, H., & Barber, S. (2011). Making transatlantic economic relations work. *Global Policy, 2*(1), 106–111.

Midwest Research Institute. (May 2006) Transportation Research Center. Retrieved from www.mriglobal.org/Pages/Defense.aspx#trans.

Minder, R. (2013, October 28). Spain summons American Ambassador on new reports of N.S.A. spying. *New York Times.* Retrieved from www.nytimes.com/2013/10/29/world/europe/spain-calls-in-us-ambassador-in-spying-scandal.html.

Mix, D. (2010). *The European Union: Leadership changes resulting from the Lisbon Treaty R41099.* Washington, DC: Congressional Research Service.

Mix, D. (2013). *The United States and Europe: Current issues RS22163.* Washington, DC: Congressional Research Service.

MM&P Wheelhouse Weekly. (2014, March 18). *TTD applauds administration for keeping maritime out of European trade talks.* Retrieved from http://bridgedeck.org/mmp_news_archive/2014/mmp_news140318.html.

Monahan, K., & Payne, C. (2014, February 20). U.S.–EU trade talks: Why financial regulation is proving a hard nut to crack. *Bloomberg Government.* Retrieved from http://op.bna.com/bar.nsf/c2723fdcff41c72485256a55005207ad/1d182a8b391a00f285257c86000643ab/$FILE/bgovttipmonahan2_20_14.pdf.

Monti, M. (2001). Prospects for transatlantic competition policy. Policy Brief, 01-06.

Morgenson, G. (2012, March 17). Barriers to change, from Wall St. and Geneva. *New York Times.* Retrieved from www.nytimes.com/2012/03/18/business/wto-and-barriers-to-financial-change.html?_r=0.

Morris, S. H., & Spillane, C. (2010). Symposium on EU's GMO reform: EU GM regulation. A road to resolution or a regulatory roundabout? *European Journal of Risk Regulation, 4,* 359–369.

Motta, M. (2004). *Competition policy: Theory and practice.* Cambridge: Cambridge University Press.

Murphy, E. V. (2013). *CRS report for congress: Who regulates whom and how? An Overview of U.S. financial regulatory policy for banking and securities markets R43087.* Washington, DC: Congressional Research Service.

Nader, R. (1965). *Unsafe at any speed: The designed-in dangers of the American automobile.* New York: Grossman Publishers.

Nasr, V. (2013). *The dispensable nation: American foreign policy in retreat*. New York: Doubleday.

NATO. (1996). Press communique: Ministerial meeting of the North Atlantic Council, Berlin June, 3. Retrieved from www.nato.int/docu/pr/1996/p96-063e.htm.

NATO. (2013). Afghanistan troop counts. Retrieved from www.nato.int/isaf/docu/epub/pdf/placemat.pdf as of 19 February 2013.

New York Times. (2009, June 4). Text: Obama's speech in Cairo. Retrieved from www.nytimes.com/2009/06/04/us/politics/04obama.text.html?pagewanted=all&_r=0.

New York Times. (2013, December 10). Volcker Rule approved by regulators. Retrieved from www.nytimes.com/interactive/2013/12/11/business/dealbook/Volcker-Rule-Approved-by-Regulators.html?ref=financialregulatoryreform.

News Desk. (2013). Monsanto steps out of Europe's GMO line. *Food Safety News*. Retrieved from www.foodsafetynews.com/2013/07/monsanto-steps-out-of-europes-gmo-line/#.UtYrEvRDt8E.

Nicolaidis, K. (2005). Power of the powerless. In T. Linberg (Ed.), *Beyond paradise and power: Europe, America and the future of a troubled partnership* (pp. 93–120). London: Routledge.

Nino, M. (2010). The protection of personal data in the fight against terrorism: New perspectives of PNR European Union instruments in the light of the Treaty of Lisbon. *Utrecht Law Review, 61*(1), 62–85.

Norris, F. (2012, May 10). The case for global accounting. *New York Times*. Retrieved from www.nytimes.com/2012/05/11/business/the-case-for-global-accounting-rules.html?pagewanted=1&_r=0.

Novak, T. (2014). The impact of the TTIP on the V4 region: Trade and investment opportunities. Retrieved from http://centraleuropenow.blogspot.com/2014/08/the-impact-of-ttip-on-v4-region-trade.html.

Nugent, N. (2001). *The European Commission*. Basingstoke: Palgrave Macmillan.

Nugent, N. (2010). *Government and politics of the European Union* (7th ed.). Basingstoke: Palgrave Macmillan.

Nuland, V. (2008). U.S. Ambassador to NATO Victoria Nuland's speech in Paris: Ambassador discusses strengthening global security for Europe. Retrieved from http://usinfo.state.gov.

Nye, J. (2011, December 6). Obama's Pacific pivot. *Project Syndicate*.

Obama, B. (2008). Barack Obama speech from Berlin, Germany, July 24. Retrieved from www.youtube.com/watch?v=Q-9ry38AhbU.

Obama, B. (2009). Barack Obama, speech on disarmament in Prague, the Czech Republic, April, 5. Retrieved from www.youtube.com/watch?v=uYcAr0ZDSlg.

Office of Science Coordination and Policy Biotechnology Team. (n.d.). Biotechnology activities. Retrieved from www.epa.gov/scipoly/biotech/pubs/bioactivities.htm.

Office of the United States Trade Representative. (2012). Promoting US EC Regulatory compatibility: Requests for comments. Retrieved from www.regulations.gov/#!documentDetail;D=USTR-2012-0028-0001 and http://ec.europa.eu/enterprise/policies/international/cooperating-governments/usa/jobs-growth/consultation-on-regulatory-issues_en.htm.

Office of the United States Trade Representative. (2013a, March 20). Letter to John Boehner, Speaker of the United States House of Representatives, March 20. Retrieved from www.ustr.gov/sites/default/files/03202013%20TTIP%20Notification%20Letter.PDF.

Office of the United States Trade Representative. (2013b). Obama Administration Notifies Congress of Intent to Negotiate Transatlantic Trade and Investment Partnership.

Press release. Retrieved from www.ustr.gov/about-us/press-office/press-releases/2013/march/administration-notifies-congress-ttip.

Office of the United States Trade Representative. (2014a). *Fact sheet: U.S. objectives, U.S. benefits in the Transatlantic Trade and Investment Partnership: a detailed view.* Washington, DC: Retrieved from www.ustr.gov/about-us/press-office/press-releases/2014/March/US-Objectives-US-Benefits-In-the-TTIP-a-Detailed-View.

Office of the United States Trade Representative. (2014b, March 27). Stakeholder consultations, investment and the TTIP. Retrieved from www.ustr.gov/about-us/press-office/blog/2014/March/Stakeholder-Consultations-Investment-and-the-TTIP.

Office of the United States Trade Representative. (2014c). Statement by U.S. Trade Representative Froman on the conclusion of the fifth round of TTIP negotiations. Retrieved from www.ustr.gov/about-us/press-office/press-releases/2014/May/Statement-by-USTR-Froman-on-Conclusion-of-Fifth-Round-TTIP-Negotiations.

OICU-IOSCO. (2014). About IOSCO. Retrieved from www.iosco.org/about/.

Olick, D. (2014). Mortgage rates fall but big banks doing less: Here's why. *CNBC.* Retrieved from www.cnbc.com/id/101576092.

Olson, M. (1965). *The logic of collective action: Public goods and the theory of groups.* Cambridge, MA: Harvard University Press.

Ostrower, J., & Van Hasselt, C. (2013, March 6). Bombardier challenges Boeing, Airbus. *Wall Street Journal.* Retrieved from http://online.wsj.com/article/SB10001424127887323628804578344680140395980.html.

Page, B., & Shapiro, R. (1992). *The rational public: Fifty years of trends in America's policy preferences.* Chicago, IL: University of Chicago Press.

Pan, E. J. (2008). Creating an advantage in global capital markets. Retrieved from www.uiowa.edu/~tlcp/TLCP%20Articles/19-3/pan.finalfinal.jyz.121610.pdf.

Panichi, J. (2013). How big tobacco's divide-and-conquer strategy exposed the EU's flaws. *Inside story: Current affairs and culture from Australia and beyond.* Retrieved from http://inside.org.au/brussels-tobacco/.

Panichi, J. (2014). Philip Morris, Australia and the fate of Europe's trade talks. *Inside Story: Current Affairs and Culture from Australia and Beyond.* Retrieved from http://inside.org.au/philip-morris-australia-and-the-fate-of-europes-trade-talks/.

Pardo, R. (2014). ISDS and TTIP: A miracle cure for a systematic challenge? *Policy Brief,* (July). www.epc.eu/documents/uploads/pub_4637_isds_&_ttip_-_a_miracle_cure_for_a_systemic_challenge.pdf.

Parker, R., & Alemanno, A. (2014). Towards effective regulatory cooperation under TTIP: A comparative overview of the EU and US legislative and regulatory systems. Retrieved from http://trade.ec.europa.eu/doclib/html/152466.htm.

Patterson, L. A., & Josling, T. (2002). Regulating biotechnology: Comparing EU and US approaches. University of Pittsburgh Center of Excellence European Policy Paper series. Retrieved from www.ucis.pitt.edu/euce/pub/policy.html.

Patton, C. (2008). No man's land: The E.U.–U.S. Passenger Name Record Agreement and what it means for the European Union's pillar structure. *The George Washington International Law Review, 40*(2), 527–551.

Pawlak, P. (2007). From hierarchy to networks: Transatlantic governance of homeland security. *Journal of Global Change and Governance, 1*(1), 1–22.

Pawlak, P. (2009). Network politics in transatlantic homeland security cooperation. *Perspectives on European Politics and Society, 10*(4), 560–581.

Pelkmans, J. (2005). Mutual recognition in goods and services: An economic perspective. In F. Kostoris & P. Schioppa (Eds.), *The Principles of Mutual Recognition in the European integration process* (pp. 83–128). Basingstoke: Palgrave Macmillan.

Pells, R. (1997). *Not like us: How Europeans have loved, hated, and transformed American culture since World War II*. New York: Harper Collins.

Peterson, J. (1996). *Europe and America: The prospects for partnership* (2nd ed.). London: Routledge.

Peterson, J. (2003). The US and Europe in the Balkans. In J. Peterson & M. Pollack (Eds.), *Europe, America, Bush: Transatlantic relations in the twenty-first century* (pp. 85–98). London: Routledge.

Peterson, J., & Pollack, M. (2003a). Introduction: Europe, America, Bush. In M. Pollack & J. Peterson (Eds.), *Europe, America, Bush: Transatlantic relations in the twenty-first century* (pp. 1–12). New York: Routledge.

Peterson, J., & Pollack, M. (Eds.). (2003b). *Europe, America, Bush: Transatlantic relations in the twenty-first century*. New York: Routledge.

Peterson, J., & Steffenson, R. (2009). Transatlantic institutions: Can partnership be engineered? *The British Journal of Politics & International Relations, 11*(1), 25–45.

Pew Initiative on Food and Biotechnology. (2007). Fact sheet: Genetically modified crops in the United States. www.pewtrusts.org/uploadedFiles/wwwpewtrustsorg/Fact_Sheets/Food_and_Biotechnology/PIFB_Genetically_Modified_Crops_Factsheet0804.pdf.

Pew Trust. (2001). Guide to U.S. regulation of genetically modified food and agricultural biotechnology products. *Pew Initiative on Food and Biotechnology* Retrieved from www.pewtrusts.org/uploadedFiles/wwwpewtrustsorg/Reports/Food_and_Biotechnology/hhs_biotech_0901.pdf.

Phillipart, E., & Winand, P. (Eds.). (2001). *Ever-closer partnership: Policy-making in US–EU relations*. Brussels: Peter Lang.

Pinder, J. (1968). Positive integration and negative integration: Some problems of Economic Union in the EC. *World Today, 24*(3), 89–110.

Polanyi, K. (1944). *The great transformation: The political and economic origins of our time*. New York: Beacon Press.

Politi, J., & Chaffin, J. (2013, April 17). US–EU talks: cuts both ways. *Financial Times*. Retrieved from www.ft.com/intl/cms/s/0/8d9d0c72-a6c1-11e2-885b-00144feabdc0.html#axzz2YwGgarKw.

Pollack, M. (2003). *The Engines of European integration*. Oxford: Oxford University Press.

Pollack, M. (2005). The new transatlantic agenda at ten: Reflections on an experiment in international governance. *Journal of Common Market Studies, 43*(5), 899–919.

Pollack, M., & Schaffer, G. (2001a). Transatlantic governance in the historical and theoretical perspective. In M. Pollack & G. Schaffer (Eds.), *Transatlantic Governance in the Global Economy* (pp. 3–42). Latham, MD: Rowman & Littlefield.

Pollack, M., & Schaffer, G. (Eds.). (2001b). *Transatlantic Governance in the Global Economy*. Latham, MD: Rowman & Littlefield.

Pollack, M., & Schaffer, G. (2009). *When cooperation fails: The international law and politics of genetically modified foods*. Oxford: Oxford University Press.

Pollack, M., & Schaffer, G. (2010). Biotechnology policy. In H. Wallace, M. Pollack, & A. R. Young (Eds.), *Policy-Making in the European Union* (6th ed., pp. 330–355). Oxford: Oxford University Press.

Pond, E. (2003). *Friendly fire: The new-death of the transatlantic alliance*. Washington, DC: Brookings Institution and European Union Studies Association.

Pop, V. (2010, March 27). EU–US Summits to take place "Only When Necessary." *EUobserver.com*. Retrieved from http://euobserver.com/foreign/29782.

Pop, V. (2011a, April 19). Privacy campaigner: EU–US Passenger Data Deal "Meaningless." *EUobserver*. Retrieved from http://euobserver.com/justice/114311.

Pop, V. (2011b, September 16). US lawmakers shun EU model on data privacy. *EUobserver*. Retrieved from http://euobserver.com/economic/113653.

Powell, D. (1999). Seminal paper on agricultural biotechnology: A summary of the science. Retrieved from http://foodsafety.k-state.edu/articles/42/ag_biotech_summary.pdf.

PriceWaterhouseCoopers. (2010). Understanding the Dodd–Frank Act. Retrieved from www.pwc.com/us/en/view/issue-13/understanding-the-dodd-frank-act.jhtml.

Putnam, R. (1988). Diplomacy and domestic politics: the logic of two-level games *International Organization, 42*, 427–460.

Putnam, R. D. (1995). *Bowling Alone: The collapse and revival of American community.* New York: Simon & Schuster.

Quaglia, L. (2013). Financial regulation and supervision in the European Union after the crisis. *Journal of Economic Policy Reform, 16*(1), 17–30.

Rees, W. (2011). *The US–EU security relationship.* Basingstoke: Palgrave Macmillan.

Reis, C. (2013). Ambassador Charles Reis in a lecture delivered at The Johns Hopkins University School of Advanced International Studies Distinguished Speaker Series, Washington, DC, April 9.

Restad, H. E. (2012). Old paradigms die hard in political science: US foreign policy and American exceptionalism. *American Political Thought, 1*(1), 53–72.

Rettman, A. (2010). US blames Lisbon treaty for EU summit fiasco. *EUobserver*. http://euobserver.com/18/29398.

Rifkin, J. (2004). *The European dream: How Europe's vision of the future is quietly eclipsing the American dream.* New York: Penguin.

Risse, T. (2008). Conclusions. In J. Anderson, J. G. Ikenberry, & T. Risse (Eds.), *The end of the west? Crisis and change in the Atlantic order* (pp. 263–290). Ithaca, NY: Cornell University Press.

Risse, T. (2012). Determinants and features of international alliances and structural partnerships. The Transatlantic Relationship and the Future of Global Governance, Working Paper (2). Retrieved from www.transworld-fp7.eu/?cat=13.

Rolet, X. (2012, July 10). Unleash the power of equity finance. *Financial Times.* Retrieved from www.ft.com/intl/cms/s/0/8e40639e-c45a-11e1-9c1e-00144feabdc0.html#axzz2rk7vBCEZ.

Röller, L.-H., & Buigues, P. A. (2005). The office of the Chief Competition Economist at the European Commission, DG Competition. Retrieved from http://ec.europa.eu/dgs/competition/economist/officechiefecon_ec.pdf.

Rosch, J. T. (2012, June 8). Can consumer welfare promote transatlantic convergence in competition law and policy? Remarks made at Concurrences Conference on Consumer Choice: An emerging standard for competition law. Retrieved from www.ftc.gov/speeches/rosch/120608consumerchoice.pdf.

Rose, R. (1985). *How exceptional is American government?* Glasgow: University of Strathclyde.

Rozbicka, P. (2013). Advocacy coalitions: Influencing the policy process in the EU. *Journal of European Public Policy, 20*(6), 838–853.

RT Question More. (2013). No more GMO: Monsanto drops bid to approve new crops in Europe. Retrieved from http://rt.com/news/monsanto-europe-gmo-food-309/.

Ruggie, J. (1994). Third try at world order? America and multilateralism after the Cold War. *Political Science Quarterly, 109*(4), 553–567.

Saadet, L., & Ballard, S. (2007). Department of Homeland Security addresses critics. *Data Protection Law and Policy, 11*, 4–6.

Sachs, J. (2011). *The price of civilization: Economics and ethics after the fall.* London: The Bodley Head.

Sackur, S. (2001). Bush wins no friends in Gothenberg. *BBC News Service.*

Sargent, T. J. (2011). United States then, Europe now. *The Sveriges Riksbank Prize in Economic Sciences in Memory of Alfred Nobel 2011.* Retrieved from www.nobelprize. org/nobel_prizes/economics/laureates/2011/sargent-lecture.html.

Scharpf, F. W. (1999). *Governing in Europe: Effective and democratic?* Oxford: Oxford University Press.

Schattschneider, E. E. (1960). *The semisovereign people: A realist's view of democracy in America.* New York: Holt, Rinehart and Winston.

Scherer, F. M. (1994). *Competition policies for an integrated world economy.* Washington, DC: The Brookings Institution.

Schmitz, G. P. (2013). State of the Union: Obama backs trans-atlantic trade deal with EU. *Speigel Online International.* Retrieved from www.spiegel.de/international/world/us-president-obama-backs-trans-atlantic-free-trade-agreement-with-eu-a-883104.html.

Schneidmiller, C. (2012). Homeland Security to extend cargo nuclear scanning deadline. *Global Security Newswire.* Retrieved from www.nti.org/gsn/article/homeland-security-extend-nuclear-scanning-deadline/.

Schott, J. J., & Cimino, C. (2013). *Crafting a Transatlantic Trade and Investment Partnership: What can be done.* Washington, DC: Peterson Institute for International Economics.

Schott, J. J., & Oegg, B. (2001). Europe and the Americas: Toward a TAFTA-South? *World Economy, 24*(6), 745–759.

Schrader, C. (2006). Passenger Name Record: Undermining the democratic right of citizens? *Social Alternatives, 25*(3), 44–49.

Sengupta, S. (2014, September 12). Nations trying to stop their citizens from going to Middle East to fight for ISIS. *New York Times.* Retrieved from www.nytimes.com/2014/09/13/world/middleeast/isis-recruits-prompt-laws-against-foreign-fighters.html?_r=0.

Serfaty, S. (2005). *The vital partnership: Power and order. America and Europe beyond Iraq.* Lanham, MD: Rowman and Littlefield.

Serfaty, S. (Ed.). (2008). *A recast partnership? Institutional dimensions of transatlantic relations.* Washington, DC: Center for Strategic and International Studies Press.

Shaffer, E. R., Waitzkin, H., Brenner, J., & Jasso-Aguilar, R. (2005). Global trade and public health. *American Journal of Public Health, 95*(1), 23–34.

Shapiro, J., & Witney, N. (2009). *Towards a post-American Europe: A power audit of EU–US relations.* London: European Council on Foreign Relations.

Sharma, R. D. (2002). Conceptual foundations of administrative culture: an attempt at analysis of some variables. *International Review of Sociology, 12,* 65–75.

Sinan, I. M., & Laciak, C. A. (2004). Current issues in transatlantic competition cooperation. *The European Antitrust Review.* www.morganlewis.com/pubs/Sinan_EU-US-Cooperation04.pdf.

Slaughter, A.-M. (1997). The real new world order. *Foreign Affairs,* September/October, 183–197.

Slaughter, A.-M. (2005). *New world order.* Princeton, NJ: Princeton University Press.

Slaughter, A.-M. (2009). America's edge: Power in the networked century. *Foreign Affairs, 88* (January/February): 94–113.

Sloan, S. R. (2011). The war on terror and transatlantic relations: Reflections and projections. *Atlantic Perspective, 6,* 4–9.

Smale, A. (2014, February 7). Leaked recordings lay bare E.U. and U.S. divisions in goals for Ukraine. *New York Times.* Retrieved from www.nytimes.com/2014/02/08/world/europe/ukraine.html?_r=0.

Smith, J. (2007). Statement of Ms Julianne Smith before the House Committee on Foreign Affairs: Subcommittee on international organizations, human rights, and oversight and subcommittee on Europe (April 17). www.fas.org/irp/congress/2007_hr/rendition.pdf.

Smith, J. M. (2007). *Genetic roulette: The documented health risks of genetically engineered foods* (4th ed.). Portland, ME: Yes! Books.

Smith, M. (2009). Transatlantic economic relations in a changing global political economy: Achieving togetherness but missing the bus? *The British Journal of Politics and International Relations, 11*(1), 94–107.

Smolar, E. (2011, June 7). Transatlantic relations and NATO. *European View, 10*, 127–135.

Speigel Online. (2007). Trans-atlantic free trade? Merkel calls for closer EU–US cooperation. *Speigel Online*. Retrieved from www.spiegel.de/international/trans-atlantic-free-trade-merkel-calls-for-closer-eu-us-cooperation-a-462160.html.

Stefanova, R. (2001). *The New Transatlantic Agenda: Facing the challenges of global governance*. Aldershot: Ashgate.

Steffenson, R. (2005). *Managing EU–US relations: Actors, institutions and the new transatlantic agenda*. Manchester: Manchester University Press.

Steinberg, J. (2003). An elective partnership: Salvaging transatlantic relations. *Survival, 45*(2): 113–146.

Steinmo, S., & Kopstein, J. (2008). Growing apart? America and Europe in the twenty-first century. In S. Steinmo & J. Kopstein (Eds.), *Growing apart? America and Europe in the twenty-first century* (pp. 1–23). Cambridge: Cambridge University Press.

Stelzenmuller, C. (2010). End of a honeymoon: Obama and Europe one year later. *Brussels Forum Papers, March*. Retrieved from www.gmfus.org/brusselsforum/2010/doc/BF2010-Paper-Stelzenmuller.pdf.

Stiglitz, J. (2013a). The free-trade charade. *Project Syndicate*. Retrieved from www.project-syndicate.org/commentary/transatlantic-and-transpacific-free-trade-trouble-by-joseph-e-stiglitz.

Stiglitz, J. (2013b). *The price of inequality* Harmondsworth: Allen Lane.

Sutton, K. (2014). TTIP negotiations: A summary of rounds 4 and 5. Retrieved from www.bfna.org/sites/default/files/publications/BBrief%20TTIP%20Summary%20Round%204-5%20(12June2014).pdf.

Swanson, E. (2013). GMO poll finds huge majority say foods should be labeled. *Huffington Post*.

Szydarowski, W., & Tallberg, P. (2013). Multi-level governance: A European experience and key success factors for transport corridors and transborder integration areas. Retrieved from www.transgovernance.eu/media/322637/bsr_transgov_task_3_2_final_9_apr_2013.pdf.

Tanaka, H., Bellanova, R., Ginsburg, S., & Hert, P. D. (2010). *Transatlantic information sharing: At a crossroads*. Washington, DC: Migration Policy Institute.

Taylor, L., & Von Arnim, R. (2007). *Modelling the impact of trade liberalisation: A critique of computable general equilibrium models*. Oxford: Oxfam.

Taylor, M. (2014). Unions say planned international trade deal poses threat to NHS. *Guardian*. www.theguardian.com/business/2014/sep/07/trade-unions-trade-deal-threat-to-nhs.

Testimony Concerning "International Harmonization of Wall Street Reform: Orderly Liquidation, Derivatives, and the Volcker Rule" by Commissioner Elisse B. Walter, U.S. Securities and Exchange Commission, US Senate (2012).

Tocci, N., & Alcaro, R. (2012). Three scenarios for the future of the transatlantic relationship. The Transatlantic Relationship and the Future Global Governance, working paper (4). Retrieved from: www.transworld-fp7.eu/wp-content/uploads/2012/10/TW_WP_04.pdf.

Torfing, J., & Triantafillou, P. (2012). *What's in a name? Grasping new public governance as a political-administrative system.* Paper presented at the 8th Transatlantic Dialogue Conference, Nijmegen, the Netherlands.

Transatlantic Business Council. (2013a). EU and US call for input on regulatory issues for possible future trade agreement; sector specific submission on financial services, January 14.

Transatlantic Business Council. (2013b). History and mission. Retrieved from http://transatlanticbusiness.org/history-mission.

Transatlantic Business Council. (2013c). Statement of Tim Bennett, Director-General of the Transatlantic Business Council before the EU–US High Level Regulatory Cooperation Council.

Transatlantic Business Dialogue. (2010). EU–U.S. financial markets: Need for cooperation in difficult times.

Transatlantic Business Dialogue. (2012). *TABD position paper: Financial market integration.* Brussels and Washington: Transatlantic Business Dialogue.

Transatlantic Consumer Dialogue. (2013a). EU and US consumer groups' initial reaction to the announcement of a Transatlantic Trade and Investment Partnership. Retrieved from http://tacd.org/index2.php?option=com_docman&task=doc_view&gid=353&Itemid=40.

Transatlantic Consumer Dialogue. (2013b). *Resolution on Trade Rules and Financial Regulation.*

Transatlantic Economic Council. (2007). *Review of Progress Under the Framework for Advancing Transatlantic Economic Integration between the United States of America and the European Union.* Retrieved from http://ec.europa.eu/enterprise/policies/international/files/tec_progress_report_en.pdf.

Transatlantic Economic Council. (2014). Transatlantic Economic Council. Retrieved from www.state.gov/p/eur/rt/eu/tec/index.htm.

Transatlantic Legislators' Dialogue. (2013). Joint Statement 74th Inter-Parliamentary Meeting, European Parliament – US House of Representatives Dublin, May 31–June 1.

Transatlantic Policy Network. (2013, July 13). TPN report: completing the strategic vision – the next step in a beautiful friendship. Retrieved from www.tpnonline.org/WP/wp-content/uploads/2013/09/TPN_Report_Final_13_07_09l.pdf.

Traynor, I. (2013, October 17). New EU rules to curb transfer of data to US after Edward Snowden revelations. *Guardian.* Retrieved from www.theguardian.com/world/2013/oct/17/eu-rules-data-us-edward-snowden.

Tyrell, I. (1991). American exceptionalism in an age of international history. *American Historical Review, 96*(October), 32–55.

UK Parliament. (2009). Documents considered by the committee on November 4, 2009 – European Scrutiny Committee contents. Retrieved from www.publications.parliament.uk/pa/cm200809/cmselect/cmeuleg/19xxx/1905.htm.

UNECE – World Forum for Harmonization of Vehicle Regulations. (n.d.). Introduction. Retrieved from www.unece.org/trans/main/wp29/introduction.html.

UNECE – World Forum for Harmonization of Vehicle Regulations. (2011). Informal document WP.29-155-38.

United Nations Economic Commission for Europe. (2012). WP.29: How it works, how to join it. Retrieved from www.unece.org/trans/main/wp29/publications/other_vehicles.html.

United States and the European Union. (2005). *Initiative to Enhance Transatlantic Economic Integration and Growth (IETEIG).* Retrieved from http://ec.europa.eu/enterprise/policies/international/files/economic_initiative_summit_05_en.pdf.

United States Mission to the European Union. (1998). *Transatlantic partnership: Action plan.*

United States Mission to the European Union – Foreign Agricultural Service. (2014). Veterinary equivalency agreement. Retrieved from www.usda-eu.org/trade-with-the-eu/trade-agreements/veterinary-equivalency-agreement.

Urbina, I. (2014, January 25). The shopping list as policy tool, news analysis. *New York Times.* Retrieved from www.nytimes.com/2014/01/26/sunday-review/the-shopping-list-as-policy-tool.html?hp&rref=opinion&_r=0.

US–EU High Level Working Group on Jobs and Growth. (2013). *Final Report of the U.S.-EU High Level Working Group on Jobs and Growth.*

US Department of Commerce – International Trade Administration. (2011). Notice. *Federal Register, 76*(85).

US Department of Agriculture – APHIS. (2013). Questions and answers: BSE comprehensive rule. Retrieved from www.aphis.usda.gov/publications/animal_health/2013/faq_bse_rule_final.pdf.

US Department of Agriculture. (2014). 2014 farm bill highlights. Retrieved from www.usda.gov/documents/usda-2014-farm-bill-highlights.pdf.

US Department of Commerce – International Trade Administration. (2011). Request for public comments concerning regulatory cooperation between the United States and the European Union that would help eliminate or reduce unnecessary divergences in regulation and in standards used in regulation that impede U.S. Exports. Retrieved from www.regulations.gov/#!docketBrowser;rpp=25;po=0;D=ITA-2011-0006.

US Department of Health and Human Services and European Commission. (2010). *Cooperation surrounding health related information and communication technologies.*

US Department of Homeland Security. (n.d.). Cargo screening. Retrieved from www.dhs.gov/cargo-screening.

US Department of Homeland Security. (2012). Container security initiative ports. Retrieved from www.dhs.gov/container-security-initiative-ports.

US Department of Justice. (2010). U.S./EU Agreements on mutual legal assistance and extradition enter into force. Retrieved from www.justice.gov/opa/pr/2010/February/10-opa-108.html.

US Department of Labor. (1998). American Competitiveness and Workforce Improvement Act of 1998. PL 105-277, 112 Stat 2681, 2681-640. Retrieved from www.oalj.dol.gov/PUBLIC/INA/REFERENCES/STATUTES/ACWIA.HTM.

US Department of State. (n.d.). Stakeholders and advisors of the Transatlantic Economic Council. Retrieved from www.state.gov/p/eur/rt/eu/tec/c33632.htm.

US Department of State. (2009a). Briefing on U.S.–EU Energy Council, November 4. Retrieved from www.state.gov/s/eee/rmk/131402.htm.

US Department of State. (2009b). Transatlantic Economic Council: Annex 2 – joint report on U.S.–EU Financial Markets Regulatory Dialogue for the TEC Meeting. Retrieved from www.state.gov/p/eur/rls/or/131045.htm.

US Department of State. (2011). Current workplan of the Transatlantic Council. Retrieved from www.state.gov/p/eur/rt/eu/tec/c33533.htm.

US Department of State – Office of the Historian. (2009a). President Barack Obama's travel, March 31–April 7. Retrieved from http://history.state.gov/departmenthistory/travels/president/obama-barack.

US Department of State – Office of the Historian. (2009b). Travels of Secretary of State Hillary Rodham Clinton. Retrieved from http://history.state.gov/departmenthistory/travels/secretary/clinton-hillary-rodham.

US Department of Transportation. (n.d.). Federal programs relations to transportation and climate change. Retrieved from http://climate.dot.gov/policies-legislation-programs/federal-org-directory.html.

US Department of Transportation. (2013). *Agency financial report: Fiscal year 2013.* Retrieved from www.dot.gov/sites/dot.gov/files/docs/508-AFR2013.pdf.

US Department of Transportation. (2014). Fact sheet: Grow America. Retrieved from www.dot.gov/grow-america/fact-sheets/overview.

US Department of Transportation – Federal Highway Administration. (n.d.). How long is the interstate system? Retrieved from www.fhwa.dot.gov/interstate/faq.htm#question3.

US Department of Transportation – Federal Highway Administration. (2004). Traffic safety information systems in Europe and Australia.

US Department of Transportation – Federal Railroad Administration. (2009). High-speed rail strategic plan. Retrieved from www.fra.dot.gov/eLib/Details/L02833.

US Department of Transportation – Maritime Administration. (2010, October 26). Groundbreaking ceremony signals start of "green" marine highway project. Retrieved from www.marad.dot.gov/news_room_landing_page/news_releases_summary/news_release/DOT_191-10_news_release.htm.

US Department of Transportation – Office of the Historian. (2009, March 1). The United States Department of Transportation: A brief history. Retrieved from http://ntl.bts.gov/historian/history.htm.

US Department of Treasury. (2008). *Blueprint for a modernized financial regulatory structure.* Retrieved from www.treasury.gov/press-center/press-releases/Documents/Blueprint.pdf.

US Department of Treasury. (2012). EU–U.S. insurance dialogue project. Retrieved from www.treasury.gov/initiatives/fio/EU-US%20Insurance%20Project/Pages/default.aspx.

US Department of Treasury. (2014). U.S.–EU Financial Markets Regulatory Dialogue joint statement: July 11, 2014. Press release. Retrieved from www.treasury.gov/press-center/press-releases/Pages/jl2564.aspx.

US House of Representatives (2011). Dodd–Frank burden tracker. Retrieved from http://financialservices.house.gov/uploadedfiles/dodd-frank_pra_spreadsheet_7-9-2012.pdf.

US Office of Inspector General. (2011). *Inspection of the Bureau of European and Eurasian Affairs for the United States Department of State and the Broadcasting Board of Directors, Report Number ISP-I-11-22.* Retrieved from http://oig.state.gov/documents/organization/161095.pdf.

US Office of Management and Budget. (n.d.). United States–European Union High-Level Regulatory Cooperation Forum. Retrieved from www.whitehouse.gov/omb/oira_irc_europe.

US Office of Personnel Management (n.d.). "Work-Life." From www.opm.gov/policy-data-oversight/worklife.

US Office of Personnel Management. (2010). *Federal human capital survey.* Washington, DC: Office of Personnel Management.

US Office of Science and Technology Policy. (1986). *Coordinated Framework for Regulation of Biotechnology.* Washington, DC: Retrieved from www.aphis.usda.gov/brs/fedregister/coordinated_framework.pdf.

US Patent and Trademark Office. (n.d.). *Geographical indication protection in the United States.*

US Senate Committee on Banking Housing and Urban Affairs. (2010). Brief summary of the Dodd–Frank Wall Street reform and Consumer Protection Act. Retrieved from www.banking.senate.gov/public/_files/070110_Dodd_Frank_Wall_Street_Reform_comprehensive_summary_Final.pdf.

US Senator Pat Roberts. (2014). Letter signed by 45 U.S. Senators to Tom Vilsack,

Secretary, US Department of Agriculture and Michael Froman, USTR, April 4 Opposing Geographical Indication Restrictions Promoted by the European Union through the TTIP, Washington, DC.

USCIS. (2000). American Competitiveness in the Twenty-first Century Act of 2000. Retrieved from www.uscis.gov/sites/default/files/ilink/docView/PUBLAW/HTML/PUBLAW/0–0-0-22204.html.

Van Rompuy, H. (2012). Europe on the World Stage, speech to Chatham House, London, May 31.

Vandystadt, N., & d'Imécourt, L. V. (2013). 14 EU culture ministers seek to exempt audiovisual sector. *Europolitics*. Retrieved from http://europolitics.eis-vt-prod-web01.cyberadm.net/social/14-eu-culture-ministers-seek-to-exempt-audiovisual-sector-art351248-22.html.

Verdier, P.-H. (2009). Transnational regulatory networks and their limits. *Yale Journal of International Law, 34*, 113–172.

Vernon, R. (1998). *In the hurricane's eye: The troubled prospects of multinational enterprises*. Cambridge, MA: Harvard University Press.

Vidal, G. (1998). The Salon Interview: Gore Vidal, January 14.

Vieuws. (2014, May 12). US Ambassador Anthony L. Gardner to Debunk the TTIP myths. Retrieved from www.vieuws.eu/foreign-affairs/us-ambassador-anthony-l-gardner-to-debunk-the-ttip-myths.

Vogel, D. (1995). *Trading Up: Consumer and Environmental Regulation in a Global Economy*. Cambridge, MA: Harvard University Press.

Vogel, D. (2012). *The politics of precaution: Regulating health, safety, and environmental risks in Europe and the United States*. Princeton, NJ: Princeton University Press.

Vogel, D., & Swinnen, J. F. M. (Eds.). (2011). *Transatlantic regulatory cooperation: The shifting roles of the EU, the US and California*. Northampton, MA: Edward Elgar Publishing Limited.

Vogel, T. (2013, December 19). MEPS to ask for suspension of EU-US data exchanges. *European Voice*. Retrieved from www.europeanvoice.com/article/imported/meps-to-ask-for-suspension-of-eu-us-data-exchanges/79123.aspx.

Wald, M. L. (2014). U.S. agency knew about G.M. Flaw but did not act. *New York Times*. Retrieved from www.nytimes.com/2014/03/31/business/us-regulators-declined-full-inquiry-into-gm-ignition-flaws-memo-shows.html?_r=0.

Walker, S. (2013, December 8). Ukraine protestors topple Lenin statute in Kiev. *Guardian*. Retrieved from www.theguardian.com/world/2013/dec/08/ukraine-opposition-viktor-yanukovych-european-integration.

Warren, Z. (2014, January 14). Major agricultural companies sue to overturn Hawaiian GMO-restrictive law. *Inside Counsel*. Retrieved from www.insidecounsel.com/2014/01/14/major-agricultural-companies-sue-to-overturn-hawai.

Weidenfeld, W. (1996). *American and Europe: Is the break inevitable?* Gutesloh: Bertelsmann Foundation Publishers.

Weiler, J. H. H. (2014, April 10). Europe's fateful choices. *European Voice*. Retrieved from www.europeanvoice.com/CWS/Index.aspx?PageID=214&articleID=80502.

White House. (2013). The 2013 State of the Union. Retrieved from www.whitehouse.gov/state-of-the-union-2013.

White House – Office of the Press Secretary. (2013). Statement from United States President Barack Obama, European Council President Herman Van Rompuy and European Commission President José Manuel Barroso, February 13. Press release. Retrieved from www.whitehouse.gov/the-press-office/2013/02/13/statement-united-states-president-barack-obama-european-council-presiden.

Wilber, V., & Eichbrecht, P. (2008). *Transatlantic trade, the automotive sector: The Role of regulation in a global industry, where we have been and where we need to go, how far can EU–US cooperation go toward achieving regulatory harmonization.* Paper presented at the German Marshall Fund Academic Policy Research Conference, Ford School, University of Michigan.

Wildavsky, A. B. (1988). *Searching for safety.* New Brunswick: Transaction Publishers.

Wilson, G. (1985). *The politics of safety and health.* Oxford: Oxford University Press.

Winters, L. A. (2009). Skilled labor mobility in post-war Europe. In J. Bhagwati & G. Hanson (Eds.), *Skilled immigration today* (pp. 53–80). New York: Oxford University Press.

Wishart, I. (2011, June 9). The regulation race. *European Voice.* Retrieved from www.europeanvoice.com/article/imported/the-regulation-race/71327.aspx.

Wishart, I. (2013, June 17). Deal reached on markets legislation. *European Voice.* Retrieved from www.europeanvoice.com/article/2013/june/deal-reached-on-markets-legislation/77554.aspx.

Wolf, R. (2009, April 5). Obama's European trip a success – and a reality check. *USA Today.*

Woolcock, S. (2007). Regional economic diplomacy: The European Union. In N. Bayne & S. Woolcock (Eds.), *The New Economic Diplomacy* (2nd ed., pp. 221–240). Burlington, VT: Ashgate.

World Health Organization. (2010). 20 questions on genetically modified (GM) foods. Retrieved from www.who.int/foodsafety/en/.

World Health Organization. (2012). Variant Creutzfeldt-Jakob Disease: fact sheet No. 180. Retrieved from www.who.int/mediacentre/factsheets/fs180/en/.

World Trade Organization. (1995a). The WTO Agreement on the Application of Sanitary and Phytosanitary Measures (SPS Agreement) – text of the agreement. Retrieved from www.wto.org/english/tratop_e/sps_e/spsagr_e.htm.

World Trade Organization. (1995b). Geographical indications. Retrieved from www.wto.org/english/tratop_e/trips_e/gi_e.htm.

World Trade Organization. (1997). Successful conclusion of the WTO's financial service negotiations. *WTO News.*

World Trade Organization. (2008). Dispute settlement: DS291 European communities – measures affecting the approval and marketing of biotech products. Retrieved from www.wto.org/english/tratop_e/dispu_e/cases_e/ds291_e.htm.

World Trade Organization. (2013a). Days 3, 4 and 5: Round-the-clock consultations produce "Bali Package." *News and Events.* Retrieved from www.wto.org/english/news_e/news13_e/mc9sum_07dec13_e.htm.

World Trade Organization. (2013b). *World Trade Profiles April.* Retrieved June 5, 2013, from http://stat.wto.org/CountryProfile/WSDBCountryPFReporter.aspx?Language=E.

World Trade Organization. (2013c). WTO trade profiles, April. Retrieved from http://stat.wto.org/CountryProfile/WSDBCountryPFReporter.aspx?Language=E.

World Trade Organization. (2014a). Agreement on government procurement. Retrieved from www.wto.org/english/tratop_e/gproc_e/gp_gpa_e.htm.

World Trade Organization. (2014b). Annex I, WTO government procurement agreement.

World Trade Organization. (2014c). USA Annex 2, Sub-central entities which procure in accordance with the provisions of this agreement.

Wytkind, E. (2013). Viewpoint: Keep air transport out of U.S.–EU trade talks. *Aviation Week.* Retrieved from www.aviationweek.com/Article.aspx?id=/article-xml/awx_08_05_2013_p0-604029.xml&p=1.

Young, A. R. (2009). Confounding conventional wisdom: Political not principled differences in the transatlantic regulatory relationship. *The British Journal of Politics & International Relations, 11*(4), 666–689.

Young, A. R., & Peterson, J. (2006). The EU and the new trade politics. *Journal of European Public Policy, 13*(6), 795–814.

Zahariadis, N. (2008). *State subsidies in the global economy*. Basingstoke: Palgrave Macmillan.

Zandonini, M. (2012). The EU and US partnership in search of leadership. In G. Grevi & T. Renard (Eds.), *Partners in Crisis: EU strategic partnerships and the global economic downturn*. Madrid: European Strategic Partnerships Observatory.

Zavodny, M. (2003). The H-1B program and its effects on information technology workers. *Economic Review*, third quarter, 1–11.

Zeff, E. E., & Pirro, E. B. (Eds.). (2006). *The European Union and the Member States* (2nd ed.). Boulder, CO: Lynne Rienner.

Zeff, E. E., & Pirro, E. B. (2011). The transport success story: Europeanization in the Czech Republic, Slovakia and Romania. *Romanian Review of European Studies, 3*(5), 48–76.

Zimmerman, J. F. (2002). *Interstate cooperation: Compacts and administrative agreements*. Westport, CT: Prager.

Index

eBooks

from Taylor & Francis

Helping you to choose the right eBooks for your Library

Add to your library's digital collection today with Taylor & Francis eBooks. We have over 50,000 eBooks in the Humanities, Social Sciences, Behavioural Sciences, Built Environment and Law, from leading imprints, including Routledge, Focal Press and Psychology Press.

Free Trials Available

We offer free trials to qualifying academic, corporate and government customers.

Choose from a range of subject packages or create your own!

Benefits for you

■ Free MARC records
■ COUNTER-compliant usage statistics
■ Flexible purchase and pricing options
■ 70% approx of our eBooks are now DRM-free.

Benefits for your user

■ Off-site, anytime access via Athens or referring URL
■ Print or copy pages or chapters
■ Full content search
■ Bookmark, highlight and annotate text
■ Access to thousands of pages of quality research at the click of a button.

eCollections

Choose from 20 different subject eCollections, including:

Asian Studies
Economics
Health Studies
Law
Middle East Studies

eFocus

We have 16 cutting-edge interdisciplinary collections, including:

Development Studies
The Environment
Islam
Korea
Urban Studies

For more information, pricing enquiries or to order a free trial, please contact your local sales team:

UK/Rest of World: **online.sales@tandf.co.uk**
USA/Canada/Latin America: **e-reference@taylorandfrancis.com**
East/Southeast Asia: **martin.jack@tandf.com.sg**
India: **journalsales@tandfindia.com**

www.tandfebooks.com